The 18th Hussars in South Africa.

Thos. Fall, Photo] [9, Baker St., W.
COLONEL EUSTACE CHALLINOR KNOX,

Commanding the Regiment from October 20th, 1899, to his death, February 18th, 1902.

The 18th Hussars in South Africa

THE RECORDS OF A CAVALRY REGIMENT DURING THE BOER WAR 1899–1902

BY

MAJOR CHARLES BURNETT

with maps and illustrations

The Naval & Military Press Ltd

The Naval & Military Press Ltd
Unit 10 Ridgewood Industrial Park,
Uckfield, East Sussex,
TN22 5QE England

Tel: +44 (0) 1825 749494
Fax: +44 (0) 1825 765701

www.naval-military-press.com
www.military-genealogy.com
www.militarymaproom.com

The Naval & Military Press offers specialist books for the serious student of conflict. The range of titles stocked covers the whole spectrum of military history with titles on uniforms, battles, official histories, specialist works containing Medal Rolls and Casualties Lists, and numismatic titles for medal collectors and researchers. The innovative approach they have to military bookselling and their commitment to publishing have made them Britain's leading independent military bookseller.

In reprinting in facsimile from the original, any imperfections are inevitably reproduced and the quality may fall short of modern type and cartographic standards.

DEDICATED,

BY GRACIOUS PERMISSION,

TO

𝔥𝔢𝔯 𝔯𝔬𝔶𝔞𝔩 𝔥𝔦𝔤𝔥𝔫𝔢𝔰𝔰 𝔱𝔥𝔢 𝔭𝔯𝔦𝔫𝔠𝔢𝔰𝔰 𝔬𝔣 𝔴𝔞𝔩𝔢𝔰,

WHOSE NAME

THE REGIMENT HAS

THE HONOUR OF BEARING.

CORRIGENDA.

Page 83, note to line 10.—Major Marling got enteric two weeks after Ladysmith was relieved, and was invalided home in May, 1900.

Pages 180, 181, 183.—Read " Uyskraal " for " *Vry*skraal."

Page 222, line 9.— Read " Leuw Spruit " for " L*eo*w Spruit."

Page 290.—Repeat Promotions *in full* where ,, ,, ,, are put.

PREFACE.

I HAVE compiled the following pages from very rough notes I made at the end of each day's work, when I was on service with my Regiment in South Africa.

Their main purport is to serve as the ordinary Regimental Records of the Regiment for that period of its history; but, as many of the incidents therein described deal with the operations of our troops generally in the eastern theatre of the War, I have published them in the hope that they may also be of interest to some of the many soldiers of other corps, with whom my Regiment had the honour to serve.

Perhaps to some those well known words, "*Hæc olim meminisse juvabit*" may apply, and on that assumption I have ventured to allow the following pages, devoid as I fear they are of all literary merit, to see the light of day.

CHARLES BURNETT.

SANDHURST, 1905.

ILLUSTRATIONS.

1.—Portrait of Colonel Eustace Challinor Knox	*frontispiece*
	to face page
2.—Tin Camp, Ladysmith	2
3.—Talana Hill	10
4.—Shelters in Banks of Klip River, Ladysmith	46
5.—Bivouac of the Regiment on the Klip River during the Siege of Ladysmith	10
6.—Squadron on Duty at Range Post, Ladysmith	57
7.—Officers of the Regiment in Ladysmith	57
8.—Wagon Hill, Ladysmith	70
9.—Cæsar's Camp—18th Hussars Entrenchment	70
10.—Manchester Fort	75
11.—Watering Horses in the Buffalo River	75
12.—Portrait of Captain Montagu Sinclair Wellby	98
13.—On the way to Lydenburg	109
14.—Rations and Forage	109
15.—Lieut.-Colonel P. S. Marling, V.C. (commanding the Regiment after the death of Colonel Knox)	149
16.—18th Hussars Patrol in Bush Veldt near Massips Drift, July, 1901	175
17.—Light Cavalry	175
18.—18th Hussars on Convoy Duty, Kaffir's Spruit, on Ermelo-Standerton Road	206
19.—Smutzog, 23rd February, 1902	220
20.—Smutzog, 14th August, 1900	220
21.—The Advance Line (18th Hussar Section) near Vlaklaagte on April 14th, 1902	233
22.—Officers of the Regiment who saw the Beginning and End of the War	236
23.—Troop Horses that went through the whole Campaign	236
24.—18th Hussars Crossing a Drift	238
25.—The Regiment *en route* to Durban and England	242
26.—The Regiment leaving Durban for England	242
27.—Lieut.-Colonel P. S. Marling, V.C., Acting Adjutant Major C. Burnett, Regl.-Sergt.-Major Simmonds, and N.C. Officers of the Regiment who were present at the conclusion of the War	243
28.—The Happy Valley : the Gully by the Klip River, Ladysmith	253
29.—Memorial erected to Officers and Men of the Regiment who died or were killed during the War	253

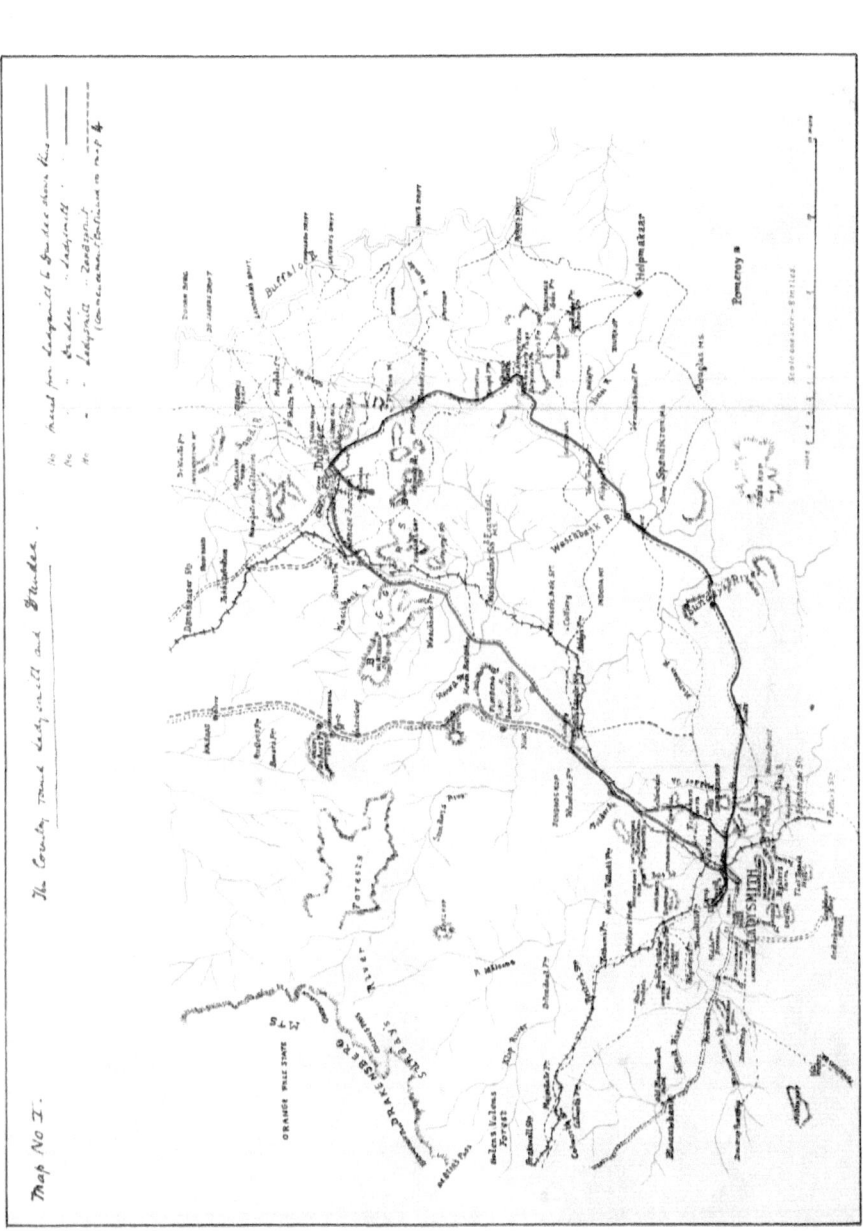

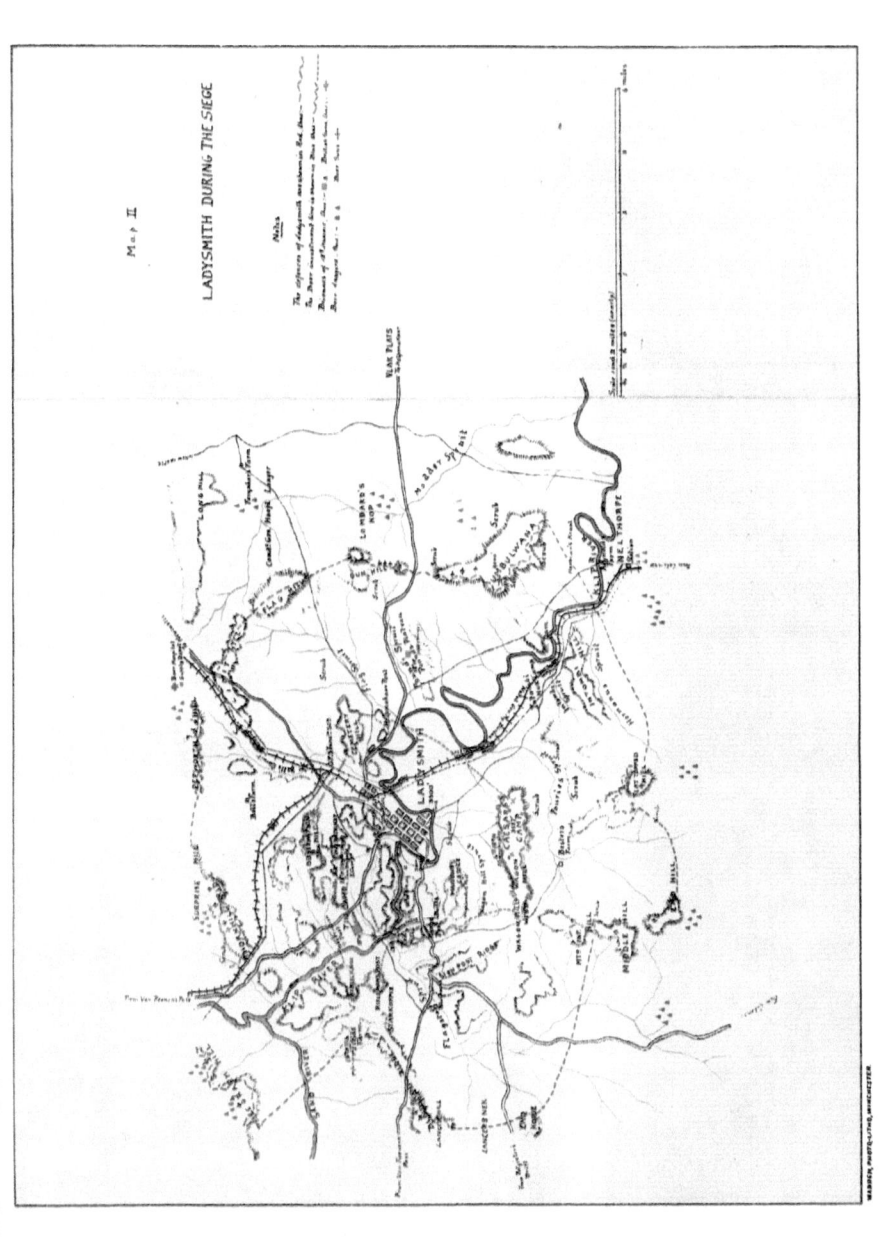

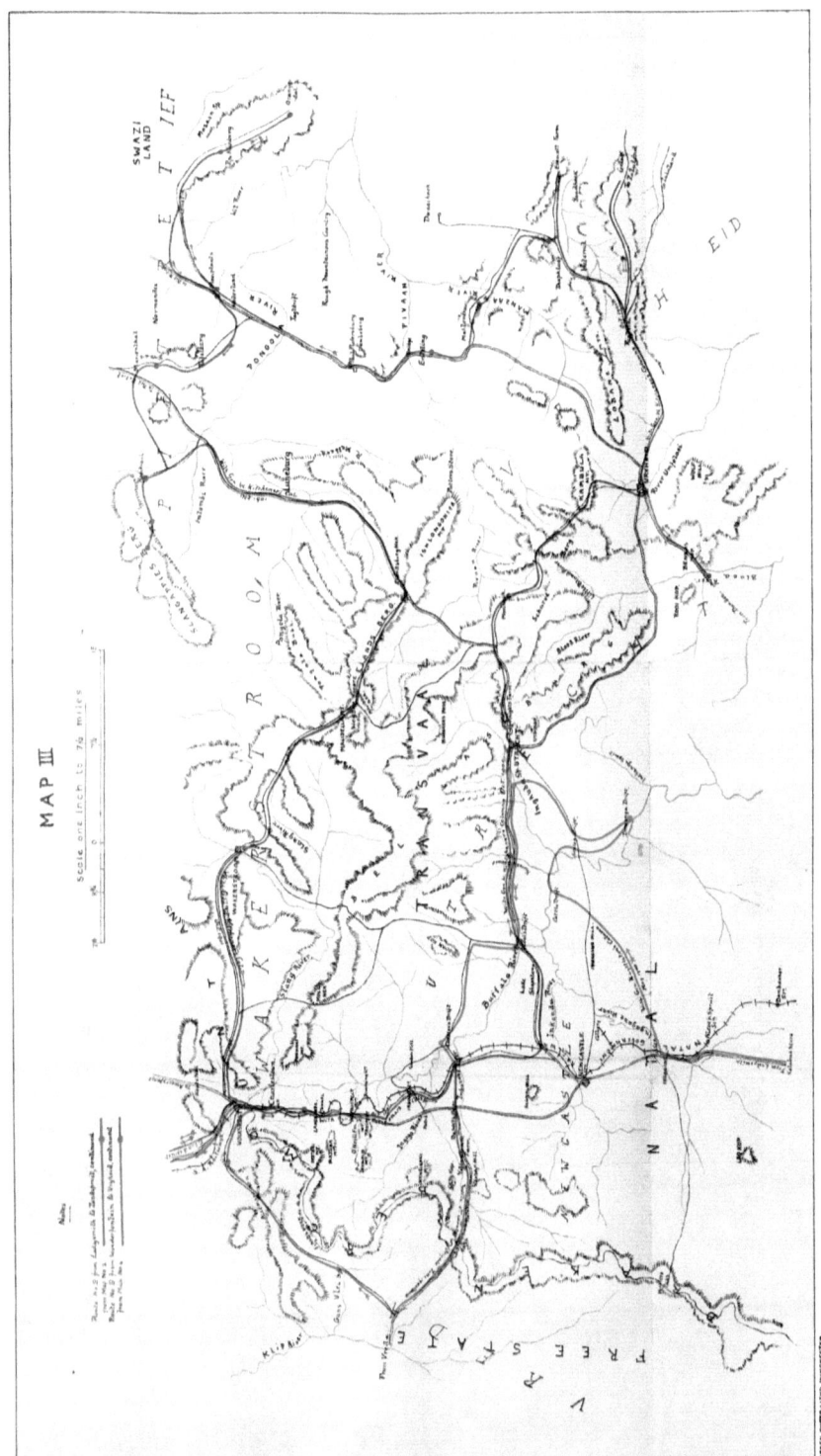

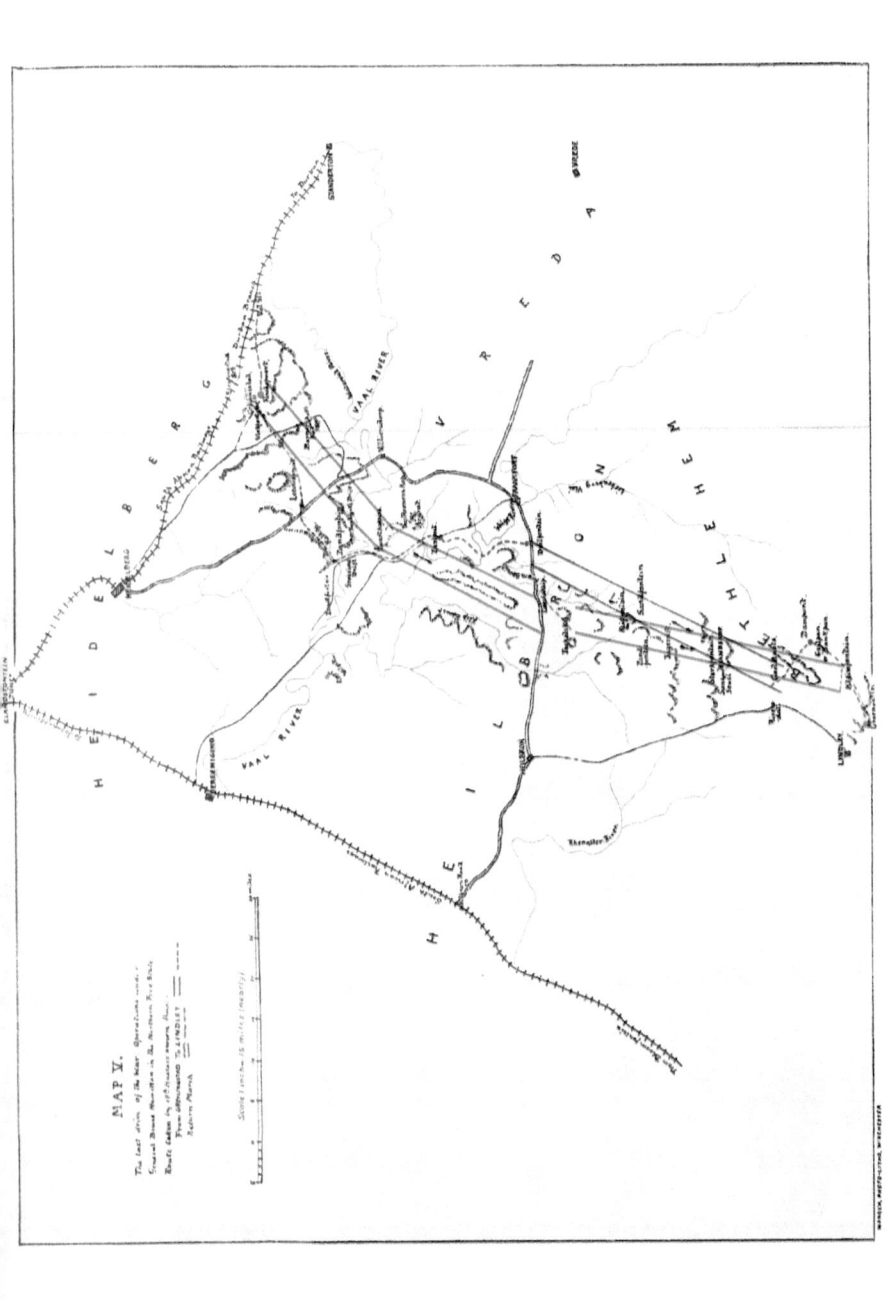

MAP IV.—NOTES

Marches Nos. 8 and 9.—With Colonel Campbell's and General Walter Kitchener's columns, September, 1902, in Northern Transvaal and South to Vryheid and Slangappiesberg (continued on Map III). Shown thus :—

Marches Nos. 13, 15, 11, *and* 4.—Drive with General Bruce Hamilton's columns to Standerton and in Free State, April, 1902. Also operations with Colonel Carleton's column round Middelburg, November, 1900. Also marches with Colonel Wing's column, March, 1902, and with Colonel Payne's column near Middelburg, November, 1900. Shown thus :—

March No. 11.—Night marches with Colonel Wing's column, January, 1902. Shown thus :—

March No. 6.—With General French's columns to Piet Relief, February to April, 1901. Shown thus :—

March No. 6.— Return march from Piet Relief. Shown thus :—

Marches Nos. 11 *and* 12.—With Colonel Wing's column to Bronkhurst Spruit, Ermelo, Standerton, Botha's Pass, etc., February and March, 1902. Shown thus :—

March No. 3.—With General Buller's columns, August and September, 1900. Shown thus :—

March No. 7.—With General Walter Kitchener's columns in Eastern Transvaal, May to July, 1901. Shown thus :—

Marches Nos. 4 *and* 7.—With Colonel Campbell's column near Middelburg, 1900. Also operations with General Bruce Hamilton's columns in Eastern Transvaal, night marches, etc., December, 1901, and January, 1902. Shown thus :—

March No. 14.—Drive with General Bruce Hamilton's column, April, 1902, along Constabulary Posts. Shown thus :—

March No. 4.—With Colonel Carleton's column to Shoedpad, November, 1900. Shown thus :—

Marches Nos. 11 *and* 12.—Night marches with Colonel Wing's column, February and March, 1902. Shown thus :—

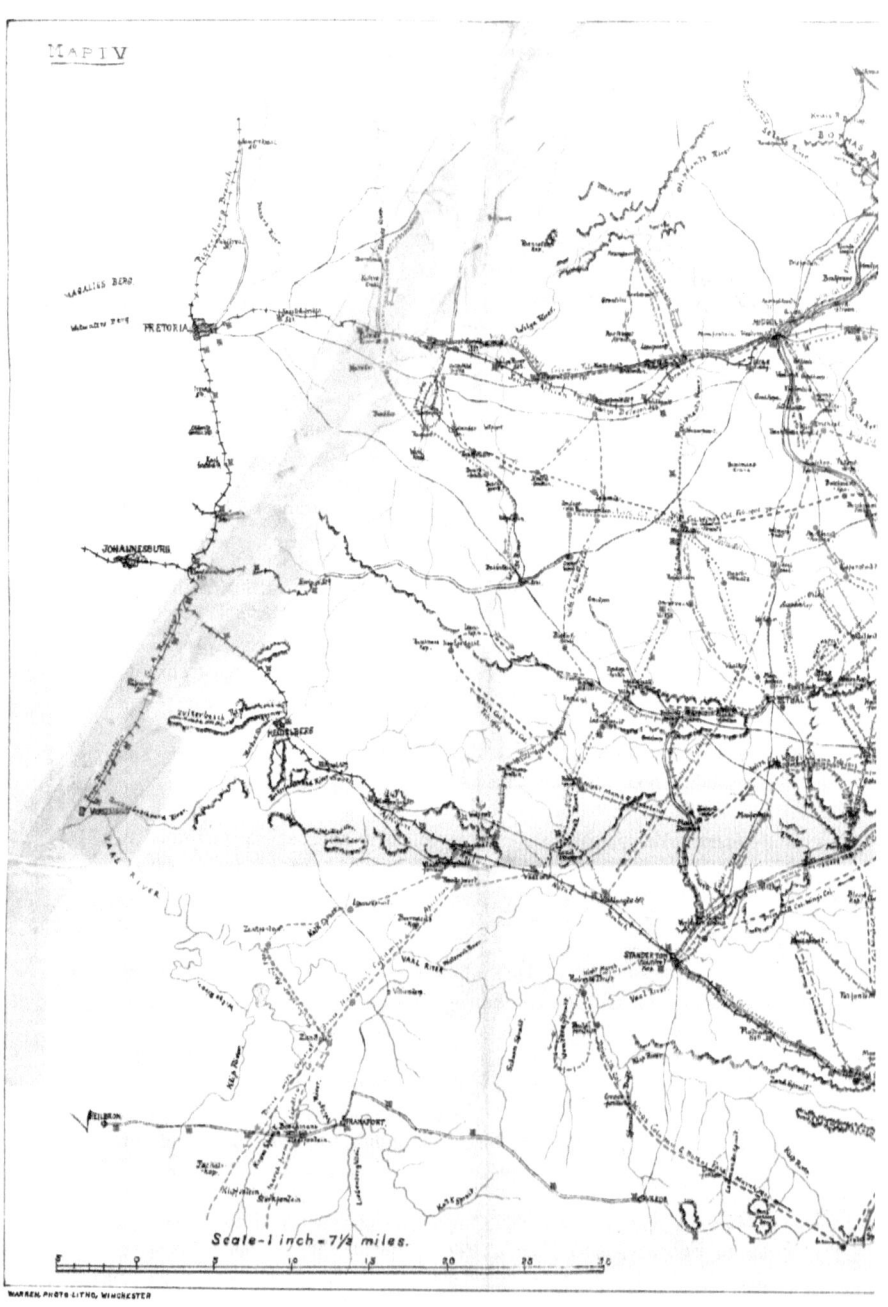

MAP IV

Scale-1 inch = 7½ miles.

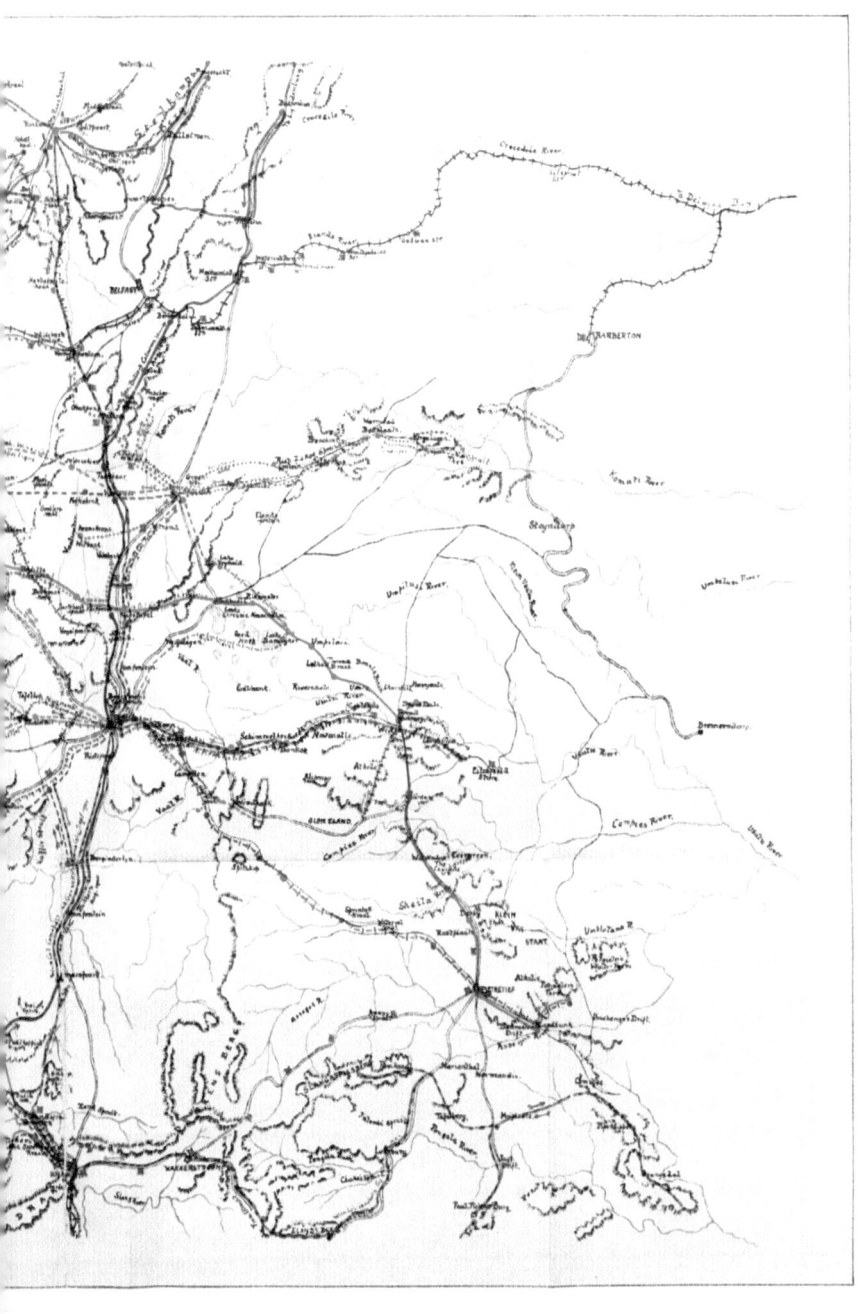

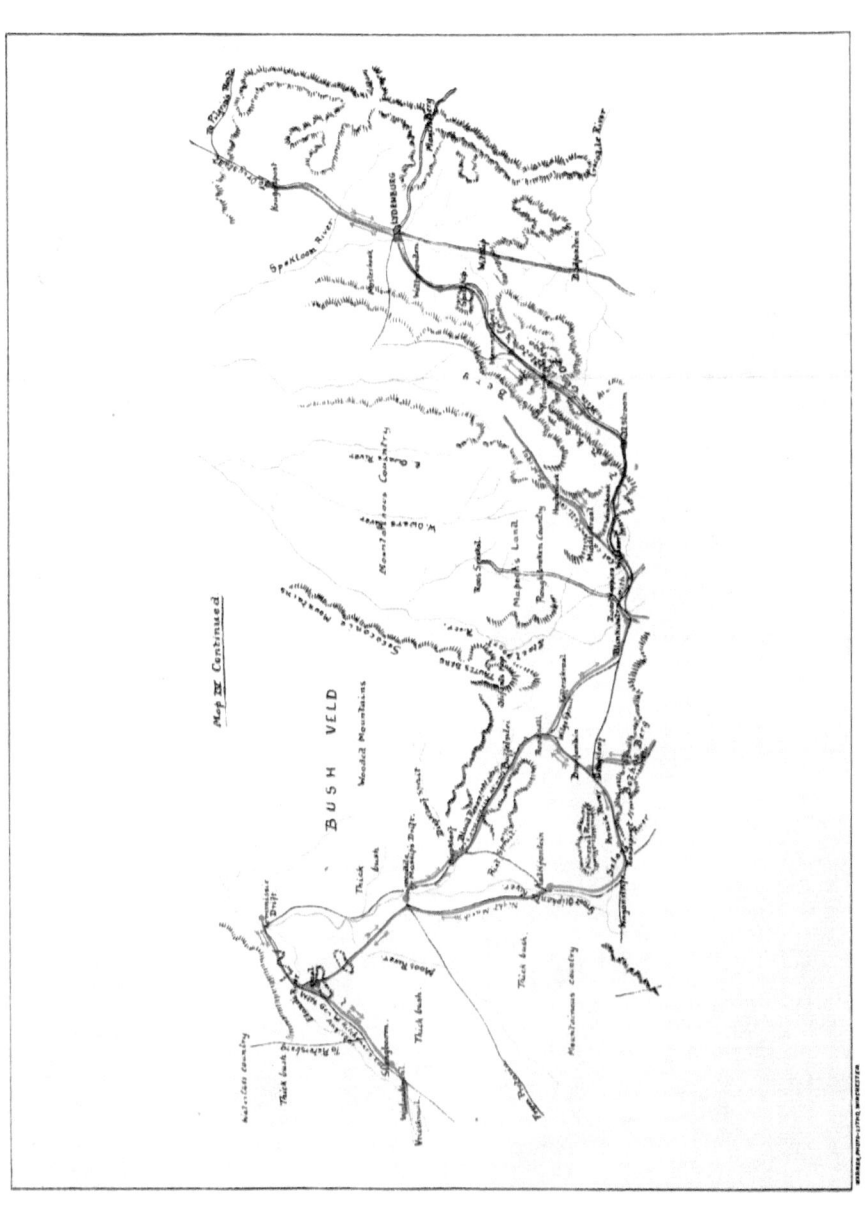

CONTENTS.

		PAGE
Chapter I.—Dundee before the War		1
,, II.—Talana Hill		10
,, III.—The Retreat to Ladysmith, October. 1899		25
,, IV.—Ladysmith during the Siege		47
,, V.—Ladysmith during the Siege		58
,, VI.—Ladysmith after the Siege, March, 1900		82
,, VII.—The Advance to the Transvaal, May, 1900		85
,, VIII.—Amersfoort, Bergendal, and Lydenburg, August, 1900		99
,, IX.—Lydenburg and Middelburg		112
,, X.—Christmas, 1900		128
,, XI.—With General French to the Swaziland Border, February, 1901		137
,, XII.--Back to Middelburg, April, 1901		150
,, XIII.—With General Sir Bindon Blood's Columns, April to July, 1901		154
,, XIV.—Wonderfontein to Vryheid		187
,, XV.—The Slangappiesberg		195
,, XVI.—Night Marches and Convoy Work		199
,, XVII.—Night Marches in the Eastern Transvaal, January to March, 1902		210
,, XVIII.—The Commencement of the Drives, March, 1902		224
,, XIX.—Drives in the Eastern Transvaal, April, 1902		231
,, XX.—Drives in the Free State, April to May, 1902		236
,, XXI.—Peace		243
Appendix A.—Extract from the Diary of an Officer		245
,, B.—Roll of Officers, showing the Engagements at which they were present		264
,, C.—Roll of N.C.O.'s and Men		265
,, D.—List of Officers mentioned in Despatches		289
,, E.—List of Officers, N.C.O.'s, and Men Killed and Died of Wounds		293
,, F.—Strength of the Regiment		301
,, G.—Officers with the Regiment in Ladysmith		301
,, H.—Strength of the Regiment leaving Ladysmith		302
,, I.—Strength of the Regiment at various dates		303
,, K.—Increase and Decrease of Horses from 1st October, 1899, to 31st May, 1902		305
,, L.—Duties performed by the Regiment at Manchester Fort		306
,, M.—Special Natal Field Force Orders		306
,, N.— ,, ,, ,, ,, ,,		306
,, O.—Proclamation to Inhabitants of South African Republic		309
,, P.—Itinerary of Marches		310
Summary of Marches made by the Regiment		319

The 18th Hussars in South Africa.

CHAPTER I.

"Dundee Before the War."

1898-9.—The regiment, 623 strong, under command of Lieut.-Colonel B. D. Moller, arrived in South Africa on October 28th, 1898, and was quartered at Ladysmith from November 9th, 1898, till September 25th of the next year.

Our quarters at Ladysmith were not pleasant ones, as a short description of that cheerless spot by one of the officers of the regiment may prove:—" The camp consists of rows of corrugated iron huts, which strike one at first sight as only wanting a tall chimney to make the resemblance to some factory complete. It lies on a patch of bare ground about a mile and a half west of the town, to reach which one must follow a dusty bumpy apology for a road through a bleak stretch of country. In spite of all attempts at sanitary improvements, the camping ground remains plague smitten, and a military funeral is almost a daily occurrence. Continually enveloped in clouds of dust, the barracks present a gloomy appearance. Rocky treeless hills overlook the cheerless camp, and the river Klip curls round it, skirting the sun-baked kopjes. In such a place you forcibly lead a monotonous kind of existence; there are no pleasures or excitements to dispel that depressing influence, which, like a dark threatening cloud, devoid of any silver lining, hangs over all. One dismal day follows another with painful regularity. It is a place to look back upon with horror, a chip from Dante's *Inferno* and one created for the damned. Such I found Ladysmith in times of peace."

Major-General Penn-Symons was, in September, 1898, in command of the troops in Natal, the towns of Maritzburg and Ladysmith forming their two stations. They had been strengthened by the addition of a couple of battalions during the months of August and September.

August, 1899.—The troops, however, were few in number, two regiments of Cavalry, three or four battalions of Infantry, three batteries of Field Artillery, and one mountain battery comprising the total force. Reinforcements, however, were on their way from India, and, chiefly owing to the anxiety of the civil authorities to guard the northern territories of Natal, General Symons, on Sunday, September 24th, ordered a force, consisting of the 18th Hussars, one company M.I.

Leicestershire Regiment, one battalion Leicester Regiment, the Dublin Fusiliers, 13th and 67th F.B.R.A., and a detachment of R.E., all under command of Colonel Moller, to proceed at once to the neighbourhood of Dundee.

In compliance with this order, the 18th had left Ladysmith at 10 a.m. on the 25th of September, after hurriedly packing up their belongings all the previous night. Colonel Pickwoad, R.A., was in command of the column, which comprised all the mounted troops of the Glencoe Field Force.

The account of their march up the Biggarsberg Pass, given here, is taken from the diary of an officer of the Regiment who took part in it:—" It was a fine morning, and many people assembled to see us off. Our first march took us past Elandslaagte, and ended at Sunday's river, about twenty miles from Ladysmith, and roughly halfway to Dundee. At about two a.m. next morning I was suddenly woken by the sound of galloping in our direction. It turned out to be a Natal Carabinier and a Natal Policeman, who had left Dundee at 11 p.m. the previous night, and had ridden hard through the inky darkness to reach us and bring us most urgent orders. We were to saddle up and resume our march on Dundee with all despatch, and try and reach the top of the Biggarsberg Pass before daylight. From information gained it was fully expected the Boers intended to occupy this pass and oppose our advance. The men were accordingly roused from their sleep, but no noise or trumpet calls were allowed. In silence the men saddled up, the transport mules were inspanned, and the guns limbered up. After a hasty breakfast at our mess cart, whilst the men were getting ready, I hurried off to join my squadron. Colonel Pickwoad had seen no cause to hurry, and seemed to pin little faith on the report just come in, so it was not much before 3.30 a.m. when we resumed our march. It was chilly and pitch-dark when we picked our way towards the road which led to the Biggarsberg. Soon after starting a spruit with very steep banks rather delayed the transport, but no further delay occurred for the next eight miles, when we halted to allow the transport to close up. It was, however, clear we could never reach the Biggarsberg in time unless we abandoned our transport, and this we could not do. It was 8 a.m. when we reached the foot of the pass. Here we halted whilst our squadron was sent forward to reconnoitre through the pass. Presently a scout came galloping back to report that firing was distinctly heard ahead, and this news was soon confirmed by another scout. The flutter of excitement caused by this intelligence was not of long duration, as shortly afterwards the pass was reported quite clear, and what had been taken for heavy firing turned out to be only blasting operations. It was quite a pretty ride

Tin Camp, Ladysmith.

through the Biggarsberg, a pleasant change from the dusty uninteresting country we had hitherto ridden over. It was, too, a matter of congratulation that our advance had been unopposed, for had the Biggarsberg been even only held by a weak party of Boers, never could we have successfully forced a passage through this very formidable pass. As we filed up the narrow track I realised the advantage we had gained, and the satisfaction we ought to feel at having met with no opposition. The pass is commanded on every side by strong kopjes, where Boers could, in perfect safety, have lain concealed. From behind the numerous boulders and trees they could have fired into us at their leisure, without our being in a position to inflict any appreciable harm in return. At midday the last wagon of our column had reached the summit, and from thence on to Glencoe was quite a short ride."

The Infantry were sent by train, the Cavalry marched up the Glencoe Pass and the guns with them, and all encamped on a ridge about a mile west of Dundee town.

During the march up from Ladysmith one of the Intelligence guides, Allison by name, brought to Dundee, where Colonel Moller and the Infantry had already arrived, a report that the Boers were advancing to hold Glencoe Pass. Allison was sent on the night of the 25th September to meet the column marching up from Ladysmith; he reached them at 2 a.m. next day, and during their march up the pass some blasting explosions near the road gave some colour to his story, but it was quite a false alarm, and would have been an impossible task for the Boers to have carried out.

On September 27th the Dublin Mounted Infantry joined the force, which was now named the Glencoe Field Force.

During the ensuing days at Dundee patrols were sent out in all directions daily, to the Navigation colleries, round Impati Mountain, to the drifts on the Buffalo River (De Beers, Landsman, Vants), to Biggarsberg Nek, and along the Newcastle Road as far as Ingagane. At night piquets were placed on all the main approaches.

The Cavalry and Mounted Infantry had hard work, as the distances were long and the weather bad, for the rains had just broken at that period in upper Natal.

One squadron of the 18th Hussars was sent to Helpmakaar, under command of Major Marling, on September 30th, to reconnoitre the country near the Buffalo and to return to Dundee next day, their object also being to restore confidence to the Police Post stationed out there.

On October 2nd, Captain the Hon. H. S. Davey took a patrol of the 18th Hussars as far as Ingagane bridge, halting for the night at Dannhauser; he found the country quiet.

On Sunday, October 1st, Major-General Symons came up from Ladysmith to inspect the camp, and returned early on Monday morning.

During this week the troops from India commenced to arrive at Durban, and were despatched up country as quickly as possible, and by the end of the second week in October the force at Glencoe consisted of the following :—

    18th Hussars.
    13th, 67th, and 69th Field Batteries R.A.
    1st Leicestershire Regiment and 100 Mounted Infantry.
    1st Royal Dublin Fusiliers and 100 Mounted Infantry.
    1st King's Royal Rifle Corps and 75 Mounted Infantry.
    1st Royal Irish Fusiliers.
    Detachment Army Service Corps.
    Detachment Royal Engineers.
    Detachment Army Ordnance Corps.
    Half the 18th and 24th Field Hospitals.
    One Troop Natal Police.
    One Troop Natal Carabineers.

making a rough total of about 3,700 men and 800 horses. There was no further increase to the Glencoe Field Force. On Monday, October 8th, Colonel Gunning arrived, and took over command of the force from Colonel Moller, but Brigadier-General Yule, arriving on Wednesday the 10th, relieved him almost at once, and on Friday, the 12th, Major-General Penn Symons, C.B., came up with his staff and took command of the Glencoe Division as it was now called, General Yule having the command of the Infantry Brigade given him, and it was designated " 8th Brigade."

From an officer's diary :—" It was on the 12th of October he, General Symons, came to stay. I remember it well. A severe thunderstorm in the night was followed by a cold wet morning, and the camp presented the usual bedraggled appearance which a real soaking produces. We had just finished breakfast, and were standing in mackintoshes and gum boots outside the mess tent, when General Symons, accompanied by his Staff, arrived. He stopped and greeted us in his usual cheery manner, and introduced us to the officers of his Staff. They had already partaken of breakfast at Glencoe Station, so declined our offer of providing them with any. Whilst we were talking a telegram was handed to the General, and, on reading it, a look of supreme satisfaction spread over his genial countenance, a look which was reflected in ours when he announced the contents. The South African Republic had declared war against Great Britain, and Mr. Egerton Green had left Pretoria. War was actually declared the previous day, October 11th. It came as no surprise, for, of course, after Kruger's impertinent ultimatum, we knew war to be inevitable."

General Symons' Staff consisted of the following officers: Colonel Beckett, A.A.G., Major Hammersley, D.A.A.G., Lieut. Murray, A.D.C. General Yule's Staff comprised Lieut.-Col. Sherston, Brigade Major; Lieut. Kenrick, Signalling Officer; Captain Vallancey, Provost Marshal; and Major Murray, Intelligence Officer.

After the heavy rain of October 12th it was found necessary to shift camp to a ridge close by, which lay between the old camp and the town of Dundee.

October 12th.—The news of the declaration of war between the South African Republics and England was received by telegram from the Government, Maritzburg, about ten a.m. on Friday morning, October 12th, and everyone seemed glad that the period of expectation was over, and that the matter was to be settled one way or the other at last.

A good many "guides" had by now assembled at the camp at Glencoe, both Natal Colonists and natives, and a great deal of information was brought in every day. The enemy had apparently been collected in force for some time back, before the declaration of war, for the most part at Zandspruit, beyond Volksrust, and between Wakkerstroom and Utrecht, and afterwards at Doornberg over the Buffalo, on the north-west of the Dundee-Vyrheid road.

The Boers on their side had much better information than we had, and knew of our every movement. About one in ten only of the local farmers round Dundee was trustworthy, and the town itself was honeycombed with spies, but we took little or no precautions to shift them.

The two bodies of Natal local troops attached to the force were now of great help in showing our mounted troops the country and in getting information from the natives, but the local population were more Dutch than English, and the information gained wanted a good deal of sifting.

On Friday, October 13th, the Dublin Fusiliers were sent off from Dundee to Ladysmith on information to hand that the Free State Boers were marching down Tintwa Pass. It was a false alarm, and the Dublins came back to Dundee at midnight on Sunday, the 15th, after a very uncomfortable journey.

For the first two or three days after the declaration of war no news of importance was gathered. On Sunday, the 15th, a patrol of the 18th Hussars, under Lieut. Thackwell, encountered about twenty-five of the enemy near De Jaager's Drift on the Buffalo, where they had crossed to loot a store on our side of the river, and had captured five men of the Natal Police there. They endeavoured to cut off our patrol, which was a weak one, but did not succeed.

Lieut. Thackwell gives the following account of what took place:—" I took a patrol to the Buffalo River and went to Landsman's Drift. Proceeded up the banks of the river to near De Jaager's Drift, where I saw a patrol of Boers, about thirty-four strong; they retreated at first, but when they saw our strength they tried to encircle us and cut us off from camp. We retired, however, through Gregory's Nek, and they followed us for about two miles and then recrossed the river. We afterwards saw a party cross Landsman's Drift. They must have been sent to cut us off if we had returned the same way as we came out."

The beginning of the week saw fresh developments. Newcastle was abandoned by the civil population, while the natives from the Navigation and Campbell collieries, and a good many from the ones at Dundee itself, commenced to trek back to their Kraals. A company of Infantry was sent to the coal mine at Dundee at Mr. Wright's (the manager) request, to give protection to those who were left.

Besides this outlying piquet, we had, at that time, a company at Glencoe Junction and one section on the road there, about a mile out of camp. By night we had piquets from the 18th Hussars and Mounted Infantry at each of the following spots (the piquets consisted of twelve non-commissioned officers and men, under an officer) :—

(1) Manager's House of South African Coalfields on Helpmakaar Road;
(2) Junction of Landman's Drift and Vant's Drift Road;
(3) Junction of Dundee-Newcastle and Glencoe-Newcastle Roads, and at
(4) Dr. Schultze's Farm on De Jaager's Drift Road.

There were other Infantry piquets besides nearer in on the approaches to camp. We had now collected about forty days' supplies of all sorts, and it had originally been intended to bring up sixty days " Woolwich Supplies " and thirty days local ones, but this could not be managed. Ammunition was short, a much needed requisition for a further supply was not attended to in time, and on its arrival at Ladysmith the line was blocked, and the train to bring it up could not get through. The Infantry had a fair supply, about 50,000 rounds a battalion, but the Artillery were very badly off.

On Tuesday, October 17th, the Boers hoisted the Transvaal flag at Newcastle, and came on at once along the railway to Hatting Spruit, where they checked for a day or two. About 2,000 of them, however, branched off from there, and were seen by our scouts, on Wednesday, the 18th, moving down the Biggarsberg Nek. On Thursday, the 19th, we sent three companies of the Dublin Fusiliers to the Navigation Collieries to bring in some 1,000 bags of mealies, which had been stacked there for the natives working on the mine. A few Boers watched them from the surrounding ridges, but they did what they wanted to, and got back to Dundee about 8.30 p.m., one company remaining at Glencoe Junction to await the arrival of part of a train from Ladysmith, which had been left at Wessels Nek Station, as the engine was unable to pull the whole train up the pass. This train, with another one, had left Ladysmith early in the day, and had been fired on at Elandslaagte Station, and the rear train had been captured by the Boers. The engine of the front train was a good deal bullet-marked, but it had to go back to Wessels Nek to bring up the portion of the train it had left behind, and at about 9.30 p.m. this portion was brought up, and the company then retired to Dundee, as the post, which at first had been occupied at Glencoe Junction, had been for the past few days withdrawn.

Piquets were out as usual on Thursday night, and at 2 a.m. information came in from the Dublin Fusilier one at Vant's Drift-Landsman's Drift post to say that some scouts of the enemy were advancing from the direction of the latter drift, and that the piquet had had to retire. On receipt of this news two companies of the Dublin Fusiliers were sent to the far side of Dundee to support the piquet, but they did not gather any more information about the enemy, and at 5 a.m. a Staff officer was sent round the various units to say that they need not "stand to their arms" any longer. They had been doing so since just before daybreak, according to daily custom since the declaration of war. However, a few minutes later, groups of men were seen lining the summit of Talana Hill and Lennox Hill, the smaller one to the south of it, and it soon became evident that they were hauling guns up the reverse side of the slope.

We learnt later on that they had crossed Landsman's Drift, some 4,000 to 6,000 in numbers, Burghers of the Utrecht, Wakkerstroom, Middelburg, Vyrheid, and Piet Retief commandoes, under General Lucas Meyer and Commandant Christian Botha, at 9 p.m. on the 19th October, and, marching all night, had reached Talana Hill at daybreak on the 20th. They had with them four field guns, two Vickers Maxims, and a detachment of Staats Artillerie. Their movement was planned in conjunction with that of a larger column which was intended to march by the Newcastle-Dundee direct road, seize Impati Mountain, and attack our camp on the 20th from that side as well, but, luckily for the Glencoe Field Force, the Boer General, Erasmus, who was in command of this second column, bungled his work, and did not arrive on Impati till midday on the 21st.

A third Boer column was to head off any sally made by

the Ladysmith garrison, and then hem in the Glencoe force from the rear; this column was, however, effectually put off its scheme by our troops at Elandslaagte.

The country round Dundee is hilly, and, though actually round the town itself the hills are undulating, a good many of the others, a little way off, are very steep and stony. About 5,000 yards from the town, and nearly west of it, lies Impati Mountain, between five and six thousand feet above the level of the sea. It is a typical South African mountain, steep at the sides and flat on the top, the summit is about a mile in extent and semi-circular in form, with the outer face of the semi-circle facing Newcastle, and the horns pointing inwards towards Glencoe, that one farthest from Dundee ending with a more gradual slope, and running in a long ridge almost up to Glencoe Junction. This ridge shuts out the main railway line and the Newcastle road, after it crosses the ridge, from the camp.

On the north and north-east sides of the town a small range of hills borders the Helpmakaar road, and a distance of about 2,000 yards separates this range from the town at the nearest point. Talana Hill forms the north-western extremity of this range, and the road to Vant's and Landsman's Drifts runs between it and Lennox Hill, the next one in the range on the south-eastern side.

Between Talana Hill and Impati Mountain the country is open, but intersected by several rather deep watercourses.

On the south side the country rises gradually to the Biggarsberg range, about five to six miles off, Indumeni Mountain, over 7,000 feet high, being almost south of Dundee and some five miles from it.

The Biggarsberg range runs nearly east and west past the south side of Glencoe Junction, which is almost four miles from camp, and it is met there by the spur running down from Impati Mountain, of which mention has previously been made.

Towards Newcastle, Hatting Spruit, etc., and towards the westward, large undulating hills, here and there broken by small rocky kopjes, roll away to the lower slopes of the Drakensberg.

Impati Mountain and Indumeni Mountain were visited by General Symons, and by all officers who could accompany him, during the early part of this week. A description of the ascent of the former, written by one of those who went with him, is inserted here:—" In the orders of Monday evening appeared a notice that the General intended to ride up Impati Mountain the next day, and all officers who cared to accompany him would be welcome. This mountain lies to the west of Dundee, and overlooked our camp. It is about 6,000 feet high, has a broad flat top nearly a mile long, devoid of trees, and on its south-eastern side its slopes are precipitous. From the summit one gets a fine extensive view of the country, the various hills and gorges, the open plains extending to the Buffalo, intersected here and there by winding spruits, and far away in the distance one catches a glimpse of the mountains in Zululand, near to which the Prince Imperial met his death. All officers who could be spared from duty collected near the General's tent at 9 a.m. that Tuesday morning. We must have numbered at least fifty, and, now I come to think of it, we ran no small risk, for had the Boers, whom we knew to be no great distance off, taken it into their heads to attack us that morning, whilst the officer commanding and most of his Staff and other officers were engaged in toiling up the slopes of Impati, things would have been mighty unpleasant for the Glencoe Field Force. Or supposing this unsuspecting party of excursionists, personally conducted by the General, had been taken prisoners, what a beginning to the war! Such a catastrophe was, no doubt, hardly likely, but not an impossibility. The half company of Mounted Infantry, who escorted us, were our only safeguard. On the way we stopped to examine the waterworks which supply Dundee with water, then a long circuitous path led us to the summit. The last part had been very steep, and a severe pull up for the ponies, but, once the top was reached, our climb was well rewarded by the glorious panorama which was spread before us. We got a magnificent birds-eye view of the surrounding country. Just below us lay the tents of the camp, and beyond them the small town of Dundee. On Impati we found a signalling post situated, a few men of the 18th Hussars under Captain Davey. We heard that, shortly before our arrival, a suspicious-looking individual had been detected watching the camp through field glasses, but that, before they could get up to him, he had mounted his pony, scrambled down the side of the mountain at the risk of his neck, and made for a farmhouse which we could plainly see below. The man, they said, was still inside the farmhouse, as they had never ceased watching it, and his pony was still tied up under a tree outside. Captain Lonsdale, of the Dublin Fusiliers, who was in command of the Mounted Infantry which had accompanied us up, asked the General whether he might ride down and try to capture this spy. The General having no objection, Lonsdale sallied forth with a few of his men. I sat down to await events, but as he had a long ride before him and I had to get back to camp, I did not wait for the *dénoument,* but I heard afterwards that the farm had been drawn blank, the bird had flown away, and the house had been found stripped of every stick of furniture."

CHAPTER II.

"TALANA HILL."

October 20th, 1899.—But to go back to the morning of the 20th.

At 5.25 a.m. an opening shot from one of the guns the Boers had brought up on to Talana Hill, combined with the view of that and the neighbouring hill to the south-eastward, lined with men watching us in our camp, very speedily convinced us what our work for that day was to be.

The first few shells fell far over our heads, but they quickly got the range and then poured them, as fast as they could, into every quarter of the camp. Luckily for us their shells were all "common shell," and the ground being a little soft, they sunk in and did little or no damage, though they created some confusion at first. But this was soon rectified. Some of the Artillery horses had been sent down to water, but the 18th Hussars had not been at all satisfied with the outlook earlier in the morning, and were ready saddled in their lines at the commencement of the shelling. They retired from the ridge the camp was on, and which was everywhere commanded by the enemy's guns, and took cover in a valley on the west side of it. The Artillery horses were hurried back from water, and one battery opened fire from camp against the enemy's guns. But the range was too far, some 4,500 yards, for our shrapnell, as we had not the "Blue fuses" in those days for the guns, and they could do no good till they advanced to another position quite close to the town. In a few minutes General Symons sent round orders to say that three Infantry Regiments, the 1st Battalion of the 60th Rifles, the Royal Irish Fusiliers, and the Dublin Fusiliers, would attack Talana Hill, aided by the 13th and 69th Batteries, while the 18th Hussars and some Mounted Infantry under Colonel Moller, would proceed to the west end of the camp and wait till he, Colonel Moller, received orders to advance, but to advance without them if he saw a good opportunity. The remainder of the Mounted Infantry were sent to guard our right flank, and patrols were despatched to Glencoe Junction, Impati Mountain, and along the Newcastle road, to gather information. The Infantry set off on their task at once, and the batteries moved away in rear of them, halting at a position at the south-east end of the town, where they at once opened a very effective fire from a range of just over 2,000 yards. The Infantry continued on through the town to their attack on Talana Hill.

Talana Hill.

Bivouac of the Regiment on the Klip River
during the siege of Ladysmith.

[See p. 56.]

Talana Hill.

As it is only intended to give here an account of what actually concerns the Regiment, so further details of the magnificent attack by the Infantry and Artillery on Talana Hill must be omitted, while the following description of the doings of the 18th Hussars, from the time we left them in the valley west of the camp, written by a senior officer of the Regiment, will show what befell them on that day :—

"*The doings of the 18th Hussars on October 20th, 1899.*"

" About 5.20 a.m. orders were received to off-saddle and water, but not quite liking the general outlook, we decided to ' stand to,' and in ten minutes a heavy Artillery fire was opened on us from the Boers on Talana Hill. We received very shortly orders to form up under cover on the Glencoe side of the camp, and we did so as quickly as possible, many of us having narrow escapes from bursting shells, but no one was hit during the process. After we had formed up the Regiment, Colonel Moller ordered me to proceed in advance with ' A ' Squadron, and try and get in rear of the enemy's position. During my advance the enemy fired on us with their guns, but they did no damage, and I got my men to an excellent position, about 1,200 yards in rear of the enemy's, and from there sent two messages to Colonel Moller, asking him to bring up the remainder of the Regiment and Mounted Infantry, and one Squadron and some Mounted Infantry were sent up about twenty minutes' later, followed later on by the rest of the Regiment, but Colonel Moller would not allow the Maxim gun to open fire, although it was in an excellent position. I was then ordered to take ' B ' Squadron forward and try and get farther in rear of the enemy, and I sent one troop, under Lieut. Bayford, on my left flank, as parties of the enemy were seen coming towards us from that direction. Lieut. Bayford sent back word to say he had captured twelve men, and I went towards him to give orders respecting the prisoners, when I observed a Boer patrol of about twenty men, supported by two other bodies of men of similar strength, advancing to rescue the prisoners, so I ordered Major Greville to charge the leading party with two troops, which he did, killing two Boers and capturing twenty, while one of his own men was wounded. Our men would have made short work of the whole of the Boer patrol had not the officers prevented them. In the meantime the other Boer patrols retired. I then rejoined Colonel Moller, who ordered me to take 2½ Squadrons right in rear of the enemy's position, and I advanced over very broken ground to the roads the enemy had used in their advance the night before. I refused to take the Maxim gun with me, as it was madness to remove it from the very excellent position it was in and risk its capture over the difficult country before me.

Soon after leaving Colonel Moller I got right in the thick of the enemy, many of whom were at that time evacuating Talana Hill and retiring by the Landsman's and Vant's Drifts roads; some 300 were on my left flank, a very large force on my right, and about eighty to one hundred in my immediate front. I forced my way through their line of retreat, engaging the enemy, dismounted in doing so, and I had one man killed, three or four wounded, and some horses shot during my progress. I also came under Artillery fire from the Boer guns, which had been removed from Talana Hill, and were in retreat towards the Buffalo, at about 2,500 yards range, but they did no damage, though one shell pitched in the middle of a Squadron which was in Squadron column. I had now become so completely surrounded by the enemy, in much superior numbers, that I had no chance of remaining in safety in one position, and it was only the rapidity of my advance which had so far saved me from capture. I therefore determined to get right through the enemy's line of retreat and let him pass me if possible, so I advanced about another two miles, and succeeded in withdrawing from the very difficult position I had had to advance to. I had then to endeavour to retrace my steps, and it was 7 p.m. before our force reached the camp at Dundee, where I learnt that Colonel Moller and the remainder of the mounted troops had been captured.

"In my opinion the Cavalry and Mounted Infantry should have been kept together on the enemy's right flank, where they had an excellent position, and could have opened fire with the maxim gun and rifles at a range of 1,200 yards on a target of some 800 Boers and ponies . . . ."

An account of the capture of part of " B " Squadron, 18th Hussars, and of the Mounted Infantry.

"In accordance with the orders issued the previous night, all the troops in camp stood to their arms at 4.30 a.m. on Friday morning, October 20th, 1899. It was one of those cold misty mornings which are occasionally experienced in Natal at that time of the year. All night it had rained incessantly, and the prospect outside was so very uninviting, that I was very loth to get up when my servant called me at a quarter to four in the morning. After struggling into my clothes I ran over to the mess tent to procure myself a cup of cocoa and a few biscuits, a very wise precaution as it turned out later.

"I was one of a group of officers standing outside the tent when Colonel Beckett, staff officer to General Symons, rode past, calling out to us we could dismiss. I heard afterwards he was on his way to a piquet of the Royal Dublin Fusiliers, which had just sent in word that Boers were advancing and firing on them, and that they were in need of support.

"Whilst conversing at the end of my squadron lines, numbers of men were pointed out to me collecting on the two hills which lay to the east and overlooked our camp. I ran to my tent and got my field glasses, and through them could see swarms of men, mostly on ponies, on Talana Hill. They were plainly visible against the sky line, and undoubtedly Boers. I could just distinguish some dark-looking objects, round which small clusters of men were gathered, and, whilst speculating whether they were guns, there suddenly came a flash from the hill top, and a shell crashed in the direction of the town. This was quickly followed by another, and soon plenty came pounding into our camp. I think the guns were being principally aimed at the General's tent, which, with the Union Jack floating from the flagstaff close by, was a conspicuous mark for the Boers. As I was in my tent, buckling on revolver and sword, whilst my horse was being brought me, a shell burst, but did no damage, a few yards off. Most of the shells were not bursting properly, no doubt due to the long range (5,000 yards) at which they were fired from; anyhow very few caused any damage. Still this unexpected bombardment on a practically empty stomach was not over pleasant, and it had the effect of hastening us out of camp pretty smartly. Whilst Colonel Moller, accompanied by his adjutant, rode off to the Headquarters Camp to get the orders, our men quickly mounted their horses, which fortunately had remained saddled up, and hurried out of camp, to form up under cover of some rocky ground, which was below the lie of the camp, and to the west of it. There was no confusion, and the officers were able to collect the squadrons and tell them off. Our guns had opened fire from the camp itself, but the range was too long a one to reach Talana Hill. Soon we caught sight of the horses of one of the batteries being led back at a gallop from the watering troughs beyond. The battery to which these horses belonged remained in camp with the Leicestershire Regiment, whilst the other two batteries were quickly on the move, making for a spot east of the town, where they came into action at a much closer range.

"And now Colonel Moller and Captain Pollok returned from the General. They had found him calmly smoking a cigarette while issuing orders, and whilst shells fell all around. He was much incensed at the impudence of the enemy daring to attack us like this.

"It was about 5.15 a.m. when the Boers began their bombardment, and barely half an hour later 'A' squadron, of the 18th Hussars, under Major Marling, v.c., received the order to move off along the Sandspruit nullah and take up a position just below a stony ridge east of Dundee, and almost right behind Talana Hill. About five minutes afterwards I was ordered to follow, with my squadron ' B,' the direction ' A ' squadron had taken and join it. Two only of my officers were with me, Captain Burnett and Lieut. Bayford, as my two other subalterns, Lieutenants Thackwell and Maclachlan, had left camp the previous night, and were still out with their patrols. Before starting to join Major Marling, Colonel Moller rode up to my squadron and ordered Captain Burnett away with a patrol to reconnoitre our left flank and the southern slopes of Impati Mountain, whose summit lay hidden in mist. Thus early in the day I lost the services of my second-in-command, for I never saw Captain Burnett again. As I trotted off towards the Sandspruit nullah the enemy's guns opened fire on me. On my way I met Lieut. Maclachlan with his patrol, and they joined me. From him I learnt that he had seen nothing of the enemy near the Navigation Colleries or on the Newcastle road. Major Laming, with ' C ' Squadron, now followed me, and, in turn, the Mounted Infantry of the Dublin Fusiliers, under Captain Lonsdale, and a section of the 60th Rifles Mounted Infantry, under Lieut. Crum, together with our Maxim gun under Lieut. Cape, and this completed our little force.

" From the ridge top behind which we were assembled we could watch the progress of the battle, admire the precision of our Artillery fire, and, later on, the dash with which the Infantry attacked. Our shrapnel was doing great execution on Talana Hill; the shells were bursting beautifully just over the summit. From the position we had taken up, and which was about 2,000 yards from the hill, we could see thousands of Boers. A great many were coming down the hill and making for a farm house at the foot of it, and from which the red cross was flying, a building the Boers had temporarily turned into a hospital for their wounded. A great number of ponies, waiting for their masters, were scattered about below Talana. Had we but had a horse battery with us, what deadly execution it could have inflicted ! Our position completely enfiladed the Boers, but the range was too great for rifle fire. Our plan should have been to remain in this position until the enemy were in full retreat, but, unfortunately, we committed the error of issuing out into the plain far too soon. We thus disclosed to the enemy our intention, and instead of sweeping down into them when they were a routed foe, they saw us in time to tell off a portion of their force to make a strong counter attack and so cover their retirement. The plain, east of Dundee, stretches away to the Buffalo river, and over it lay the enemy's line of retreat. This impatient eagerness of ours to intercept and cut off the

Boers was the primary cause of our ultimate discomfiture. My squadron was to act as advance guard, and Major Knox accompanied it. It was still drizzling slightly, and the fog had not lifted as we descended into the plain, followed at some distance by the remainder of the regiment and the Mounted Infantry. I picked my way through the fog, moving in a north-easterly direction, with scouts thrown out well to the front and flanks. No enemy was visible, and but for the rattle of musketry fire, which could be distinctly heard, there was no sign a fierce battle was raging close by. After advancing some little way Knox ordered me to halt whilst he galloped back to see what the Colonel proposed doing. My advanced parties were under the command of Second Lieutenant Bayford, while Maclachlan was galloping for the commanding officer. Presently one of my scouts returned to report that a small party of Boers were gathering in a spruit about three-quarters of a mile away, and to my right flank. I sent him back, telling him to keep a sharp look out and report any further developments. It was about this time that I noticed some Boers advancing towards a Boers' ambulance waggon, which, with its staff of doctors, had halted in the open veldt. Owing to the fog these latter Boers were unaware of the presence of my squadron, and it came quite as a surprise to them when they caught sight of me advancing on them at a gallop, for I quickly made up my mind to charge. It was all over in a few seconds, and out of the thirty Boers one was killed, about eight wounded, and the remainder taken prisoners. Had I not shouted to my men to give quarter few would have escaped death. The men's blood was up, and it was their first introduction to the Boers, and their desire to lay about them was only natural. Besides, these very Boers had previously fired at us from off their ponies as we were advancing towards them. But once we got amongst them they were a wretched, miserable, cringing lot, pleading for mercy. Some took off their bandoliers and held them up to us, others threw their rifles to the ground and prayed for their lives. These we made prisoners. I then saw a young Boer, a mere lad, deliberately fire at one of my men, who had purposely spared him on his begging for mercy. He shot him through the body, but this was my only casualty. I then retired with my prisoners towards the Boer ambulance, and despatched their doctors off to attend to the wounded. Dr. Hardy, our own doctor, also assisted. The prisoners were handed over to a guard of mounted infantrymen, who, with the remainder of the 18th, had come on the scene. These Boers were a funny crew. Their shaggy beards, slouch hats, and unkempt appearance reminded me forcibly of the brigands portrayed in burlesque.

"Colonel Moller now ordered me to halt and dismount; my squadron was to remain with him and the Mounted Infantry, whilst 'A' and 'C' squadrons, under Major Knox, moved away in a south-easterly direction. Lieut. Bayford was still out with his troop scouting, and he, with his men, eventually joined Knox.

"I was next ordered to mount my men and accompany the commanding officer, but after proceeding a short distance we returned to the Mounted Infantry, whom we found dismounted close to a road, and lying down ready to fire to cover our retirement had it been necessary. It was then a message from Major Knox was brought me, bidding me rejoin him with my squadron. However, it was not to be, for the Colonel, thinking Knox was advancing too far towards the Buffalo, ordered me to remain with him; but he sent Veterinary-Lieutenant Shore, who was acting as galloper, to ask why Knox required my squadron. Unfortunately Shore was unable to deliver the message owing to large parties of Boers now blocking the way and separating us from Knox.

"The Boers were now advancing on us in numbers. My scouts had warned me of their approach. They had collected in batches in the spruit before alluded to until they were sufficiently strong to attack us. The Mounted Infantry fired a few volleys and the Maxim gun also opened fire, but the range was still a long one, and many ant hills gave the Boers good cover; besides the heavy fog assisted in keeping them concealed.

"The Boers steadily increased in numbers, and the flanks of our small force were threatened, so the Colonel ordered a retirement. I am inclined to think my squadron might then have been advantageously employed; a charge into the flank of the enemy at this period, though costly no doubt, might have checked the enemy, and even caused them to fly. I was not, however, in a position to dictate orders, and I had to obey those I received.

"After retiring nearly a mile we were again halted, and besides the Mounted Infantry, one troop of my squadron was ordered to dismount and take up a position to check the enemy's advance. It was difficult to tell exactly how many Boers were attacking us, but there is no doubt we were greatly outnumbered. The position taken up on the open veld, with only a few ant hills to give cover, was really no position at all, and when the Boers began to work round our flank we were forced once more to fall back. We now had to cross a deep spruit, and here my horse stumbled and rolled over with me, but I managed to keep hold of him, and, being none the worse for my spill, I was quickly up again in the saddle and with my squadron. A good deal of wire fencing

Talana Hill.

had now to be cut through, but sending on a few men with wire cutters to clear a way for us, we were not much retarded. It was at this spruit our casualties began. Our Maxim gun got stuck in the muddy bottom. This I heard afterwards, and also how pluckily Lieut. Cape and the gun detachment had behaved. But in their endeavour to extricate the gun from its perilous position, all the detachment were either killed or wounded. Lieut. Cape was himself severely wounded, shot through the throat, and the Boers quickly closing in captured the gun. All this was related to me afterwards. A portion of the Mounted Infantry had been told off as escort to the maxim, but, for some unaccountable reason, had been removed, by order of the commanding officer, before the gun got into difficulties. Being the only officer with my squadron I had not left it, and so the sad gun episode, which had occurred on the right flank whilst I was on the left, had not attracted my notice. My trumpeter, a smart lad, had been wounded before we got to the spruit, but now the poor lad was hit again and killed.

"Men were beginning to drop, several riderless horses were careering about, and Boers were firing from closer quarters. Lieutenants Crum and Maclachlan were wounded. Both the latter managed to get back to camp without further mishap. Bullets were whistling past us and the fire was getting hotter, but, considering the excellent target we must have presented while riding through the narrow openings made in the wire fence, the Boer's markmanship was very erratic.

"Once more we dismounted, and this time the whole of my squadron, besides the Mounted Infantry, were dismounted and sent into the firing line. An ant hill here and there offered cover, but many men had to lie down and fire fully exposed. The Boers have a wonderful knack of keeping concealed, and it was only very occasionally during the whole of our retirement I actually caught sight of one.

"Captain Pollok and myself had imprudently ridden up into the firing line, with the result we almost simultaneously had our horses shot under us. Remaining mounted, we had drawn the enemy's fire on to us. Whilst in the act of dismounting from my wounded horse, who was bleeding profusely, a bullet passed through the end of my right boot, but it avoided my toes most miraculously, and another took a small snick out of the heel of the same boot. I soon captured another mount, a Boer pony, which was trotting about riderless. Meantime the order to mount and retire was again shouted out, as Boers were beginning to outflank us and render our present position no longer tenable. I had not even the time to unstrap my cloak from off my dead horse or even empty the contents of the wallets, in which, amongst other things, lay my flask. I had barely time to draw my sword and secure my field glasses.

"The Boer pony I had managed to catch seemed a willing enough beast, but I found having to ride in a saddle with only one stirrup, and that one quite four holes too short, a not altogether comfortable predicament to be in.

"I soon caught up the squadron and Mounted Infantry, who now retired through a narrow defile, and struck west round Impati Mountain, with the intention of regaining the camp *viâ* the Newcastle road. We could hear no more firing from the direction of Dundee, and fighting was evidently over. By this time we had shaken off the enemy. The Colonel trusted in getting safely back round by the Navigation Collieries, which neighbourhood Maclachlan had reconnoitred early in the morning, and reported clear of Boers at 6 a.m. Our luck was, however, dead out, for we had not proceeded far when my advanced scout reported the presence of Boers in the vicinity, and I soon myself observed parties of them descending the slopes of Impati. It was now clear to push on further in the direction we were taking was but to court disaster. We were heading for a new Boer commando, which had taken no part in the battle of Dundee. Thereupon the Colonel decided in taking up as strong a position as could be found handy and holding out until nightfall in the hope of slipping away in the dark. I considered this a most injudicious plan, and was all in favour of retracing our footsteps the way we had retired, now the Boers, who had harassed us all the morning, had sheared off and given up the pursuit. Had we done so and returned to camp *viâ* the Sandspruit nullah we should have escaped the sad fate which awaited us. By taking up a position then our mobility no longer stood us in good stead; we became Infantry and isolated Infantry, caught like a rat in a hole. There seemed little chance of deliverance, and it was with a feeling we were all doomed men I entered Adelaide Farm, for I never expected to leave it alive. It was about 1.15 p.m. when the Colonel settled on this farm as our last stand. Hills which were spurs of Impati Mountain lay at the back; on them the Mounted Infantry were posted. Scarcely had we dismounted and got into our places when the Boers, with their customary alacrity, collected from all sides and opened fire upon us. The position we had taken up was the best we could select, and which the country we were in afforded us. It gave the men good cover and a clear field of fire, but it had the drawback of giving an insufficiency of cover for the horses, and the presence of a nullah, stretching along the front and flanks, only about 750 yards away, which was quickly occupied by Boers, and from which they fired unceasingly for over two hours, was a great disadvantage."

The Defence of Adelaide Farm.

"The position we had selected to defend was a small farm, the front of which was faced by a stone wall 3ft. 6in. high, and about 80 yards long. This wall was about twenty yards from the house. The house itself was quite a small brick building, with a tin roof, on which bullets were heard to rattle unceasingly. It contained but three small rooms and a front and a back door. A small stable, also of brick, stood about thirty yards to the right, and an ox waggon lay halfway between the two buildings. A wire fencing, which completed the enclosure behind, we cut down on entering the farm. My men were posted behind the wall, whilst our horses were placed behind the house and stable, which latter was able to accommodate a couple only. The Mounted Infantry of the Dublin Fusiliers occupied some rocky ground on a hill to the right, which commanded the approach to the farm. The section of the 60th Rifles Mounted Infantry, took up a position on a small hill overlooking the place. Behind us rose Impati Mountain, on whose stony slopes lay the Mounted Infantry as well.

"From behind the wall we could see no Boers, but the continual whizzing of bullets over our heads made us aware of their presence. The Mounted Infantry, being on higher ground, could occasionally catch a glimpse of a Boer moving about, and they would seize those opportunities to fire a volley, and, as their shooting was good, they accounted for several of the enemy. The Boers' fire never showed signs of slackening; the expenditure of ammunition to them did not matter, besides they were plentifully provided, whereas we had to carefully nurse ours. I could see nothing of the enemy, and my men had to content themselves in remaining crouching behind the wall, wet through and shivering from cold. But they behaved splendidly, as they did all through that trying day. Not the slightest symptom of fear or wavering was ever shown, all orders were cheerfully and bravely carried out. The men were on their mettle, and seemed to realise their case was a desperate one, but a firm desire to do their duty to the last filled the mind of each defender. Once we experienced a bitter disappointment. We had observed a body of men approaching, and in the distance had mistaken them for British troops; our hopes of being rescued were, however, quickly dispelled on finding them to be Boer reinforcements. At about 1.45 p.m., and after we had been about half an hour in the farm, a gun opened fire on us, but the shell dropped short of the wall.

Only one shot was fired, and at the time I could not understand why no more followed. Meanwhile the Boers were actively employed firing off their Mausers. Though none of us had yet been hit behind the wall, the rain of bullets which poured into the farm enclosure made it very unsafe to move out, even but a few yards away from the wall. Bullets were pattering into the roof of the house and stable, and occasionally a horse was hit. The house was too small to completely hide the horses from view, and unfortunately a good number had to stand unprotected from the enemy's fire. It was a sad sight to see the poor brutes shot down one after another, and exasperating to feel we could do nothing to prevent this massacre. We tried shifting some of the more exposed ones from behind the house to the back of the stable, but whilst moving them across the bit of open ground which separated the buildings several were struck, the Boers firing with increased energy when they came into view. A corporal of my squadron, who was leading a horse, was knocked over, and at first I thought he was killed. He was picked up and carried into the house through the back entrance. He had been badly wounded, the bullet having entered the right side of his body, struck a pocket book, which saved his life, for it caused the bullet to glance off a vital spot.

"The owner of the farm was discovered, with his wife, lying under the bed, too terrified to render any assistance to the wounded man. The latter was put to bed and the best done for him, and a man told off to remain by his side. From time to time I looked over the wall to try and catch sight of the enemy, but not a single Boer could I see. It was necessary, however, to keep a sharp look out, as the Boers might at any moment emerge from the spruit and try to rush us. Their firing never relaxed a moment, but as far as we were concerned it did us no harm. The Mounted Infantry fared less well, and a few of their men were struck. Our horses, too, were frequently knocked over. A few turkeys and chicken were pecking away in the farm quite unconcerned. A bullet would often strike the ground with a thud right in their midst and cause a little skipping, but they would soon resume their grubbing, regardless of the consequences. The Mounted Infantry were now beginning to run short of ammunition, and matters were getting serious. The fire was now not only directed at our front, but our flanks were also beginning to catch it hot. The Boers had crept along the spruit, which formed nearly a complete semicircle round our position. When we eventually capitulated we found the enemy had worked right round and gained the heights of Impati to our rear.

"But if matters had previously looked bad for our small force, they looked doubly more so when, at 3.45 p.m., a couple of Krupp guns opened fire on us at a range of only 1,500 to 2,000 yards. The first shell struck the rocks above the ground where the Mounted Infantry were lying, but the second fell amongst them, killing one of the Dublin Fusiliers and wounding several others. The third, I believe, did no harm, but the following one fell amongst the horses, killing several and causing the remainder to stampede. The guns were making excellent practice. Every second I expected a shell to come ploughing into us, and it was hardly a pleasant sensation to experience. One hit the stable plump, killing a horse inside, another carried away part of the wall, behind which we were, smothering the men with earth and stones, but hurting no one.

" Our casualties increased. I saw one poor fellow struck by a shell which caught him below the shoulder blades, and which also killed the horse he was holding. Another man, though riddled by splinters of a shell, was still conscious and groaning piteously. We were having a bad time of it, and I had resigned myself to the fate which awaited us, and from which there seemed no escape. It was then the Colonel decided to surrender.

" Seventeen of our horses had been shot down and the others had stampeded. The Mounted Infantry had fired their last round. To continue a hopeless resistance entailed a mere useless sacrifice of life. For over two hours we had held out against heavy odds. If those guns had not appeared on the scene we might, perhaps, have lasted out until dark. We were told by the Boers afterwards that the first time they had fired a gun at us was from their laager, but that on finding the range was too long a one, they had brought their guns up much closer. Whilst the guns were being fetched, and until their arrival, the Boers had, by their incessant rifle fire, kept us boxed up in the farm.

" Out of a total of 187 men, the following is a correct return of our casualties on October 20th :—

	Killed.	Wounded.	Officers Wounded.
18th Hussars	3	8	2
Dublin Fusiliers M.I.	3	6	—
60th Rifles M.I.	2	3	1
Total	8	17	3

" A sheet, which someone had fetched from the house, was attached to a pole and raised over the wall. Above, on the hill, the bugler was sounding the ' cease fire ' . . . . we had given in !

" There was a short pause and a few seconds for bitter reflection, and then, as if by magic, Boers sprang up from everywhere. From all sides they galloped up to us, waving their arms and yelling to us to lay down our arms. There were quite 500 of them, and as their laager lay not far off, it would have been easy for them to summon up more men had they required assistance. I don't mind confessing that when I saw this howling calvacade approaching, I was foolish enough to imagine we should all be shot down."

The following is an account of the disaster which befel the maxim gun and the detachment with it, consisting of the under-mentioned:—Lieutenant H. A. Cape, in charge; Sergeant Batten, Corporal Sexton, Private Waterson, Private Lock, and Private Wolfe:—

"To relate again the events of October 20th, 1899, in detail would be labour in vain, so I commence my narrative from the time when Colonel Moller began his retirement, which eventually led to such disastrous results. The small force of Boers which came against the two troops of 'B' Squadron, the Mounted Infantry and the machine gun, under command of Colonel Moller, was evidently an off shoot from the main body under Lucas Meyer, and they had viewed us in the open plain after 'A' and 'C' Squadrons had been detached under Major Knox. As they approached us I was ordered to take up a position in the open with the Mounted Infantry, and this I did. I opened fire at about 1,700 yards range, and remained in position some time. As far as I could see there was little to fire at, and it was almost impossible to watch the effects of the shots. I then received an order from Colonel Moller to retire, the Mounted Infantry doing likewise, and I again took up another position, but before I had time to come into action yet another order reached me to retire again, the Mounted Infantry already having done so. Naturally by the time we had got the horses up and hooked on we were the last to leave, and I saw the Mounted Infantry on my left, and the two troops of 'B' Squadron in front, fast disappearing over the crest of a slight rise. We then saw Captain Pollok on our left endeavouring to get Trumpeter Salmon on to his own saddle, he evidently having lost his horse, but almost immediately the trumpeter fell off again, so we stopped the gun and took him up, and on we went again, bullets flying around like hailstones, and the squadron and Mounted Infantry still going on farther and farther away. After going about two miles, as near as one could judge, I saw a deep spruit in front, and as the horses were by now completely done and one had been shot in about four places, we knew all was up. As we approached I turned round and emptied my revolver at the fast approaching Boers, and as by some extraordinary piece of good luck I managed to knock one man over, it had the effect of checking them for an instant. The last words

I heard poor Trumpeter Salmon shout out were 'Well done.' Down into the Spruit we all plunged and then they were all around us, so I shouted to the men to save themselves, but I knew it to be too late. Sergeant Batten, before he was killed, and Corporal Sexton, before he was wounded, succeeded in disabling the gun, and Private Waterston, 'C' Squadron, behaved most gallantly. He seized Sergeant Batten's revolver after he had been hit, shot one Boer's horse, and then knocked him on the head with the empty revolver. Private Waterson himself was hit in three places, but managed, by lying perfectly still, to escape detection, and made his way back into camp that same evening. Out of the gun detachment Sergeant Batten, Private Lock the driver, and Trumpeter Salmon were killed; Corporal Sexton, Private Waterston, and myself were wounded; Private Wolfe, whose horse was shot, was taken prisoner at the same time. On seeing the Maxim gun in their hands, the Boers almost at once gave up the pursuit of Colonel Moller and his force, and came crowding round, stripping us of everything we possessed. They then took out the horse that was so badly shot and harnessed in a pony, and so we were taken back, picking up one wounded man of the King's Royal Rifles, whom we placed on the gun, into the midst of the now retreating Boer forces, to whom we were a great object of interest. Whilst we were in amongst the Boers we saw our own batteries of Artillery come up into the nek at Talana Hill, over which the main Vryheid road ran, unlimber and whip round their guns. Every moment we expected to have shells hurtling over our heads, but not a shot was fired. It was a magnificent opportunity lost, as the Boers were crowding in masses, and the whole of the Staats Artillery was standing there, the men off the horses and wandering about with their hands in their pockets. We were not kept long here, but we were sent off in a Cape cart to the farm at the base of Talana Hill on the Vryheid side, which had been turned into a Boer Hospital. I was put into a room eventually, which was crowded to suffocation with about twenty-five wounded Boers, and the sights, sounds, and smells were truly awful. Captain Hardy came out from camp and did what he could for us. After a night, the like of which I never wish repeated, and during which several of the Boers had died, we awoke with hopes of ambulances or doolies coming for us from camp, but it was long past one o'clock before eventually we got off, and were taken back to our own Field Hospital through a most appalling thunderstorm. The journey back in hospital tongas was a very severe trial, and caused excruciating agony to some poor chaps who were badly wounded. On arrival in camp we met with a distinctly cold reception from our own people, as we were placed on the wringing wet ground in tents through which the rain poured. Our friends the enemy, however, gave us a warm enough one to make up for it, for no sooner had we reached camp than they commenced shelling the Hospital Camp, about which they could see the Doolie bearers moving, from Impati Mountain. Their shells were, however, more alarming than harmful, but, I fear, sadly tried the already too highly strung nerves of the wounded. Here I found McLachlan shot in the leg, and from him gleaned much welcome news. Besides being at times full of shells, the air was full of rumours too of reinforcements coming from Ladysmith and also of our success at Elandslaagte. At daybreak, on the 22nd October, the Boers commenced shelling the hospital again, and continued doing so throughout most of the day whenever they saw any movement of any sort. In the evening General Symons received a message from General Yule, saying that he was sorry he could not come into camp to bid him goodbye, and that the column was leaving that night for Helpmakaar. Unfortunately this news was kept so secret that no one knew of it until the following morning, when it was too late to make a bold bid for liberty. Had we known this on the Sunday night I am convinced that there would have been a few absentees from the Hospital Camp on the Monday morning."

The casualties of the regiment on October 20th, 1899, were as follows:—

		Officers.	Other Ranks.
Killed	(a)	—	6
Wounded	(b)	3	14
Missing	(c)	4	81
		7	101

(a) Sergeant Batten, Trooper Salmon, Privates Lock and Bushell, Trumpeters Shrubsole and Grieve.

(b) Of these numbers thirteen men remained in the hands of the enemy, three were sent into Ladysmith during the investment (Lieut. McLachlan, Lieut. Cape, and Corporal Franklin), and one remained at duty (Lieut. Bayford).

(c) Colonel Moller, Major Greville, Captain Pollok, and Veterinary-Lieut. Shore.

A Squadron, 16 non-commissioned officers and men.
B Squadron, 60 non-commissioned officers and men.
C Squadron, 5 non-commissioned officers and men.

On October 21st Sergeant Farrier Shepherd was shot through the arm by a fragment of a shell when on parade with the Mounted Infantry, to which he was attached.

CHAPTER III.

"The Retreat to Ladysmith."

October, 1899.

The death of General Symons, or rather the mortal wound he received, and the total disablement of nearly all his staff, left things in a very disorganised condition at the close of the battle.

In consequence the taking of Talana Hill by our Infantry was not followed up by the pursuit and capture of a considerable body of the enemy as it might have been. They left the hill, Lucas Meyer's men, at about 12.30 p.m., and presented a large target to our Artillery, who were coming up by the main road, but, for some reason or other, the guns, on reaching the summit of the hill, did not open fire, Colonel Pickwood, who commanded them, respecting, apparently in too charitable a manner, a flag of truce which, accompanied by many Boer ambulances, was sent out from the range beyond Talana. This was undoubtedly a ruse on the part of the Boers, and one we were not quite up to at that early period of the campaign. However, it answered its purpose, and the Boers retreated unmolested, slowly in knots of twenties and hundreds, retiring out of our sight towards the drifts on the Buffalo across which they had advanced, no doubt in anticipation of an easy victory, early in the night of the preceding day.

It is needless to explain the reason they were allowed to do so by our Cavalry, after reading the account of what the 18th Hussars and the Mounted Infantry they had with them did during the whole of that day.

The Infantry got back to camp about 3 p.m., and arrangements were at once made for burying their dead, the 60th Rifles and the Royal Irish Fusiliers being the heaviest losers, though the Dublin Fusiliers had suffered pretty severely too. General Symons and nearly all his staff having been either killed or wounded, we were left with General Yule in chief command; Major Murray, of the Intelligence Department; Lieut. Murray, A.D.C. to General Symons; Captain Vallencey, Provost Marshal, and Lieut. Kenrick, Signalling Officer. As none of these officers had had any experience of the mixed troops now left under General Yule's command, it was nearly impossible to pick up the strings and work the machine at the point General Symons had left off at.

October 21st.—Patrols and piquets were sent out nearly as usual during the night of October 20th, additional ones being sent to our rear, Rhodes Colliery and the south side of Dundee town being the positions these latter took up. The night passed off quietly, and in the morning patrols from the 18th Hussars were sent off down the Newcastle road, round the east side of Impati Mountain, and to other places as well, besides parties to the battlefield of yesterday to continue burying the dead. About 11 a.m. information was sent in from Lieut. Thackwell, who was out with a patrol of the 18th Hussars on the east side of Impati Mountain, that the Boers were bringing five guns up the northern slopes of the hill, and later further information was sent in by Major Marling, who was out with his squadron in the Newcastle direction, that men from General Joubert's commandos were detraining a big gun at Hatting Spruit.

General Yule decided to move the camp from the ridge it was on to another undulating ridge south of the railway, just on the west side of Rhodes' Colliery. We commenced to do this about 2 p.m. in the afternoon, the Infantry and Artillery moving across the railway, together with all the transport. The Cavalry and Mounted Infantry were still out, most of them, under Major Knox's command, having gone along the Newcastle road in support of the squadron which had been sent out earlier in the day. Rain came on with great violence at about 3 p.m. and delayed matters in camp for a while, but camping grounds and lines of entrenchments were, however, marked out as rapidly as possible; still, before either could be completed the Boers had got one of their big guns on the slopes of Impati, near where the Newcastle road crosses the spur of the hill.

It had evidently not been contemplated that the new camping ground would be within range of Impati, but it easily was. The Boers opened fire with two heavy guns about 3.30 p.m., and kept it up till dark, causing a great deal of confusion among our troops, who were compelled to move camp a second time, the one first chosen having proved to be absolutely untenable. To add to our confusion night was coming on apace, the weather was unfavourable, our own guns were unable to reply as they were outranged, and the hastily improvised staff was quite incapable of competing with the sudden emergencies which fate had thrust upon it.

As can be seen from the description of the country around Dundee, previously given, the Biggarsberg range crops up on the southward at no great distance from the town, and the undulating country commences to change to that of a more hilly nature some distance away from the range itself. Towards this broken country General Yule was compelled to look for a more suitable spot to fix his camp in, the long rolling ridges he was now on giving no cover to his troops from the elevated position near Impati Mountain, where the Boers had brought their guns to. About 2,000 yards southeast of Rhodes' Colliery there was a farm belonging to a man called Tom Roone, with a rough kopje on the south-east of it, and many more hills and dongas on the Biggarsberg side of the farm. There was plenty of cover here both from view and fire, and just before sunset choice was made of this spot for the Glencoe Field Force to occupy as soon as it possibly could. The regiments were very much scattered at nightfall, as the new camp they were first to occupy had been only partially laid out, and the guns, with half a battalian Royal Irish Fusiliers and the Dublin Fusiliers, had been disposed in front of the camp to defend it whilst the other troops and baggage were moving across. Whilst this was taking place the Boer gun opened fire, and though at first it did no damage, still it was evident that the position was a bad one, and the decision for moving further to the southward had to be come to, and fresh orders issued for the move. These were arranged, but the communication of them to the different regiments was a more difficult matter, and it was found impossible to move the force to the second camp selected till the morning. The transport, both regimental and A.S.C., a very large mass of baggage for so small a force, was sent to the cover of the kopje near the freshly selected camp with half a battalion of the Royal Irish Fusiliers as escort, to hold the hill during the night. The remaining regiments were ordered to proceed to the new camp at an hour before daybreak. The guns and their escort of the Dublin Fusiliers, and half-battalion Royal Irish Fusiliers, were to go there from their position in front of the camp first fixed on, the 60th Rifles from where they had formed up in quarter column under protection of some ground close to Rhodes Colliery, awaiting orders since the commencement of the change of plans, and the whole of the Leicester Regiment from the line of branch railway which ran to Rhodes' Colliery, and which they held during the night.

The Cavalry were not back in camp, or rather at Rhodes' Colliery, till dark on the night of the 21st, when they returned from their reconnaissance in the Hatting Spruit direction, in close touch with the Boer advance guard, now rapidly advancing on Impati Mountain. No orders were issued to them on that night, and they had to select their own spot for a bivouac; in the morning they were directed to patrol the country in the immediate vicinity of the new position our troops had taken up, and also to hold some ridges which lay on the south side of this position, and which it was necessary to occupy for the safety of the new camp.

We all spent a most uncomfortable night; no one knew for certain what was required for the morrow, or whether we had any plan of campaign good enough to frustrate the enveloping tactics the Boers were using against us with such success. We had practically abandoned to the mercy of the enemy some six weeks' supplies, all our tents, kits, a considerable quantity of ammunition and our hospitals, in fact our whole camp, with the exception of what little we could carry on our horses and persons, and what our regimental and supply wagons could bring away. We had retired from one position to another, and still we were in range of those guns which had so assiduously followed us up since half-past three o'clock in the afternoon, and which no doubt would recommence their harassing tactics at daybreak.

The inhabitants of Dundee were getting alarmed, and several came to us during the night for protection, thinking that we were leaving them to their fate, and altogether a feeling of uncertainty, and perhaps a little despondency as to future events, caused most of us to think that we were not altogether in an enviable position. All had had a long day, however, and, in spite of the discomforts of the night, slept soundly enough where they were, the Infantry on the ground they were occupying at nightfall, and the Cavalry alongside their horses, under the kopje by T. Roone's farm.

October 22nd.—Before dawn on the 22nd all regiments commenced to move up towards the farm, and as soon as light availed they were placed along the ridge in position, the 60th Rifles, Royal Irish Fusiliers, and Leicestershires on the ridge above the farm, and the Dublins in reserve; the 18th Hussars were sent out in the direction of Glencoe Pass, and the Mounted Infantry towards Helpmakaar.

By daylight it was seen that the new position we had taken up was commanded by many points on the south side, especially by the hills adjacent to Indumeni Mountain, and also that the water supply was a poor one. A conference of commanding officers of regiments was, in consequence, called at about 6 a.m., and after a short discussion Colonel Carleton, of the Royal Irish Fusiliers, and his brother, Col. Carleton, of the Leicestershire Regiment, were requested by General Yule to draw up a scheme for the day. They were both in favour of an immediate retreat on Ladysmith, and their arguments in support of this were, briefly, that the British forces in Natal were too few to be split up and encounter with success the large forces the South African Republics were pouring into the country, that gun ammunition was running very short, there only being sufficient for one more fight, that Ladysmith could not send us reinforcements, and that Dundee was not tactically capable of withstanding a siege. These were weighty arguments in favour of a retreat, and they carried the day, for truly a retreat seemed the only possible course to pursue. However, just as the orders had been made out for an immediate retirement on Ladysmith, a telegram was received, *viâ* Helpmakaar (the direct line had been cut for the last two or three days), to say that the Ladysmith garrison had attacked and defeated a force of the enèmy, who had taken up a position close to Elandslaagte Station, and had captured a good many of them and two of their guns. On receipt of this news the orders for our retreat on Ladysmith were not given out, and other dispositions for the day were made.

A part of our force, two batteries of Artillery, the 60th Rifles, Royal Irish Fusiliers, and the 18th Hussars, were ordered to proceed at once to the head of Glencoe Pass to cut off any fugitives passing up that way to join the main Boer army. The troops set off at once in compliance with this idea, and on nearing the head of the pass the right of our column came under fire of the enemy's guns on Impati Mountain, to which again we could not reply, as the distance was too great, and the unsuitability of the ground prevented a nearer approach. The Boers, too, on seeing our apparent intention of seizing the head of Glencoe Pass, despatched guns and an escort along the ridge on the west side of the railway to a hill directly commanding the exit from the pass, the one we used to hold with a company during the first period of our stay at Dundee.

The 18th Hussars, together with one battery of Field Artillery and the remainder of the Mounted Infantry, were sent in advance, under the command of Major Knox, to cover the approach of our troops to Glencoe Station. Major Laming's Squadron " C " was in advance, and the account of his movements is given below. The mounted troops were unable to seize the head of the pass, for they were forestalled by the enemy as previously stated, and in consequence they conformed to General Yule's change of plan, and acted as rearguard to the force on its retirement to camp.

Report of the movements of No. 4 Troop, " C " Squadron, 18th Hussars, on 22nd and 23rd October, 1899.

" From Officer Commanding ' C ' Squadron 18th Hussars to the Officer Commanding 18th Hussars :—

" On October 22nd, 1899, I was ordered to proceed with my squadron to Glencoe Pass, together with a battery of Field Artillery, for the purpose of shelling and pursuing any fugitive Boers who might be escaping that way after the battle of Elandslaagte.

" No. 4 Troop of my squadron, under command of Acting Sergeant-Major, Sergeant Baldry, formed my advance guard. On arriving at the head of the pass the guns and main body changed direction, while the advance guard turned down the pass. Sergeant Baldry states that he proceeded some way down the road before he became aware of the change of direction of the main body. He then attempted to return, but the enemy had appeared in force on the west heights at the head of the pass. Finding he could not return this way, he moved again down the pass and reached Waschbank, at its southern entrance, only to find that the lower ground was also in possession of considerable numbers of the enemy. He again turned back into the pass with the intention of regaining the Dundee camp under cover of dark, but the enemy had by this time got complete possession of the higher outlet, and had advanced some way down the pass itself. He came across them some two miles from the summit, whereupon they put up a white flag, of which he took no notice, but finding both exits of the pass blocked, he wheeled to his right and turned up a valley, which runs into the pass from the westward, at the point he had reached. This valley was, he soon found, also occupied by Boers, and he came under fire both from these fresh Boers and from those who had put up a white flag just before. However, by striking up the hill sides diagonally, he succeeded in crossing the heights and getting clear of the hills just before dark, pushed on and reached Sunday's River, near where the Dundee-Ladysmith road crosses it, that night and bivouacked there. Before daylight on the 23rd he marched to Elandslaagte, where he obtained information that there were parties of the enemy still between him and Ladysmith, and that the railway line had been torn up near Modder Spruit. He proceeded along the line with a view to stopping any train coming that way, and when at the level crossing on the Ladysmith side of Modder Spruit the enemy opened fire on him, and at the same time he observed a train coming from Ladysmith towards him. He rode towards the train and stopped it, and the officer in charge of the train took on board two men whose horses were exhausted and one man whose horse was shot at the level crossing. From this point onwards he marched his troop into Ladysmith without further opposition. Sergeant Baldry's casualties were three men and three horses missing. Private Clegg was severely wounded and taken back to Dundee by the enemy, and eventually sent into Ladysmith during the investment. Corporal Padwick was taken prisoner and sent to Pretoria. Private Morgan was with Corporal Padwick's patrol, but managed to evade the enemy; he made his way to a German Mission Station, where he was provided with civilian clothing. Later he was arrested and sent to Pretoria, but released after a few days, having been treated as a civilian. The wounded horse was afterwards recovered and brought into Ladysmith.

"Sergeant Baldry's troop consisted of thirty-one non-commissioned officers and men.
"(Signed)   H. T. LAMING, Major.
"18th Hussars."

In forwarding Sergeant Baldry's name for mention to the Commander-in-Chief, the Commanding Officer, Major Knox, drew attention to the determination and resource shown by this non-commissioned officer in extricating his troop from a most difficult and perilous position. It is evident the enemy considered they had them securely trapped, and that the hoisting of the white flag was to give them an opportunity to surrender. The timely warning the patrol gave to the approaching train no doubt, too, saved it from derailment and capture.

In view of the signal service rendered by Sergeant Baldry, the Commander-in-Chief conferred the award of the Distinguished Conduct Medal on this non-commissioned officer.

Corporal Padwick's account of the experiences of No. 4 Troop " C " Squadron on the 22nd October, 1899.

"On Sunday, the 22nd October, we (that is No. 4 Troop, 'C' Squadron), under Sergeant Baldry, moved from our camp at Dundee in the direction of Elandslaagte. I don't think any of us knew where we were going to; the extent of our knowledge was that we were the advance troop of the squadron, and had to reconnoitre towards Glencoe. It was raining heavily as we entered Glencoe Pass, and we halted when we had got about three miles down it. Sergeant Baldry then sent me with two men to keep a look out on the right, with orders to rejoin him as soon as the main body came abreast of my post. I waited about twenty minutes, and saw no signs of connecting files or main body, but I did see what I was sure were parties of Boers on the opposite side of the pass, on the very ground I had seen our left flank scouts on a few minutes before. I was about to send the information to Sergeant Baldry, when the latter came back up the road, and I rejoined him, and we proceeded up the pass to join touch with the main body. On nearing the summit of the pass we heard guns firing, and soon found our road blocked, and that we were cut off from our squadron. The only course left us was to make back again down the pass in the hope of reaching Elandslaagte and joining up with any of our troops there, who might have stayed behind after the fight of the day before.

"All went well till we reached Wessels Nek, where I and two men, who had been sent on with me as advanced scouts, found a Boer fugitive in the police hut, and we took him prisoner, and I kept his pony with the intention of riding it to save my own horse, which had hardly been unsaddled for three days, but it proved to be so dreadfully done up that I could hardly get it out of a slow walk! I little thought that the slowness of this same pony would eventually land me in Pretoria for over six months as a prisoner of war. I went on nearly to Elandslaagte, where I could see nothing of our own troops; the red cross flag was flying from some buildings, and what appeared to be a burial party was moving about on the battlefield. I learnt from a Kaffir that our men had withdrawn to Ladysmith the previous day, and then I withdrew to rejoin my troop. I met Corporal Randall on the way, and he told me that Sergeant Baldry had determined to try and get up the pass again, and that I was to bring the prisoner along. As the troop was trotting it was impossible for me and the prisoner on his tired pony to keep up, and I soon got left a long way behind. As we neared the centre of the pass, Sergeant Birkett came back to me and said Sergeant Baldry would wait for me at a spruit there was ahead, and I soon came in sight of the troop halted about $1\frac{1}{2}$ miles in front. Almost at the same moment I saw a mass of men and what appeared to be guns on the summit of the pass, and they very quickly opened fire on our troop beneath them. I waited, fully expecting the troop to retire back towards me, but they turned straight to the west, through the opening I had been posted on earlier in the day, and with great difficulty, as I heard later, reached Ladysmith on the following day. This left me and another man, Private Clegg, with the prisoner alone in the pass. There was only one thing to do, namely, to let the prisoner go and retire again. The Boers were already between me and the troop, and in a few minutes would have been in the road behind me if I hadn't galloped pretty sharp. We reached the Elandslaagte Collieries at dusk and found the manager there. The latter gave us food and shelter, and we put our horses up for the night. At daybreak we moved off again, intending, if possible, to get to Ladysmith. All went well till we got just past Modder Spruit, where we almost ran into a Boer patrol. We also saw several other parties of Boers across our front. We tried in several places to get through, but the Boers seemed to be in front of us everywhere, so at last we gave it up and decided to wait till dark and try and get through Glencoe Pass somehow, hoping, if we were detected, to be able to gallop through in the darkness. We little thought that by this time the Dundee column had left and was then on its way to Ladysmith, and that by going back to Dundee we were going practically into a Boer laager.

"We got within sight of the pass at dusk, and we were passing a Kaffir kraal when two men came out from it. They were dressed in khaki with slouch hats, and had no arms.

They struck me at first as being Natal carbiniers, but on coming up closer to them we found that only one of them could speak English, and that they both had Transvaal crests in their hats. We were just drawing our carbines, but before we could do so two shots came from the kraal, but they missed us, though I can't think why, as the range could not have been more than thirty yards. I saw one of these decoy men later on when I was a prisoner, and I asked him how he accounted for the bad shooting. He said that one of the men who fired first had been wounded at Elandslaagte in the arm, and so was unsteady, and that they were also afraid of hitting their own men who were close to us. However, we got clear away, and they did not attempt to follow us. I should think there were ten or twelve of them in the kraal. After we were out of range we came across an old shed, and as it was now dark and raining heavily we decided to rest ourselves and the horses for an hour or two before making our fourth and last attempt to get through. This was the most miserable night I spent during the whole campaign. We had nothing to eat since the morning, and one of us had to hold the horses and look out whilst the other tried to get a little sleep. At last, about 11 p.m., we started again for the pass; we made a wide detour of the kraal from which we had been fired upon, and shortly commenced entering the pass. We made the horses walk very slowly, and as the road was muddy we made no noise at all, and except for the moon showing through the clouds occasionally, it was quite dark. We went along very well for about two miles, when we evidently disturbed something a little to our right, and although it might only have been cattle grazing, we decided to halt where we were till the moon came out, so that we could see among the bushes and make sure. Presently there was enough light to see a group of ponies grazing, and here and there a saddle with men lying about, evidently all asleep. We decided to move off very slowly as we had come, in the hope of leaving them undisturbed. This we managed to do, and it was a great relief to get away from them without being discovered. The suspense was, however, dreadful, as we did not know at what moment we might run into another post and perhaps be discovered by them first. Soon afterwards we crossed a spruit in about the middle of the pass, and could not avoid making a certain amount of noise doing so, but we got over it all right and moved on, but had not gone more than forty yards before someone shouted in my ear, in Dutch, 'Who goes there.' All suspense was now at an end, and there was only one thing to do, so I shouted to Private Clegg to gallop, and at our first stride they opened fire. I could hardly say which of us was hit first, for at the same moment that I felt as if someone had smacked my ear,

Clegg fell across my horse's croup, shot through the chest. I could do nothing but go on, as they kept firing up the road. Clegg's horse followed behind mine, which was lucky, for my horse seemed to be going very lame, and I dismounted a little further on, and found that he had been shot in the near fore, and that I had two scratches, one in the thigh and another in the ear, so I mounted Clegg's horse and pushed on at a gallop, which was now necessary, as any other piquets in the pass would certainly be on the alert. However, nothing happened till I reached the top of the pass, when I was fired on from the right. I heard afterwards this was from a post with a gun in position. After passing this post I saw nothing till I arrived at the colliery near Dundee, and as it was breaking day, but still dark, I thought I would wait till it was lighter, and then have a look round to see where our troops were. As it gradually got lighter I could see mounted men moving about our camp, and on closer inspection I saw they were Boers, and no matter which way I looked it was the same. Above Glencoe Station I could see their laager. They were coming down the Newcastle road. They were all over the town of Dundee; in fact they were everywhere. Although no doubt they could see me, they probably took me for one of their own men in the uncertain light, so I turned round with the intention of hiding in the colliery until I could find some way of getting away from them. When about fifty yards from the colliery a party of Boers came from behind it, and although I attempted to get away, they, with their fresh ponies, soon overtook me, formed a circle right round me, and so I was taken prisoner. I had always thought that falling into the hands of Boers meant very harsh treatment, and I was very much surprised when they offered me, first of all, a bottle of whisky and then food, which they had evidently just looted from the town. I was very thankful for the food, having had nothing since the morning before, and after the fatigue and excitement of that last day and night, I appreciated it all the more. Many of these Boers could speak English, and they informed me that our troops had evacuated Dundee, leaving all their guns behind, and that it was only a matter of hours before Lucas Meyer overtook them and captured the lot. They took my horse and put me on a little white Basuto pony, and took me to their laager above Glencoe Station. There I was brought before the commandant, a very big dark man in a velvet jacket, who, when I arrived, was at breakfast on the end of a very comfortable waggon. He offered me some of the beef he was eating and some coffee, and as I sat at the end of the waggon a crowd very soon collected round me, and I appeared to be an object of great curiosity to them. As they began to get a nuisance, asking all manner of silly questions, the commandant sent them away, and had me taken over to the ambulance to get my wounds dressed. There I learned that Clegg was very seriously wounded, and the doctor said he did not think he would get over it, but luckily he eventually did. When I got back to the laager, which, by the way, looked very much like an old-fashioned country horse fair at home, I found out that there were a good many men who had fought at Elandslaagte attached to it. One man showed me his rifle, which was cut through the wood and partly into the barrel. He said a lancer had made a cut at him with his sword, and he had saved his life by holding his rifle with both hands above his head. About mid-day I was driven in a Cape cart to Hatting Spruit Station. We passed several laagers on the way, and at each of them we stopped, and I was exhibited for a few minutes. At one they told me that a lot of our men, pointing to the colours in my helmet, had been captured a few days before, and had been sent to Pretoria. When we arrived at Hatting Spruit we found several commandos round the station, and a lot of the Staats Artillery with their guns, awaiting transport to Ladysmith. They then put me into the pantry of the stationmaster's house with a sentry on the door, and later in the day another prisoner, a corporal of the Royal Irish Fusiliers, was put in with me. He had been left behind when our troops evacuated Dundee. We were left till about nine o'clock the next morning, when a Boer, who I afterwards learnt was General Botha, came in to see us, and with him an old gentleman, rather stout, with a long square beard almost white. He was introduced by General Botha as follows:—This is Commandant General Joubert, and he wishes to ask you a few questions, which, as prisoners of war, you are not obliged to answer. Then, turning to me, he asked, ' Do you know if there is any ammunition buried in Dundee?' I replied ' I don't know.' Again he asked: ' There are two wires running from a tent in Dundee camp; do you know if they are connected with a mine?' I replied ' I don't know, but they might be.' I knew quite well the wires he meant; they were telegraph wires running from the Brigade Office. After these questions General Joubert said: ' I am sending you to Pretoria, and as long as you give no trouble you will be treated with respect and no one will interfere with you.' After this interview we were marched out to the platform. We had been standing there a few moments, when a train came into the station, and exactly opposite us was a truck with a very large gun on board, which one of our guards informed us was ' Long Tom.' On the other trucks there was a searchlight and several other guns. Next to the engine of the train was a closed truck, and into this they put us, and as three-parts of it was full of Long Tom shells, we sat on these whilst they conveyed us back to Glencoe again.

We got out of this train at Glencoe and were put into an old room in the stationmaster's house. During the day a civilian was put in with us; he had been taken as a spy because he was riding through Dundee town on a bicycle. As night came on it got very cold and wet, and we found some old dresses in a cupboard, and with these we covered ourselves up, and had just got to sleep when we were awakened by a dreadful noise. We found out it was the stationmaster's piano, supplemented by captured drums and brass instruments, in the hands of not very competent Boer musicians. The next morning a train was made up for Pretoria, and we were put into this in a closed cattle truck with two Boer sentries. Our first stop was Newcastle, and as soon as the truck was opened we had a crowd of burghers round it. They treated us with civility, and were most anxious that we should have the latest news, and, as it was the same thing always between here and Pretoria, I will relate what the latest news was:—'Ladysmith had been taken that morning. They had cut off the water supply at Kimberley, and expected it to fall at any moment, whilst Mafeking would succumb to the first attack.' One of our guards, an old man, was present at Majuba in 1881, and as we passed it he pointed it out, and tried to give us his version of the fight, but his knowledge of English was so slight that we did not understand him very much. About 6 p.m. we arrived at Volkrust and were now in the Transvaal, a country I did not again quit till the end of the war. As the train went no further that night we were marched to the jail to be housed till morning. Arriving there we were put into a large room, in which there were already two civilian prisoners. One of them, a bank clerk, had been arrested as a spy whilst leaving the Transvaal a few days earlier. His bag had been searched at Volkrust, and a photograph of a man in the uniform of the 17th Lancers had been found in it. It was the photograph of a friend of his, but the Boer official said that it was his (the clerk's) photo, and with this he was arrested on suspicion. The other prisoner was a French Jew; he told me that he had for some time been employed in the Transvaal secret service, but lately he had been employed by the English, and that he had been arrested near the border just before war was declared. He said he had been taken out to be shot two days earlier, but they had brought him back again to the jail. He seemed quite confident that though they had threatened to shoot him they were afraid to do so. I was surprised to read in a *Standard and Diggers* newspaper, a week or two later, a graphic account of the shooting of this very man. It was the 25th of October when I met him, and the paper was dated October 22nd! We were awakened the next morning at 3 a.m. and taken to the station at six o'clock by six men of the

Johannesburg police, who were staying in Volkrust on their way down to Ladysmith. We left Volkrust at 6 a.m. and reached Pretoria at about nine at night, having been exhibited on the way to very inquisitive crowds of Boers at all the roadside stations. Their chief questions were the date of General Buller's arrival and the effects of lyddite shells. The corporal of the Fusiliers gave them a most exaggerated description of the effects of the latter, which seemed to amuse the more enlightened amongst them, but evidently impressed the majority, judging by the way they translated it to their friends who did not understand English. We were escorted solemnly through the town of Pretoria by a dozen mounted police to the jail, and lodged that night in a room the Reform prisoners were in in 1896."

But to return to the narrative of the events of October 22nd :—

We were unable to prevent the enemy reaching the head of the pass, as they had a considerably shorter way to get there, and as it was not General Yule's intention to attack the Boers just then, he decided to discontinue his advance towards Glencoe, and to retire again to the farm and ridge he had occupied in the morning.

One regiment, the Leicesters, and a battery of Artillery had remained behind in camp to protect the transport, and wagons were sent early to our old camp under Impati to remove tents and stores, but they could not approach the neighbourhood of the camp even, as the Boers opened a very hot fire from five guns on the top of Impati Mountain and drove them back.

By the time our force, which had been towards Glencoe Junction, arrived back at Roone's farm, the Infantry with it had had a ten mile walk to no purpose, and the gun horses some heavy work pulling the guns and limbers over spruits the rain had made very boggy. The troops rested during the afternoon, it being about midday when they got back to their last night bivouac.

General Yule was uncertain now what course to pursue, but an interview with Colonel Dartnell, in the garden of the farm, again convinced him that a retreat, and a retreat at once, on Ladysmith was the only feasible course, and about 3 p.m. it was decided to retire *viâ* the direction of Helpmakaar. The Glencoe Pass road was practically in the possession of the Boers, and the old road over the Biggarsberg was reported unfit for waggon traffic. The route *viâ* Beith in the direction of Helpmakaar was a circuitous one, but at present it was open, and should it not remain so all the way to Ladysmith, there was always an alternative line of retreat left through Greytown to Maritzburg.

A transference of our force to Talana Hill had been suggested, but it was not considered a good scheme. At the same time the idea was allowed to get abroad, as it was not desirable to let anyone know our real intention.

October 22nd.—It was determined to start our proper march at 9 p.m., and orders were issued about 4 p.m. for all to be ready to move at the former hour. At about 9.30 p.m. the column moved off in the following order :—60th Rifles, Royal Irish Fusiliers, half 18th Hussars, two batteries of Artillery, Regimental Transport, Supply Column, half 18th Hussars, Royal Dublin Fusiliers, 1st Leicestershire Regiment. The column was about four miles long, and the march lay past the east side of Dundee town and along the Helpmakaar road by the collieries to Blesboklaagte, a deep ravine nine miles from Dundee, which was reached by the advanced guard at 4.30 a.m. on the morning of the 23rd. The 18th Hussars and what remained of the Mounted Infantry all under command of Major Knox, with Captain the Hon. H. S. Davey as his adjutant, took up their position as day broke to cover the front, flanks, and rear of the column. Before leaving Roone's farm as many wagons as could be collected by the Army Service Corps were sent, under Major Wickham, to the old camp at dusk, to collect what stores they could carry on them, and then to join in with our column on the march from Dundee. They found the old camp quite deserted and everything standing as we had left it, a few Kaffirs only having entered it since our departure, and taken a little loot therefrom. Our field hospitals we had to abandon, and with them nearly all those who had been wounded at Talana Hill on the 20th, including General Symons, who died very shortly afterwards, and Lieutenants Cape and McLachlan of our own regiment.

The Boers placed a good many shells round and about the Field Hospital during the 22nd and on the morning of the 23rd, till they discovered that we had gone, but apparently they did not hit anybody inside.

One of the inmates writes as follows :—

"Our feelings that morning, 23rd October, when we heard of the departure of the column, may be better imagined than described. 'Left,' hopelessly 'left,' is what we felt, and prisoners of war to all intents and purposes as well. The light of subsequent events of course shows that there was no other alternative, but when it came it was a bitter pill to swallow. The Boers, too, were completely surprised, as they had no idea the column had moved off, and at daybreak commenced shelling us again. This, however, was soon put a stop to by one of the medical officers, Captain Milner, R.A.M.C., riding out to them with a flag of truce and explaining that they were only firing on the hospital, and that the British column was away. At first they were very incredulous, but later on, towards afternoon, they came down from the hills and practically took possession of the camp and hospital, helping themselves to everything they wanted and going through all the hospital tents collecting arms and ammunition. Their bearing towards us was, however, most chivalrous; no boasting, no swaggering, in fact they behaved like gentlemen, sharing their loot from the town with some of the men. At 6 p.m. to-day poor General Symons died, his death casting a profound feeling of sorrow over the camp.

"Tuesday, 24th October, found the camp of the column overrun with Boers, who helped themselves to everything, enlivening proceedings by weird blasts on the musical instruments they found and beatings of drums. No news of our ultimate fate, but in the evening Joubert's A.D.C. and the P.M.O. of Joubert's Commando dined with the medical officers in the hospital camp.

"Wednesday morning, 25th October, saw yet more Boers everywhere, and waggons arrived to carry off their loot. In the afternoon Private Clegg, of 'C' Squadron, was brought in badly wounded, and told us of the dashing exploit of No. 4 Troop, 'C' Squadron, under Sergeant-Major Baldry.

"Thursday was an uneventful day, but on Friday, 27th October, we were all moved into houses in Dundee by order of Joubert. This was indeed luxury after our camp, which was by now a perfect quagmire. Here we stayed until Friday, 3rd November. Meantime many rumours reached us, all of which we know now were vastly exaggerated. One of them was that Sir George White had been killed, hit by a bullet in the stomach; these rumours and the uncertainty as to our fate did not tend to keep us very cheerful. Our wounds were, however, given a chance of healing somewhat.

"On 2nd November those who were slightly wounded, and could travel, were ordered to go to Pretoria, and on the next day the remainder, with the exception of those who were too bad to be carried, were put into a train *en route* for Ladysmith. We were told to be ready to start at about 6 a.m., but it was 4.30 p.m. before we got off, a truly motley crowd, many only having a suit of blue hospital clothes and some Boer blankets. That evening we got as far as Glencoe Junction, and there they kept us the whole night, five of us in a filthy dirty Dutch carriage, myself the only one able to move, all with wounds that required dressing, and nothing to eat. The next day, after much talking and making of plans, we got off, and arrived at Elandslaagte about midday, after a terrible journey. Here we were kept until the arrival of the baggage, which came down in a second train some hours afterwards. Eventually we proceeded on our way, and finally were deposited on the veldt about three miles beyond Elandslaagte Station, where we awaited the arrival of Boer transport, to take us the remainder of the journey into Ladysmith. Before taking us on, however, we were taken to Pepworth's farm, where the Boers had established a hospital, and it was here that Major Kerin, R.A.M.C., said that he would undertake that none of us should fight again during the campaign. Little did he or any of us realise what this would mean; however, we have all since had the bitter experience of being "Sleeping partners of the chase." On our arrival at the Orange Free State junction outside Ladysmith, we were met by a piquet of the Liverpool Regiment, and an application was sent in for our transport, which eventually deposited us all in the various hospitals in the town, in the midst of a terrible thunderstorm. Our joy at being once more amongst our own people was somewhat marred when we heard that next day we were to be sent to Intombi Camp. However, the pleasure of seeing one's brother officers and hearing all the news made partial amends.

"It was 4.30 p.m. on Sunday, 5th November, when we first saw Intombi, and it was then a small hospital camp, having accommodation for about 200 sick and wounded. What it developed into later on may be imagined when, at one time, there were over 2,300 sick and wounded there, and on 8th March, 1900, 650 poor men had been laid in their last resting place in the cemetery close to the camp, as many as twenty-three being for burial in one morning. These numbers are not complete, because after that date there were many more buried there, bringing the total up to, I believe, nearly 700."

To return to the Glencoe Field Force. The entire evacuation was carried out very quietly, but of necessity very slowly. The road was carefully explored during the afternoon and the surrounding country too. No mention was made to anyone of our destination, and it was generally believed that Talana Hill was the new position we were going to take up; the Dundee townspeople, with a few exceptions, also clung to this idea, and looked towards Talana next morning with the expectancy of seeing us lining the summit of that hill, but on Monday morning, the 23rd, all trace of our column had vanished, and Boers and townspeople alike looked for the Glencoe Field Force in vain.

October 23rd.—No opposition to our march was encountered, and at daybreak part of the 18th Hussars and two batteries crossed Blesboklaagte and took up a position on the far side to cover the crossing of the whole force. The ravine was passed and the column halted for breakfast, at about 9 a.m., for two hours, about a mile on the far side of the

The Retreat to Ladysmith. 41

spruit, the Infantry thoroughly tired out with their long night march after the work they had to do on the preceding day.

Only a two hour halt was allowed here, as we were still in sight of Impati Mountain, from which the Boers were signalling to us, mistaking us for some of their own people coming up from the Vryheid district. At 11 a.m. we moved on past the Dutch church at Beith to Vlakfontein, at the top of the Mohawala or Van Tonder's Nek pass, on the Ladysmith road, about two miles beyond the church. Here we halted for rest and food

General Yule had sent on messengers in the morning to Helpmakaar to wire the following message to General White at Ladysmith:—"Propose camping at Beith to-day, and march to Sunday's River, Beith-Ladysmith road, to-morrow, starting at 2 a.m."

This plan was altered in regard to the time of departure, for Lieut. Thackwell, with some colonial guides and a troop, having explored during the afternoon the road down the pass, and General Yule being persuaded to start off at 11 p.m., we were all on the march again at that hour, descended the hill by a fairly good road all through the night, and as day broke we debouched on the lower ground which lies under the Biggarsberg on the Ladysmith side.

October 24th.—Very soon after leaving the range in our rear the country became more open, and the baggage was able to close up and move several wagons abreast, thereby lessening the length of our column.

We had intended to take the road on the west side of Spion Kop, or Job's Kop as it is sometimes called, but our guides reported it out of repair, so we took a more easterly one instead. At 9 a.m. we reached Waschbank River, close to where the Imbusi River joins it, crossed it, and halted on the far side, as the baggage animals and Infantry had had enough for the present. Here the Infantry halted all day, taking up a position on the ridge on the left bank of the river till the afternoon. The 18th Hussars and two batteries of Artillery were sent out at about 11 a.m. in the direction of Elandslaagte, heavy firing having been heard somewhere in the neighbourhood of Modder Spruit Station on the Natal railway. This, as we found out later, was the fight at Reitfontein, undertaken by the Ladysmith garrison to withdraw the attention of the Boers from our retrograde movement. Our reconnaissance was productive of no result, as it was found that the fight was a great deal farther off than we had imagined at first, and the mounted troops, after a tiring day, did not rejoin the others at Waschbank River till night was setting in. One of the advanced patrols of the 18th Hussars, under Lieut. Clarke, had lost touch with the main body during the reconnaissance, as the following account will show :—

Account of the doings of a patrol of " C " Squadron, 18th Hussars, on October 24th, 1899.

" My patrol originally consisted of one corporal, three men, and a guide, who was a Natal carbinier. Our object was to push on to some high ground about three miles beyond the main body, to try and discover a position for the guns to shell any Boers who might be retiring in front of Sir G. White. We discovered no signs of retreating Boers, though we pushed on some way beyond the high ground, and two messages were sent back to that effect. On our return we fell in with another patrol, whose horses were dead beat, and they asked us to reconnoitre towards Glencoe Pass for them. This I did with Corporal Overton and the guide; the other man's horse being beat, I sent him back. We passed through Wessels Nek, which was deserted and looted, and having discovered no signs of the enemy towards Glencoe commenced to withdraw about 3 p.m. Soon after this a terrific storm burst, the rain being so heavy it was impossible to see more than a few yards. Owing to this we lost our way, the guide knowing nothing of the country, and accounting for his ignorance by saying he had only lived ten years' in the neighbourhood. Eventually, at 10 p.m., we again found ourselves at Wessels Nek. We got some mealies for the horses and one tin of condensed milk, the only eatable thing in the place for ourselves. The station being all wired in, we judged it would be safer to sleep out on the veldt, which we did, keeping watch in turn. Three horsemen passed us during the night, but it was impossible to say who they were. At daybreak we made another effort to find the column, but not being successful, I judged it best to strike for Ladysmith. We struck the line at Sundays River, and proceeding along it, passed the battlefield of Elandslaagte, strewn with dead horses, and reached Elandslaagte Station about nine. Here we found a coolie cook, and although the place had been looted and used as a hospital, he managed to find us some cocoa and tinned fish. All the Kaffirs here were unanimous that the Boers·had absolutely left the neighbourhood. We now proceeded along the main Newcastle-Ladysmith road, and saw an ambulance going along just in front of us; galloping up, we found that it was a Boer ambulance going to the scene of the battle of the previous day. The driver gave me the first authentic account of our men who had been lost at Talana, but vouchsafed no other information. Pushing on, we reached a spot on the road where the Modder runs under the railway, about six miles from Elandslaagte, when we saw a low kopje about 400 yards in front, which was covered with men. Looking at them through the glasses I saw they wore slouch hats, on which the guide at once said, 'Oh! they are carbiniers out to meet the column.' At this moment two mounted men left the kopje and galloped out towards us. As they approached I saw they were Boers. We reined up and looked at one another. Not quite knowing what to make of them, I asked them if they were looking for dead and wounded from the fight. 'No,' they said. 'What do you want then?' 'Our commandant has sent us to examine your ambulance to see there are no armed men concealed in it, as we were fired on from your ambulances yesterday.' I now saw we had fallen into a hornets nest, and several more men were beginning to gallop up from the kopje. I took the only chance and said 'All right, you can go and examine our ambulance' (the Boer ambulance, which they mistook for ours, was now about 400 yards in rear), and as they galloped off we dashed down into the spruit, crossed the line under the bridge, and galloped for all we were worth. After going some way I turned round, and saw a great discussion evidently in progress round the ambulance. Fortunately no one seemed to think of pursuing us, as our horses were so beat we had to dismount after about a mile. We met no more Boers after this, and eventually reached the line of outposts thrown out by the 19th Hussars some six miles out of Ladysmith."

From now till we reached Ladysmith rain fell nearly incessantly. All through the night of the 24th storm after storm swept over our bivouac and drenched everyone through and through, but go on we must, and at 4 a.m. on the 25th we had to resume our march.

The country now was bush veld, and the road a poor one through mimosa bush and over rocky ground, a good deal intersected by watercourses. At about 10 a.m. we descended a rather deep ravine the Sunday River flows through, crossed it by a good drift, and halted some two miles on the Ladysmith side to allow the baggage to come across. Some of the 18th Hussars, under Major Marling, v.c., went on about three miles in the direction of Ladysmith, but the country was clear of the enemy, and though full of Kaffir kraals and natives, we could gain no information from the latter about the Boers. Half the "18th" and some Mounted Infantry, with two batteries and two Infantry Regiments, remained on the north side of Sunday River, the Cavalry patrolling the banks till the baggage had all crossed, which it had done by about 1 p.m., when all the force outspanned and off-saddled at the place the leading troops had reached in the morning, and piquets were put out to guard the camp for the night.

At 4 p.m., however, "A" Squadron of the 5th Lancers arrived at our bivouac, Lieutenants Dugdale and Purdey with it, carrying orders from General White that we were to push on if possible to Ladysmith at once. Information also reached us at the time that the Boers had just occupied the camp we were in the night before.

We had to hurriedly collect the transport animals and inspan before night came on, orders being issued at once for the resumption of the march at 6.15 p.m.. At that hour we started off in order of march for the night, the Infantry leading the column, and a few Kaffir scouts, who knew the road, were sent in front of them again. It soon got dark, and at about 8 p.m. a furious storm of thunder and lightning broke right on us, the road itself, a poor one, was hard to find, as there were many tracks through the bush, and we progressed slowly, halting very often for the column to close up. At Vlakplaats the head of the column came in touch with some Natal irregular troops, who were holding the kopjes there, and who had come out from Ladysmith to support us.

By this time the road had become quite a quagmire, and the transport animals were having a very bad time of it indeed, but they behaved magnificently, and only one wagon had to be abandoned in the mire. From Vlakplaats the precautions which we had employed were somewhat relaxed, as a considerable force had come from Ladysmith to Modder Spruit to assist our retreat, and they had piqueted the road, so units were ordered to push on as best they could through the mud and rain to a farm near Modder Spruit.

The advanced guard halted for half an hour at the farm, and arrived at Modder Spruit at 3.30 a.m. on the morning of the 26th, but it was some hours after this before the transport and rearguard reached that spot. The torrents of rain everyone had had to put up with, and the mud they had had to plough their way through, made the different regiments scarcely recognisable in the early hours of the morning. However, the weather cleared on the 26th, and after halting at Modder Spruit to collect stragglers and reform regiments, every corps set off as soon as possible for Ladysmith, distant some five miles. The "18th" arrived there about midday, and proceeded to their old quarters in the Tin camp, some 2½ miles north-west of the town.

The total distance we had covered in our round-about march from Dundee was some seventy miles. We left Dundee at 9.30 p.m. on the 22nd, marched twenty-two miles to Beith with a two hours' halt, halted from 1 p.m. to 11 p.m. on 23rd, then marched sixteen miles to Waschbank River, halted from 9 a.m. 24th to 4 a.m. 25th, marched twelve

The Retreat to Ladysmith. 45

miles to Sunday River on 25th, halted from 10 a.m. on the 25th to 6 p.m. same date, then marched fifteen miles to Modder Spruit by 3 a.m. of the 26th, halted till 10 a.m., and arrived at Ladysmith about twelve noon. Roughly we marched the seventy miles in eighty-eight hours, with halts altogether of about forty-eight hours for the head of the column, but very few of the Infantry got as much rest as this, for the column was a long one, and the time required for the rear to catch up was often reckoned by hours. Again on the 24th, at Waschbank River, the troops were out nearly all day, and very few on the 26th reached Modder Spruit before 6 or 7 a.m. The 18th Hussars were practically in the saddle all the march for very nearly four days, and their horses had little or no rest. Food for ourselves and horses was fairly plentiful, but the difficulty was to find time and opportunity to serve it out.

The whole march back had been well planned, and carried out with a dogged persistency which spoke well for the troubled future looming ahead. The last night was indeed a climax to the ordinary exertions which might be called for from a retreating force. Though unmolested by the enemy, the troops found that nature had contrived to bring enough obstacles in their path to glut the most persevering appetite. That pitch-dark toilsome march through mud and mire, with animals and men mixed up in one unsortable mass, with constant halts and dashes to close up the broken column, vivid flashes of lightning and deafening peals of thunder, and with weariness and hunger thrown in, must often come back as a nightmare to the memory of those who have been through it, and who yet, by the will of God, live to tell the tale.

An officer thus shortly relates his experience of the few days' march :—

"At night we were ordered to move to Talana. It turned out, however, that our real destination was Ladysmith, but the matter was kept a profound secret. We none of us knew at the time where we really were going to, and in consequence left all our kits in the old camp, to be very shortly in the hands of the Boers. We marched till 7.30 a.m. on the 23rd, and resumed our march at about 10 a.m. a.m. on the 23rd, and resumed our march at about 10 a.m. without molestation, as the Boers did not believe that we had really left Dundee, but thought we were laying an ambush for them. We finished our march at 4 p.m. and bivouacked on the top of Van Tonder's Pass. At 6 p.m. I was sent down the pass with three men to see if it was occupied. It was pitch-dark and you could see nothing, so consequently we had to depend on our ears. I got down within one and a half miles of the bottom (total length of pass about five miles), when I met one of our guides, who told me that the remainder of the pass was open, so I went back and reported it clear to the General. At 9 p.m. the column marched through the pass and arrived at Waschbank River at 10 a.m. next morning. There we halted till about 1 p.m., when we heard heavy firing in the direction of Elandslaagte, so one battery and the regiment procceded out to try and cut in, but we saw nothing, as it was too far away. Most of us got back at 4.30 p.m., when a terrific thunderstorm came on, and lasted well into the night; we were all soaked. We moved our camp about half-a-mile further up the river and took what rest we could. The Waschbank River rose about ten feet in an hour, and went down almost as rapidly; it cut off for a time a patrol we had under Cawston on the left bank. On the morning of the 25th we moved off at 4 a.m. and marched to Sundays River, on the far side of which we halted. Here we were met by a squadron of the 5th Lancers, who brought us orders to go on to Ladysmith at once, and as we heard that the Boers were close on our heels, we set off again at 6 p.m. on our march. At about 7 p.m. it came on to pour with rain, and the road became a perfect quagmire, so that the rear of the column was constantly losing touch. We hardly made a mile's progress by 10 p.m., owing to stoppages and overturned waggons; it was bad enough for the guns and ourselves, but goodness knows how the Infantry fared. However, we got into Modder Spruit in some kind of order, reformed there, and reached our old camp at Ladysmith at 12 noon, a place when we were at Dundee we never wished to see again, but now were only too glad to do so. It was a long and tedious march, the last part under very bad conditions, but all through the whole force had behaved splendidly."

Shelters in banks of Klip River, Ladysmith.

CHAPTER IV.

"LADYSMITH DURING THE SIEGE."

ON October 26th, the day we arrived back, Ladysmith was very full of troops. The following were the different regiments assembled there, not including the Dundee troops:

    5th Lancers.
    5th Dragoon Guards.
    19th Hussars.
    1st Brigade Division Royal Artillery (21st, 42nd, and 53rd Batteries).
    10th Mountain Battery.
    2nd Battalion King's Royal Rifles.
    1st Battalion Gloucestershire Regiment from Allahabad.
    1st Battalion Devonshire Regiment from Jullundur.
    1st Battalion Liverpool Regiment from Capetown.
    1st Battalion Manchester Regiment from Gibraltar.
    2nd Battalion Gordon Highlanders from Solon, India.
    1st Battalion Royal Irish Fusiliers from Egypt.
    2nd Battalion Rifle Brigade from Crete.
    About 500 Imperial Light Horse.
    Detachments of Natal Carabineers.
    Natal Border Rifles.
    Durban Naval Brigade.
    Durban Light Infantry.
    100 Mounted Infantry of Leicestershire Regiment.
    Fifty Mounted Infantry of the 1st K.R.R.
    Two 4.7 naval guns and two twelve pounder guns, with a detachment of the Naval Brigade.

The 2nd Battalion Rifle Brigade and the naval contingent did not reach Ladysmith till the 30th October. The Dublin Fusiliers, of the Glencoe Field Force, were sent off immediately after their arrival at Ladysmith to hold Colenso railway bridge.

This left a total available fighting force in Ladysmith of, roughly, 6,500 men and about 2,500 horses, or, with the Glencoe Field Force added, some 9,000 men and 3,100 horses.

The "Eighteenth" remained in their quarters at the Tin camp on the 27th and 28th, and on the 29th they went out with most of the other mounted troops on a reconnaissance in the Modder Spruit direction.

This reconnaissance was productive of very little result; patrols from "B" Squadron proceeded to Limit Hill and Lombard's Kop, and a few Boers were sighted, but enough information was to hand from various sources to show that the Boers were now in considerable strength along Pepworth Hill and Long Hill, while Free State commandos were encircling Ladysmith on the western side.

October 30th.—Acting on the information he had obtained

of the dispositions of the Transvaal Boer forces on the north side of Ladysmith, General White determined to attack them whilst, as he was informed, they were separated from the Free State commandos, who had trekked round the west side of the town to take possession of the Colenso railway bridge. The inglorious encounter at Farquhar's Farm and the surrender at Nicholson's Nek were the unprofitable result of the day's fighting.

The 18th Hussars took part in these operations, and started out from Ladysmith camp at 2 a.m. to Limit Hill, where they were joined by the 5th Dragoon Guards and Imperial Light Horse, and waited there till daybreak under the command of Brigadier-General Brocklehurst. The battle commenced with an Artillery duel, and when that had slackened off a little, at about 7.30 a.m., General French, who was in command of the mounted troops, decided to take all the Cavalry to the right flank, and the 18th Hussars and General Brocklehurst's other troops proceeded to Lombard's Kop. The 18th dismounted there and lined the summit and sides of the hill, where they came under a heavy fire from the Boers, who were posted on a ridge in front of them. The cover was good however; there were no casualties, and the Boers eventually retired out of range. The Regiment remained for some hours at Lombard's Kop while the Infantry attack by Farquhar's Farm on Long Hill was developing, but the country beyond the kop was too difficult for the Cavalry there to be of any assistance in the Infantry's forward advance, and at the same time the position they were in was too far back from the right flank of the Infantry to cause their presence there to be any check to a commando of Boers, which had quickly outflanked our Infantry's right.

As they could make no further forward progress they were ordered, about midday, to withdraw, and the mounted troops on Lombard's Kop covered their retirement. In performing this duty they were most ably assisted by the batteries of Artillery, who effectively prevented the Boers gaining possession of Lombard's Kop when the Cavalry had at last to leave it. The "Eighteenth" got back to Ladysmith about 2 p.m. The report by General Brocklehurst on the action of the Cavalry under his command is given below.

REPORT ON ENGAGEMENT AT LOMBARD'S KOP.
30TH OCTOBER, 1899.

From Brigadier-General J. F. Brocklehurst, M.V.O., Commanding Cavalry Brigade.

To the Chief Staff Officer, Natal Field Force,
Ladysmith, 30th October, 1899.

Sir,
I have the honour to report that I arrived at Ladysmith by train at 3 a.m., and proceeded at once to Limit Hill, where I joined

my Brigade, consisting of 5th Dragoon Guards, 18th Hussars, and Imperial Light Horse. The remainder of the Cavalry being on the extreme right, under command of Major-General French.

At 7.40 a.m. two squadrons, "I.L.H.," under Major Doveton, took up a position behind three kopjes on the extreme left, a little to the east of Observation Hill, to check the enemy who were attempting to outflank our left. The enemy retired north. About 11 a.m. the remainder of the "I.L.H." were ordered to report to Sir George White, Commander-in-Chief, and passed out of my command. I attach Major Davis's report, and would bring to your notice the action of Lieut. and Adjutant Fitzgerald, 11th Hussars, therein described.

About 8 a.m. I received an order from the Commander-in-Chief to proceed to the right. The Chief Staff Officer accompanied the Brigade. On arriving at Lombard Kop I heard heavy firing, and received an order from Major-General French to reinforce him with all I could. Two squadrons 5th Dragoon Guards advanced to the eastern slope of Lombard Kop and acted dismounted. I attach Major Gore's report, and would bring to your notice the conduct of Second Lieut. Norwood and Private Sibthorpe therein described.

The 18th Hussars, on arrival at the valley below Lombard Kop, sent one squadron to reinforce the 19th Hussars, holding the north end of the western slope. The remainder of the regiment held the position on the right of the 5th Dragoon Guards, on the eastern slope of the valley.

The whole of the Cavalry were engaged in a warm fire action until the Infantry had retired about one mile. The Brigade then withdrew by the Helpmakaar Road, arriving at camp about 1.30 p.m.

I attribute the little loss in retiring to the accurate fire of our batteries firing through the Nek, which kept down the enemy's rifle fire, and prevented his advancing to Lombard Kop.

The 19th Hussars and 5th Lancers were not under my command. The reports of the Officers Commanding these two Regiments have been rendered separately.

I have, etc.,
    (Signed)   J. F. BROCKLEHURST, Brigadier-General,
                           Commanding Cavalry Brigade.

The regiment was fortunate in escaping without any casualties on October 30th, for Colonel Grimwood's Brigade of Infantry close by had suffered very severely.

October 31st was a quiet day, given up to getting the women and children out of Ladysmith; the Eighteenth turned out at 4.30 a.m. to a rendezvous near Cove Redoubt, where the Cavalry Brigade, under General Brocklehurst, assembled on this and subsequent days till the 10th of November, so as to be ready for any emergency in the early mornings. After parade the regiment returned to the Tin camp for the remainder of the day and night, but our occupation of this spot was destined to be of short duration.

The Boers were putting up guns all round the town and rapidly encircling it, but so far the railway was intact, and remained so till the 2nd of November.

It is not intended in this book to give any description of the general disposition of our troops, during the subsequent siege of Ladysmith, nor yet to recount any of the collective actions of the Natal Field Force besieged there, which do not directly affect the regiment. The services of the latter only will be hereafter referred to, together with the particular localities they garrisoned, the duties they had to perform, and the manner in which they executed them.

The 18th Hussars were now brigaded with the 5th Lancers, 5th Dragoon Guards, and 19th Hussars, and placed under the command of Brigadier-General Brocklehurst, M.V.O., who had to help him on his staff; Major Wyndham, 16th Lancers, Brigade Major; Lieut. Lord Crichton, R.H.G., as A.D.C.; and Captain Harrison, 11th Hussars, as Provost Marshall.

November 1st was spent quietly, except for the Boer bombardment of the town, which proceeded intermittently throughout the day.

Early on the morning of **November 2nd**, at 2 a.m., to be accurate, the regiment turned out and proceeded to the iron road bridge over the Klip river, and waited there till daybreak, when they, together with the rest of the Cavalry Brigade, some Natal Mounted Volunteers, and one Battery Royal Artillery, proceeded off along the Maritzburg road as far as Range Post, with the intention of seizing a Boer laager on the west side of Ladysmith. At Range Post the force turned south and occupied the Nek just north of Bester's Farm, and the one to the west of it. From here the 5th Lancers went on a little further, and our guns were brought into action to shell the laager, which lay on the east side of the Maritzburg road, and about three miles from Bester's Farm. A few rounds were fired at it and a certain amount of uproar created therein, but our attack was not pressed home, and the whole of our force was soon withdrawn to camp, which we reached about 10 a.m. General Brocklehurst's report on the morning's work is as follows:—

SKIRMISH NEAR MIDDLE HILL.
2ND NOVEMBER, 1899.
From Brigadier-General J. F. Brocklehurst, M.V.O., Commanding Cavalry Brigade.
To the Chief Staff Officer, Natal Field Force,
Ladysmith, 2nd November, 1899.

Sir,
I have the honour to report that my Brigade and the Natal Mounted Volunteers, and one battery, rendezvoused at the Iron Bridge under Major-General French, commanding Cavalry, at 4 a.m. The force advanced across Long Valley.

The Volunteers, under Colonel Royston, and one section "R.A.," held the Nek between Waggon Hill and Middle Hill. From here a laager of the enemy could be seen, but it was out of range from that point. The remainder of the force advanced to the Nek between Middle Hill and End Hill; one squadron 5th Lancers held the ridge dismounted.

The remaining four guns and two squadrons 5th Lancers pushed on about 3,000 yards through the Nek, and the guns placed about ten shells into the laager. The enemy lined a ridge and opened rifle fire, their guns also coming into action.

Major-General French having effected his object, withdrew the guns and the force retired, reaching camp before 10 a.m.

    I have, etc.,
        (Signed)   J. F. BROCKLEHURST, Brigadier-General,
                            Commanding Cavalry Brigade.

During our absence from the Tin camp the Boers had been getting to work putting up guns in position to shell it, and no sooner had we returned than they opened fire on us, and we had to withdraw with our horses to the gully, where the footbridge to the rifle ranges crosses the Klip river, and there we remained till dusk.

November 3rd.—Next day we proceeded to the same spot instead of going to Cove Redoubt, as the Cavalry Brigade was undertaking another reconnaissance along the Maritzburg road, an account of which is given in the accompanying report. The 18th Hussars were ordered out at about 11.30 a.m. to join the remainder of the Brigade which had started from Ladysmith early in the morning.

From Brigadier-General J. F. Brocklehurst, M.V.O., Commanding Cavalry Brigade.
    To the Chief Staff Officer, Natal Field Force,
                           Ladysmith, 3rd November, 1899.

The Brigade rendezvoused at the old transport lines, and was disposed, so as to support the Helpmakaar Post in case of an expected attack at dawn.

At 9.45 a.m. patrols reported enemy moving west of Ladysmith.

The Brigade rendezvoused at once at Range Post. The following is the report rendered on the day's operations:—

"At 10 a.m. the 19th Hussars, 5th Dragoon Guards, and the 21st Field Battery assembled at Range Post. Four squadrons 'I.L.H.' were already about one mile to the front, in the direction of Lancer's Nek, and had located the enemy with one gun on the ridge to their front.

"At 11.15 a.m. I advanced the battery, with escort of one squadron 5th Dragoon Guards, direct on the hill reported to be held by the enemy; with the other two squadrons 5th Dragoon Guards on the right rear of the guns. The 19th Hussars advanced over the Long Valley to the ridge to our left and outflanked the enemy's left. I sent orders to the 18th Hussars to turn out and watch the right rear of my advance. I requested General Hamilton to guard my left rear, and he occupied the detached hill one mile south of Caesar's Camp with two companies of Infantry, and sent one company Mounted Infantry to a large round topped hill east of Colenso Road.

"At 11.40 a.m. the enemy opened fire. My battery advanced to effective range, and in about four shots silenced the enemy's gun. It then turned its fire on a kraal enclosure, in which some enemy appeared to be laagered.

"At 12.15 p.m. the 19th Hussars reported Artillery fire to their right at about 2,000 yards range, and they halted under the ridge and occupied it with dismounted fire. The 18th Hussars halted still more to the right behind the kopje near the nek on Van Reenen's Road.

"I sent back then to headquarters for two more batteries. About this time it appeared to the officer commanding 'I.L.H.' that the bulk of the enemy had retired from the ridge, and dismounting his men he advanced close up to it. The advance was most gallantly made, but being unsupported, it was an error of judgment, and I would not have sanctioned it had I been aware that it was contemplated. The enemy returned to the ridge, and our guns had to fire on the ridge and a green kopje to our left to keep down their rifle fire.

"In order to facilitate the retreat of the 'I.L.H.,' I ordered Major Gore, commanding 5th Dragoon Guards, to send one squadron forward to take up a position to cover their retirement, which he did, finding shelter in a nullah 1,000 yards to my front.

"At 1 p.m. the Natal Mounted Rifles, under Colonel Royston, came up, and I sent them on the high hill to my left, where they became warmly engaged till the withdrawal of the force.

"Two more batteries also arrived. The 42nd was sent to the right to silence the enemy's gun there, and to act with the 19th Hussars. The 53rd came up in line with the 21st.

"At 1.30 p.m. a large body of the enemy was reported by the 18th and 19th Hussars trekking east to west. The officer commanding 19th Hussars called up the battery on the right, and the enemy came under their fire and that of the dismounted men, and suffered considerable loss. At about 4 p.m. I concentrated the Artillery fire on the ridge, and the 'I.L.H.' withdrew behind the guns at a gallop in extended order. About fifteen minutes later the squadron 5th Dragoon Guards withdrew in the same manner.

"I decided to attempt nothing further till assured that Colonel Royston had entirely cleared the hill on the left, but, on his signalling that the enemy was advancing in great numbers, I turned the Artillery fire on the green kopje which was bringing a cross fire on the Volunteers, and ordered a retirement from the left. This was carried out with the greatest steadiness. The enemy was too distant for the heavy rifle fire they kept up to molest us, but again opened fire with their guns from front and both flanks.

"I would like to mention the excellent practice made by our Artillery, and the capable way in which Colonel Royston, with the Volunteers, secured my left. I also wish to commend the able way in which Major Heneage's squadron, under direction of Major Gore, advanced and covered the withdrawal of the 'I.L.H.'

"General Hamilton brings to my notice the judgment shown by Captain Bridgford, commanding the Mounted Infantry, Manchester Regiment, in covering the retirement.

"I regret the great expenditure of Artillery ammunition, but it was necessary to keep down the enemy's rifle fire to avert considerable loss to the 'I.L.H.' and Major Heneage's squadron, 5th Dragoon Guards.

"I attach reports of General Hamilton, Colonel Jenkins, Colonel Royston, and Major Davis."

I have, etc.,

    (Signed)   J. F. BROCKLEHURST, Brigadier-General.

The siege had now regularly set in in earnest, the railway line had been cut the day before, and the Boer commandos completely encircled the town. We were cut off from the outside world, though we then hardly realised it, and when we did give it a thought, we reckoned that it was only an incident in the war, and our further offensive operations would be resumed at a very early date.

The regiment got back to the Tin camp about 5 p.m., and spent the night there, parading again next morning as usual under Cove Redoubt.

November 4th.—The Boers sent our wounded officers and men, who had been left behind at Dundee, into Ladysmith, and took advantage of this to send one of their Staats Artillerie men as a waggon driver with a red cross on his arm to spy out our defences, and we did not become aware of the ruse till after it was too late to take the man prisoner.

It was unsafe to occupy the Tin camp any longer by day, so we bivouacked instead in the gully by the footbridge during the day time, and retired to the Tin camp at night. This procedure we continued for a few days, but the Tin camp very soon became unsafe at night as well as day, and we had to make a permanent camping ground of the gully instead.

The next few days were uneventful, the Boers regularly shelling the town and outskirts intermittently during the daytime, and our patrols were regularly shot at when they went their usual useless rounds to the different points of the compass they were ordered to go to, and which by now were well-known to the Boers.

On **November** the **9th** the usual monotony of the siege, which we were becoming quite accustomed to by now, was broken by a more vigorous bombardment on the part of the Boers, and by two distinct attacks executed by them on Signal Hill and Caesar's Camp. The attacks were easily repelled, and the mounted troops did not take part in the fight.

Cavalry are certainly an anomaly in a beleaguered town, and during the commencement of the siege of Ladysmith there is no doubt that the regular Cavalry assembled there was a puzzle to the Staff to dispose of. On the face of it it would appear to have been more practical to have come to a sweeping decision before the siege commenced, and despatched a greater portion of the Cavalry to Escourt to await there the relieving army, retaining in their place the battalion of the Dublin Fusiliers sent to Colenso after the retreat from Dundee. For the mobility of the Cavalry within Ladysmith was practically no greater than that of the Infantry had the latter been placed on waggons; the roads were the only routes they could move along at any pace, for the country was too steep and rocky to move fast over, moreover the Cavalry force available was too small a one to launch at the enemy unsupported by other troops, and so it was tied down to the Ladysmith enceinte, and its every movement therein was an immediate object for the attention of the Boer gunners, and one they seldom failed to take advantage of. However, after the beginning of November, the die was cast, it was too late to get rid of the regular Cavalry, and for a time something had to be found for them to do, and headquarters puzzled their heads to find the something. As the siege wore on and actual men for the defences became scarcer, the problem automatically solved itself; there was no question about what the horses would be wanted for, and work for the men was plentiful enough in the latter days of the siege.

A small camp was arranged for the Regiment at this period in the gully by the footbridge, and a few tents and cook houses were rigged up, and the men and horses made as comfortable as it was possible to be in that confined area.

So events progressed without much excitement out of the ordinary until the 14th of November was reached, when another of the many fruitless " reconnaissances in force "— an ill-omened term which we got to regard with dire suspicion long before the end of the war—was undertaken by the Cavalry Brigade, again along the Maritzburg road. Lieutenants Thackwell and Dugdale were sent out very early in the morning in the direction of Middle Hill and End Hill, where they reported that a Boer gun epaulement was erected, and that it was pretty certain that the epaulement contained a gun. Their report was, however, received with credulity until subsequent events lent weight to their story. The whole Cavalry Brigade and two batteries of Artillery proceeded out at daybreak to attempt the capture of a gun the Boers put up on Blaubank ridge, and all went well till a position was reached near the peach trees on the Maritzburg road.

The Blaubank gun was apparently silenced by fire from our batteries, and all that remained was to storm the position on foot and capture the gun. But the Boers on Middle Hill and End Hill, and those at Hussar Hill, held us in check with Mauser fire, supported by guns on End Hill and Telegraph Hill, and the Cavalry Brigade was not considered strong enough to go through with the fight. A retirement was soon ordered, and we were treated to a very heavy shelling on our way back, crowded on the narrow surface of the Maritzburg main road, and it has always been a puzzle to us why we escaped as lightly as we did. There were practically no casualties; shells came from every point of the compass and fell right among the troops, but as usual the Boer shrapnel fire was a minus quantity, and the " common " ones burst under our feet with little or no damage. We got back to our bivouac at 4 p.m., not at all pleased with the importance of the " arme blanche " when opposed to rifle and gun fire in a trappy country.

That night the Boers varied proceedings by a midnight bombardment, and in spite of the annoyance of having our well-earned rest broken, we could not help admiring the weird effect the bursting shells had in the inky darkness of the night.

For some days after this we pursued the even tenor of our way in the " Happy Valley," as we called the gully we were bivouacked in, without anything of note occurring to personally affect us. Our patrols were regularly fired on, and had some miraculous escapes.

We lived, too, in constant fear that our hiding place, none too secure a one, would be eventually discovered, and our fears were very soon to be most abundantly realised. A description of the adventures of one of our patrols, under charge of Sergeant Hamilton, may be of interest at this period :—

Patrol Work in the Siege.

"One day, in the early part of November, 1899, I was sent on the usual daily patrol, which went out in the direction of Blaubank kopje, on the Van Reenen's road. As soon as we reached the open ground in the 'Long Valley' the sergeant in charge sent me on as 'advanced scout,' telling me at the same time that a small hill to my right front, known to us as 'Star kopje,' had been reported clear in the early morning by a patrol of the Mounted Infantry.

" I had proceeded about half a mile, when, on a small kopje, about midway between ' Star kopje ' and ' Blaubank,' I saw two or three figures moving about, and one of them commenced to wave a white flag, or what appeared to me to be one. I was then about nine hundred yards away from them, and having no field glasses with me, I cantered back to the sergeant and asked him to look through his and see if he could distinguish what the objects were. He did so, and told me they were only Kaffirs. So going on in front again I continued to advance until I had reached the right rear of the kopje, from where I could see parties of Boers travelling to and from ' Blaubank ' and ' Field's Farm.' The figures on the hill still continued to wave the flag and swing their arms about, and as I saw the sergeant looking at them again through his glasses, and got no further information from him, I concluded they were Kaffirs, as there were Kaffir kraals at the foot of the place they were on, so thinking they wished to give me some information, I started to go over to them, and as soon as they saw me making towards them, they also commenced to come down the side of the hill, and I soon found myself face to face with three typical Boers. They understood very little English, but their idea seemed to be that it was Sunday, and all shooting was postponed for the day. They sat down quietly and began to smoke, and were soon joined by three other of their friends. They seemed very anxious to know when we were going to surrender, and tried to impress on me that they would very soon take the town when they really set to work. I waited with them till I saw the rest of my patrol within supporting distance, then I quietly retraced my steps, and we returned towards camp, halting for a short time near ' Star kopje,' about which the sergeant wished to take some notes.

"The Boers had, however, now occupied the position, and we very soon had to hurriedly depart to camp."

The gully we occupied on the south side of the Klip river, near the Tin camp, was well enough in its way, but it gave little cover from the direction of Surprise Hill, and in those days one wanted cover all round.

On **November 20th** we were bivouacked there as usual, spending our time at the usual routine, and in the afternoon, about 3 p.m., we were in our tents, or shelters we had rigged up in place of them.

The Boers had meantime " spotted " our retreat, and at that hour opened fire from Surprise Hill with a forty pounder Howitzer, dropping some twenty shells most accurately into the narrow valley we were in. There was nothing for it but to clear out, and as we were pretty used to shell fire at that time, we did so in a most orderly manner up the road to the rifle range, halting in rear of some kopjes, which lie between the Colenso road and the Klip river, until we could select a more suitable spot for our permanent camp. Although the forty pounder shells had landed, everyone of them, in the midst of the regiment, before they moved off and as they were doing so, yet only one effected any real damage; this one lit in a temporary cook house we had rigged up by the banks of the river and knocked it down, wounding four men, one of them, Private Cawthorne, seriously.

We had previously marked down what looked like a good place for a camp in the valley of the Klip river, about halfway between the Tin Camp-Rifle range road and the commencement of Ladysmith town, where the river flows through a gorge, the cliffs on either side being nearly precipitous. On further examination we found that with a little trouble we could make a very fair road down to the river bed on the south side, and that alongside the river was a stretch of grass, some 300 yards long and about eight to ten yards broad, a sort of ledge of flat ground about six or eight feet above the level of the river. The bank above this rose fairly steeply, but contained a few small level ledges here and there; there was plenty of shade, the soil was good, and cover was excellent.

Squadron on Duty at Range Post, Ladysmith.

Officers of the Regiment in Ladysmith.
[See p. 65.]

Ladysmith during the Siege.

Here we took up our new quarters, the General Officer Commanding 2nd Cavalry Brigade allowing us to remain here on our representing that from this spot we could reach any threatened portion of the defences as rapidly as we could from anywhere else.

We quickly made the place habitable, building all sorts of shanties and levelling ledges to pitch the tents on. The horses did well as long as we were able to feed them, and did not suffer at all from horse sickness, and the men of the regiment were far more healthy than those of any other corps. The whole regiment remained in this spot till the end of January, and after that date we still kept a squadron here to look after what remained of the horses. Our duties were fairly light, each squadron in turn had to remain for twenty-four hours on duty at Range Post, a point where the road from the Tin camp to the rifle range crosses the Ladysmith-Colenso road, leaving their horses in the river bed. Besides this we had one or two other small piquets to furnish.

For some time past the Staff had an idea that it was possible to make a dash from Ladysmith on some Boer convoys which were supposed to pass round the west side of the town, and every day a look out post on Observation Hill was employed endeavouring to find some likely-looking string of wagons suitable for the Cavalry Brigade to move out after. But it was an impracticable idea; the route the Boer wagons took was, roughly, some seven miles distant, where they crossed the Zandspruit, they then converged in a little to where their line of circumvallation crossed the Colenso road, then bore still further away to reach the positions they had taken up between Colenso and Ladysmith. To reach them our mounted forces would have had to break through the encircling cordon, a feat which could have probably been done at many points if done quickly, but by the time the distance to the convoy had been covered, a very considerable force of the enemy could have been collected to bar the return journey, and it is very doubtful if any great number of our mounted troops would ever have been able to get back. The harm they could have done to a Boer convoy would also have been infinitessimal, knowing as one did the nature of such convoys. The country to be moved over was most unsuitable for fast Cavalry work, as we well knew, though, looking at it from a distance, it appeared quite level and the best of good going. We knew it, however, and were not at all sanguine for this particular performance of cutting out convoys, and were well enough pleased when, towards the end of November, the subject seemed to be dropped and we had no longer to stand to, all saddled up, ready to turn out at a moment's notice for one of these wild rides over some of the most treacherous ground in South Africa.

CHAPTER V.

"LADYSMITH DURING THE SIEGE."

LIFE passed as pleasantly as we could hope during the early days of the occupation of our new home. We had soon made things quite ship-shape, and built a good road to enable us to get quickly out of the river bed, and later on we turned our attention to making the squadron we had on duty at Range Post as comfortable as circumstances would permit, by excavating platforms for tents to be placed in and rigging up other shelters of sorts. Our horses were still in very good condition; we had saved back grain when it had been issued lavishly to us at the commencement of the siege, and, for exercise, we took the horses out for about an hour's trot every evening just as night was closing in.

In the day time there was little to do but watch the progress of the bombardment and visit other parts of the defences, while at night we occasionally had concerts.

The officers built themselves a small mess-house close to the river, but their judgment in the selection of a spot was not good, as on two occasions the Klip rose rapidly and swept their wooden constructions away.

On **November 20th** the Boers varied the monotony of the siege by shelling us at night, and at frequent intervals they repeated this practice. We were endeavouring at that time to open up communication with General Buller's army by means of flashlight signals on the clouds at night, and to retaliate in some sort of way the Boers replied by bursting their shells over the town. Our position in the river bed was, however, safe from anything but an erratic shell; it was invisible to any of the heights on which the enemy had their guns, and though now and again a ricochet would bound over or into the Klip river close by us, there were so many more tempting objects for them to aim at that we felt pretty safe.

On **November 24th** the Boers captured some 200 of our slaughter cattle as they were grazing near King's Post, and they would have got a good many more if it had not been for some of the Mounted Infantry, aided by our standing patrol under Sergeant Baker, of " A " Squadron, which went daily to " Direction Post " on the Van Reenen's road, driving the remainder of the herd back within our defences under a heavy shell fire.

Nearly every day we saddled up and stood to arms in expectation of attacks, authentic reports of which we were daily kept informed of by our local intelligence department.

On **November 28th** we expected to take part in a strong sortie on Blaubank and End Hills, but the reinforcement of these positions by the Boers altered our plans, and nothing came of it.

On **December 2nd** an unlucky shot from a gun the Boers had just put up on Gun Hill split up on the edge of the river bank near our camp, and fragments of it alighted among our tents, wounding Private Owen so seriously that he shortly afterwards died of the injuries he had received. We turned out at 8.5 p.m. this night and rendezvoused at the convent with the 5th Lancers and Imperial Light Horse, the 7th and 8th Infantry Brigades doing the same in the town, but apparently it was only a practice affair, and we were sent back to our camps by 1 a.m. the same night. We turned out again on December 5th at 11 p.m., and again returned to our bivouac, but on the night of December 7th we received orders to saddle up at 3.45 a.m. next morning and await orders. At 4.20 a.m. we were told to proceed at once to the examining post on the Newcastle road, and we made the best of our way there with " A " and " C," and what was left of " B " Squadron, leaving an officer and the dismounted men to take care of the camp.

At the examining post we got our orders, and went off with the 5th Lancers down the Newcastle road, crossed the Free State and Transvaal railways at the level crossings with " B " and " C " Squadrons, " A " turning up on the east side of the Free State line to near Bell's Farm. After crossing the Transvaal Railway, " B " and " C " Squadrons turned along the line, while the 5th Lancers, who were accompanying us, went on by the Newcastle road. The Boer guns on the slopes of Pepworth Hill and on Bulwana opened fire on us as soon as we reached the level crossing, but they did no damage. We crossed Bell's Spruit and held the kopje on the left of Limit Hill, between the Newcastle road and the railway, with part of " C " Squadron, while the rest of " C " and " B " advanced back across the line to a low kopje on the west side of it, and a little in advance of the hill the other part of " C " Squadron were on. In the meantime " A " Squadron was guarding the Free State line and our left flank. Beyond these points it was impossible for a small force to advance; there were a considerable number of Boers in the low hills lying all round Pepworth's Hill, and they were momentarily increasing in numbers, and endeavouring to get on to some hills which lay between our centre and " A " Squadron, who were on our left. To repel this attack we sent a part of " B " Squadron, under Lieut. Thackwell, to hold the intervening space, and this stopped the forward movement of the Boers for a time.

At 6.45 a.m. we received orders from General White to

retire. The orders for this retirement had reached the 5th Lancers, who were on Limit Hill on our right, some time previously, and our position was becoming a precarious one, as Limit Hill was evacuated, and it completely commanded the position we were in. We were unable with the centre party to re-cross the line at the spot we had originally crossed it by, as the Boers swept the railway with rifle fire from very close range, so we had to keep on the west side till we came to the culvert under which Bell's Spruit runs, and by rushes of a few men at a time, cross there and rally on the Ladysmith side, "A" Squadron at the same time retiring along the west of the Free State line the way they had come out.

By 8.30 a.m. we were all back in camp, where we learnt that a sortie made by part of the "I.L.H." and Natal Carabineers, under command of General Hunter, on the guns the Boers had lately put up on Gun Hill, close to Lombard's Kop, had been a very successful one; two guns, one a Long Tom, were destroyed, and a Maxim brought into camp. This success had saved us a considerable amount of shelling, which otherwise we would have encountered, as our route lay very much exposed to the Gun Hill position. As it was, we had Bulwana and the two guns to our front under Pepworth's Hill to reckon with, and the fire of the Boers in the laagers round the foot of the hill. Our casualties were few until the retirement commenced. "A" Squadron on the left escaped with no casualties, but "B" and "C" suffered considerably from the close fire they were exposed to on the kopjes by Limit Hill, and in their retirement under the Bell Spruit culvert. Two men, Lance-Corporal Robert Claridge and Private James McHardy, were killed, and Lieut. Thackwell, Squadron Sergeant-Major Power, Lance-Sergeant Howard, Lance-Corporal Watson, Lance-Corporal Sheehan, Privates Deal, Ewart, Meekings, Webster, Stewart, and Maton were wounded; Lance-Corporal John Weir, Private Leonard Gould, Private William Halliday, and Private Harry Woodley were also wounded, and died from the effects of their wounds. Two other men were injured by falls from their horses, which were shot under them, and at the same time we had four horses killed and thirty-one wounded.

It would have been an impossibility to have made a further advance, as the Boers were in considerable numbers in our front, having been rather needlessly put on the *qui vive* by a midnight raid by a squadron of the 19th Hussars along the Newcastle road, and they were collecting from all quarters. Our objective, the Modder Spruit terminus of the Netherland's Railway over the summit of Pepworth's Hill, was impossible to reach by daylight and with the enemy alarmed. We might perhaps have got to Modder Spruit, but never back again, and we were lucky to escape as lightly as we did. The 5th Lancers on our right had very few casualties, and the 5th Dragoon Guards, with a battery, did not proceed further than the examining post on the Newcastle road.

Most of our wounded were moved as soon as possible to No. 18 Field Hospital, and next day to the big hospital at Intombi.

The report of the day's proceedings, sent in by Major Knox to the Brigade Major, 2nd Cavalry Brigade, is as follows:—

RECONNAISSANCE UNDERTAKEN BY THE 18TH HUSSARS
ON 8TH DECEMBER, 1899.

From Officer Commanding 18th Hussars.
To the Brigade Major, Cavalry Brigade.

Ladysmith, 8th December, 1899.

At 4.20 a.m. I received orders to take my regiment to the rendezvous, the examining post on the Newcastle road, and at 4.40 a.m. I arrived there and received orders to reconnoitre in a northerly direction, keeping on the left of the 5th Lancers, who were advancing along the Newcastle road, and, if possible, to destroy the telegraph wire and railway. I understood that I was afterwards to move round the west of Long Hill. I ordered one squadron to cross the Orange Free State Railway at the level crossing, about 500 yards north-west of the junction, to keep on my left and close in as we advanced towards the west of Long Hill.

With the remaining 1½ squadrons I proceeded along the Newcastle road, crossed Bell's spruit, and proceeded due north till nearly in line with Limit Hill. At this point we crossed the railway and took up a position with one squadron about 400 yards south of a farm (not marked on map, but situated near a level crossing with white gates) close under Limit Hill. Whilst advancing we came under a heavy rifle fire and also fire from two guns, one a Vicker's Maxim. I had previously sent on an officers' patrol, who reported the enemy in considerable strength in a strong position about 700 yards north of the farm before mentioned. I was anxious to ascertain the strength of the enemy, and opened fire from a good position which I had taken up. The enemy now advanced in order to take up a position on a hill commanding our left flank, so I ordered up my remaining two troops I had kept in reserve to move forward quickly and take the hill first. This they did, and opened fire on the enemy at a distance of about 400 yards, forcing them to retire. It was difficult to estimate the numbers of the enemy, but in my opinion there were about 200 in the farm, and in the laagers round about, and the same number some 1,200 yards north-west of the farm.

At 6.45 a.m. I forwarded a message to the general officer commanding Cavalry Brigade, informing him of my position. Shortly after this I received orders to retire, and I gradually withdrew my troops in open order under a very heavy fire, keeping on the west of the railway, and crossing it at Bell's spruit in order to avoid the fire from the Vicker's Maxim gun.

My left squadron proceeded to a point about half a mile north-east of a small farm, which is itself half a mile east of Bell's Farm, where they came under heavy fire and were unable to advance any further, the enemy being in a very strong position. A number of the Boers in front of the squadron were here seen dressed in khaki, and it was difficult to tell whether they were friends or foes. There were no

casualties in this squadron, but amongst the remaining 1½ squadrons the casualties were:—
Killed: Two men.
Wounded: One officer and fourteen men.
Injured: Two men who had their horses shot under them.

Amongst the horses the casualties were:—
Killed: Four.
Wounded: Thirty-one.

I should like, in conclusion, to bring to the notice of the General Officer Commanding the gallant conduct displayed by Captain W. E. Hardy, R.A.M.C., both on this occasion and also at the battle of Talana Hill. During the retreat to-day and after the troops had left the position Captain Hardy remained attending to and bringing in the wounded under a very heavy fire directed at him from several points.

(Signed) E. C. KNOX, Major,
Commanding 18th Hussars.

Copy of circular memorandum from the G.O.C., 2nd Cavalry Brigade, on "Reconnaissance from Ladysmith," on December 8th, 1899:—

"The G.O.C., Cavalry Brigade, has expressed his admiration for the gallantry displayed by the Regiment during the reconnaissance this morning, and his regret that so many brave men should have been killed and wounded."

"*Extract from Brigade Orders dated Ladysmith, 11th December, 1899:—*

"On the report of the reconnaissance of the 8th inst., rendered by the G.O.C., Cavalry Brigade, the Commander-in-Chief has made the following note:—'I regret the number of casualties, but I was an eye-witness, and it was inspiriting to see the keenness and dash with which a dangerous duty was carried out by officers and men.'"

For some time after December 8th matters were fairly quiet in Ladysmith, the Boers confining their attention to General Buller's army on the Tugela river. On the night of December 10th four companies of the Rifle Brigade, under command of Colonel Metcalfe, took and blew up a howitzer gun on Surprise Hill, but they suffered rather severely on the way back, having fifty-five casualties. This gun was the one which so effectively drove us out of the valley by the Tin camp, and we rejoiced at its death.

On **December 14th** we could hear distant firing in the Colenso direction, but there was not much of it. On the 15th it commenced again very heavily at about 5.30 a.m., and went on to 11.30 a.m., our spirits rising at first with every round, but the little movement there seemed to be among the Boers round Ladysmith after a time rather damped our ardour, and we began to think things were not quite as rosy as we hoped. Firing went on after 11.30 a.m. in an intermittent manner and then gradually died away altogether, but it was not till Sunday, December 17th, that we gathered information to the effect that General Buller had met with a reverse, and it was a long time before we got a really true account of his fight. Meantime a notice posted in the town to the following effect warned us that we should have some time longer to wait.

SPECIAL NATAL FIELD FORCE ORDER.

BY LIEUT.-GENERAL SIR GEORGE S. WHITE, V.C., G.C.B., ETC., COMMANDING.

Ladysmith, 17th December, 1899.

The General Officer Commanding Natal Field Force regrets to have to announce that General Buller failed to make good his attack on Colenso; reinforcements will therefore not arrive here as early as was expected.

Sir George White is confident that the defence of Ladysmith will be continued by the garrison in the same spirited manner as it has hitherto been conducted, until the General Officer Commanding in Chief in South Africa does relieve it.

(By Order)   A. HUNTER, Major-General,

Chief of the Staff, Natal Field Force.

Sunday was always most religiously observed by the Boers, and they seldom worried us on that day with shell fire, unless they noticed that we were putting up a gun in a new site or relying too freely on their observance of the Sabbath by remaining in any exposed position. In consequence the officers generally took advantage of the comparative peace and rode round to many of the advanced works, and had opportunities of witnessing the changes and improvement in the defences as the siege progressed. Most of the outlying works to the north, north-east, and north-west of the town had assumed by this period of the siege some good proportions; the east of the town towards Bulwana Mountain was flat, open country, excellently guarded by its flatness and the tortuous course of the Klip river which flowed through the valley on that side; the western side, too, towards Blaubank and Onderhook was naturally well defended by Red Hill and the open ground to the west, but Caesar's Camp and Wagon Hill to the southward, the very key to the whole position, eminently natural fortresses in themselves, were left almost as Nature had made them, strong in their own way for those who had immediate possession of them. This we could not help noticing in our rides round Ladysmith, and we marvelled at our own consummate trust in providence, as we had marvelled before at the prehistoric scheme for one of our squadrons to hold Van Reenens Pass, another Cundy's Kloof, and the third the Biggarsberg passes, which was the idea before the war broke out; and again as we had wondered at the rooted objection there seemed to be to make any of the natural hill fortresses, lying around the one place in Natal, which had been, wisely or unwisely, selected as our main stronghold, into modern siege works worthy of the name.

Caesar's camp and Wagon Hill were unique though, even in comparison with the other defences which had been thrown up to guard the approaches from other points of the compass. To an ordinary observer in those days, there was nothing there to prevent the Boers seizing the outer ridge of the hill and commanding the flat top, till their superior numbers had worked their way across the level, if necessary, inch by inch, and when once the hill was in their possession Ladysmith was doomed. That they knew this and intended working on their knowledge was proved to us later on; had they been European foes gifted with the Boers' adeptness in picking our brains, our fate would have been soon settled; the natural discipline of European armies would soon have enabled weight of numbers to capture this commanding position.

A sad contrast between our hopes and our fears revealed itself about this time in the publication of some special orders.

On December 14th special Natal Field Force Orders were issued, providing for the establishment of a flying column, under the direct orders of the Lieut.-General Commanding, which was to carry four days supply, and was no doubt intended to complete the enemy's defeat after their dispersal by General Buller. The 18th Hussars formed a part of the Cavalry Brigade of this flying column, together with the 5th Lancers, 5th Dragoon Guards, and Imperial Light Horse, all under command of Brigadier-General Brocklehurst. On December 17th, however, quite a different tone was given to our orders, and special ones, issued on that day, assigned to all troops their positions in the defences, and what steps were to be taken in case of an alarm, and the flying column orders were put on one side.

One squadron of the 18th Hussars, the one whose turn it was to be on duty at Range Post, was detailed to assist in Section "C" of the defences, under Colonel Ian Hamilton, this section comprising the country between the east end of Caesar's camp and Range Post. The remainder of the regiment was to form, with the rest of the Cavalry Brigade, part of the "reserves." On the alarm sounding (or red lamp being run up on the hill above the Headquarter Office and on Cove Hill) all troops were to stand to their arms, the Cavalry saddling up.

After December 17th the Boers considerably increased their shelling, and on the 18th a shell from Telegraph Hill gun landed very close to the officers' mess, fragments of rock hitting several officers, but no harm was done. Again on December 22nd an unlucky shell fell in the 5th Lancers bivouac, which was a few hundred yards higher up the river than ours, wounding four officers of that regiment, while another one killed five men and wounded fifteen more of the Gloucesters.

Ladysmith during the Siege.

Beyond the shelling there was nothing of note to record about this period of the siege.

December 25th.—Christmas Day was observed in the orthodox Sunday manner by the Boers, with the exception of those who were round the Bulwana gun; they added insult to injury by sending us a plum pudding inside a "Long Tom" shell, the original and proper stuffing having been first removed. We tried our best to supplement this extraneous ration by an extra allowance of anything we could scrape up, so that the men could have a Christmas dinner of sorts, but rations were already running rather low, and it was not possible to make it an elaborate meal.

After Christmas Day the Boers continued to shell us with renewed activity, and one officer of the Devons was killed and seven wounded by a shell which struck a shelter they were using as a mess house.

On December 29th we had very heavy rain, and the Klip river rose at a great rate; the lower part of our bivouac rapidly became untenable, and we had to make very speedy efforts to rescue and remove to places of safety what tents, shelters, and kit we had on our low-lying bivouac. It was a dark night, and the roar of the rapidly rising water was the first intimation we had of our danger. We lost a considerable amount of odds and ends, which there was not time to save, and the officers' mess building was carried bodily away; the tents were knocked down, but the ropes and pegs held them in their places, and when the river went down next day we were able to recover them. Next morning it was necessary to construct fresh ledges higher up the banks of the river to put our tents on, and for a time this kept us busy, as the work among the rocks was very laborious.

Towards the end of December sickness increased considerably in Ladysmith, and the numbers in Intombi Hospital were rising daily; by the 30th they had reached about 1,100. Our own regiment had so far been extremely fortunate, we had suffered considerably from enteric during the year before the war, and had no doubt got a good deal hardened to it, and this, aided by the gravel soil we were camped on, and the great care taken to keep the ground as clean as possible, no doubt saved us many lives. Major Marling had been unwell for a considerable time, and had only just been able to be present at the reconnaissance of December the 8th, and on December 24th he was admitted to Intombi Hospital, where he remained till the end of the siege suffering from a very bad attack of dysentery. Captain Wellby took over command of "A" Squadron in his absence. On January 1st Captain Davey took over command of "B" Squadron, and Captain Burnett acted as Adjutant for the remainder of the war.

The beginning of the year saw matters moving in much the same strain, and up to the night of January 5th nothing particular happened.

January 6th, 1900, had, however, been decided on by the Boers for their great attack on Ladysmith, and taking advantage of their knowledge of the unprotected state of Caesar's camp and Wagon Hill, they chose those spots for their supreme effort. From our camp we could hear heavy musketry fire at a very early hour in the morning, and we learnt later that they had, about 2.30 a.m., rushed the dismounted piquet of the " I.L.H.," which held Wagon Hill, and established at the same time a firm foothold on the southern crest of Caesar's camp, driving back the piquets of the Manchester Regiment, which were guarding that circle of the defences. The firing continued all the morning, and all the big guns, both Boers and British, which could take part in the attack and defence, joined in at daylight. One battery of ours, with the 5th Dragoon Guards as escort, was sent out at dawn over Range Post; they remained by Sign Post ridge all day with a smaller escort, and though they did not fire very much after they first got out, their presence there served to check reinforcements of Boers from Blaubank reaching their friends at Middle Hill *viâ* the " Long Valley," thereby compelling them to make a long detour to do so.

Another battery took up a position in the scrub jungle to the east of Caesar's camp, and from there was able to harass the Boers who were descending the hill on the opposite side of Bester's Spruit to join their comrades on Caesar's camp itself, and they inflicted severe losses on those Boers who attempted this and on others as they retreated. But in spite of these two flank protections, Caesar's camp was being constantly reinforced by Boers pressing up from " Flat-topped Hill," Bester's Farm, and Middle Hill direction.

Though nearly all the " I.L.H." piquet on Wagon Hill were killed at the first rush, a few managed to join a supporting piquet of their own regiment, and these, together with some Engineers, who were engaged at the time in putting up a 4.7 gun of ours on Wagon Hill, managed, though very hard pressed, to hold a part of the hill until reinforcements could reach them. The fight swayed backward and forward all the morning, the Boers being practically in possession of the southern edge of the entire hill all the time.

The 18th Hussars were ordered out at 10 a.m., and proceeded to a little beyond Range Post in small parties, so as to avoid the fire of Blaubank and Telegraph Hill guns. From here " A " Squadron went on to the foot of Wagon Hill, while " B " and " C " remained near Highlander's Post. The advanced guard reported that Wagon Hill was only held by a few of the " I.L.H.," and that the Boers were on the outer edge of the hill, and round the corner to Bester's

Farm and on Middle Hill. At 11 a.m. General Hamilton ordered " B " and " C " Squadrons to return to camp, but at 12 noon they were again sent for to proceed to Wagon Hill. " A " Squadron had in the meantime dismounted and held the extreme western end of the hill, and the slopes towards the nek which lay between Wagon Hill and Middle Hill. " B " and " C " on their arrival were dismounted, and held in support at the foot of the track leading to our howitzer's emplacement. At about 1 p.m. the Boers made a determined effort to sweep our men off the top of the plateau, and some of the enemy penetrated as far as the gun sangar which was erected near the centre of the hill. Here Major Miller Wallnut, of the Gordon Highlanders, was killed, and the men still on the summit, consisting of small parties of Gordons, Naval Brigade, and I.L.H., being apparently left without a leader, began making their way by twos and threes down the slope on which we had " B " and " C " Squadrons in support. Their retirement soon became a rush, and Major Knox had only just time to order up our squadrons to take their places. This was effected, however, and " A " Squadron extended along the whole of the top, while " C " took the east end and slopes of the hill, and " B " remained close to the summit on the northern side. At the same time we endeavoured to collect the detachments which had previously been holding the hill, and to send them off to their own regiments.

The rush made by the Boers had, however, been ineffective; those who reached the gun sangar were all killed, and the others for some time after this contented themselves with pouring as heavy a fire as they could on to the hill from all points, especially from Middle Hill and the south-western extremity of Wagon Hill, opposite Manchester Fort, which was higher than our part of Wagon Hill, and which they had had possession of all day. At the same time their gun on Blaubank kept pouring very disconcerting shells into our backs, as the north face of Wagon Hill was completely exposed to its fire. At 3 p.m. two companies of 60th Rifles came to reinforce us, and took up a position on our left, prolonging the line to beyond the howitzer's old emplacement, where they suffered considerably from the fire of the Boers on the south-eastern end of the hill. The day up to now had been very hot and oppressive, but great masses of clouds rolling up from the eastward warned us that a heavy storm was coming, and about 4 p.m. it burst with great intensity over our position. At first it was a typical South African hailstorm, enormous lumps of ice falling, then heavy rain set in for an hour and a half, such a volume of water descending that the most insignificant dongas were rendered impassable torrents for some time after the rain had ceased.

At nearly the commencement of the storm a great number of the 60th Rifles left the firing line, mistaking a command of "cease fire," which had been given them, for "retire," and "B" Squadron, who were in support, were ordered to take their place. The men of the 60th, seeing they had made a mistake, then returned to their original positions. During this storm the Boers slowly moved off the hill, and a gallant charge of the Devon Regiment at the other end of the position cleared off any who were still left in that quarter. The light was, however, very bad, and it was hard to see the enemy retreating in the scrub country below the hill to the southward, nevertheless our men searched the hillside and country beyond with incessant fire, and this, combined with the swollen nature of Bester's Spruit, must have made the retreat by no means a happy one for the heroic remnant of the Boer commandos, who had clung so obstinately to Caesar's camp and Wagon Hill all through that day.

By half-past five or six o'clock the firing had gradually died away to a spasmodic shot or two, and our squadrons and the 60th Rifles, left in possession of the hill, set to work to make rough sangars all along the crest line, and to arrange reliefs for the coming night. We had been worried by the heat and exertion of perpetually climbing the hill side, a very rocky one, during the earlier part of the day; later on we had been drenched to the skin by the tropical downpour, now we were shivering with cold, the temperature having dropped many degrees, and, to add to our discomfort, water was lying in pools all over the hill, and we had nothing but wet ground to rest ourselves in, no food and no mackintoshes or great coats to keep us warm, and, as the excitement died away, we all felt indeed far from comfortable, though well content that we had done what was required. Parties were sent off to get rations as soon as the fight was over, but owing to the distance we were away and the darkness of the night, they were many hours in reaching us. Early next morning we expected a repetition of the attack, but no shot was fired either by the Boer guns or by riflemen. We were well prepared, as at about 8 a.m. on the night before two squadrons of the 5th Dragoon Guards had come up as a further reinforcement. Major Gore was in command of them, and as he was senior to Major Knox, the command of that part of the position fell on him.

About 7 a.m. on the morning of the 7th January the Boers appeared from the direction of Middle Hill with a white flag, and we sent down an officer to halt them outside the piquet lines. They wanted permission to arrange an armistice and come to the hill and collect their dead. The armistice was arranged, but their dead were collected by our men, and carried down to them on their side of the hill. We collected about forty from our immediate neighbourhood, and carried the bodies of our men who had fallen in the fight at the same time to the Ladysmith side of the hill. Their casualties must have been very heavy, while on our side some 150 were killed and 250 wounded. In the " Eighteenth " Sergeant Henry Webb was killed about 3 p.m. on the eastern slopes of the hill, and Lance-Corporals Gill and Ward and Privates Davis and Bailey were wounded. Major Knox's report on this action is inserted here :—

REPORT ON THE PART TAKEN BY THE 18TH HUSSARS IN THE DEFENCE OF WAGGON HILL.

ON THE 6TH JANUARY, 1900.

From MAJOR E. C. KNOX, Commanding 18th Hussars.

To Brigade Major, 2nd Cavalry Brigade.

At 10 a.m. on January 6th I received orders to turn out at once and proceed to the foot of Waggon Hill to support the Imperial Light Horse. I proceeded there with one squadron, the remaining 1½ squadrons halting close to Highlanders' Post for a short time, and thence joining the leading one at the foot of Waggon Hill. At 10.45 a.m. "A" Squadron, under Captain Wellby, remained at this position while the others retired back to their bivouac post close to Range Post. At 12 noon an order was received for the whole regiment to go to Waggon Hill to protect the right flank and guard the 4.7. naval gun, which was lying on waggons at the foot of the hill, from surprise and capture. "A" Squadron was now sent further forward, to hold dismounted the ground at the foot of Waggon Hill, and towards Mounted Infantry Hill, whilst "C" Squadron, under Major Laming, and part of "B" Squadron under Captain Davey, were kept behind in reserve, the horses being back about 600 yards.

At about 1.30 p.m. we observed that the Gordons at the top of the south-west extremity of Waggon Hill were being hardly pressed, so I at once ordered the reserve (1½ squadrons) to reinforce them. Captain Wellby's Squadron was also ordered by General Hamilton to move up the hill to their assistance. The 18th Hussars now occupied the firing line on the right of the position, keeping one squadron in reserve close up to the north-west slope of the hill. At this time there were a good number of Boers at the foot and on the sides of the hill looking towards Colenso, but it was difficult to say how many.

At about 3 p.m. two companies King's Royal Rifles were sent to reinforce us, and took up their position in the firing line on the left of the 18th Hussars. At about 4 p.m., during a severe hailstorm, a large number of the King's Royal Rifles left the firing line (retiring towards the north-west side of the hill), owing, I was told, to the men mistaking the command "cease fire" for "retire." I at once ordered the squadron of the 18th Hussars, who were in reserve, to move forward into the firing line, which they did in excellent order. The King's Royal Rifles, seeing they had mistaken the order, moved forward with the 18th Hussars and re-occupied their position, and the Boers during this period retired under cover of the scrubs round Besters Farm. At about 7 p.m. Major Gore, 5th Dragoon Guards, took command of the position from me. The 18th Hussars remained in the firing line and spent most of the night in throwing up temporary works to give head cover, as there was none on the hill, and it was most urgently required. During the engagement the officers, non-commissioned officers, and men of the Regiment behaved with the greatest coolness, the men being under excellent control.

At about 9.30 a.m. on the morning of the 7th the Regiment was relieved and ordered back to its permanent camp. Return of casualties, etc., have already been forwarded; 6,731 rounds of small arm ammunition were expended by the Regiment during the day.

(Signed) E. C. KNOX, Major,
Commanding 18th Hussars.

Ladysmith, 8th January, 1900.

The Boers we met below the hill were very reticent, but it was most apparent that yesterday's fight had told immensely on their spirits. We, in spite of our discomforts and heavy losses, were full of confidence and happy at our success, though we regretted not having been able to inflict as great or greater loss on the enemy with more immunity to ourselves, as we should have done had the defences of the hill been at all adequate; on the other hand, no doubt, the Boers would have fought shy of attacking the position if it had been strongly entrenched, and the fight, a great victory for us, would never have come off.

At 11 a.m. we collected our bedraggled squadrons and marched back to our camp, but hardly had we got there when we received orders to send up one squadron as a permanent garrison to Manchester Fort, on the western end of Caesar's camp proper, and "A" Squadron, under Captain Wellby, was detailed for this work.

In addition to this, and the squadron on duty at Range Post, we now had also to furnish a piquet of twenty-eight men daily on Leicester Post, where they acted as a reserve to other outlying piquets on that hill.

After the 7th January matters ran their old course; intermittent shelling from the Boer guns and constant alarms of night attacks continued, and an increasing shortage of food for both men and horses set in. The horses indeed were now in a fairly bad plight, which we endeavoured to alleviate by cutting grass for them from the hillsides.

There was now very little real fighting, but on our side greater efforts were made to thoroughly entrench our positions.

Matters dragged on till **January 17th**, when the sound of heavy gun fire to the south and west put us all once again on the alert. For the next few days firing went on in an intermittent manner, dying away altogether on the 21st, which was a Sunday, and starting again on the Monday morning. It continued in a desultory fashion on Tuesday and Wednesday, and on Thursday culminated in what we could no longer mistake for anything else but an attack on the Boer position some way beyond Onderhook. From the top of Caesar's camp we could watch the shells, presumably our own ones, bursting all over the summit of a particularly high plateau on the heights overlooking the Tugela. A Boer

Wagon Hill, Ladysmith.

Cæsar's Camp—18th Hussars Entrenchment.

laager had been placed behind this hill and on our side of it, and we could easily discern through telescopes the commotion going on inside. The firing continued on the 25th, but as it never got any closer, and the Boer laager remained in its original spot, our hopes did not rise very high. The next day all firing had ceased, and we learnt, on Saturday, fairly full details of the Spion Kop fight.

We had been relying on this second attempt of General Buller, for people who knew the country said that that was the way round, and we knew that if it could succeed, then the Ladysmith garrison would be of some sort of use in the pursuit of the enemy to their own passes. Now we felt a touch of despair; two attempts had failed, why should not a third? And we did not enjoy contemplating what would be our fate should all efforts to relieve us be frustrated. However, few among us ever allowed our thoughts to rest on that bitter subject. What worried us was the fact that we and our horses would daily get weaker, and we should be of little use to the Natal Army when they did relieve us.

On **January 29th** the supply of forage had reached such a low ebb that a conference of Cavalry commanders was called to decide what was to become of our horses. As a result of this conference it was resolved to keep 300 Cavalry horses, seventy-five out of each regiment, and the remainder were to be turned out to graze on the outskirts of Ladysmith, under a grazing guard, and driven into kraals at night. This decision was hardly a happy one, as in our regiment and the 5th Lancers there were a considerable number of very good horses whose retention in the Army was worth a great deal more than that of almost any of the horses brought over from India by the regiments arriving since the declaration of war. Ours were Colonials and South Americans, the latter thoroughly acclimatised, and hardly ever have a better stamp of horses been in the possession of a Cavalry regiment. They could do any amount of work, and keep fit on a very small allowance of forage, and were, withal, weight carrying horses possessing pace, qualities we tried in vain to find in the many hundred horses we had given us afterwards to make our numbers up. As it was, we were allowed to keep our seventy-five, and the remainder were driven out to find for themselves and to be daily diminished in number as the requirements of the Chevril factory grew more and more exacting. Those that were driven out to graze got unfortunately irretrievably mixed up the first evening as they were endeavouring to drive them back to their kraals, for no proper arrangements had been made for dealing with so large a mob of horses suddenly turned loose, many were lost altogether, and the rest got so mixed up, corps among corps, that it was a very difficult matter to catch and sort them again. We thus lost some of our really good horses which would have been of incalculable service to us at no very distant part of the war.

Captain Davey had had to be placed on the sick list immediately after the fight of the 6th January, and at the end of this month he was in a very critical condition, but he recovered a little in February and slowly got better. Major Marling had also undergone a very bad attack of dysentery at Intombi Hospital, and Lieut. Cawston had shortly to go there suffering from the same complaint. A good many of the non-commissioned officers and men were also beginning to succumb to this most prevalent disease, and already it was rare to find anyone who was altogether in robust health.

On **February 1st** we left eighty men and horses under command of Major Laming, with Captains Gosselin and Baker, Lieutenants Wood, Clarke, and Cawston, in our old camp in the bed of the Klip river, and marched up the remainder of the regiment, dismounted, to Manchester Fort. Major Knox, Captains Wellby and Burnett, Lieutenants Stewart, Field, Thackwell, Bayford, Dugdale, and Purdey, with Captain Hardy, R.A.M.C., and 226 non-commissioned officers and men, comprised the total we could muster. This included the officers and men of the squadron who had previously been on duty at that post. Manchester Fort was to be our quarters for the next month, and we had to become Infantry for the time being. We were placed between the Manchester Regiment, under the command of Colonel Curran, on our left, holding Caesar's camp proper, and the 2nd Battalion of the Rifle Brigade, under command of Colonel Metcalfe, on our right, who held the Wagon Hill extremity of the plateau. Their numbers had become so diminished by losses that the Cavalry had to be employed to aid them. About a thousand yards of front on the southern edge of Caesar's camp fell to our share, to be guarded by an almost continuous line of sangar trenches, while behind this line we had supports at night, and on the Ladysmith side of the hill we held Manchester Fort itself, and in a deep cutting there was there we placed our tents and shelters, and withdrew most of our men to it by day.

General Ian Hamilton was in command of all this portion of the defences, and Major Murray, who had been with us at Dundee as General Symon's Intelligence Officer, acted as his Brigade Major.

We found the whole extent of front very badly entrenched, and during all the time we were there, especially at the commencement, we were almost constantly employed in digging and making obstacles along our front. Manchester Fort itself was a good work, and so were also some others erected on the Ladysmith side of the plateau, but the outer face of the hill gave us constant employment, and the hard nature of the soil, mostly solid rock or huge stones embedded in hard ground, told severely on our men, who were by this time far from robust. The enemy's guns which caused us particular annoyance were a Long Tom on Bulwana, two field guns on a white rocky kopje in the Onderhook direction, and a gun on Middle Hill. The sentry on duty at Manchester Fort had orders to watch these guns, and, when any of them fired, to call out the name of the gun so that our men could take cover accordingly. The Bulwana gun made very accurate practice at our fort, placing two shots running one day right into the fort itself, whose dimensions were a bare thirty yards by twenty, while the range was close on 8,000 yards. The ninety-four pounder which the Boers had on Telegraph Hill was moved by them to their Tugela positions early in February. Had it not been, its fire would have annoyed us considerably, as it lay direct to our rear, and the deep cutting we most of us lived in did not give so much cover on the Ladysmith slope of the hill.

The rain at this period of the year was very heavy, and we had difficulty in keeping our shelters clear of water, and the outlying piquets at night were often drenched to the skin.

So matters dragged on. One day we heard General Buller's army shelling some part of the enemy's position, the next all was quiet again. On February the 5th he seemed to be making another attack nearer Colenso and close to Keat's drift, and on the 6th cannonading still went on, but died away next day; later on we heard that this was the Vaal Krantz attack. After the 6th there was comparative peace, the Boers shelled us a little whilst we were perfecting our defences, and the usual alarm of night attacks kept us well on the alert. Our duties were heavy. Out of our 226 non-commissioned officers and men we had to keep forty-six every night in the sangars directly in front, forty-six in support, and thirty-eight more in other isolated posts round Manchester Fort, more than half our full strength actually on duty at one time.

It was not till **February 23rd** that General Buller's army wakened within us more hopeful sentiments. On that date cannonading went on all day, and we soon learnt that our forces had established themselves on Hlangwani and Monte Christo, and this seemed to give us closer touch with the outside world than we had had for a very long time. From the 23rd onward General Buller's army seemed to remain stationary, but reports reached us that all was going well, and instead of the fire slackening, as it generally did after two or three days, it still kept steadily on. The Boers annoyed us in Ladysmith less and less. A large number no doubt had already gone to the Free State and others to repel General Buller's army at Colenso, while even threats of night attacks began to grow less prevalent. Our chief amusement at this period was to watch a twelve pounder naval gun of ours, which was mounted in an emplacement on Caesar's camp, shell a gigantic dam the Boers were making across the Klip river below Intombi Hospital, with the intention, apparently, of flooding the low country to the east of the town.

On **February 26th** we heard of Lord Roberts' success in the Free State, and on the 27th General Buller's guns were at it harder than ever, and the musketry fire could often be quite distinctly heard. On February 28th, about 2 p.m. in the afternoon, it was reported that the Boer wagons were trekking back to their own countries, and every telescope was at once in request on Caesar's camp and Observation Hill to watch this pleasing sight, and though earlier in the siege we should have liked to have gone after them, we had come to think that to see the last of them was the most pleasing occupation that could fall to the lot of mortal man. All afternoon, and probably all night too, the long train of wagons slowly trekked along the Van Reenen's road and from behind Lombard's Kop in the direction of Modder Spruit siding, and just as night was closing in some mounted men, part of the Imperial Light Horse and Natal Carabineers from General Buller's army, rode over the drift on the Klip, where the old Ladysmith-Colenso road crosses the river, into the town, and our communication with the outside world was once more an established fact.

The weather was bad all night; incessant thunder and storms of rain went on, while our big guns added to the din, firing away the remnant of their precious store of ammunition at the Boer Long Tom on Bulwana, a prize we had always hoped would fall to our share if the siege was ever raised. But the Boers had very little trouble in removing the gun; our men could hardly have walked so far to prevent them, and the darkness of the night hindered our gunners making accurate enough practice to impede them, and in the morning the gun was gone.

The siege had lasted 118 days, and how much longer we could have stood it is, of course, pure conjecture, for we hardly realised how weak as a fighting machine we had become. This was, however, rudely brought home to us when a small picked force was sent out to follow up the retreating Boer army, for the distance this force was able to cover was microscopically small.

Provisions and forage had been plentiful in Ladysmith at the commencement of the siege, and we had never imagined that under any circumstances could the investment drag on so very long. In consequence we had been rather too lavish at the start, and when the disasters of

Manchester Fort.

Watering Horses in the Buffalo River.

[See p. 86.]

Ladysmith during the Siege.

December came on us, we had to at once commence a much severer course of banting, which rapidly reduced our strength in the unsalubrious surroundings we were compelled to exist in. January saw all the grain ration ended for our horses, and at the beginning of February it was a question of preserving a certain number of them for food for the garrison, for as we could no longer hope to keep our animals in condition, the best we could do was to keep them alive. At the commencement of the siege we had 288 horses, and up till the end of January we only lost ten, nearly all of these during the reconnaissance of December 8th, while at the end of February we had seventy-one left, so great a number had strayed, died of exhaustion, or been killed for food during the last month of the siege.

With respect to our own rations, the allowance for all ranks at the end of the siege was naturally a very meagre one, as the ordinary ration does not divide up for long in half and quarter shares to yield a satisfactory sustenance. We had always sufficient meat of sorts, but this qualifying phrase was enough to condemn it, and hard, lean, tasteless meat with no vegetables, its only accessories being bad coffee and mouldy mealie meal, was enough to tell on the strongest constitution in spite of the quite liberal supply of the meat itself. Every man had that pinched look and dull expression on his face towards the end of the siege, which one generally expects to find on those who, having been buffetted about in this world, come to the end of their tether, and do not much care what more hardships fate may have in store for them. Water was hard to get on Caesar's camp, and the want of it soon reduced our men's clothes to a lamentable condition. The soaking rain and heavy work in digging trenches, felling trees, and putting up barbed wire entanglements, dirtied and destroyed their kit, while the rough ground made short work of their boots. It was a strange sight to contrast the bronze healthy faces and dirty serviceable uniforms of the relieving force with the pale cheeks and the threadbare clothes of the besieged men.

LIFE AT INTOMBI HOSPITAL DURING THE SIEGE.

From the Commencement of the Siege of Ladysmith, from the Diary of an Officer who was there.

We lived a life of absolute monotony, but gradually, as our wounds healed, we were able to go about and do what we could to help the already sorely overtaxed hospital. Of course we got the full benefit of every shot that was fired from "Long Tom" on Bulwana Hill into Ladysmith, and the effect of this on some of the wounded was very bad. Each morning, about 7.15 a.m., the train from Ladysmith bringing us our supplies used to arrive, and at 5 p.m. every evening it returned. By it came what little news we ever heard, the most welcome being news of the regiment. The sick and wounded used also to be sent out by this train, and during the early stages of the siege these numbered very few; latterly, however, when times were blackest, as many as eighty have arrived by this train in the morning. On these days very often they were kept in this train until 4 o'clock in the afternoon, and then only dragged out and laid on the floor of some probably wringing wet marquee, which was put up after a fashion by the hospital authorities, and which in more than one instance blew down, and, I fear, ended the career of many a poor man. Several times a recurrence of such a catastrophe was only averted by the strenuous exertions of a few of the more or less sound ones amongst us.

I may here point out that the camp itself was divided into four separate hospitals, viz., one British Station Hospital, two British Field Hospitals (from India), and one Volunteer Hospital. The staff of each comprised in the main hospital officers of the Royal Army Medical Corps, assisted by civil practitioners and nurses both army and civil, in the two Field Hospitals, officers of the R.A.M.C. and native attendants, and in the Volunteer Hospital, Volunteer doctors and nurses.

As far as possible the distribution of the sick was as follows:—All serious cases of enteric, dysentery, wounds, etc., were sent to the Station Hospital; slight cases were sent to the Field Hospitals, and all cases of Volunteers to the Volunteer Hospital. From this it will be seen that all the hospitals were entirely separate, separate staffs, separate commanding officers, chaplains, nurses, etc., but the whole were under Lieut.-Colonel Mapleton as Principal Medical Officer. The administration and arrangements in the Field and Volunteer Hospitals were excellent, everything possible being done for the patients; the nurses in the latter simply devoted themselves entirely to their patients, as also did the doctors. No body of men or women throughout the campaign did more service than these nurses throughout the whole of this trying period. I am sure, had it not been for them, with their ever cheery presence and willing hands, the mortality would have been far heavier than it was. No praise is too high for them and no reward could be too great.

The Hospital was situated on either side of the railway, about $3\frac{1}{2}$ miles from Ladysmith, at a point where the Klip River, after making a bend to the east, comes back again towards the railway, preparatively to forcing its way through the gorge which lies between Bulwana Mountain and the hills which run on the west side of Nelthorpe station.

In the early days of the siege food was more or less plentiful, but as time wore on we suffered severely from the lack of supervision, and waste that went on during the early period. Our rations, of course, were gradually reduced, as were those of the troops in Ladysmith, and one can readily imagine the effect of a diet of horseflesh, and bread (?), made out of sour mealies, and such similar fare on the emaciated frames of the wretched patients. Scurvy and starvation played terrible havoc, and these, with the addition of enteric and dysentery, were far deadlier foes than any " Long Tom " or other shells. Words fail me when I try to describe the scenes that one strove to avoid witnessing, but to glean any idea of what Intombi was like, one must picture to oneself a vast collection of tents, both large and small, and the same filled to overflowing with men in every stage of disease and illness—the middle of some stifling night in February—the whole place reeking with most nauseating odours—frail skeletons of men, strong in their delirium, fighting and wrestling with gentle nurses—weird groans and sounds from everywhere, and in the morning a mournful procession of men, carrying on stretchers lifeless forms of poor souls, wrapped in Government blankets, to their last resting place, the bearers halting many times through sheer exhaustion during the walk of a few hundred yards which separated the cemetery from the camp. It was a poor look out for any, save those of the strongest constitutions and wills, who got really ill during the latter part of the siege, as in addition to there being practically no food, spirits, drugs, and medical comforts of every sort gave out. It was not a question of getting better, but of being kept alive at all.

As an instance of the force of mind over body, I may mention that the mortality was considerably affected on the days we received bad news, but on the receipt of any reassuring rumours the men seemed to pull themselves together and make up their minds not to die. From this one can gather that our life was one of the utmost monotony, and was only broken by such excitements as midnight salvos, etc.

On reference to my diary I find that on the night of the 15th November the Boer guns fired a salvo into Ladysmith, which of course was somewhat disturbing to us, but probably more so to those inside the town. I also note that this was the first date that the relieving column was supposed to be due? Again on Sunday, 19th November, about 12.45 a.m., the Boers made night hideous by firing into the town, and that day those who were wounded in the armoured train disaster at Frere were brought into camp by the Boers from Nelthorpe. Our hopes just about this time were very high, and the air was full of rumours. St. Andrew's Day was celebrated in the most orthodox manner, though we were forced to make our limited quantity of "Mountain Dew" go farther than one is wont to. At the beginning of December the number of sick that were sent out daily from Ladysmith increased greatly, and this fact, added to the bad news we received about Methuen's reverses, made our spirits drop somewhat.

On 7th December all or nearly all of us who were wounded at Talana, were shifted from the Station Hospital to the 26th British Field Hospital, which was commanded by Major Kerin. I fancy the officer commanding the Station Hospital was somewhat relieved at our departure, as many of us who were well on the road to recovery were rather a trial to him, in so much as we did our best to rectify the errors and omissions of his staff, and thereby, from his point of view, made ourselves generally objectionable.

On Friday, 8th December, we heard the action of Limit Hill in the distance, and the next day heard details of it from the wounded that were brought in, viz., Privates Woodley, Ewart, Meekings, Gould, Stewart, Watson, Maton, Deal, Halliday, and Corporal Weir. These men were all put into one tent, and in the evening there was a fearful storm, and it was only the united efforts of some of us officers that this tent, which had been erected, I cannot say pitched, by some of the hospital staff, was saved from collapsing entirely on the top of some twenty or thirty patients. We succeeded in fastening the tent, however, and the storm, after a while, abated, but I much regret that Corporal Weir and Private Gould both died during the evening.

On Sunday, 10th December, there was much joy in camp as we received some newspapers, dated 5th and 6th December, which supplied us with food for conversation and discussion.

On Tuesday, 12th December, the number of sick and wounded from Ladysmith reached sixty-three, and this number was much exceeded the following day, causing congestion and discomfort in camp.

On 15th December heavy firing was heard in Colenso direction, and it continued for five hours, but on the 18th December our hopes, which were somewhat high, were dashed to the ground on the receipt of most depressing news, viz., that we had to hold out for some time longer, possibly six weeks or so. This, added to the fact that one had to conceal one's own feelings as much as possible from the men, and also from the nurses, and the fearful heat of the days, served to make one sorely depressed. However, I am thankful to say that I had a certain amount of manual labour to keep me occupied. Amongst other things the water supply for the camp was most inefficient and bad, and I did what I could to reorganise this, and am glad to say was able to keep the supply of fresh drinking water up to the demand.

On 21st December General Hunter came out and visited the camp. We also received news of the battle of Colenso, which helped to drive our spirits down to zero.

On the 23rd I felt rather seedy, and from now on to the end of the siege I was not fit for very much, worse luck. Our Christmas Day was indeed a curious one. There was no service in camp, but in the evening some hymns were sung to the accompaniment of shells from Long Tom on Bulwana. In the evening we had a Christmas dinner, which was a sort of expiring effort on the part of those entrusted with the culinary operations, but was, I believe, a grand success. McLachlan and I shared a bottle of " bubbly wine," which was most generously and kindly sent out to us from the Regiment, and much did we appreciate it.

On the night of the 29th the Boers turned their searchlight into the camp for the first time.

1900 was ushered in to the tune of guns, Colenso way, which was a good sign for the new year, but there was very little news to be gleaned just now, and life was terribly tedious and monotonous. At 3.30 a.m. on Saturday, the 6th January, we heard the reports and saw the flashes of the Boer rifles and guns, as well as our own, as the attack on Caesar's camp commenced. A terrible fusilade was kept up all day, and our anxiety to know the result was intense. The next day we heard a certain amount, but it was not till some days afterwards that we learnt of the severity and determination of the Boer attack and the gallant defence made by the garrison. When eventually we heard further details and the severity of the death roll, our grief at the loss of so many real good friends was somewhat mollified by the reports of the excellent work the Regiment had performed during the day. Wood most kindly sent me a graphic account of the whole action, as did Dugdale too. The severe knock the Boers took had the excellent effect of keeping them more or less quiet for the next few days, and there was little firing.

On the 11th January we heard of the gracious message sent to the garrison by Her Majesty the Queen. Rumours were very frequent now, and on the 16th January there was a very strong one that the camp of the relief column could be distinctly seen from Waggon Hill. Would that it had been so. Firing towards Colenso was heard daily, and on 18th January, about 4.30 p.m., the heaviest cannonade that we had up to the present heard from that direction commenced, and continued with the greatest violence for three-quarters of an hour. From now on our hopes ran very high, and every day the news got better and better, so much so that after the incessant firing we heard on the morning of the 24th January, which started at 3.30 a.m. and kept on continuously till 11.30 a.m., relief was only a question of days, and finally only a question of hours.

There was, however, a strange and irksome delay and absence of news on Friday, the 26th January, and at last, on Sunday, 28th January, our hopes, which till then had remained at boiling point, suddenly sank to zero, and far below, as we then heard that Spion Kop, which had been won on the 24th instant, was lost to us. Knowing, as one knows, what feelings of depression and consternation this loss filled people at home with, can it be wondered at that the effect on the sick at Intombi was disastrous. Men, who up to now had been buoyed up with hopes and had lived on from day to day in the hope of immediate relief, seemed to entirely "chuck up the sponge," and the mortality throughout the camp was gruesomely and depressingly heavy. A strong will was indeed a thing to be thankful for, as it did more to prolong one's existence than the effect of any drug on the shattered and emaciated frames of the poor souls, whom ill-fate had ordained should be inmates of this delightful and salubrious spot.

From now on rumours and counter rumours flew about daily, and it was impossible to gather anything definite one way or another, but the most significant fact was the further reduction of the rations (such as they were) for the sick. Half a pound of bread per diem made from sour mealies, with an unlimited amount of horseflesh, are hardly the best hospital comforts for men in the last stages of scurvy, dysentery, and enteric; however, it was either that or nothing. On the morning of 5th February our hopes again began to revive as the welcome sound of guns from Colenso was once more heard, and on 7th February it was distinctly nearer. On 10th February the only news we heard was that Buller was too busy to send us any, which was most excellent.

The weather just now was most oppressively hot, and, I fear, told considerably on us. On Sunday, 18th February, there was more very heavy firing from Colenso direction, and the fact of it being Sunday made it more than ever welcome. On the evening of 19th February the camp was swept by a very violent storm of rain and wind, and as usual some of the marquees collapsed, and, I fear, put "paid" to the account of many a poor man.

On 21st February our guns fired very heavily into the nek, where the Klip River runs out towards Colenso. We learnt afterwards that this firing was directed against the Boers who were working on the dam, which they were building across the river at this point, presumably with the intention of first of all flooding us out at Intombi, and eventually of submerging the whole of Ladysmith. It was a mercy that this ingenious scheme of theirs was effectually frustrated by our relief, otherwise the consequences might have been disastrous. This same day we heard the extraordinary rumour that the whole of the Ladysmith garrison, as soon as it was liberated, was to be sent either to India, the Mediterranean, or home. Subsequent events, however, effectually put a stop to any such piece of good luck for some time.

On Thursday, 22nd February, we heard of the capture of Cingolo and Monte Christo, which cheered us up immensely, but there was still a terrible wave of depression over the whole camp. The following day there were more good signs, viz., our naval twelve pounder and 4.7 guns fired many rounds at the men working on the dam, and also the bread ration was again increased. The next two days brought no fresh developments, but on Monday, 26th, the firing was distinctly nearer, and apparently there was much betting in the town as to the actual date of our relief. The odds were four to one that it would be at midnight on Sunday, 4th March. On Tuesday, 27th, we heard of the capture of Cronje by Lord Roberts, and on Wednesday, 28th February, 1900, we had the unique experience and unbounded satisfaction of seeing a small body of our own troops,—we learnt afterwards they were 200 men of the Natal Carabineers and Natal Police,—come down the hills by the civil camp and gallop on towards Ladysmith. We then knew we were at last free men again, after 118 days of inaction and ennui. The following day, Thursday, 1st March, we had the gratification of seeing Buller himself and his magnificent army march through the camp on their way to Ladysmith.

As regards the ultimate fate of Intombi, and the time it took to remove all traces of it, I know nothing, as six days after our relief I bade goodbye to it, and was on my way down country *en route* for England. There is, however, one trace there which will remain, I trust, for ever, and that is the all too sorrowful collection of white crosses and mounds in God's acre. These mark the last resting place of many a brave man who gave his life, not only in combating the onslaughts of the Boers and helping "to keep the flag flying," but also of those whose fate it was to be struck down by the hand of that far more deadly enemy, disease.

CHAPTER VI.

"LADYSMITH AFTER THE SIEGE."

MARCH, 1900.

DURING the next two and a half months there is little to chronicle of the doings of the 18th Hussars. Nearly the whole period, from the relief of Ladysmith to the 23rd of May, the day we set out again on our journeyings northward, was taken up in collecting remounts, refitting ourselves with stores and clothing, getting ourselves fit again after our privations, and endeavouring to work the regiment up to its normal condition, so that it should be ready to move when called upon.

On **March 3rd** the regiment left Manchester Fort and marched down to the ground under Cove Redoubt, where the Cavalry Brigade was stationed, a camp become by this time a very unwholesome one, and we were sorry to leave the high plateau we had been on for so long, awkward though it was in many respects for getting supplies to, for the foul smelling precincts of the Cavalry Brigade, inured as we were at that period of the war to smells of all kinds. Here we had managed to collect 118 horses, and we were by far the strongest regiment in this respect, as the others only had about fifty each.

Letters and stores from now onwards kept pouring in upon us, and the following day was an experience we shall never forget. "The greater part of the mail," writes one of the regiment in his diary, "arrived this morning, and you never saw such a pile; simply glorious to get so much news. Everyone has been awfully good in writing and sending things out; loads of stores, etc., sent to the mess by kind people. The *Daily Telegraph* sent a really handsome present, and all the married people of the regiment at Maritzburg sent boxes. Lady White's present also arrived, and was much appreciated by all ranks."

The regiment remained for a few days in its insanitary camp by the Cavalry Brigade, and in the meantime chaos reigned supreme at Ladysmith. Nothing was known of the future moves, what columns would be formed, what objective would be given us, or under whose command it would be our fate to serve. Everything at present gave way to the importation of stores, arms, and ammunition into the sadly denuded town, and train after train of transport wagons followed one another with ceaseless regularity from Colenso bridge.

Officers and men were being despatched down country to recover from the effects of the siege as fast as arrangements could be made for their journey, and many of our own officers found their way to Capetown or Durban to get a little fresh air into their lungs again. Major Marling, Captains Davey and Burnett, Lieutenants McLachlan, Bayford, Cape, Dugdale, and Cawston were now all obliged to leave Ladysmith, all, with the exception of Lieutenants McLachlan and Cape, being incapacitated by illness from further work. Major Marling, Captain Davey, and Lieutenant Cawston very shortly found their way to England, and Captain Davey did not again rejoin the regiment during the war. Major Marling came back to South Africa in the spring of 1901, and Lieut. Cawston was only away for a short period in England. Lieutenants McLachlan and Cape, as prisoners on parole, were debarred from taking any further part in the war, and the regiment did not see them again till it was over, while Captain Burnett, Lieutenants Bayford and Dugdale, found a voyage to Capetown and back sufficient to pull them together for further field work. Many of the remaining officers left Ladysmith too for short periods of leave at Durban or elsewhere in Natal, and as many of the non-commissioned officers and men as could be spared were given leave if they required it.

March 12th.—The regiment left the Cavalry Brigade camp and encamped till the 11th of April at Field's Farm, about a couple of miles west of the Tin Camp, on the right bank of the Klip River. The farm had been completely destroyed by the Boers, and every particle of wood removed from it, but there were acres of new clean veld stretching around it, and everyone was pleased to get there after the insanitary camp they had been in for the last few days.

Major Knox had been given the temporary rank of Lieut.-Colonel during the latter part of the siege, and the home authorities confirmed his acting appointment as commanding officer of the regiment, until he could be gazetted as such on Colonel Moller's retirement on half-pay.

March 12th to April 11th.—The days passed uneventfully at Field's Farm; our unaccustomed liberty was sufficient for us to think of and grow used to, while men and horses spent most of their time making up for former deficiencies in the food supply. Busy cooking parties were at work all day, and one could seldom look down the lines without seeing small columns of smoke ascending in every direction. Our duties were light, a night piquet on Telegraph Hill (one officer, one sergeant, and twenty-three men) and daily patrols towards Spion Kop summed them up. Meanwhile one squadron was sent to just beyond Devon post, under command of Lieut.

Gosselin, and Lieutenants Stewart and Thackwell accompanied it.

This squadron remained at Devon Post till March 24th, when it was ordered to move to General Warren's camp and act as divisional cavalry to his division. The remainder of the regiment rested at Field's Farm till April 11th, when they received orders to move to Pound's Plateau, the open piece of ground lying north-east of Ladysmith, under Bulwana mountain. As the order was not received till 1 p.m., and there was nearly ten miles to cover after the camp had been packed up, it was long after dark before Pound's Plateau was reached, and everyone spent a most uncomfortable night in heavy rain in the open.

A fresh batch of remounts, one of the many which had arrived for us just lately, had come just as we were leaving our old camp, and they still further delayed our departure that afternoon. Next morning we got ourselves straight, and fixed our camp alongside the 5th Lancers and 19th Hussars, the other regiments of the 2nd Cavalry Brigade, which was still under the command of General Brocklehurst.

April 18th.—A composite squadron from the Brigade was sent to Vaal Plattz, to act as an advanced post on the road to Helpmakaar, and it occupied a farm there was there. Lieut. Webster was sent with it to take charge of our men who formed part of the squadron.

Officers and men now commenced to rejoin the regiment again from sick leave, and our numbers rose daily, but there was little to do beyond getting the batches of remounts we kept daily receiving fit for work, and sending a few patrols in the direction of Sunday's River to watch if the Boer forces came down from their position on the Biggarsberg.

April 18th to **May 22nd.**—So matters went on for a little over a month, until Lord Roberts advance in the " Free State " called for a similar move from the British troops in Natal.

CHAPTER VII.
"THE ADVANCE TO THE TRANSVAAL."
MAY, 1900.

ON the evening of **May 22nd** we, together with the 19th Hussars, received orders to march to Modder Spruit Siding on the Transvaal line, and early on the 23rd we set off once more from Ladysmith to try our fortunes to the northward, this time for good, and gladly we shook its dust off our feet.

The regiment left with three complete squadrons. " B " Squadron had been made up to nearly its full strength again, it having consisted of only two mounted troops during the siege, and a total of 107 of all ranks.

Colonel Knox was in command of the regiment, Major Laming in command of " C " Squadron, Captain Wellby in command of " B " Squadron, and Captain Gosselin in command of " A " Squadron. Lieut. Thackwell and fifty-eight non-commissioned officers and men were detached as Divisional Cavalry to the 4th Infantry Division, under General Lyttelton.

The other officers accompanying the regiment were as under:—Captain Burnett (Acting Adjutant), Captain Haag, Lieutenants Stewart, Wood, Field, Dugdale, Clarke, McClintock, and Webster, the two latter having joined the regiment on appointment soon after the siege of Ladysmith. Lieut. Purdey was with Lieut. Thackwell at Elandslaagte. Captain and Quartermaster Baker also accompanied us.

May 24th.—We marched to Sunday's River and intended going up the pass over the Biggarsberg the same day, but the baggage of the 1st Cavalry Brigade took so long getting up that we had to wait the night below the pass. On the 25th we had a long pull up Biggarsberg Nek, and had to halt for the night at De Aar's farm on the top, our baggage not arriving in camp till long after dark. Next day we made a short march to Kalabash Store, and on the 27th reached Ingagane, bivouacking opposite the hotel and store there is there.

Here we met General Lyttelton and the 4th Division, and were at once attached to a mixed force he was collecting. This consisted of two squadrons of the 18th Hussars, one regiment of Mounted Infantry, four squadrons of Irregular Horse, two batteries of Field Artillery, one Howitzer battery, two pompoms, two 12 pounder naval guns, and an Infantry Brigade under General Howard, composed of the Gordons, Liverpools, and 1st 60th Rifles.

On our way up through northern Natal we found the country absolutely laid waste by the Boers, the stores and the railway bridges had all been destroyed, the latter most artistically, while the private houses had been looted of everything valuable and the stock driven out of the entire country. We, on the other hand, had many orders, varying in tenor and strictness, issued to us regarding our behaviour in the enemy's country we were approaching, and they were generally to the effect that we were to touch nothing at all, or pay for what we wanted if the inhabitants were willing to sell the same.

Captain Gosselin and Lieut. Stewart were left at Ingagane with half " A " Squadron, and as the remainder of that squadron was detached as Divisional Cavalry, we were left with two squadrons only. With these we marched at 5.30 a.m., on the morning of the 28th, as advanced guard to General Lyttelton's force towards Cattle Drift on the Buffalo River, where we halted for the night on the Natal side.

The country through which we passed was very deserted, but we saw some 200 Boers on the other bank of the Buffalo near Stales Drift. At 6 a.m. next morning we crossed Cattle Drift, and set foot for the first time in the Transvaal. Our two squadrons turned down the left bank of the river, passed Stales Drift, and halted close to Inchanga Drift with the main force for the night. The weather now was getting very cold after sunset, and we found the stone walls and outhouses of a farm there, close to the Drift, most welcome shelter.

May 30th.—The next day we were to go further along the left bank of the Buffalo River to Doornberg, where the Boers were supposed to be collected in some force, but from later information it appeared that they had left, so our course was changed, and we moved back up the left bank of the river instead, and again passed Stales Drift, left the river there for a while, and crossed the Ingkalba Spruit about five miles south-west of Utrecht. Here we met General Hildyard's force, which had marched from Newcastle to seize Utrecht, and we camped close by him.

The next day we halted, sending " B " Squadron, under command of Captain Wellby, as escort to General Hildyard, who was going to receive the surrender of the town. The town of Utrecht lies under the Drakensberg, and many wooded ravines run up the hillsides close by. In these the Boers secreted themselves, and though they surrendered the town readily enough, it did not count for much, as they fired on our troops when we attempted to occupy it. However, the surrender was accepted, and as it was not part of our plan to attack the enemy just there, we withdrew again to our camp at Inchanga Spruit, the Boers no doubt " re-taking " the town as soon as our backs were turned.

June 1st.—We continued our course northward, and halted for the night at Wool's Drift, near the bridge over the Buffalo, a few stray Boers exchanging shots with our patrols on the right flank. Next day we went on to Coetze's Drift, where we joined up with Lord Dundonald's and General Clery's forces, who were encamped on the slopes of Imquala mountain, their advanced piquets coming in for a certain amount of shelling from a "Long Tom" perched on the summit of Pogwani Mountain. We halted here for the next few days whilst plans were being formed for the crossing of the Drakensberg, and a short rest was very welcome to all.

On **June 6th** we left General Lyttelton's force and marched to De Wett's farm on the Vrede road, where we were again formed, with the 19th Hussars, into the 2nd Cavalry Brigade under General Brocklehurst, and as such we were attached to General Hildyard's Division, consisting of the South African Light Horse, two 4.7 guns, four twelve pounders, three field batteries, one Howitzer battery, two pompoms, and the 2nd, 10th, and 11th Brigades of Infantry, in all some 12,000 men and many miles of wagons. A considerable part of General Hildyard's force had already seized some outlying spurs of the Drakensburg, which commanded the road up Botha's Pass at its lower part; while next day (June 7th) they seized Van Wyck's Hill, which still further aided us in obtaining a good position for our guns to shell the edges of the Berg which lay in front of us. After the occupation of this hill we were ordered to advance nearer the pass, and about 3 p.m. left De Wet's farm for Yellowboom Farm, which we reached at nightfall, and our baggage some considerable time after us. During the night all preparations were made for storming the pass on the following day, and at an early hour on June 8th our guns commenced systematically searching the top of the Drakensberg where the Vrede road crosses it. From our position at Yellowboom Farm we had a magnificent view of the advance.

Up till 11 a.m. the bombardment went on, eliciting no reply from the Boers, and, as to whether they intended holding the pass or not, we were quite uncertain till our Infantry had scaled the hill sides, and, beyond meeting with inconsiderable opposition on the right flank, made it apparent that they had either retired from the head of the pass or had never properly occupied it. About 11 a.m. all the Cavalry were ordered to advance, and we proceeded up the winding road which follows the stream as it issues forth from the mountains.

The large number of guns supporting our advance no doubt overawed the few light guns and pompoms the Boers had at that point to oppose us, and prevented them bringing them to the edge of the Berg, but as our troops topped the summit they opened fire from two guns and a pompom posted behind ridges, which lay further back from the Berg. We halted at a farm just under the last rise the road goes up in ascending Botha's Pass, until our field guns and all the Cavalry were ready to move on, and about 3 p.m. we dashed up this last ascent and out on the rolling plains of the Free State beyond, drawing, as we did so, fire from the Boer guns, now not far ahead of us. However, there was fair cover in the dips of the ground, and we suffered no harm.

We now completely commanded the head of the pass, and the baggage column, heavy guns, etc., could start at once their entry into the open valley which lies under the pass on the Natal side. Four guns had ascended the road with us, and they quickly got into action against the Boer ones, and after a few rounds the latter's fire stopped altogether, and it was soon evident from the grass fires the enemy were lighting that they were moving off. The 19th Hussars and a field gun, with ourselves in support, were sent in pursuit, but night was quickly coming on, and after going some three miles from the head of the pass and firing a few rounds at shadowy horsemen flitting over the tops of neighbouring ridges, half-hidden by the smoke of the grass fires, we retired back to the pass and down it again to the homestead just under the last ascent, leaving Infantry at various strategic points along the summit to hold it till the morning. Below we passed a cold night, with frost, dew, wind, and fog to contend with.

June 9th.—All next day was employed in getting our train up the pass, and when we had done so we encamped near some water close to the summit on the Free State side. The "18th" were on outpost duty most of the day on the north and north-west side of our position. Our patrols visited some of the surrounding farms, and found among them a certain amount of provender and a few Dutchmen who had decided to surrender.

The weather was much colder on the high veld we were now on, and the nights and early mornings were far from pleasant, chiefly on account of the thick mists which rolled along the hillsides and quickly penetrated what scanty cover we had.

June 10th.—We started at 6.30 a.m., in a fog, along the road to Alleman's Nek and Volksrust. The fog lifted about 10 a.m., and we crossed the Klip River soon afterwards, and learnt from the inhabitants of a farm there that a considerable number of Boers had retreated in front of us to Alleman's Nek, and that the Vrede Commando was on our left flank in the southern slopes of the Gemsbokhoeksberg.

Our road now bore round to the north, and the South African Light Horse, who had been covering the advance of

General Hildyard's Division, while the 2nd Cavalry Brigade looked after the left flank, reported to us, at about 1 p.m., that a greater portion of their regiment had got rather hotly engaged with Boers on some kopjes, which lay to our right front, some four miles east of Gansvlei Spruit.

To help them we sent " B " Squadron, under Captain Wellby, to move round the west side of the ridge and engage the Boers in that direction until the South African Light Horse withdrew, and as it was too late in the day to continue an advance, we contented ourselves with supporting " B " with our other squadrons on their left and rear. " B " Squadron came under a heavy rifle fire as they attempted to approach a kopje from which they could engage the Boer right, and they had to retire and make a larger detour to gain their object. A long wavy ridge ran out from the hill on either end of which the South African Light Horse and Boers were, and under cover of this ridge " B " were ultimately able to approach the enemy's position and conceal their horses there, advancing on foot to the northern extremity of the ridge, where an open donga prevented any nearer approach to the kopje the Boers were on. However, they could open fire from here, under cover of which the South African Light Horse were able to withdraw. A succession of small rises along the ridge " B " Squadron had taken up a position on had been occupied by rushes of a few men at a time, and it became rather a difficult job to retire from the more advanced ones when towards nightfall it was necessary to do so.

The uncertain light aided us somewhat, but it was 8 p.m. before the regiment got back to the camp at Gansvlei. During this skirmish " B " Squadron had Trumpeter Herniman, Corporal Eade, Privates Cooper and Sawtell wounded, but none of them severely, and altogether the squadron escaped fairly lightly, as they were under a smart fire for three hours at a distance of about 600 yards from the nearest body of Boers. The cover was good, however, and the men knew well how to take advantage of it. The South African Light Horse had three men killed and eleven wounded.

June 11th.—As there were evidently a certain number of Boers in the country to the westward, the 2nd Cavalry Brigade were ordered next day to cover the left flank of the advance whilst the guns and Infantry negotiated the passage of Alleman's Nek. So on June 11th we went off to the ground we had been fighting over yesterday, and found that the Boers had retired to some hills further to the north-west, where we did not follow them up, as they were too far off to retard in any way the passage of our column up the Nek. Six Boers were buried by our troops on the hill the South African Light Horse had been fighting on the day before, and this went to prove that our efforts had not been in vain. Further evidence was supplied by a farm house close by, which we learnt had suffered considerable losses. The owner was killed, a friend staying with him wounded and dying, his brother wounded, and his son a prisoner in our hands. The consternation of this family when they learnt, rather late in the day, the true state of affairs, after giving us to understand that their relatives had gone away, having inflicted considerable loss on us, can better be imagined than described.

Alleman's Nek was gallantly taken by the Infantry, well supported by the guns, towards nightfall, our losses being sixteen killed and 105 wounded, mostly among the Dorset Regiment, on whom had fallen the stiffest share of the fighting. The Nek at the top of the pass is some three miles long, and the country off the road extremely difficult, so that a small force of Boers left behind as rearguard were sufficient to hold in check our troops till darkness closed in. No pursuit was attempted, and it seemed a pity that a halt should have been made on the southern side of the pass, as, in spite of our long day, we were equal to pushing on to its northern exit, unoccupied as it undoubtedly was, the Boers having fled many miles that night. From the northern exit we should have had complete command of the railway, and this, when we did obtain it, was of little use to us through the lateness of the hour at which, next day, we debouched from the pass itself.

June 10th.—It was late at night before we got back to the bivouac General Hildyard had halted at after his attack on the Nek. We had remained out to cover the rear of the column as it slowly advanced to the foot of the hill, and at no very early hour next morning (June 11th) we continued our march in rear of the column over the pass. However, at 10 a.m., we got orders to move up to the front, and we trotted up to the northern entrance of the defile and advanced into the open country the railway there runs through. The Boers had set alight to the grass all over this district in their retreat the day before, and the presence of some half-charred corpses on the north-west slopes of the pass proved that the retreat had been a hurried one.

Volksrust, with its tin roofed houses, all of which displayed white flags, lay before us soon after we left the pass, and a few mounted troops were sent on to take possession of the town. Of the Boer army nothing was to be seen; they had scattered towards Standerton and Amersfoort, and our slow advance had prevented us from securing any of the Netherland trains, the last of which had only left Volksrust early that morning.

June 12th.—About four miles west of the town we halted for the night and marched on next morning, the 19th Hussars and ourselves, to Charlestown, and the remainder of General Hildyard's Division to Volksrust, while General Clery's force came up along the railway over Laing's Nek.

Charlestown village was in a filthy condition; the Boers had completely ransacked the place and stabled their horses in the rooms of some of the houses, which they had not burned down. We got a certain amount of shelter in the large railway goods shed and unoccupied houses round about, and this we appreciated, as the weather was, as it almost always is on the top of the Berg, cold, misty, and wet.

We halted at Charlestown till June 21st, and amused ourselves by visiting Majuba and the recent defences the Boers had thrown up on Pogwani, while the large sheds enabled us one night to hold an excellent concert, at which Colonel Bethune's Mounted Infantry joined in as they were passing through.

June 19th.—In the night we detached "B" Squadron, under Captain Wellby, to Laing's Nek to furnish patrols there, but they rejoined us again next day, and moved on with the regiment on the 21st, when we received orders to march through Volksrust to Zandspruit. We saw no Boers during our stay at Charlestown, and very few now remained in that neighbourhood; they had all cleared farther into the Eastern Transvaal.

The 19th Hussars did not accompany us to Zandspruit, but remained at Volksrust to furnish the necessary mounted troops there, our joint duty being to protect the communications along the railway line, whilst General Buller's troops opened up the rest of the railway to Elandsfontein.

As it was probable that we should be at Zandspruit for some time, we set about making ourselves as comfortable as circumstances would permit, the railway line coming to our aid most advantageously. On our arrival there we met part of General Hildyard's Division, which had marched *viâ* Wakkerstroom, taking and evacuating that town in the manner which was so common to our plans at that stage of the war. They left us the same day, and the 13th Battery of Field Artillery and the Dorset Regiment alone remained with us as the garrison of Zandspruit and the country for a ten mile radius around. The 18th held the outlying posts while the guns, including a naval twelve pounder sent to us from Volksrust, the Infantry and squadrons not on duty, encamped on the right bank of the Zand Spruit, near the railway station. Our piquet duties consisted of one permanent post of a troop on a hill about two miles south of the railway, a post on the road to Hout's Nek, and a post, during the day time, on one of the southern spurs of Grass Kop, a high commanding hill some five miles north of Zandspruit station. Besides these three permanent posts we had to send patrols at uncertain hours and by varying routes to connect up with patrols of the 19th Hussars from Volksrust, on either side of the line, and also with the Mounted Infantry at Paardekop, the next station on the line towards Standerton, and some twelve miles off. The railway line itself had also to be patrolled every morning early before the train could start.

Grass Kop was our most vulnerable point, as the hill was too large and too far off for us to occupy, and behind it the Boers could collect unseen in any numbers. The high ridges to the north of Dublin Hill, which itself lies close to and on the north side of the railway line, were also good stalking grounds for the enemy. As most of their commandos had retired in the direction of Amersfoort, the north side of the line was more likely to be the scene of the next fight than that to the south, where our intelligence led us to believe that the Boers were not collected in any great numbers.

Up till **June 25th** nothing of importance occurred, beyond an occasional false alarm that the enemy were collecting in the neighbourhood. On the 25th we were ordered out at 9 a.m., ourselves and one battery, to move in the direction of Amersfoort and try and discover what force of Boers were laagered in that neighbourhood, while the naval gun, with one company of Infantry as escort, supported us as far as the lower slopes of Grass Kop. "C" Squadron furnished the screen, and about seven miles north-west of Zandspruit they discovered a piquet of some twenty to thirty Boers on a kopje which was a continuation of the Dublin Hill ridge. Major Laming, in command of "C" Squadron, moved part of his squadron round the Boers' right, Captain Gosselin protecting his left flank as he swung round, and the remainder of "C" prepared to hold the enemy in front till the guns got into position to shell them; but they had no intention of stopping, and took to their ponies, our men knocking three or four out of their saddles as they retired, but they had time to stop and get their wounded away before we could completely seize the hill. After their retirement we brought the guns on the top of the ridges and shelled them as they retreated still further off, whilst our patrols examined the country to the north and north-west for three miles or so, but could discover no parties of the enemy. At 3.30 p.m. we retired back to Zandspruit, and the Boer piquet we had dislodged galloped back to their old position and fired as fast as they could at our rearguard as they left the ridge, but a few parting shots from our guns in the open soon induced them to keep quiet.

The Advance to the Transvaal. 93

The enormous distance to which modern bullets carry was proved to us at the point where the guns fired from at the close of the day; the range they were firing at, calculated by the range takers themselves, was 3,200 yards, and at this distance the Boer bullets were falling among and beyond the guns.

Our only casualty on this day was one horse shot, but our object had hardly been obtained, and the information we gathered could have been procured more easily by a small patrol or native scouts. It would not have been a wise proceeding on our part to have advanced further in the Amersfoort direction, as we knew full well that to do so would have at once brought on a retaliating attack from the Boers, when they thought we had come far enough for their purpose, and our strength was much too small for any success to be expected. However, at Volksrust, it was evidently imagined that what we had been unable to do with our small force would speedily be accomplished by a stronger column from there, and on June 28th a squadron of the 19th Hussars, two regiments of Infantry, one battery of Field Artillery, and two twelve pounder guns, all under command of Colonel Coke, arrived from Volksrust to help us out. But this sanguine expectation was not to be fulfilled.

June 29th.—Next morning we went out to the ground we had skirmished over on the 26th, taking the battery with us. The Boers were very near to their old position, but they made off a long way in front of us in small parties towards Amersfoort. Captain Wellby, with " B " Squadron, was covering our front, and a part of one of his patrols, consisting of Corporal Arnold and another man, mistaking some scattered parties of the enemy for scouts of the 19th Hussars, who were in front of Colonel Coke's column, which was moving on our right on the direct Volkrust-Amersfoort road, approached them too closely before they recognised their mistake, and on their endeavouring to withdraw the Boers opened fire on them, mortally wounding Corporal Arnold and capturing the other man, whose horse was blown.

We held the ridges on Colonel Coke's left front and flank whilst he endeavoured to approach Amersfoort by the main road, but the Boers rapidly brought up a considerable force, and held a strong position some five miles south of the village, and Colonel Coke, estimating their numbers at over 2,000 men and three guns, did not feel qualified to setting to and turning them off with the force at his command, so at dusk he retired to Grass Kop, the " 18th " remaining out till he had done so, though very few Boers were met with on our side.

June 30th.—Colonel Coke took most of his force back to Volksrust, leaving the Dublins and two 4.7 guns to hold the end of the ridge, now called "Dublin Hill," on the north of the line. He had had two men killed and five wounded on the previous day.

This was the last of our expeditions for some time, as it was seen that they did not result in very much good if always followed by a retreat back to our original position at the close of the day.

On **July 17th** the Boers got a gun up on Grass Kop, and dropped some shells pretty close to our camp, but no one was hit, and on our turning out they withdrew from the hill, and endeavoured to get us to follow them on to the ridges we had manoeuvred over before. But we had no intention of doing so, and when they found that we would not come on, they unmasked two or three guns they had concealed there and shelled us on the lower slopes of Grass Kop. Lieut. Stewart, who had proceeded out beyond Dublin Hill post with a troop, encountered a considerable number in his front.

On the same day the Boers captured one of our men who was scouting for a patrol we had to send towards Hout's Nek to meet the 19th Hussars patrol on that side.

By **July 20th** we had made ourselves fairly comfortable at Zandspruit, and had just got tents up by rail, but on the 21st we were ordered off on our former light baggage scale, and we were not to see these tents, or very much food either, for some considerable time to come.

A general advance was about to take place, and three columns, under General Hildyard, were to take part in it. We were attached to the left column, which consisted of four companies of Mounted Infantry, under Colonel B. Stewart, two squadrons of Irregular Horse under Major Gough, two naval twelve pounders, 13th Battery R.F.A., and half a battalion each of the Dublins and Lancashire Fusiliers. The general plan was that Grass Kop was to be taken and held, and the enemy driven out of the country round Amersfoort.

Very few Boers had surrendered to us at Zandspruit; they had no faith in our ability to protect them from the vengeance of their own commandos, and they were quite right, our authority extending only to gun range of our own outposts. Had this been otherwise we no doubt would have received many surrenders at that period.

July 21st.—In the night we encamped under Dublin Hill, and next morning advanced along the Mooimatjesfontein heights towards Meerzicht, the Boers retiring in front of us to Rooi kopjes, where they had their guns, and on our opening fire with a pompom on their position, they retaliated, and fired heavily at us till our big guns came up and silenced them for a time.

The Advance to the Transvaal.

We did not advance any further that day, but halted for the night at Meerzicht, our baggage not reaching us till late in the evening. We were joined here by General Hildyard with most of the troops of the other columns; they had captured Grass Kop and garrisoned it on the way.

On **July 23rd** we employed our time shelling Rooi kopjes, preparatory to attacking the position next day, and on the 24th the regiment moved out to cover the left flank of our attack.

General Brocklehurst had taken command again, and he reformed the 2nd Cavalry Brigade, which at present consisted only of ourselves and the 19th Hussars. We advanced as leading regiment a long way to the north-west, getting round the right flank of the Boers, who held the long line of Rooi kopjes. Some Mounted Infantry covered our left flank, and the 19th Hussars supported us in rear. The attack by our Infantry on the south end of the kopjes was somewhat delayed, and we were unable to maintain for long our very forward position, as the Boers crept up the dongas, which lay to our north in considerable numbers, so we had to move off to the westward, while two troops of " B " Squadron held a farm we had occupied as our most forward position, and covered the retirement of the rest of the regiment.

A good part of the ground we had to cross in our retreat was greatly exposed to fire from a Boer pompom, but though the enemy kept up a continuous stream of shells whilst our men were crossing, none of them were hit. Some of the Boers made a dash for the farm " B " Squadron were holding, thinking we had all left it, but they received a very warm reception, and lost several men, retiring again quickly, and enabling the two troops of " B " Squadron to join us on the left flank. A footing having by this time been gained by our Infantry on the more central portion of Rooi kopje, an advance was made by ourselves and the Mounted Infantry on the Boer right, and this time we succeeded in occupying the nearer hills, but as the ridges in rear were equally good positions, the Boers did not withdraw far, and intermittent fights went on till after dark. Throughout the day we had covered the left flank, and as night fell we collected in our scattered parties and withdrew towards Meerzicht, as this was only to be another of the many days on which we marched out apparently more for the amusement of the thing than for anything else. We always enjoyed the outward journey, but it was not generally so pleasant coming back. Fortunately, on this occasion, the light was too bad—it was pitch-dark long before we got back—for the Boers to follow us up and harass our retirement.

In the early part of the day Private Grover, of "B" Squadron, was wounded, and we had also a few horses shot, but on the whole we were lucky in having so few casualties.

July 25th.—The next day we halted, and sent in to Paardekop to get some forty remounts which had arrived there for us. We might almost as well have left them alone, as in three weeks time there were only two of them left. They had come direct from the ship to Paardekop, and having immediately to take part in heavy work on indifferent food, had no chance whatever of keeping alive.

On **July 26th** we made another reconnaissance, and again one on the 28th, the first to the north-east and the second to the north-west. On the 26th we found the Boers holding a well defined range of hills covering Amersfoort, and when they opened fire on us with several guns, we retired back to camp. On the 28th we explored the country for about twelve miles to the north-west, and found a considerable amount of stock, which we drove in, the Boers appearing in small parties to the northward.

July 29th.—On the 29th we halted. On the 30th we received orders at 6 a.m. to turn out at 9.30 a.m. Two of our own squadrons, together with two squadrons of the 19th Hussars, four companies of Mounted Infantry, and Lieut.-Colonel Wing's Battery of Field Artillery, accompanied us, while two twelve pounders and an Infantry Battalion followed, as a support, a certain distance on our way, which lay in the Amersfoort direction. Our two squadrons were assigned to the right front and flank, and "B," under Captain Wellby, with the addition of Lieut. Stewart and Lieut. Wood, were given the advanced duties to perform, Major Laming following in support. Our route lay over Witkopjes, but very few of the enemy were met with till we reached the southern part of the hills, which lie some five miles on the south and south-west side of Amersfoort. The enemy left the southern part of this ridge and we occupied it. Captain Wellby, taking with him Sergeant Butcher and a few men of Lieut. Stewart's patrol, who had been scouting to the right flank, now proceeded down the Schalk Spruit, a stream running in a north-east direction towards Amersfoort, and which is met some four miles south of that place by another stream coming in from the direction of Grass Kop. Whilst he was engaged shooting at some Boers who were retiring from the ridge our troops were on, others attacked him, advancing up the main stream he was close to. He took up a position in a kraal, and succeeded in keeping them well at bay until a larger party of some thirty Boers, taking advantage of the Grass Kop spruit, advanced under cover to a very close range,

The Advance to the Transvaal.

and he was only aware of their plan as they were completing it. However, he had time to bid the men with him mount and gallop for their lives whilst he kept off the advancing Boers.

When all his men had cleared, leaping on his horse, he attempted to follow them, but the Boers were within ten yards of him, and, on his indignant refusal to their appeal of "hands up," they fired, mortally wounding him in the stomach. Of those who were with him Sergeant Butcher got away in safety. Private Gover was shot through the thigh and had his horse captured, and Privates Tomlinson and Feehan were also captured and their arms taken from them, both their horses being shot.

The regiment was meanwhile holding the right of the long line of hills which lie some five miles south-west of Amersfoort, and from where it was not intended to make any further advance that day. The Boers were in considerable numbers to our front and left flank, and shelled us till our own guns put a stop to their fire; but our perpetual policy of going out a short way only to retire at dusk was so well-known to them that they did not condescend to withdraw to any great distance.

And at 3.30 p.m. their expectations were fulfilled, and all our troops retired towards Meerzicht, the Cavalry on the left doing so a great deal too expeditiously, for the Boers who were concealed in front quickly occupied the high ground they had been on, and somewhat interfered with the leisurely movements of our retreat. The rather heavy firing we had been indulging in during the day had, however, brought out of camp other troops, and a few rounds from their guns quickly silenced the Boer fire, and we marched back to camp without further incident, reaching it soon after dark.

Our ambulance, with Captain Hardy, our Medical Officer, remained behind to see after Captain Wellby, whom it was found impossible to move.

Next day, **July 31st**, we were joined by the 5th Lancers, and this made General Brocklehurst's 2nd Cavalry Brigade up to and above its original strength, for it now comprised the 5th Lancers, 18th and 19th Hussars, with one battery Royal Field Artillery, two pompoms, and four companies of Mounted Infantry.

On **August 1st** General Hildyard and the 5th Division Headquarter Staff went back to Volksrust, and General Howard commanded at Meerzicht till General Buller's arrival.

The troops were now collected for the advance to the northern line *viâ* Ermelo, and no more "reconnaissances in force " were undertaken from Meerzicht. But any probability of the Boers being taken in by the thoroughness of our next manœuvre was pretty well put aside by the immense preparations we had to make for the move.

At Meerzicht we halted till August 7th, very much incommoded by the exceptionally bad water supply for our horses, for the springs at that altitude nearly the highest part of the Transvaal were then very nearly dry.

On **August 5th**, at 3.30 a.m., Captain Wellby died after forty-eight hours' unconsciousness. He was brought in on August 2nd from a Kaffir kraal he had been taken to on the day he was wounded. For the first few days he seemed to be making fair recovery, but it was found that he was never out of danger, and the wound rapidly proved itself to be a mortal one. His funeral was arranged to take place the same afternoon at Zandspruit, and he was buried there, near the railway station, at 3.30 p.m., all the officers, non-commissioned officers, and men of the regiment who could get away, together with many officers of other corps, including Generals Hildyard and Brocklehurst, being present at the little cemetery by the railway line. In Captain Wellby the regiment lost one of its best officers, and his help in the more independent operations Cavalry could engage in, in the later phases of the war, would have been invaluable to us. His exploits in exploration and travel are too well-known to be here even lightly touched on. Confident, as we all were, that he would in years to come have earned for himself a still greater prominence in this particular service, we all sorrowed to think that this, the first casualty among our officers, should not only be a loss to ourselves as a regiment, but also a great one to England, for it is not given to all of us to command success in such adventurous expeditions as he had undertaken with marked ability and so great a promise of far-reaching results.

CAPTAIN MONTAGU SINCLAIR WELLBY.

CHAPTER VIII.

"AMERSFOORT, BERGENDAL, AND LYDENBURG."

AUGUST, 1900.

On **August 7th** General Buller had collected the large force he was to lead across the Eastern Transvaal, and orders were issued on the evening of the 6th for our advance next day. His column consisted of the following troops :—

2nd Cavalry Brigade, composed as before described.

Lord Dundonald's Cavalry Brigade, composed of Bethune's Mounted Infantry, Strathcona's Horse, Natal Irregular Troops.

Artillery: Two 4.7 naval guns, two 5in. guns, four 12 pounder naval guns, one Brigade Division Royal Field Artillery, "A" Battery Royal Horse Artillery, and one Howitzer Battery.

Infantry: 7th Brigade, under General Kitchener, consisting of the Gordons, Manchesters, Devons, and Rifle Brigade; 8th Brigade, under General Howard, consisting of 1st Battalion King's Royal Rifles, Lancashire Fusiliers, Leicesters, and Inniskillings.

General Lyttelton was in command of the Infantry Division.

Besides the baggage of the various staffs and the Regiments, there were also over 400 wagons in the supply column, carrying ten days' food and forage; three days' more was carried on the regimental wagons, and one on the man and horse, making a total of fourteen days in all.

Lieut. Thackwell joined us on Sunday, the 5th, from General Hildyard's headquarters at Volksrust, bringing his men, who had acted as Divisional Cavalry, back with him. They were a welcome addition, as our numbers were few, and, in spite of the remounts we had already received since leaving Ladysmith, we were still badly off for horses. The remounts indeed proved of little value for the work they were expected at once to do, and since May 23rd we had got through some 200 horses.

On **August 7th** we commenced our advance at 8.30 a.m., Colonel Lord Dundonald's Brigade having to come up from Paardekop into line with us before we could move. The general idea was that the force should first seize Rooi kopjes, then wheel to the right and advance on Amersfoort.

We had always hoped that a different scheme would be adopted, and the Boers held on the Rooi kopjes side whilst a strong Cavalry column, supported as rapidly as possible by Infantry, kept in concealment by Grass Kop, advanced directly through Amersfoort, and thereby cut off the Boer guns from their probable line of retreat to Ermelo. However, the other plan was adopted, and the Cavalry advanced to Rooi Kopjes and found them practically unoccupied, the Boers being in their old positions south-west of Amersfoort. The 18th Hussars, during this first advance, covered the front of the Cavalry Brigade, and on the occupation of Rooi Kopje had to halt to allow the left column to swing round to the right. Whilst halted, orders were received for the 2nd Cavalry Brigade to rally and proceed to the right of our main line of advance. The " 18th " were ordered to hold the easterly end of the ridge we had occupied on July 30th, when Captain Wellby was wounded, while the remainder of the 2nd Cavalry Brigade attacked the ridge on our left.

The Boers, rapidly grasping the fact that we meant coming on this time, did not remain long on the ridge, but, retiring their guns after a few shots, withdrew, burning the grass as they went, through Amersfoort and across the country to the west of it. As some of our Cavalry was posted on the right flank and some on the left, while a good bulk of it executed an Infantry attack on the centre, it became a difficult matter to collect it and follow the Boers up. Within about three miles of Amersfoort we joined the rest of the 2nd Cavalry Brigade, and moved forward to within about two miles of the town; as the Boers retreated, there we halted from 4 p.m. till 9 p.m., whilst Dundonald's Cavalry and some Infantry moved on to bivouac at Amersfoort for the night. It was cold work waiting about, and at 9 p.m. we were glad to get orders to move on to the same place, which we reached at 10.30 p.m. that night, our road well lit up by the continuous grass fires the Boers had kindled earlier in the day. We were little better off here, as there was no sign of any baggage, and we had long ago eaten all our food, and as the thermometer registered many degrees of frost, there was no other way of keeping warm than to march all night up and down the deserted so-called streets of this little tin-roofed stone-built Transvaal town. Our own casualties during the day had been very light, only one man being hit by a spent bullet and two horses wounded, while, altogether, the force had two officers and sixteen men wounded.

Next day, **August 8th**, we halted at Amersfoort to let the baggage come up. Our own had started to trickle in at 1.30 a.m., but many of the wagons did not do so till daylight, and as the supply train was still wanting in the morn-

Amersfoort, Bergendal, and Lydenburg.

ing, "C" Squadron was despatched back to the country to the eastward to guard against any advance by Boers from that direction, but none of the enemy were encountered. A few "snipers," however, began to open fire on our horses as they were being watered at the spruit close to the town, and apparently, not realising that we had a strong outpost close by them, they waited too long in the farm they were shooting from, and five of them were collared. A few fighting townspeople, who were caught by us in the town, were also annexed, and the whole sent back under escort to the line.

On **August 9th** we continued our march towards Ermelo, moving off towards the Vaal River at 7 a.m., the 2nd Cavalry Brigade on the right and right front, and Dundonald's Cavalry on the left and left front, while the Mounted Infantry covered the rear. The 18th Hussars were in support this day, and no Boers were seen. We halted for the night at Mooifontein farm after about a twelve mile march. Next day we started at 8.30 a.m., and marched as far as the Vaal River. Our regiment was on the left flank, and found plenty to do provisioning our rather scanty larders from the resources of the country. As the baggage column had to cross the Vaal by the road bridge at Berginderling, the operation was a long one, and it was 7.30 p.m. before we were to tie our horses up in our bivouac for the night.

The Boers had made good their retreat, some in front of us towards Ermelo and Carolina, others to the Piet Retief district, and they did not seem to be in the humour to make any further stand at present.

The wind got up in the night, and it blew next day as it only can blow in South Africa, and the freshly-burnt grass added its most unwelcome smuts to the many particles of dust we were usually treated to on those occasions.

We camped on **August 11th** at Vlakfontein, and scarcely had pitched our camp, or rather laid down the horse lines, as we had no tents, and outspanned the wagons, before someone in a neighbouring camp set the grass on fire, and we had to move for safety on to a burnt spot, where we spent a very uncomfortable and dirty night. Ermelo was reached on August 12th, and the town impressed us as being quite the best built and prettiest place we had seen in either Northern Natal or the Transvaal, and as such it always remained till its destruction by our column in September, 1901.

Nothing of importance occurred during the next two days, **August 13th** seeing us at Sterkfontein, close to which are the sources of the Vaal and Komati rivers, the one flowing into the Atlantic and the other into the Indian Ocean.

On **August 14th** we reached Vaalbult, about six miles west of Carolina, and into the latter small town parties of Strathcona's Horse rode that day and received a rather warm reception. At Vaalbult the Cavalry Brigade camped some miles ahead of the rest of the column, but we reunited on the 15th at Twyfelaar, crossed the Komati River, here an insignificant stream, and camped on the left bank, with our outposts in touch with Lord Roberts' army, which had then reached Wonderfontein on the Delagoa Bay line. From here the Boers were reported to be in considerable force at and around Belfast.

We halted at Twyfelaar till **August 21st**, and each day furnished strong observation posts and supports to them over different sections of the country, a squadron being detailed in turn for this work. We were also ordered to send an officer and fifty men to General Lyttelton's Division to act as Divisional Cavalry, and Lieut. Stewart and fifty non-commissioned officers and men of " A " Squadron were ordered to undertake this duty. Our strength at this period was as follows :—

"A" Squadron, non-commissioned officers and men, 145; horses, 92.

"B" Squadron, non-commissioned officers and men, 148; horses, 105.

"C" Squadron, non-commissioned officers and men, 143; horses, 105.

Total number of horses :—In the ranks 302, out of the ranks 28, sick 29, absent 3, grand total 362. So to furnish the Divisional Cavalry we had to break up " A " Squadron.

On **August 21st** we marched from Twyfelaar to Van Wyck's Vlei, with " B " and " C " Squadrons out as advance guard to the main force. A part of Dundonald's Cavalry were expected to prolong our right and cover the right flank, but they kept such a long distance in rear that they were not of much support to us. The country to the eastward which they had to march over was very bad going, and exceedingly tricky, and this delayed them considerably. On the left there was little chance of any fighting, as Lord Roberts' army was close by, and only " C " Squadron on the right met any Boers.

About three miles east of Van Wyck's Vlei, where the country begins to dip in a succession of ledges to the valley of the Komati, Privates Evans and Bee, who were the leading men of a patrol of Lieut. Field's troop, came suddenly on a number of Boers who were very artfully concealed near a farm. The Boers opened fire, hit both Privates Evans and Bee, and captured Private Bee and the horses, but Evans, seeing that the Boers were lying in wait at this spot, where the ground kept dropping so sharply that their presence could not be detected, and that part of a company of the

Amersfoort, Bergendal, and Lydenburg.

Gordon Highlanders were rapidly advancing into the same trap as he had fallen into, managed, in spite of his wound, to wave his helmet and shout to the Gordons, preventing them advancing to probably the same fate as he had met.

VAN WYCK'S VLEI, 22ND AUGUST, 1900.
To Brigade Major, 2nd Cavalry Brigade.
Sir,
I forward herewith a statement from Lieut. and Adjutant Shee, 19th Hussars, concerning No. 4,480, Private Albert Evans, of the Regiment under my command.

Private Evans was employed as a scout yesterday in front of his Squadron " C," and was wounded severely while reconnoitring near a farm. I have the honour to request that you will bring the conduct and behaviour of this man to the notice of the General Officer Commanding for favourable consideration.

(Signed) E. C. KNOX, Lieut.-Colonel,
Commanding 18th Hussars.
Sir,

With reference to your memorandum of to-day, asking me to give the particulars in the case of Private Evans, 18th Hussars, I have the honour to state that yesterday afternoon, the 21st of August, I was walking across the plateau above the farm, two miles east of this camp, and met a company of the Gordon Highlanders advancing to the edge of the ridge overlooking the farm. About 500 yards off, on the left flank of the Gordons, a man was waving his helmet whilst lying on the ground, and the officer commanding the advanced party of the Gordons asked me to find out what he wanted, and I did so. I found the man to be a private of the 18th Hussars, who was wounded in two places. He told me that he had waved his helmet in order to attract attention, and let the Gordons know that the enemy were holding the farm (about 400 yards from the ridge), and that if they, the Gordons, advanced to the edge they would walk into a trap, as they would show up against the sky line with no cover. I galloped back and told the officer of the Gordons before mentioned, whose name I do not know, and then went back and brought Private Evans in to the doctor. He informed me on the way that one of his patrol had been killed close to the farm, and that when he was wounded he had crawled away over the ridge and lay there until the Gordons advanced.

(Signed) M. ARCHER-SHEE, Lieut. and Adjutant,
19th Hussars.

Lieut. Field, seeing that his patrol had got into a tight place, went forward to their aid, and finding Evans severely wounded, endeavoured to get him away out of fire, but in doing so he was hit himself in the shoulder, and had difficulty in crawling away under the heavy fire he had provoked. As the country in this direction was very difficult, and it lay some distance on our right, it was not deemed advisable to continue a fight in that direction without plans for pushing it through, especially as orders had been received to take up a line of outposts considerably closer in to Van Wyck's Vlei farm, where the main body was halting for the night. All the regiment was out till after dark in support of the outpost line we had been ordered to take up, and the afternoon was enlivened by frequent skirmishes, principally on the right and right front. Some Mounted Infantry got into rather a warm corner near the farm " C " Squadron's patrol had been to earlier in the day, and a squadron of the 5th Lancers and a pompom were sent to their aid, but the country again proved very awkward, and it required a battery and four companies of the Gordons to support them. With this force a desultory fight went on till dusk, no apparent advantage being gained, as the ground was so eminently suited to Boer tactics. The casualties of our force were six killed and twenty-six wounded at the close of the day, and it was 9 p.m. before our last squadron could get back to camp.

August 22nd.—We halted next day to enable a stronger force to drive the Boers off the edge of the high veld they were taking such advantage of, but they were only playing a waiting game, and had no intention of remaining for a battle. Our regiment did not take part in this advance, but we sent " B " Squadron and Lieut. Wood, with what remained of " A " Squadron, to do outpost duty on the southeast side of the camp.

Yesterday we had lost eight horses killed or seriously wounded by the enemy.

On **August 23rd** we continued our march to Geluk, the Boers clearing off after firing a few shots from the country to our right and front, and falling back on their Dalmanutha and Bergendal positions, where they had retreated in front of Lord Roberts' troops, who were now in occupation of Belfast, with General Pole Carew's column at that town, and General French's Cavalry between us and them.

We halted at Geluk on the 24th and 25th, keeping up intermittent affairs with different parties of the enemy as they endeavoured to probe into our line. They had several guns in front of us, and shelled the hills which lay around our camp, but the stream we camped by ran through a fairly deep valley before it disappeared in a steep gorge to the northward, and there was plenty of cover for our troops. The outpost line was, however, very closely situated to the Boer positions, and a good lot of digging had to be done to render our position secure. On the north side the abundance of rock and broken ground gave plenty of cover to the enemy's skirmishers, and they made it unpleasant for any who exposed themselves in that direction.

On **August 26th** it fell to our lot to escort to Belfast a large convoy, consisting of many empty wagons of the supply column and all our sick and wounded. We saw the convoy to within the outpost line at Belfast, and then returned, having received orders to guard the left flank and rear of General Buller's column, which was engaged in making a reconnaissance of the Boers' position at Bergendal.

There was a great deal of big gun firing on both sides, and the Boers made a determined attack on General Buller's right flank late in the day, but were driven off. The fight went on till after dark, and we had to remain in our positions on the left and rear of the column all night, and it was not till 8 a.m. next morning that we managed to fall in with our baggage and get something to eat. The weather was still very cold at night, and sleeping out in the open on the burnt veld, with our horses to hold as well, was by no means a pleasant job on that elevated part of the Transvaal.

The Boers seemed to either have no wish to meet our troops again in a stand up fight, or else to be endeavouring to draw us down into the low country, far away from our communications, and on the 27th they had left many of the positions they were occupying the day before. Their retreat, we learnt afterwards, could not be stayed by their leaders, and they were already hurrying past Machadodorp, but a considerable body of the Johannesburg police, commonly called " Zarps," determined that they, at any rate, would not retire any further, and accordingly re-assembled to hold a kopje at Bergendal. This they had previously selected, through its unequalled capacity for defence, as a suitable position to hold. It consisted of a strong out-crop of rock, with a glacis-like approach, along which the distances were marked out, so that the ranges could be estimated, and as the ground shelved off in rear it would enable them to quietly disappear out of sight when the time for retreat came. This kopje, close to the southern side of the railway, was an ideal position if the edge of the high veld running southward had also been held, as it was by a strong Boer force on the previous day; for any approach from the other or north side against the kopje would have been most difficult on account of the deep ravines which flanked it.

But, as we have seen, the Boers commenced to evacuate the country to the southward, and this kopje, held by some 300 Johannesburg Police and Staats Artillerie with a pompom, was soon converted into an isolated fort, which was rapidly invested by our troops.

Owing to the heavy fighting there had been on the previous day on the right flank, and the difficult nature of the country there, it was apparently not considered advisable to despatch the mounted troops in that direction for the purpose of cutting off any Boers who might retreat down the line of railway to Machadodorp. For this would appear to have been a plan which had on the face of it the most promising results. Instead the 18th Hussars, together with nearly all the other mounted troops, were collected in rear of a ridge running at right angles to the railway, some 3,000 yards from the Boer position, which General Buller had determined to attack with his Infantry.

It was an heroic deed on the part of these police to attempt to withstand the enormous odds which were now to be brought against them, and could they have got away when they realised our numbers, no doubt they would have done so; but it was then too late, the guns completely commanded the short line of retreat, which they had to traverse before the dip of the ground to the low country would give them shelter from our fire. After a most furious bombardment by every conceivable class of gun we possessed, turning the kopje for a short time into a veritable Vesuvius, our Infantry, the Rifle Brigade from the west, and the Inniskillings from the south, advanced against it. The Boers had, in spite of the cannonading, reserved themselves for this attack, and the Infantry lost over 100 men, the Rifle Brigade suffering most severely in their advance over the open. When they were within a hundred yards of the kopje, the Boers, seeing that they could hold out no longer, hoisted a white flag and surrendered, and it speaks volumes for the generosity of our troops that they, the remnant of Boers then left, escaped alive. As soon as it was apparent that the kopje and pompom were in our possession, the Cavalry were ordered forward to follow up the Boer retreat on Machadodorp, but Cavalry, so few in numbers as we were, could do little good in that execrable country. We advanced for some distance and kept up a running fight with the rearguard till dark, then withdrew back to Bergendal for the night, the "18th" escaping on that day with only one horse wounded.

What had happened to Lord Roberts' army no one seemed quite to know, but it was very apparent that General Buller's had walked straight across their front and engaged and driven off the Boers from before them. A more profitable policy would appear to have been to allow the Pretoria column to hold the Boers in front, whilst General Buller essayed to reach round their left flank and rear by marching on Machadodorp direct from Twyfelaar.

On **August 28th** our entire column marched on to Machadodorp, a wretched collection of tin shanty buildings, the 18th Hussars taking the left flank and capturing two Boers on the way, but very little was seen of the main Boer army, which was rapidly making its way towards Lydenburg and Komati Poort.

On **August 29th** we left Machadodorp, and after some fighting with the Boer rearguard on the uphill winding road, we found ourselves back again on a spur of the high veld, and we halted for the night after a ten mile march at Helvetia, a spot which later on gained an unenviable notoriety as the scene of the capture of one of our 4.7 guns by the Boers. At Helvetia we met many of General Pole-Carew's and General French's troops, the latter *en route* for Weltre Vreden, which lay a few miles to the eastward, overlooking the steep and wooded valley of the Elands River, down which the railway ran to Komati Poort, and which we had just left on our way up from Machadodorp.

On **August 30th** and **31st** we halted at Helvetia while General Pole Carew's force marched on to Waterval Onder, and some of General Buller's troops joined General French at Weltre Vreden, in time to see the British prisoners, some seven officers and 1,800 men, come up the hillside from Nooitgedaacht after their release by the Boers.

On **September 1st** we set out at 7 a.m. along the Lydenburg road, and soon met the troops of General Buller's column who had gone to rescue the prisoners. These troops took on advanced guard duties from the 18th Hussars, and our column, which had left Helvetia as a separate one, had to halt to allow the Nooitgedaacht one to get on first. Lieutenants Thackwell, Dugdale, and Bayford, with their troops, were, however, at the moment we received orders to halt, engaged in following up small parties of the enemy retreating into the valley of the Crocodile River, and orders to halt did not reach them till they had pursued the Boers right up to the bridge over it, where, if they had been supported, they would have cut off some Boer wagons crossing the bridge. Our column reached the river in the afternoon, the baggage taking a long time to descend the long and dusty road leading down to the lower bushy country which lies in the valley. On the edge of the hill we had descended we left twenty men, under Sergeant Bond, of " A " Squadron, to supplement a small post of half a battalion of the Inniskillings and two guns, which was established there.

On **September 2nd** our column crossed the Crocodile and endeavoured to ascend on to the Lydenburg plateau by the road which goes up a long steep slope for some miles after leaving the river. But the Boers had taken up a very strong position on the top, and, allowing our troops to come as close as they could, they then opened fire on them from several guns they had placed at the head of the ascent. The mountains ran out on both flanks from their position, and this enabled them to overlook our advance from both sides, and rendered the position a very formidable one to attack. The " 18th " were engaged in protecting the left flank, and so did not take much part in the day's affair. At nightfall our column retired to camp, the Royal Horse Artillery battery and leading mounted troops having had a long day in a far advanced position, from which they found it impossible either to advance or retire till dusk. That night we received orders for the 2nd Cavalry Brigade to join General Ian Hamilton's force, which was moving on Lydenburg from Belfast *via* Dulstroom.

September 3rd.—At 5 a.m. next morning we set off, our regiment doing rearguard and right flank guard, " C " on the right, " B " in rear. We outspanned at midday on the top of the hill where the Inniskilling post was, and reached Helvetia at 4.30 p.m. in the afternoon, after a very tiring march for the transport animals. Here we halted for half an hour and then went on, along the road General Pole Carew's troops had advanced by from Belfast, for another five miles, the track a very bad one, greatly cut up by watercourses, and covered with large stones. It was now 8 p.m., and as our transport was miles in rear and the animals dead beat, we could get no further, and had to halt on the top of some rugged hills, known as the Zwart Kopjes, for the night. Early next morning (September 4th), at 5 a.m., we continued our march to catch up General Ian Hamilton, who had left Belfast on the 3rd. The 18th Hussars led the way, and before long we got orders to push on from the baggage column by ourselves, and join General Hamilton as quickly as possible. This we managed to do, after marching about fifteen miles, and overtook him at Dulstroom, a collection of about a dozen houses near the source of the Crocodile River, as he was outspanned there. We pushed on to his front and took up advanced guard duties from a very small body of C.I.V. Mounted Infantry, who had previously constituted his entire mounted force.

The country after leaving Dulstroom was exceedingly trappy, and for Cavalry very difficult, the flank patrols being often compelled to either come right into the centre of the advance, or else to take a route so far away that they were altogether out of support, while the advance guard had great difficulty in thoroughly examining the country before the advance of the head of the main column, so many were the natural obstacles the winding road passed through. Only five miles were accomplished beyond Dulstroom when we halted for the night, and left two troops of " B " Squadron out on piquet. The column we had joined consisted of the C.I.V. Mounted Infantry, four guns of a Canadian Battery, a " cow " gun, so called as it was pulled by oxen, a twelve pounder naval gun, a pompom, and three Infantry regiments. During the latter part of this day's march some of the horses

On the way to Lydenburg.

Rations and Forage

[See p. 145.]

had quite given out; they were a poor lot on the whole, and the present hard work was thinning them down considerably. As many of the weak ones as we could we left to come on with the baggage column, but in spite of this three men got left behind, their horses being quite done up, and the Boers coming on them, as they were trying to drag their weary horses along, killed one of our men, Private Caddis, of " B " Squadron, and took the other two men prisoners, taking their rifles and horses, which latter they were welcome to, but the men themselves they let go. They were picked up by the baggage column, which came on later, and Private Caddis was buried at Dulstroom, where the column halted for the night.

September 5th.—At 6 a.m. we continued our march on Lydenburg, scouting all round for General Hamilton's column, but meeting with very little opposition. That night we halted at Wemmer's Hoek, where our belated baggage reached us. Next day we had some difficult country to march through, but the approach to Lydenburg, by the road we were on, gave us command of the higher ground, and the possession of this no doubt induced the Boers to quit their position in General Buller's front, for we were rapidly threatening their right flank.

Major Laming, with " C " Squadron, reconnoitred the road itself as it wound down round Spitz Kop, a conical hill at the foot of the pass, standing out in the Lydenburg plateau, which lay considerably lower than the country we were coming from. Captain Haag and Captain Gosselin took their men along the ridge overlooking the right of the road, and from which the road itself could be commanded, and where, by means of a mountain path, a descent could be made on to the Lydenburg plateau without using the main road. Very few Boers opposed our advance; they were busy getting their guns away through Lydenburg and up the steep hill towards the Mauchberg, which we saw their wagons ascending as we debouched on the plain. Lieut. Thackwell, with his patrol on the ridge on the right flank, was able to establish communication with General Buller's force at Badfontein, in the deep valley of the Crocodile, and very soon our column was swarming down the Spitz Kop pass, and General Buller's one up the steep hill which separated him from the Lydenburg plain, and our turning movement had accomplished its object with little or no loss.

We, the Cavalry, went on to Lydenburg town, which was practically deserted by the Boers, but we were fired on from a gun they had got half-way up the first hill on the Mauchberg road, and we retired again out of range and halted with the rest of the column some three miles outside the town for the night.

In descending the pass earlier in the day, a collision occurred between our men and some of our friends. Part of " B " Squadron got to the bottom of a goat's track they were moving along, galloped for a farm house which lay at the opening of the valley up which the main road ran, hoping to be able to cut off any Boers who might be retiring by the road itself, and occupied it. The 19th Hussars advanced down the road at the head of our main column, and, seeing this farm occupied, began to attack " B " Squadron, whilst at the same time parties of Strathcona's Horse, advancing up from the Badfontein valley, joined in from their side, not knowing that we had come round by another road and reached a spot where they had previously seen no one but Boers. We quickly impressed on them the mistake they had made, and got them to turn their attention elsewhere. Luckily their shooting had not been as accurate as it ought, and we suffered no loss.

Next day, **September 7th**, both General Buller's and General Hamilton's columns entered Lydenburg, General Hamilton's halting on the south-west side. The Boers had by now all retreated along the Mauchberg road, and apparently we considered they were done with for a time; but they had more surprises in store for us, and as it did not seem to be anybody's business to ascertain if the roads to Lydenburg, and places we were choosing for our bivouac grounds, were within range of the hill top the Boers had just disappeared over, no consideration was given to a safe selection for camp. The Boers, no doubt, knowing our urban proclivities, had posted two of their " Long Toms " on the summit of the range to the eastward, and, waiting till enough of our baggage and column had arrived to give them some fun for their money, first sent us an offensive heliograph message to tell us to look out, and then opened fire for the rest of the afternoon at any tempting target that offered itself. The range was a long one, nearly 11,000 yards, and only one man was killed on our side, but the annoyance they put us to was considerable, and one which a more judicious selection of ground would have saved us from suffering.

Our regiment was that day guarding the front and right flank, but as General Buller's column came up along the Machadodorp road, which ran on our right, we had not much to do, and the young wheat and barley which was just then coming up in that fertile country enabled us to gather considerable supplies of forage during the day. Our column was the first to reach the outskirts of Lydenburg, and we watched from some rocky kopjes, on which we had taken up a position, the approach of General Buller's one from Badfontein. The irregular mounted troops were covering the advance, and we were anxious to observe what the approach of one of our columns looked like from the front. It was indeed a peculiar sight, and not quite what we had imagined. All thoughts of the enemy had apparently vanished from the minds of those gallant troopers, whose one idea seemed to be to reach Lydenburg before it was thoroughly looted; first by twos and threes, then by twenties and thirties, and afterwards by whole squadrons, they came dashing along the main road with their led horses and light carts following as best they could, not a scout anywhere, no formation of any kind that one could see, simply Lydenburg and a square meal of some sort written in their faces. It was evident that we had chosen the wrong day for our observation of their scouting capabilities. The baggage of this column, following along after these impetuous horsemen, first tempted the Boers to unmask their guns. To the top of the hill the enemy were on was, however, a matter of five miles, and it was too long a job for us to undertake to turn them out that afternoon, and our own big guns having to fire up at such a height, were able to give us little help.

As the Boers commenced to shell us again early next morning (September 8th), General Buller attacked the range they were holding and advanced with his own troops on the left of the road, while General Hamilton took the country to the right, and the 2nd Cavalry Brigade watched the right flank and rear. Early in the day an unlucky shot from one of the enemy's guns landed among the Volunteer company of the Gordon Highlanders, killed two men and wounded thirteen more. On seeing our advance the Boers withdrew their big guns, covering them very skilfully with a pompom as they did so. In our own immediate neighbourhood we met with only a few Boers, whom " B " Squadron, under Captain Haag, chased for a long way, but they did not succeed in catching them. Between us and the country the Boers were retiring over was an immense ravine with precipitous sides, quite impassable in that neighbourhood for Cavalry, and as our duty was to remain at Lydenburg and not go on with General Buller's troops after the enemy, we contented ourselves with guarding the right flank till the position in front had been captured.

General Buller, leaving half a Brigade of Infantry, a battery, and the 2nd Cavalry Brigade at Lydenburg, went on after the retreating foe, whilst General Ian Hamilton took his own column back to Machadodorp.

General Buller had undertaken a hard task, for the country by the Mauchberg and on to Pilgrim's Rest was exceedingly difficult, immense mountains separated by deep ravines, the road one in name only, and position after position suitable for a small force to hold back for an infinite time one numerically superior, made up its component parts.

CHAPTER IX.

"LYDENBURG AND MIDDELBURG."

WE halted at Lydenburg from September 7th to October 9th, and found it a much more pleasant spot to live in than most South African towns.

On **September 12th** we sent " C " Squadron, with Major Laming, Lieutenants Dugdale, Clarke, and Webster, to Badfontein on convoy duty, and this reduced our numbers very considerably. On the 5th of the month Sergeant Warren, of " A " Squadron, had been wounded whilst patrolling round Schoeman's Kloof, the place on the Machadodorp road, at which we had left Sergeant Bond and twenty men; two troopers who were with him had been captured by the enemy at the same time.

Up till this period of the war we had rarely been called upon to furnish night outposts, but now that the columns were beginning to get smaller in size, we had to take our turn with the Infantry, and after a long day in the saddle, a further stretch of night work was not what we wanted. Observation posts, patrols to various points of the compass, and parties to fetch in forage, employed our time for the first few days at Lydenburg.

On **September 16th** Major Laming's squadron returned, bringing with them what was always the one thing we looked forward to most throughout the war, namely, two or three week's mails.

On **September 21st** we again had to send an escort to a convoy as far as Wit Klip, a short distance on the Machadodorp road, Captain Gosselin, Lieutenants Wood, Bayford, and McClintock accompanying it. Lieut. Wood did not return with this squadron, as he was sent on to Badfontein to take command of about seventy of our men who were there. These included some fifty men who had reached this spot in the train of Lord Roberts' army, having been released from Pretoria in June, formed into a squadron there, and attached to the force which marched up from Pretoria to Belfast in August. From among them Private Langlands, of " A " Squadron, had been killed at Badfontein on September 18th, and Private Barnes, of " B " Squadron, badly wounded in the shoulder.

On **September 30th** the Cavalry Brigade, including two squadrons 18th Hussars, under Major Laming and Captain Haag, with six companies of Infantry and four guns Royal

Lydenburg and Middelburg.

Horse Artillery and a pompom, were ordered to proceed to Kruger's Post, distant some fifteen miles to the northward.

We had escaped doing baggage guard very well up to date, but it fell to our lot to do it on this day, and we had an uneventful march. The country was quite different to anything we had yet been through, and the scenery magnificent, with well-wooded mountains and splendid gorges, but the climate rapidly altered, and lacked that invigorating keenness there was in the air of the high veld. We crossed a pretty stream, called the Speckloon River, and after about five miles of wooded country came out on the fertile valley, in which the few farms called Kruger's Post are situated. The 5th Lancers had been doing advanced guard to the column this day, and the folly of trusting to a lance as a weapon of defence in such a country as we were now marching through was unhappily only too plainly proved. Four of their scouts, seeing a couple of Boers galloping away from them through the bush, started off in pursuit, whereupon one of the Boers quickly dismounted and picked off one by one three of the Lancers as they advanced, lances in hand, in pursuit.

There were a few Boers with a pompom at Kruger's Post, but they retired north-west on our approach, after firing a few rounds at us, and we outspanned on the Origstadt road, where it crosses a small range of hills on the north side of the village. Erasmus' Farm was situated in this valley, and we found in it a great store of forage for our horses, and round about many fields of young wheat in excellent condition.

We took up a position on the Origstadt road to cover the advance of General Buller's force which had been marching through Pilgrim's Rest, and was returning to Lydenburg *viâ* Kruger's Post; but, either our anxiety to do only just what had been ordered, or our usual fatalistic disregard for neighbouring hill tops, prevented us from following up the retreating Boer pompom, and ascertaining if it had really cleared off or not. The next day we found out the true state of the case in a manner we did not quite expect, and General Buller's troops must have wished they had fallen in with a less happy-go-lucky reinforcement.

October 1st.—The head of their column began to approach next morning at about 9 a.m., and continued coming in, wagon by wagon, along the narrow mountain road, up till 4 p.m. of the same day, and naturally thinking that, as we had been there since the day before, the spot was a safe one to camp in, they prepared to rest in comfort for the night. But the Boers were as usual only waiting till a sufficiently large target was offered them before opening fire, and at 4 p.m. they started shelling our different camping grounds in turn with a "Long Tom," a Howitzer, and another gun, all of which they had put up in position on some high hills about four miles off. Our own guns, we had some heavy ones with us, were away down in the hollow where the Kruger Post farms are situated, and from that low ground they could do very little to keep down the fire of the Boers. Luckily our own horses were scattered over the fields of young wheat, enjoying an afternoon's grazing, and an intermediate kopje fairly well screened them from the enemy. Our lines, however, came in for a good share of the shelling, and we had to take cover in neighbouring dongas till another part of the camp attracted the Boers' attention. Some of the 6in. shrapnel shells bursting on the ground at one end of the horse lines, scattered their bullets all along the row of saddles, which were just behind the ropes the horses were to be tied down to, and no doubt their effect on the latter, had they been there, would have been disastrous, judging from the holes which were made in the saddlery. Just before dark the fire slackened, and we thought it was over for the day, but the afternoon's performance was only a preliminary for one at night, and when our fires were well lighted the Boers started again, gave each bivouac they had got the range of in the afternoon another dose in the darkness of the night, and kept on at it for about an hour altogether. Had it not been for the extraordinary accuracy they showed in aiming their shells, the spectacle would only have appealed to us as a marvellous firework display. It was one of those beautiful nights, which one so often gets in South Africa, and one could not but watch with admiration the distant flash of the enemy's guns, the shrieking approach of the shells, and the violent explosions as they burst, some among the many bivouac fires which dotted the hillsides in every direction, others high up or low down in the sky, like exaggerated rockets at some peaceful fête.

General Buller's troops suffered some casualties through this nocturnal shelling; one officer of the Devon Regiment and two men of the South African Light Horse were killed, and one man of the Devons and eight men of the South African Light Horse were wounded, besides a number of horses and oxen. But, although we did not know it at the time, this was the last our regiment was to see of those obnoxious 6in. Creusôt guns.

To retrieve our remissness in allowing the enemy to occupy the commanding position they had fired from, the 2nd Cavalry Brigade was called on to furnish Volunteers to make a night attack on the Boer guns, and the Howitzer, being the nearest, was selected as our first objective. As very nearly all the regiment wanted to go, we had to tell off four officers, Captain Haag, Lieutenants Bayford, Dugdale, and Clarke, and 115 men for the work, only 250 being wanted for the

Lydenburg and Middelburg.

entire party. They started just before midnight, and rode their horses for about three miles, then dismounted, and after a rough climb over very rocky ground, arrived at the place the gun had been firing from, but, beyond the boxes the cartridges had been in, they found no trace of the gun itself; for the Boers had marched off to the westward as soon as they had finished their evening gun fire. There was nothing to do but to retire back to Kruger's Post, and our men rejoined their regiment at 6 a.m. in the morning, and both columns retired the same day to Lydenburg, General Buller's taking with it a few prisoners they had captured near Pilgrim's Rest and a great quantity of sheep, the only stock our slow moving large columns could come up with in those days. The sheep, poor beasts, died by hundreds as we drove them along in our endeavours to keep them in front of the rearguard of our column.

We did not move out of Lydenburg again till our final departure. General Buller, together with Strathcona's and the South African Light Horse, were now to leave us, Strathcona's to go to Canada and the South African Light Horse to be disbanded, and on October 6th we all lined the Machadodorp road side as they passed out of Lydenburg on their way to their homes. We knew it would be a long time before we should be directing our steps in the same course, but we wished them a hearty farewell all the same. We then employed our time for the next few days in removing a great quantity of oat hay from around the Kaffir location, about three miles north of Lydenburg, bringing it into the town for the use of the garrison who were to be left there.

On **October 8th** Lieut. Stewart and the men of "A" Squadron were sent back to us from their divisional cavalry work, and next day we were ordered to form part of General Lyttelton's column, which was to move, *viâ* Dulstroom, on Middelburg. General Brocklehurst and his staff had left on the 6th with General Buller for England, the 5th Lancers had been despatched to Belfast, and the 19th Hussars distributed along the Machadodorp-Lydenburg line, so that the 2nd Cavalry Brigade of the Natal Army now ceased to exist, and our own colonel, Colonel Knox, took charge of the mounted troops during our march from Lydenburg to Middelburg.

General Lyttelton had been put in command of the communications from Middelburg eastward, and, leaving General Howard with some Mounted Infantry and the Rifle Brigade at Lydenburg, he marched with the 18th Hussars, two companies of Mounted Infantry, three regiments of Infantry, and a few guns back to his headquarters at Middelburg.

We left Lydenburg at 8 a.m. on the **9th October**, and marched along the Belfast road, the same way we had come with General Ian Hamilton. At Spitz Kop, where the road commences to ascend to Wemmer's Hoek, we found a few Boers posted on the commanding positions the country there abounds in. Major Laming, with "C" Squadron, scaled Spitz Kop, and from its lofty summit he effectively scared off what Boers there were in front of "B" Squadron, which, under Captain Haag, was covering the front. It was not intended that the column should ascend the pass that day, a fact not fully understood by some patrols of "B" Squadron on the left front, who had ascended the hills on the southern side of the road, and got a good deal away from the support. Private Dineen, of "B" Squadron, was out scouting from one of these parties, and he was not seen again after they reached the top of the hills. A little firing took place between the patrols and a few stray Boers there were in the neighbourhood, but no one was an eye-witness of any mishap befalling him. Later on in the year we got information through the Boers that he had been shot close to the pass, and that they had buried him there.

We camped for the night below the pass, and Lieut. Wood and the men who had been at Badfontein joined us there during the day. This was our first meeting with those who had been taken prisoners at the fight on October 20th at Talana the year before.

October 10th.—Next day the Infantry advanced up the hills on either side of the pass in case they might be held by the enemy, but the latter were not collected in any numbers in this part of the country, and we had an uneventful march, past Wemmer's Nek, to a spruit some ten miles north of Dulstroom. One of our men, Corporal Morecom, of "A" Squadron, who was with Captain Gosselin and the advanced guard, was slightly wounded in the foot during the march.

The rains were now beginning to set in, and we already had had some wet days at Lydenburg. The country in consequence was commencing to look green, and we were no longer troubled with grass fires, but in their stead we had the violent thunderstorms for which South Africa is notorious.

On **October 11th** we reached Dulstroom, and a good deal of sniping went on on the right flank during most of the march, the Boers collecting on that side in more considerable numbers. Next day we marched from Dulstroom to Witpoort over very difficult ground, for in this neighbourhood the high veld was broken by many deep dongas which intersected the country. Our advance guard came on the enemy very soon after leaving Dulstroom, and from then till 4 p.m. in the afternoon we kept up a running fight, having to turn, by flanking moves, very strong positions on three or four occasions. The firing, though pretty continuous, was at long ranges, and our men escaped with no loss, and it was impossible to see whether we inflicted any on the enemy or not.

Our Infantry were not so fortunate, as on nearing Witpoort they lost one man killed and six men wounded. We outspanned half-way and halted for an hour or so, as it was a long march over bad roads for the transport. On continuing our advance we had to leave the broken high veld we had been marching over, and descend to the commencement of the bush veld on the north side of the Steelpoort valley where Witpoort lies. The descent to this valley was by a narrow track which just gave room for one vehicle to move at a time, as it wound down a small ravine. On the bush covered slopes of the opposite side of a larger valley this one ran into, the Boers had taken up a position awaiting us. There were, however, two roads leading down the hill, and they had apparently expected us to take, what was to us, the left-handed one, and had posted one of their pompoms completely commanding it, but their plan was spoiled by our taking the right hand one instead. Our scouts had reported considerable numbers of Boers on ahead during our outspan, and in consequence the Infantry were sent forward to help clear the way, the country off the track being impassable for mounted men unless they led their horses.

The Infantry started to carry this out, but time was not given them to get sufficiently ahead of the column, and the Boers, who were hidden in the bush of the opposite side of the valley we were descending into, saw their advantage, and caught the troops at the head of the column in solid formation. It did not take long for the latter to open out and advance against the wooded country in front, causing the Boers to rapidly retire, and very nearly making them leave their pompom behind them. They had been firing, too, at our regiment as we came down from the hill-top and marched on Witpoort, entering as we did so the zone of country exposed to their fire. The enemy must have suffered considerably, as a heavy fire was very quickly brought to bear on them in their retreat, and we heard, later on, that they lost one of their best Generals, named Govette, on this day; he was shot in the leg, and the wound mortifying, caused his death. Some of the Boers did not retire far that night, and next morning, October 13th, we met them again on the right and right front, and one of our patrols, starting at 4 a.m., nearly succeeded in catching one of their piquets, which was not too wide awake.

A good many Boers had gone off with their guns to Roos Senekal to the north-westward, and others, collecting behind us, considerably annoyed the rearguard till they had got out of the thick scrub which lay close under the hills. The country became more open as we left Witpoort and entered the Steelpoort valley; this we followed for about five miles, and then crossed the river of that name by a good drift at Blinkwater. Only small parties of Boers followed, and these were scattered on both flanks and in rear.

During our march this day, Private Beatwell, of "A" Squadron, was wounded, but this was the only casualty we had. The work we had to do was very hard on Cavalry, the country being so bad just there for horses, and the small number of mounted troops, only ourselves and the two companies of Mounted Infantry, made the drain on our resources a heavy one. On the night of the 13th we camped just under the high hills, which overlook the Steelpoort valley on the south side, and form the edge of the high veld, which runs out northward from Middelburg.

Next morning, **October 14th**, we continued our march up the hill, a big pull for the transport, and arrived once again on the rolling high veld, where we found ourselves more at home. Scarcely had we ascended the hill when our scouts brought word of some cattle, sheep, and wagons away to the east, and we hurried on after them. They had evidently stumbled across us on their way to the Steelpoort valley, and had then tried to turn off to the eastward, but we came on too quickly for them, and they, trusting to our usually misplaced generosity, now decided to stop with their cattle and surrender, instead of bolting for it and leaving their stock to its fate, so we captured nine Boers and a considerable quantity of cattle and sheep, and brought them along with us to Middelburg.

On **October 15th** we marched through Elandslaagte, where we found a small store, with a few useful articles in it, and on the 16th we entered Middelburg, having seen little or no fighting with ~~our friends~~ the enemy on the last two days.

At Middelburg we found Captain Pollok awaiting us, and with him twenty men, who had just returned from a march to Barberton. They all belonged to that portion of "B" Squadron which had been captured at Dundee, and we had now got back nearly all those who had been taken prisoners on that occasion. Our total strength at this period was 470 non-commissioned officers and men, but only 250 horses were fit for work, so we set about, as quickly as we could, to collect some more remounts or horses of any description we could lay our hands on.

The following is a copy of a letter received from General Lyttelton, commanding 4th Division, dated Middelburg, 16th October, 1900:—

On the termination of the operations of the last week the General Officer Commanding wishes to convey his thorough satisfaction with the manner in which the 18th Hussars carried out the responsible duties assigned to them.

The fighting was not severe nor the losses serious, but the country was very difficult, and in the opinion of the General Officer Commanding, it was much due to the perception of Lieut.-Colonel **Knox** of the proper functions of Cavalry in such ground, and the dash and intelligence of all ranks under him, that the operations have been carried out with such slight loss.

General Lyttelton would feel himself fortunate if, under similar circumstances, he had so good a regiment under him.

We found Middelburg a very clean, well-built little town, but absolutely devoid of stores of all kinds, which was unfortunate, as the long round we had lately made by Lydenburg had pretty well run us out of anything we possessed. We camped on the south side of the line near the reservoir, and, with the Mounted Infantry, had to arrange for the patrolling of the country on that side and the safety of the railway line as well. As it seemed to be intended that we should remain some time at Middelburg, we made ourselves as comfortable as we could, and had just procured some tents, when the wet weather set in in earnest with a very smart hail storm, and we were thankful that we had got shelter in time. There were a good many Boers on both sides of the railway line, but those on the north did not give much trouble. The ones on the south were, however, a more enterprising lot, and our patrols, which usually consisted of a squadron, often had a skirmish with them.

On **October 26th** a patrol of the Liverpool Mounted Infantry got entangled on the south side, and we had to turn out and go to their help, but the Boers had departed before we reached the scene of action, and we could only collect what remained of the Mounted Infantry; they had lost one man killed and six wounded, and had had fifteen rifles and seventeen horses captured.

It was determined to form a small column and endeavour to strike a blow at this enterprising commando which, from information we had, laagered as a rule some fifteen to twenty miles south of the town.

So on **November 1st** the 18th Hussars, with the Mounted Infantry, totalling altogether about 500 mounted men, together with the Duke of Cornwall's Light Infantry and four guns R.H.A., the whole under command of Colonel Payne, of the D.C.L.I., set out early to explore the country to the southward. We marched through Rochdale, Good Hope, and Eikeboom farms, halted at the latter to get any information an Englishman, who was in charge of the coal mines there, could give us, and then resumed our march to the south-west in the direction of Roodepoort, meeting a few Boers on the road, who retired before us. We halted at Klipfontein Farm for the night, about fifteen miles in a direct line from Middelburg. During the evening the weather took a turn for the worse, and a storm accompanied by cold wind and rain broke over us and kept on intermittently as long as we were out.

On the morning of the next day, the **2nd November**, Colonel Payne, seeing that the Boers were playing their old tactics, determined to retire again to Middelburg and endeavour to arrange for more than one force to make a joint movement against them, as their elusive tactics made it a useless waste of time and horseflesh advancing with only a single column. The morning of the 2nd was by no means a cheerful one; the cold was intense, and we were wet through by a night in the open. However, as there were some Boers watching us from the direction of Roodepoort, we determined to advance first in that direction, and drive them away whilst our Infantry and wagons got on their way towards Middelburg. The weather was so thick that our advance did little good, as we could not see far enough to know whether we had driven the Boers away or not, and the inaccuracy of our gun fire—the battery with us lacked range finders—so convinced the enemy that they need not do so, that, on our starting to retrace our steps, they commenced in their usual way to swarm after us in even a bolder manner than usual, greatly aided by the drizzling rain, which still kept on. "B" Squadron were covering the direct rear, and during our retirement to rejoin the column, which had started on its way back, one of their men, Private Reid, was shot at close range by a Boer, who had cleverly followed up the rear scouts, and Private Stewart, of the same squadron, was nearly captured as he was stopping to have a few parting shots at the advancing foe. His horse was shot and he himself was badly wounded, but Sergeant Collier and Private Bracey, seeing the danger he was in, galloped back, and with great difficulty got him away on one of their own horses.

Sergeant Collier's account of this matter is as follows:—

On November 3rd we were retiring back to Middleburg, and my troop, under Lieut. Bayford, was doing rearguard to the squadron. During the retirement my half troop was holding a ridge, when a mounted man came over the ridge we had just left, and we immediately fired a volley at him, but fortunately without hitting him, and he still came on quite leisurely. Corporal Valpy, who was looking through his glasses, said he made him out to be one of our own men. Just then two more men came up on the same ridge; they dismounted and fired, and we all saw the man fall forwards on his horse's neck. I jumped on my horse, and taking Private Bracey with me, we galloped out to assist him, but unfortunately his horse made off to the right, as the man lying on the horse's neck was clinging to the off reins, but we caught him up, and found it was Private Stewart. I could tell he was badly hit somewhere, but we could get nothing from him, as he appeared partly unconscious. So we lifted him on to the front of my saddle, and Bracey took his horse and rifle. The Boers meantime tried hard to get round us, but after a hard gallop we managed to get past them, and reached the regiment safely.

Lydenburg and Middelburg. 121

We reached Middelburg about 5 p.m., none too pleased with our outing. We got a little consolation next day, when the Boers sent into our lines for a doctor to come out to look after their wounded men, and we hoped we had inflicted more damage than we had suffered ourselves.

We halted at Middelburg after this for a few days, sending, on **November 7th**, Lieut. Stewart and thirty men to hold, together with some Infantry, an outlying position on Aasvogel Krantz, about five miles north of Middelburg, and Lieut. McClintock and twenty men to another post at Gun Hill, one of the outer defences of the town. All the Cavalry, chiefly details of different regiments, which had been at Middelburg before our arrival there, had now been sent away; the Mounted Infantry had gone too, the latter to Oliphant's River and Pan, the two next stations up and down on the railway, and so it fell to our lot to do all the Cavalry work which might now be required. Next day, **November 8th**, we had to send Lieut. Field and thirty-two men to Bronkhurst Spruit, to be joined there by Lieut. Cawston and eighteen men from Pienaar's Poort. Lieut. Cawston had just recently set out to rejoin the regiment from sick leave, having been invalided to England after the siege of Ladysmith. The men with him were the balance of the prisoners captured at Dundee who had not yet rejoined us. Lieut. Clarke and thirty men had also to be sent to Wilge River Station. The troops who had been doing the mounted work at all these stations were withdrawn elsewhere. We had managed to obtain 180 horses as remounts just lately, and this compensated us for these losses, but we were lamentably short of officers at headquarters itself.

On **November 13th** a combined move was arranged, with General Smith Dorrien's column at Belfast, against the Boers who were collected in some force in the Steelpoort valley and country round Roos Senekal, their quondam seat of government. At 2 a.m. that morning we set off from the south side of the town to rendezvous at Gun Hill with 200 of our men, Major Laming, Captains Haag and Pollok, taking the three squadrons they were divided into. Here we were joined by the 21st Battery Royal Field Artillery, one pompom, a 5in. gun, six companies of the Leicesters, and four companies of the 60th Rifles, the whole under Colonel Carleton, of the Leicestershire Regiment. We marched that day to Elandslaagte store, sighting a few Boers on the way and some wagons many miles in the distance.

On **November 14th** we continued our advance to Schietpad Farm, on the edge of the high veld overlooking the Steelpoort valley. About 200 Boers were in front of us all the way, and we managed to catch them, with our advance squadron and the pompom, in one of their retirements, knocking over a few of their horses and riders as they galloped away, but they always showed great gallantry in carrying off their wounded men, and they did so again this time under a heavy fire. As we reached the edge of the high veld it looked as if they meant to make a stand to cover the retirement of their wagons, and Lieut. Dugdale with his troop, which was leading the advance, came under a smart fire they opened on him from the top of the Berg. Our pompom and 5in. gun, however, quickly decided them to retire, and our men, galloping up to the position the Boers had just left, dismounted and hurried their retirement considerably as they disappeared into the wide Steelpoort valley which stretched in front of us many hundred feet below. General Smith Dorrien's column was meanwhile advancing from Belfast, and we could mark its course from the heights we were on by column after column of smoke ascending from the farm houses on its course. The inhabitants were removed, and the buildings burnt to render them useless as future rallying posts for the Boers. Our columns were too far apart to render one another any real support and to properly hem in the Boers, probably about 2,000 or more in numbers in that district, at least three more columns coming from the north, west, and east would have been necessary, for the country was hostile, the enemy had no communications to keep up, required no regular supplies of rations or forage, and could always vanish into space if he was seriously threatened.

We took no prisoners on this expedition and captured but few cattle, still our movement considerably harassed the Boers, and made them feel that their pastoral plans in the fertile valleys by Roos Senekal were very liable to rude interruption. We halted the night at Schietpad, and returned during the next three days by slow marches to Middelburg through Bothaville and Bankfontein farms, a more easterly road than the one we had come out on. On our way we cleared as much of the produce of the country as we could, and removed the few inhabitants there were.

Our policy in this latter respect was in those days constantly undergoing changes, as there were no concentration camps ready for the Boer women and children and those men who chose to surrender. At one time we seemed inclined to let the Boers look after their own families and be put to the trouble of feeding them, at another we decided to bring them in, as many as we could collect, to towns like Middelburg. They might be brought in by one column with what few goods they could bring with them, only to be sent out again in a few days with a message to the nearest commando to come and take care of them. Their phlegmatic nature seemed outwardly to take either course as a decree of fate, but inwardly they must have heaped anathemas on the heads of the hated English.

As far as our policy was concerned, no doubt the removal of the women and children from the farms did us very little real good, except perhaps just at first. A few peace-loving Boers came in and surrendered; then, probably goaded on by their wives, later on escaped again to their commandos. At the same time, to a small extent, their comfort was interfered with by the loss of their homes and the necessities their women folk could find for them. The removal of the natives from the entire high veld, a project not easy of accomplishment, but still quite practicable, would on the other hand have debarred them from the use of the whole of that part of their territory when the current year's supply of food had run out, and would have practically reduced the country to a wilderness in the shortest possible time.

On **November 17th** we were back again at Middelburg, where Lieut. Wills, a few men, and some thirty horses, the latter always a welcome reinforcement, had joined in our absence. We rested at Middelburg, doing the usual patrol duties, till November 28th, when two small columns were formed, one under Colonel Carleton, consisting of 2½ squadrons of the 18th Hussars, 21st Battery Royal Artillery, a twelve pounder gun, a pompom, and six companies of the Leicesters, and the other under Colonel Payne, consisting of half a squadron of the 18th Hussars, two guns of "G" Battery, and the Inniskillings. Captain Haag and Lieut. Bayford went with the latter column, and the other officers, with the exception of Major Laming, Lieut. Stewart, and Captain Hall, who remained at Middelburg, proceeded with the first one.

The following description of the nature of the work which fell to the lot of the Cavalry to perform on these expeditions may be of interest:—

Sergeant Collier's account of the " trek " with Colonel Payne's force.

On November 29th, 1900, we went with a column under Colonel Payne. The mounted troops consisted of fifty men of "B" Squadron, under Captain Haag. On the 30th we marched to Goodhope. There was a good lot of sniping when we started, and it appeared as though one of the kopjes in the direction we had to go was strongly held. All the guns were brought to bear on it, and then Captain Haag, with about thirty men, made a dash for it; we had one man wounded in going across the open veld. We dismounted and climbed to the top of the kop, with the usual result; you could just see what few Boers there were disappearing in the distance. We arrived in camp at 1 p.m. without further incident. At 2 p.m. a party of thirty men of the Infantry, with about fifteen wagons, was sent to a farm about three miles away, beyond the outposts, to bring in mealies, etc. I went with this party with six men, and after scouting through the farm and the ground beyond it, I retired to a small wood, where we could keep a good look out without being seen ourselves. We had been there about 1½ hours when two parties of Boers, about thirty strong, came out of a donga, two miles to our front, and galloped towards us. Mounting one of my men to go and warn the officer in charge, I took up a position at the edge of the wood with the others. When they arrived about 1,500 yards from me they halted, and sent three or four men on in advance whilst they came on slowly in rear. We waited until their scouts arrived within 500 yards, when we put a volley into them and then fired " independent " as fast as we could at both parties, with the result that they all galloped away to their right, leaving two of their horses behind them. Whether the men were wounded or not I could not tell. I sent Private Bowman to my left flank to watch them, and in the meantime the officer came up at a double with a few men, and I told him the strength of the enemy, and he said he should retire at once, and that I was to try and keep them back till he reached the outpost. Private Bowman came in to tell me that the Boers were working round my left flank, so leaving one man to watch my right I took the others to the left. As soon as we appeared in the open we were met with a very sharp fire, but quickly dismounting and sending the horses out of range, as there was no cover, we kept up a steady fire whilst the wagons were reaching camp. As soon as we commenced to run to our horses the Boers came galloping after us, so we quickly dropped down again, and after firing a few rounds at them, they took cover, and we retired once more with the same result, but this time they reached the wood we had previously occupied, and I signalled at once for the horses to come to us, and we made a run for it. One of the horses was shot before we could get mounted, but putting the man up in front of another, we just waited a bit to give him a start, and then made a rush for it, and I don't think anyone was sorry when the outpost was reached. All the men worked very well, especially Private Dorey, who was holding the horses (it was his first time under fire), and Private Bracey. On December 1st we retired to Middelburg, having one man, Corporal Cluer, slightly wounded on rearguard on the way.

Colonel Carleton's column marched to Oliphant's River on Nov. 28th, and picked up twenty-five Mounted Infantry there. Next day we marched through Geluk and one of the Pretorius' farms at Roodepoort, meeting about forty Boers on the ridges by his house. We missed catching Pretorius himself by a narrow margin. He had great difficulty in getting away, as we commanded the exit from his house on the road he had to get his light wagon along, but the country was bad, and we could not advance quick enough, so, in spite of delaying him by killing one of his oxen with a pompom shell, he managed to get off into some rocky country to the northward. We camped the night at Pretorius' farm, and next day marched on to Kranspoort, overlooking the Waterval drift on the Wilge River. The country here falls rapidly away to the bush veld, and so abominable a district was it, that it had come to be called by the unflattering subriquet of " hell." In old days the Boers had had great difficulty in expelling the natives from the broken gorges the river dashes through on its way to join the Groot Oliphant. Here we were effectively brought up, though we knew there were Boers on the road to the drift, and that they had wagons with them.

General Paget's force was engaged all this day on the western bank of the Wilge with a large body of Boers under Vilgoen and Muller, and it seemed as if we ought to be easily able to press the Boers who were in front of us on to him if he would aid in blocking the drift on his side. But General Paget's column was not having it all their own way on their side of the river, and it was only after some very hard fighting by General Plumer and his mounted men, who were with General Paget, that the combined column was able to make much headway, and even then they were many miles off our drift, and we could not get communication with them by signal. Our own course was, however, a very tame one. It was open to us to attempt the capture of what Boers there were in front of us by an advance to the river bed, before they could cross the river itself, but instead of doing so we encamped at Kranspoort and shelled the retreating wagons, while a few carts, tents, and cattle, which the Boers had not been able to get away, fell into our hands. One of our men was captured here by the Boers and released after they had taken his arms from him.

Next day we retraced our steps back towards Oliphant's River, halting on the night of December 1st at Hartebeestefontein, after a seventeen mile march, during which we had burned a great many farms and done a considerable amount of damage. On December 3rd we marched into Middelburg, encountering on the Uityk ridge about forty Boers who had taken advantage of our absence from the town to make a raid on it. They were rather disconcerted to find us coming up on their flank, and they beat a hasty retreat.

Our other half squadron had had a little fighting whilst with Colonel Payne's column, but had not accomplished anything in particular.

We halted in Middelburg till **December 7th**, when we were again despatched out to Kranspoort, this time under Colonel Campbell, who brought the 60th Rifles with him, in place of the Leicestershire Regiment. There were the same number of Boers again about Roodepoort, and we skirmished with them up to the difficult country around Kranspoort, making one march of it this time from Oliphant's River station to Kranspoort farm. Sergeant Batchelor, with six men of "B" Squadron, were following up the Boers into the rocky country which lies to the west of Kranspoort, and had advanced some distance from the main body of "B," who were leading the advance, when about forty of the enemy, having collected together, made a furious attack on him; he had good cover, however, handy, and taking every advantage of it, he held his own in the rocks, knocking over several Boers as they incautiously dashed on what they thought was their certain prey. Private Bee was wounded and one of the horses was killed, two more were wounded, and the rest stampeded before other troops could come to their assistance and drive the Boers off into the rough country by Waterval drift. Corporal Wilson too was accidentally shot whilst with a party of the rearguard on this day.

We halted for two days at Kranspoort to explore the difficult country on the way to the drift and join up with General Paget who was now camped, not far off, on the opposite bank of the river. On **December 9th**, the next day, we went a certain way through the bushland, over the rocks, to the drift, four of the Infantry being wounded en route, and on the following day "A" Squadron, supported by some Infantry, opened out the road the whole way down, the Boers who had been there retiring by some tracks we had no knowledge of. At the drift we communicated with some of General Plumer's Australian troops, who had also advanced as far as the river.

The weather was getting uncomfortably hot in the middle of the day, so next morning, having to get back to Middelburg, we started at 2 a.m. and went part of the way, as far as Roodepoort, in the cool. We halted there that night and went on next morning, at 2 a.m. again, to Oliphant's River, followed as usual by a few enterprising Boers, who appeared always from the hollows they hid in as soon as our main body marched off. At Middelburg we now halted for some time without anything of much note occurring. Every morning we had to send a squadron at daylight to occupy Uitkyk Hill, where there was a railway siding about half way to Oliphant's River. Before we occupied this and signalled that the country was clear no trains were allowed to start from Middelburg. It was a very exposed piece of ground, approached on the western side by many dongas which led up to it from the Groot Oliphant's River. We had always advocated a permanent post being established there, but the supply of troops in Middelburg was not at that time thought to be sufficient to permit of this being done. A small force daily approached this height, and, unable to vary its route to any appreciable extent, was almost certain to meet with an ambush of some sort before very long.

On **December 21st** Colonel Knox left us to go to Pretoria and take over command of the 2nd Cavalry Brigade (the one belonging to the main army, not the Natal Field Force one) in place of Colonel Broadwood who had gone to England. Needless to say we were all very sorry to lose him, even for a while, but we knew at the same time that he would have a splendid column and gain more opportunities for advancement where he was going, than in the junior capacity of a regimental commander. Major Laming now took command of the regiment, Major Pollok, who had just been promoted, having " A " Squadron, Captain Haag " B," and Lieut. Wood was transferred from " A " to command " C," as Captain Gosselin was on the sick list, and Lieut. Stewart was sent as A.D.C. to General Lyttelton, a post he occupied till the end of the war. At the same time we had our numbers strengthened by the arrival of Lieut. King and a few men from Maritzburg, the former joining us for the first time on appointment to the regiment.

CHAPTER X.

"Christmas, 1900."

On **December 24th** we sent a squadron as usual at daybreak, or rather a little before, to see if they could catch any Boers coming up to the Vitkyk ridge, Lieut. Wood and "C" Squadron performing the duty on this day. They remained there till about 9 a.m., when, all seeming quiet, they were relieved by Lieut. Thackwell and a troop of " B " Squadron, for, as it was very improbable that the Boers would attack the line in any force late in the day, we always reduced the outposts if nothing was seen of them in the morning. However, this was a faulty move on our part, and the Boers, knowing it, took advantage thereby. They had been collected at Van Niekerk's farm, a couple of miles away on the Groot Oliphant's side, since before daylight, intending to attack the line, blow it up, and capture our outpost and a train if possible when our squadron should retire. As soon as they ascertained that the squadron had done so, and before their own whereabouts had been discovered by our men, they determined to attack Lieut. Thackwell and his troop, which consisted of thirty-four men, and set about doing so at once. About eighty of them, supported by others to cover their retreat, advanced up the dongas from the Groot Oliphant's direction, a few men at the same time being sent by the north to cut off the post from Middelburg. Lieut. Thackwell had very few men available to defend himself with, a good many having to remain to hold the horses close to the siding itself. The Boers attacked with great dash, opening at the same time a heavy fire on the outnumbered piquet. They succeeded in stampeding the horses, the greater number of which galloped back to our lines in Middelburg, where already a messenger from Lieut. Thackwell had arrived asking for assistance. This was sent as quickly as possible, but before reinforcements could come up the Boers had completely overpowered the piquet, and as we advanced to the rescue were rapidly disappearing a long way off on the Bethal road.

Lieut. Thackwell and his men had fought it out most gallantly till the last; he himself was badly wounded in two places, and Lance-Sergeant William Howard, Privates Walter Birkett, James Collyer, John Pritchett, and William Talbot, all of " B " Squadron, were killed. Sergeant Coxen, Sergeant Stephens, and three other men were captured, their clothes pierced by several bullets. Eight horses and three more men who were in charge of them were taken prisoners;

the remainder of the party were able to retire on the support which came out from Middelburg to their aid. The Boers were with difficulty kept by their leaders from shooting Sergeant Coxen, as he had fired till they were on the top of him, killing one of their men a few paces distant; but their better feelings prevailed, and we found all the prisoners they had taken, together with our dead and wounded, on the plateau on our arrival there. The following is the account of the affair by the Officer Commanding the regiment to the General Officer Commanding at Middelburg :—

Lieut. Thackwell proceeded from camp at 8 a.m. this morning with thirty-four non-commissioned officers and men to Uitkyk to relieve Lieut. Wood and a squadron, which had been there since before dawn (leaving camp at 2 a.m.).

Lieut. Thackwell had posted Sergeant Stephens and three men on his right by the siding, a centre party on the highest part of the ridge, and a left party by the wire entanglement. Sergeant Stephens posted his men, and very shortly after doing so one of them, Private Talbot, pointed out to him about sixty Boers in Van Niekerk's farm on the north side of the Oliphant's River road. These men at once proceeded to send a party to the line to blow it up, and the remainder advanced to attack Sergeant Stephens. He sent back word to Lieut. Thackwell, who came up, and information was also sent to camp by heliograph that the Boers were blowing up the line. A few men were sent to reinforce Sergeant Stephens from Sergeant Coxen's post, and Lieut. Thackwell decided to hold on to the ridge till reinforcements arrived. Lieut. Wood and his squadron had, however, gone too far to hear the firing, and arrived back in camp just as the information came in to say the line was blown up.

The Boers attacked from three sides, up the two valleys which run from the south-west to Uitkyk, and up the spur which lies between them, making their strongest attack up the valley on the right. Our men held out there until five were killed and Lieut. Thackwell wounded in two places, when the remaining men, viz., Sergeant Stephens, Corporal Tatford, and Private Hopkins, were taken prisoners. Meanwhile Sergeant Coxen and Private Speight on the left were captured as they were covering the retreat of the left and centre parties, who managed to get away. Privates Leith, Bowman, and Carmichael had also to surrender with a few led horses, although most of the latter, attacked by another party of Boers sent to cut them off from Middelburg, had already stampeded. The casualties of Lieut. Thackwell's party were as follows :—Five men killed, one officer wounded, eight men and eight horses captured.

On Lieut. Thackwell's message being received in camp I at once turned out a squadron and a half with a pompom, and proceeded as rapidly as possible to the scene of the fight, picking up on my way the remainder of Lieut. Thackwell's troop. Lieut. Thackwell estimates the actual attacking party at seventy, which was reinforced to 120 after his position was taken. The Boers retired through Good Hope to Boshoff. I counted eighty leave the former farm. Our support arrived at Uitkyk at 11 a.m., and we halted there till 1 p.m., at which hour the Boers left Boshoff and disappeared to the south-west.   (Signed)   H. T. LAMING, Major.

Commanding 18th Hussars.

Our men were buried that afternoon in the cemetery at Middelburg.

We had reason to think that the loss inflicted on the Boers had been greater than our own, as they had exposed themselves a great deal in their dash up the hill.

AN EXPERIENCE WITH THE "UITKYK PATROL."

At 7.30 a.m. on the 24th December, 1900, Lieut. Thackwell, with our patrol of thirty-two non-commissioned officers and men of "B" Squadron, relieved "A" Squadron, which, under command of Lieutenant Wood, since 2 a.m. had been holding a position near the colliery to the east of Uitkyk Station, distant about three and a half miles from Middelburg. Reaching the colliery, we dismounted and relieved the different posts, and our horses, led by the number threes, were placed under cover. We had not taken up position more than ten minutes when we saw Boers moving about amongst the trees surrounding Van Niekirk's Farm, then we saw a waggon, which, with the Boers, was making towards the railway line. Lieut. Thackwell was occupying a position commanding the line, the ground affording little or no cover, with the exception of a few small ant heaps. Looking through my glasses I saw another party of the enemy threatening our left flank and rear, so sent Private Collier with a message to that effect to Lieut. Thackwell, meanwhile placing the five men (Privates Speight, Slinger, Seppings, Kempster, and Jackson) and myself well extended to resist a flank attack. By this time the Mauser bullets were flying thick and fast, and we could hear Lieut. Thackwell's party hard at it as well, for they were only about two hundred yards away. Then we heard three loud explosions, which we at first thought were from the guns at Oliphant's River, but soon discovered they were caused by the charges of dynamite placed under the rails, which resulted in blowing up the line. As soon as this was accomplished the Boers (who certainly numbered 130, some say 150) devoted their whole attention to us, and as they had to advance for some distance up a gentle slope they made a fair mark, and we made it rather warm for them. We held on to our positions for quite an hour and three-quarters, then a shrill whistle sounded, ponies appeared as if by magic, the Boers were in the saddle in a twinkling, and they rushed us, yelling like fiends as they came. Slinger, Seppings, Kempster, and Jackson managed to reach their horses, but, to tell the truth, I did not miss them until I heard them shouting to Speight and myself, for they were bringing our horses up; but I waved them back, for I saw that it would mean the whole of us being captured, as the Boers were too close upon us. Speight and I went on firing as quickly as we could, still hearing Lieut. Thackwell's party doing the same. When the Boers were within about one hundred yards of us we opened cut-offs and commenced magazine fire, the last shots ringing out when they were about ten or twelve yards away. The next second I was jerked on my feet by two burly Boers seizing my bandolier, my carbine wrenched out of my hand, and I saw that Speight had been served in the same manner. We were then marched down into a hollow towards Van Niekirk's farm by four of them and two armed Kaffir boys, the remainder pursuing the four men who had got away, but they fortunately did not succeed in wounding or capturing one of them. In about a quarter of an hour they returned, and then there was a big palaver, and very excited they seemed to get. Luckily Speight and I did not understand Dutch, or we certainly should not have been so unconcerned. Just then they were joined by a man in a white jacket, who evidently seemed to be someone in authority, although his appearance and dress would not have proclaimed it. They had a long talk with him, and we heard the name of "Jansen" frequently mentioned, and angry faces were turned towards us as they pointed at us. Ultimately we were told to go, the man in the white jacket coming a little distance with us, saying to us before leaving that we should consider ourselves lucky for his timely arrival, as the majority of the Boers were for shooting us, on account of firing until the last moment, instead of laying down our carbines and putting our hands up. We then walked up the slope, where we were met by Sergeant Stephens, Privates Leith and Hopkins, Stephens telling us that Lieut. Thackwell was wounded in two places, through the left thigh and lower part of left shin; the butt of his rifle was also blown to splinters, by an explosive bullet I should imagine. This was not the worst though, for Sergeant Howard, Privates Collier, Burkett, Pritchett, and Talbott were lying dead where they had fallen, all of them being shot through the head, with the exception of Talbott, who was shot through the breast. These were not the only wounds, however, for all of them were hit in three or four places. Sergeant Stephens had a very narrow escape, a bullet going through his helmet and the handkerchief which was inside it, passing within an inch of his head. By this time the sun was getting strong, and Lieut. Thackwell needed water badly, so Private Leith went over to the station to get some. At that moment a Boer leader rode up (I don't know if it was Trickardt himself) and asked Lieut. Thackwell if he felt much pain. Noticing a water bottle on his saddle I asked him for it, and he willingly gave it. Then recollecting having seen some sheets of corrugated iron three or four hundred yards off, I went and fetched two pieces, which we bent into a V shape, and so improvised a rough shelter for him from the heat of the sun. The Boer then said: "Well, I must be off, as I see your ambulances are coming out." He then wished Lieut. Thackwell the "Compliments of the season," which were heartily returned, and rode away. Soon afterwards Surgeon Captain Hardy arrived, dressed the wounds, and we lifted Lieut. Thackwell into the ambulance. During the whole of the long weary wait he had not uttered a word of complaint, or given vent to a groan. Just before being lifted into the ambulance I heard him say, "Hardy, don't let them cable that I'm wounded if you can possibly help it, for it will spoil all their sport at Christmas at home." We then waited for the other ambulances, into which we lifted our dead, and after seeing them in the mortuary tent at the field hospital, made our way to camp. I had rather a narrow shave myself, five bullets through my jacket, two through my pants. Not one of these touched my skin, although I was hit through the muscle of the leg below the calf, but not bad enough to go sick with, and it healed entirely in about a fortnight. In conclusion I heard from three different sources, one of them being a Boer who was himself in the attack, and was captured some months afterwards, that the Boers had nine killed and nineteen wounded, five of the latter subsequently dying. "Jansen," I discovered, was one of Trichardt's leading men, and was amongst the killed.

H. H. COXEN, Sergeant, 18th Hussars.

The reductions of the garrisons of both Belfast and Middelburg had quite prevented us making any combined movements against the enemy in the Eastern Transvaal for some time back, and in proportion to our quietness the enemy's activity increased. Attacks on the line were becoming daily occurrences, trains were getting captured and the patrols harassed in all directions, and on Christmas Day, 1900, we seemed, in our part of the country at any rate, to be making very little progress indeed. For all this we determined to celebrate Christmas Day in as befitting a manner as possible, and we had sent to Durban some time before for a supply of provisions, which, together with some beer from Pretoria, luckily escaped the vagaries of the railway and reached us in time for all to have a good dinner on that day. The Boers, however, did not keep Christmas, and either jealousy on their part, or a thought that we might indulge too freely on that occasion, always led them to become particularly obnoxious as that time of the year approached. This year was no different to other ones, and they celebrated it by blowing up the line at many different points.

On **December 26th** all the " 18th " had to go out at daybreak towards Pan, to rescue a train which had there been derailed and plundered by the Boers, but before we could reach it it had already been set on fire and partially destroyed. We put the fire out, pursued some scattered parties of Boers from the neighbourhood, and spent a very hot day on the dry up-lands which lie west of Pan.

We remained at Middelburg till January 22nd of the incoming year, and very little of importance happened during this period in our immediate neighbourhood. The Boer activity at the end of the year increased to a great extent, and, after several small successes, culminated in a concerted attack delivered in the middle of the night at the beginning of January on six different posts which were situated along the line near Belfast. At only one of the posts were they successful, and even there they received a very warm reception. This repulse and the gradual formation of many columns at different points between Belfast and Standerton caused them to draw off a little from the immediate neighbourhood of the railway line, and, after the first week in January, there was comparative peace round Middelburg. General French was now concerting his plans for sweeping the whole of the Eastern Transvaal to the Swaziland Border, and many columns were being formed in pursuance of this idea. A few changes had in the meantime taken place in the regiment itself. Lieut. Dugdale had left to go as A.D.C. to Colonel Knox with the 2nd Cavalry Brigade, and on January 14th Captain Corbett, Lieutenants Pilkington, Lyon, and Lichtenberg, with ninety-one non-commissioned officers and men, joined from England.

Our camp we had shifted on **January 17th** to a fresh site under " Western Kopje," and we had employed our time in putting the kopje we were under in a thorough state of defence, the late night attacks executed by the enemy putting us very much on our guard. We had also a small post to entrench at Klein Oliphant's River, a short distance out of Middelburg on the road to Pan.

Christmas, 1900.

On **January 21st** the regiment set off at 8 p.m. to lie in wait at a level crossing near Pan for some Boers who were reported to be about to cross the line there from the south side to the north. There is little doubt that our departure from Middelburg, though kept as secret as possible and not commenced till well after dark, was communicated to the Boers by their friends in the town, as none of them attempted to cross the line that night, but, knowing that we should hardly do the same thing two nights running, crossed in safety on the following one. The regiment spent a night in concealment by the crossing, all ready saddled up, and in momentary expectation of a midnight charge, until the first break of dawn showed too plainly that no human being, friend or foe, was abroad on those desolate plains. There was nothing to do but to wait at Klein Oliphant's river for the arrival of our baggage, and have breakfast there in the meantime, for we were to march that day to Pan, *en route* for Wonderfontein, there to join General Smith Dorrien's column, and it was out of our way to return again to Middelburg. We were only taking two squadrons on this expedition, but a pompom under Captain Poole, R.A., who had been with us on many of our late excursions, accompanied us as well. Major Laming went in command, and Major Pollok and Captain Haag led the two squadrons our men were divided into, " A " and " B " only being with us. " C," under Lieut. Wood, was left at Middelburg for garrison work. Besides these officers, Captain Corbett, Captain Burnett, Lieutenants Bayford, Cawston, Lichtenberg, Lyon, Pilkington, Wills, and Captain Hardy, R.A.M.C., accompanied us.

We marched in two days to Wonderfontein, arriving there on **January 23rd**, a few Boers hanging about our right flank between Pan and Wildefontein. At Wonderfontein we halted till the 25th, and were placed under the orders of Colonel Henry, who commanded the mounted troops of General Smith Dorrien's column. These mounted troops consisted of 200 of the 18th Hussars, 50 19th Hussars, 250 5th Lancers, 300 2nd Imperial Light Horse, and 450 Mounted Infantry, total 1,250 mounted men. The rest of the column was composed of three 5in. guns, two batteries of Field Artillery, three pompoms, and four Infantry regiments, by far the strongest force collected in these parts since General Buller's advance in the preceding year.

Our object was soon known to be Carolina, and at five a.m. on **January 25th** we set off as far as Twyfelaar in that direction. At Grootpan we halted for a couple of hours to allow the transport to overtake us, as the country was very waterlogged, the wagons heavy, and their pace very slow. During the outspan our regiment was sent to the westward to drive off some Boers who were hanging about the right flank, but we did not go far in that direction, and soon returned to form a support to the advance guard, which shortly afterwards came across the Carolina and Ermelo commandos, who had collected at Lilliefontein to bar our advance over the Komati River. They had taken up a strong position, and it was necessary to attack them in force, as the ground was much of the same nature as that we had found so difficult in our advance with General Buller in the previous August. The enemy, too, had a considerable force with them, including two guns and a pompom, so the Suffolk Regiment, with a battery, one of the 5in. guns, "A" Squadron of the 18th Hussars, and some of the Imperial Light Horse, were directed to engage them while the remainder of the Cavalry was collected on the right flank, as the country higher up the river was easier, and a crossing could better be effected on that side. The enemy were very strongly posted, and took little or no notice of our fire, which probably did them no great harm, as the ground dropped rapidly behind them and afforded excellent cover.

Rather late in the day, not till 4.30 p.m. (it was about 2 p.m. when we began to find out the enemy's position), a strong force of our mounted troops were sent over the Komati River above Twyfelaar with orders to get between the enemy and Carolina. Almost as soon as the Boers divined our intention they left the Lilliefontein position, retiring their guns very coolly under as heavy a fire as our own guns were able to bring on them. The light was bad, and a heavy thunderstorm helped them to retire in comparative safety, and long before our mounted troops had got round to intercept them they had disappeared into the gloom in the direction of Carolina.

One of our men, Private Bott, of "A" Squadron, had been wounded during the fight, and several horses had been hit; among the other troops one officer of the Suffolks had been killed and five men wounded, while a trooper of the Imperial Light Horse had been killed by lightning, and two other men and one or two horses were knocked over by the same agency.

We spent a wet night at Twyfelaar, and marched early next day (January 26th) to Carolina, with the 18th Hussars as advanced guard, and met with a little opposition from a few parties of Boers who had retired on the previous day in the direction of Ermelo. On entering Carolina we found the town practically deserted; about a dozen wounded Boers were in the hospital there, and these, with one or two other prisoners, represented our total capture.

January 27th.—We left Carolina at 9.30 a.m. next morning and marched back again to Twyfelaar, our regiment again in advance. The Boers, who were as usual waiting for this move on our part, soon put in an appearance from the Ermelo direction and considerably annoyed the rearguard, which consisted of the Mounted Infantry, and some of their men were taken prisoners during the retirement. For a while a brisk fight went on, and a considerable number of the "18th" were ordered back late in the day to take part in it, but it was nearly dark when they got back, and the fight was then almost over. The weather was again very bad, rain falling nearly incessantly all through the day, and it was late, 9 p.m., before we got back on that night to a very wet bivouac on the north bank of the Komati River, with our horses very weary after their long day. One of our men, Private Owen, of "B" Squadron, a reservist, was so badly wounded during our advance in the morning that he died next day.

On the following day, **January 28th**, the "18th" had to return again over the Komati and take up the duties of rearguard for the day, and at 3 a.m., after a short rest, we retraced our steps to the further side, and held the right bank until our column had cleared off sufficiently far in the direction of Wonderfontein. A considerable number of Boers kept advancing to see if they could rush us at any point, but with the aid of a 5in. gun on the northern bank we kept them at a distance and they swung off lower down the river, crossed it, and attacked the left flank of the column as it was moving along on the far side. After a short but heavy cannonading against the Boers immediately in rear of us, we took an opportunity of comparative calm to slip back over the river to the north side and continue the skirmish from there, but the enemy did not attack us with any vigour, most of them having gone off to join in the attack on the left flank, which was protected by the Imperial Light Horse. They were, however, beaten off after a short fight, with the loss of a few men wounded on our side.

We halted at Grootpan for some time on the way back to rest the transport and to leave some of the troops there. The remainder, including ourselves, marched on to Wonderfontein, where we arrived at 9.30 p.m. that night, wet through and pretty tired, having been in the saddle since three in the morning. The object of this march to Carolina and back did not impress us as being very laudable. It savoured too much of the many former ones we had taken part in, which resolved themselves into guarding an immense convoy through the enemy's country, at first driving the foe before us, and later on being driven by the foe in their turn, and what the scheme had to do with General French's advance eastwards we were not clever enough to discover. General French's move was, however, now to be put into execution, and we were ordered back to Middelburg to form the mounted portion of a column which, in connection with it, was there being formed.

On **January 29th** we marched as far as Pan on our road back, and during the day two of our men, Privates Faulkner and Hall, of " A " Squadron, who were scouting on the left flank, came suddenly on two Boers, who were lying up in the grass waiting for them; luckily Faulkner saw one of the Boers before the latter could take good aim, and, drawing his sword, at once galloped at him and ran him through, the Boer firing and wounding Faulkner's horse as he did so, whilst the other Boer, who ran up to his rescue, was shot by Hall before he could do anything. Our two men had to gallop for it, as these Boers were supported by a party of about thirty others close by.

Middelburg was reached next day, and on **February 1st**, after a day's halt, we again marched off with Colonel Campbell's column to take part in the great " drive " eastward. Two columns, under General Paget and Colonel Plumer, had most unfortunately to be taken from the places which had been assigned to them, and sent off to Cape Colony to repel De Wet, then making an incursion into that territory. To fill this gap our column was hastily improvised, but it was a small one, and consisted only of 200 18th Hussars, 100 Mounted Infantry, 800 Leicestershire Regiment, one twelve pounder, and one section 21st Battery Royal Artillery. We took practically the same officers and men as before, Lieutenants Woods and Webster joining us in place of Captain Haag, who went to take up an appointment in the South African Constabulary, and Lieutenants Bayford and Pilkington were left at Middelburg to do duty there.

CHAPTER XI.

"WITH GENERAL FRENCH TO THE SWAZILAND BORDER."
FEBRUARY, 1901.

THE scheme we were now joining in was one which we had always hoped would be undertaken, as it represented the advance of a nearly unbroken line over an immense extent of country. But the loss to us of two columns was a most serious blow, and the distance from ours to Colonel Alderson's, the next one on our right, was much too great, and only equalled by the distance to General Smith Dorrien's on our other flank. The other columns were not, however, so far apart, and they were too of greater strength.

The general idea was to advance straight east and drive the enemy into the low country of Swaziland and Zululand, where their horses would suffer from horse sickness, and they would be far from their own districts, and certain to be more ready to surrender if at all cornered in a tight place. At first no doubt they did feel very insecure at the sweeping tactics we were adopting, and this was shown by General Louis Botha's readiness to come in and see what terms he could get; but as they learnt more easily to avoid our columns, with our broken lines and the big gaps between them, they grew obstinate again, and it was to take more closely knitted cordons to bring them in the end to surrender.

On the night of **February 1st** we halted at Bankfontein Farm, a few Boer outposts being visible that day. At 6 a.m. next morning we set off in a south-easterly direction, and almost immediately got in touch with a few of the enemy skirmishing on the hills by Roodepoort farm. Major Pollok, with "A" Squadron, was leading the advance, Lieut. Cawston's troop being out on the left front, taking the ridge of high ground which flanked the road on that side, and two troops of "C" Squadron, under Lieut. Wood, supported this advanced troop.

The ridge on the left ultimately met another ridge at right angles, the latter crossing the road, and being known at that point as Roodekop, the highest ground about that part of the country. On this kop the Boers had concealed themselves, partly in a shallow pan of water there was there, and partly along the ridge itself in the long grass and mealie crops. It was impossible to see what positions they were exactly taking up, though our troops knew that they were sure to be met with before very long. Lieut. Cawston, in his eagerness to discover what ground they were occupying, rode on with the scouts of his troop, and nearing the pan on the top of the hill was met with a furious fire from the Boers who were concealed in that position, supported by other parties of the enemy defending the length of the ridge where it crosses the main road, along which our centre was advancing.

Possession of the ridge running on our left, and especially its point of junction with the one in our front, was at once seen to be a vital necessity. Unfortunately our guns, which had for a long time covered the advance of our leading troops, imagining that our men had gained the crest, a supposition to which the convex nature of the ground led them, were advancing to a closer position, and could not at once open fire in support of Lieut. Cawston's troop. But the pompom and the supporting troops of " A " Squadron, together with a section of the Mounted Infantry, under Lieutenants Crum and Reed, at once opened fire and went to their assistance. Lieut. Cawston was among the first to be hit, and Sergt. Baker thereupon took over command of the twenty odd men composing the troop, and, acting throughout with great gallantry and judgment, managed to save his troop from complete annihilation.

The Boers had allowed the advance scouts to come right up to their position before opening fire, but Sergeant Baker, who was with the main body of the troop, received information from one of the scouts, Private Stork, who had cleverly located the Boers, of the proximity of the enemy, and just had time to dismount his men and get them in position before the Boers opened fire. The ridge was immediately swept by their bullets, and any movement on it was difficult in the extreme. Nearly all the advanced men were laid low, and the Boers, attacking most gallantly, threatened to overwhelm the rest of the troop. Sergeant Baker now received a wound in his right arm, of so serious a nature that amputation was shortly afterwards necessary, but in spite of this he rallied his men and opposed such a determined front to the Boers that time was given to our support to make a counter attack, and a section of the King's Royal Rifles Mounted Infantry, gallantly led by Lieut. Reed, making a slight detour to our left, came on the enemy with a heavy fire at close quarters. This counter attack, combined with the fire of our own support, and the pompom at a range of about 1,200 yards, first checked the Boers, and finally caused them to slowly retire, covered by their comrades' rifle fire from the pan on the top of the hill.

As we slowly advanced they were ultimately compelled to leave the ridges where their rearguard had so skilfully delayed us, and they were rapidly disappearing through Roodepoort Farm, some 1,500 yards on the south side of the ridge, when

LIEUTENANT C. F. CAWSTON.

our leading men gained the crest. The fight had not been a long one, but whilst it lasted was of a very furious nature, and Col. Campbell, who was then directing the central advance, checked for the moment by the strong position in front, saw the importance of the left-hand ridge, and sent up two companies of Infantry to aid in the capture of the ground by the pan. This had helped to make our task a comparatively easy one, and we were able to establish ourselves all along the ridge, shelling the Boers as they retreated through Roodepoort Farm, but the small number of mounted men we had with us forbade any attempt at pursuit.

Unless the enemy chose to come and fight us, we, as on many occasions before, had no voice in the matter, and had to be content with a march in solemn procession, more as an escort to the baggage and convoy than anything else.

We encamped that night at Roodepoort, and collected our dead and wounded to the farm there.

Of our own corps, besides Lieut. C. F. Cawston, who had been wounded in two places, and who died next day from the effects of his wounds, Lance-Corporal Charles Gill, Privates William Nicholls, Thomas Birkenshaw, and Frank Tindle, all of " A " Squadron, were killed, and Sergeant Baker, Privates H. Hughes, W. Gibbons, and A. Sheehan were wounded, and five of our horses were killed and two wounded. The Mounted Infantry suffered almost as severely. Lieut. Reed was wounded so seriously that he died in two days' time, and they had besides four men killed and four wounded. That the Boers suffered a good deal more severely we had accurate information later on to prove, but at the time we only found two of their dead on the ground. They adopted various devices, and would run any risk to get their killed and wounded men away from the field, and this time they dragged some of the former off with ropes tied to their ponies' saddles.

Next afternoon we buried our dead in a small cemetery we made for the purpose close to the farm. All were good men and a great loss to us. Lieut. Cawston had on this and other occasions shown proof of exceptional bravery in action.

A PART OF MAJOR LAMING'S REPORT ON THIS SKIRMISH.

To BRIGADE MAJOR, CAMPBELL'S FORCE.
Zandbank, 1st March, 1901.

Sir,—I have the honour to bring forward the names of the undermentioned non-commissioned officer and man for special service rendered at Roodepoort by them on February 2nd, 1901, together with particulars of the case.

No. 2,703, Sergeant H. Baker. This non-commissioned officer was with Lieut. Cawston and his troop when that officer was mortally wounded, and four men were killed and four wounded out of the troop of some twenty men. Sergeant Baker himself was among the latter, and lost his right arm through amputation on account of the wound he received. Lieut. Cawston had halted his troop, and had himself ridden up close to the leading scouts to examine the position. Sergeant Baker acted independently with great judgment in dismounting the men of the troop on information he received from one of the scouts, who reported the Boers close by hidden by a fold of the ground. Hardly had he done so when a very hot fire was opened on the troop, causing Lieut. Cawston and several men to fall, on which Sergeant Baker rallied together the remainder of his men and withstood the Boers, who were advancing most determinedly, thereby enabling a counter attack to be delivered by a section of King's Royal Rifles Mounted Infantry, who were in close support, which successfully drove the Boers off. I consider that Sergeant Baker's conduct is specially deserving of mention, as he was suffering at the time from a very severe wound. He has throughout the war proved himself to be a gallant man, and I believe was specially commended by Major-General Howard for services performed when attached to his staff at Meerzicht in July, 1900, but this recommendation was not forwarded through the regiment.

No. 4,796, Private Stork, at the same time and place described in the above account, showed conspicuous bravery. He was one of the scouts of Lieut. Cawston's troop, and very cleverly located the Boers, who were hiding in the long grass and a slight depression of the ground. He at once brought his information in, and Sergeant Baker acted on it. He then returned dismounted to the spot from which he had observed the enemy, and in spite of their fire, which was then very heavy, from this position, he was able to enfilade their advance and prevent them encircling the flank of the troop.

H. T. LAMING, Major.
Commanding 18th Hussars.

The next day was Sunday, and we halted at Roodepoort so as not to get in front of the line of columns advancing from the westward. The Boers, who perceived this advance, and had also got information of the small size of our column in comparison with that of the others, thought it a wise move to endeavour to overpower us, and thus gain an open tract of country for their forces to retire through if pressed from the westward. In pursuance of this policy, and imagining that we would only hold Roodekop with a small piquet (camped as we were on the southern side of that hill and advancing in a south-easterly direction), determined to move round our flank and seize the ridge in our rear.

On first seeing their column of some four to five hundred men moving round our right flank, we imagined that they must belong to Colonel Alderson's force, which was then supposed to be about ten miles to our south-west. But their suspicious movements put us on our guard, and we opened fire on them as they moved round to our rear, but it was hard to see if our guns did them any harm. Colonel Campbell had already posted at Roodekop a strong piquet of half a company of Infantry well entrenched, in the manner the Leicestershire Regiment always took good care to carry out, and very little anxiety was felt for the ridge; but, as an additional support, some Mounted Infantry and a company of Infantry were sent to aid in the defence should they be required. The Boers advanced to the attack, hidden from us by the Roodepoort ridge and from aimed fire of our guns, but the Infantry and Mounted Infantry, well posted in their chosen positions, waited for the attack and easily drove them off, and after a short time they gave up all hope of annoying us from that quarter, and retired out of range and view to the westward, contemplating, as we learnt afterwards, a night attack on our camp. But Commandants Chris Botha and Grobelaar, who were directing the Boer operations in that quarter of the Transvaal, began to fear for the safety of their vast herds of cattle, retreating by Ermelo to the Swaziland border, and already threatened by the move southward of General Smith Dorrien's forces from Wonderfontein, and so, instead of remaining in our neighbourhood, they determined to retire and attack the more easterly column, which they did on the following night.

On **February 5th** we set off from Roodepoort to Morsom's store, and met at Boshmansfontein a commando of Boers, under Chris Botha, who had been between us and Colonel Alderson's column since daybreak. Our troops seized the western edge of a large pan of water there is there, and held the outer circumference of the pan for the remainder of the day, while the Boers occupied the ground on its other side. The ground there was higher, but, like most of the rolling plains in those parts, it was convex in shape, and afforded neither side a large field of fire. If Colonel Alderson's troops had been able to come up on Chris Botha's rear he would have been caught between us. We had met his patrols earlier in the day and fired at them, thinking they were Boers, and on their way back to his column they had lost most of their men through mistaking Chris Botha's force for their own column; but our connection with Colonel Alderson was not well enough established to allow of any reliance on his support. The fight continued till dark, the "18th" holding the flanks and rear whilst the Leicesters held on to the front, but they could not advance far beyond the western side of the pan. At nightfall the firing died away, and the main Boer forces hastened off for the daring night attack they were to make on General Smith Dorrien's force, which was encamped by the shores of Lake Crissie, some forty miles away.

Next morning, **February 6th**, we expected to renew the fight, but on pushing on beyond the positions we had occupied the day before, it was soon very evident that the Boers had left, and beyond small isolated parties, who kept a respectful distance away from our 5in. gun, we met with no further determined opposition on the whole of this "trek." Our route now lay through De Witte Kranz, on the Klein Oliphant's River, to Klipfontein on the source of the Komati, and on from there to Lake Crissie, where General Smith Dorrien was awaiting us with a convoy. We had orders now to collect all women and children, seize as much stock as possible, and destroy anything which might be of use to the enemy, but not actually to burn farms, though we might do so with out-houses, etc., in fact we were to convert the country into as much of a wilderness as we could. This was only possible over a small area, as our front was a narrow one, and time was not our own; we had to do a certain distance by nightfall, and in spite of all our efforts there were still left the Kaffirs, practically servants of the Boers, whom we had to leave behind, ready to repair a good deal of the damage we had done.

The country we were marching through was very fertile, and, though only lately settled in by the Boers, for some twenty years previously there was hardly a farm on it, was now covered by prosperous homesteads, growing most abundantly all kinds of produce, and it was well wooded where trees had been planted. It possessed, too, a climate exceptionally suitable for white men, quite different to that most justly maligned and semi-tropical portion of South Africa which lies round Ladysmith, and where we had spent most of our time.

Before reaching Klipfontein on **February 6th** we saw in the distance large parties of Boers halting on Klipstapel; they were resting there after their attack of the night before on General Smith Dorrien, and his pursuit after them of that very morning. But long before we came anywhere near they had disappeared northwards, and they remained a force still to be reckoned with, and one which we had to leave in our rear. We learnt from two Dutchmen, who surrendered to us at this spot, that the Boer casualties had been heavier than we supposed in the fights we had with them on February 2nd, 3rd, and 4th, and that they totalled altogether 57 killed and wounded.

By marching to Lake Crissie on **February 7th** we joined up with General Smith Dorrien's column, and learnt of the night attack he had repelled, but with serious loss to himself, the night before. His casualties included twenty-four killed and fifty wounded, while a great number of horses, chiefly belonging to the 5th Lancers, had stampeded. On our way to Lake Crissie we found eleven wounded Boers, most of them too badly hit to be able to be moved, while a good many killed were also picked up by General Smith Dorrien's troops, and buried alongside our own men at the Lake.

Lieut. Clarke and ten men and horses awaited us here, as they had not been able to join us before we marched from Middelburg.

To the Swaziland Border. 143

We halted at Bothwell, on the shores of Lake Crissie, till the 9th. Heavy rain fell nearly all the time we were there, and increased considerably the volume of water in this so-called lake, for it was only a shallow and nearly dry pan when we had first reached it.

From here we were to march to Amsterdam, more or less in touch with General Smith Dorrien's column on our left, but some way from Colonel Alderson's on our right.

On **February 9th** we started off over lovely grass lands and through a country at first thickly interspersed with large lakes, and afterwards by many rapid flowing streams, a land once almost entirely occupied by Scotchmen, and called by them New Scotland, but latterly given over more and more to encroaching Dutchmen, no doubt well backed up by friends at Pretoria. It seemed to us a pity that England had not marked these lands as fit spots for future colonisation, and at all events stipulated for their retention after the war of 1881, populated as they were by so many of our own countrymen.

The march was a pleasant one, but our column met with little or no opposition, and all we had to contend with was the heavy nature of the country we were marching through. The general direction of our march lay through the farms of Blauwater, Hamilton, Umpilasi, Bonny Brook, Churchill, Westoe, and thence to Amsterdam village. On our way an Englishman, named Baxter, and his three sons surrendered to us; the latter had been fighting against us, and were rather more Dutch than English, all of them being Transvaal subjects. One Boer we also captured at Westoe, where the road we were on crosses the Usutu River. From Westoe to Amsterdam we descended rapidly to the Compies River valley, leaving the healthy high lands we had been roaming over for the last few days. General Smith Dorrien had met with more success than we had, having captured a great number of cattle and wagons, several Boers, and an immense quantity of sheep, whose fate, poor beasts, was destined always to be a tragic one; the whole country was in fact covered with sheep, and we suffered no privations on this " trek " from lack of very excellent mutton.

Amsterdam is very prettily situated under the high ground which runs out on the east to the Swaziland border, but we found the temperature very high at that period of the year, and the fruit crop which we had left hardly ripe in the Lake Crissie district was almost over in this part of the country.

We halted for one day at Amsterdam and then set out, accompanied by the Mounted Infantry, a 5in. gun, two fifteen pounders, and a pompom for Wolvenkop, about fourteen miles along the Piet Retief road, where a small force of mounted troops from Colonel Alderson's column was encamped. We were now in the middle of the rainy season, and so far had been lucky to encounter nothing much worse than intermittent storms, but our good fortune was to forsake us, and we were soon to learn how nearly akin the climate of the eastern edge of the high veld was, at that time of the year, to the western ghauts in India, when the monsoon first breaks over them.

We were to endeavour at Wolvenkop to capture a small body of Boers who, separated from the other commandos, which had broken back through our lines, had been driven into the rough country which there borders Swaziland. The rain prevented us putting this plan into operation at once, for almost as soon as we left Amsterdam a steady downpour set in, and continued, almost without intermission, until the 27th of the month, at one time coming down in torrents, at another drizzling with a heavy mist, which completely shut out the landscape from our view. In spite of the weather we had to try and take these obstinate Boers who, rightly or wrongly, preferred to trust to the doubtful friendship of the Swazis and many hardships from hunger and bad weather in the inhospitable fastnesses they had hidden in, than to surrender and gain security, though not much comfort, in our camp. The latter was by now nothing more or less than an extensive bog; it was of no use changing its site, for in five minutes the new ground became as much of a quagmire as the old. The horses churned it up into great rivers of mud, and, without tents and with very few shelters of any sort, we sat huddled up under what cover we could extemporise during the periods we had of rest from outpost duty and scouring the surrounding precipices in search of our friends.

It was truly proved, we took it, by our experiences during this and the following month, that however depressing this vast country might be, and to some people a subject for little love, its climate was nevertheless a truly miraculous one, for no matter what extremes of heat and cold, wet or dry weather one was subjected to, harmful effects were scarcely ever felt by those who kept on the move and lived in the open.

During our few days at Wolvenkop we were out most of the time exploring the country to the eastward, and pulling our horses after us up and down some of the most precipitous and rocky ground it had so far been our fate to encounter. The weather was generally so thick that it was hard to see the exact nature of the region around, but, when the clouds did roll aside for a short space, we caught a glimpse of the rugged type of country we had come to. To the eastward of our camp, after passing a few lofty kopjes covered with bush and broken into ledges by the action of water for many generations, one suddenly came to the edge of the plateau on which Wolvenkop was situated. The ground broke away at once in enormous precipices, cut into here and there by the streams and rivers, which flow down in cascades from the high veld, while dense vegetation was spread over the more gradual slopes and grew in impenetrable thickets in the small dongas which cut into the hillside. Far away below bushy country, thickly sprinkled with rough kopjes and cut up by deep worn dongas, swept away to the north-east, east, and south-east until mountains, as high as the ground we stood on, shut out the view in those directions. A few zigzag paths led down the mountain side, used by the Boers and natives for driving their cattle down to and up from the hot country, where, in the cold winter months, good grazing was always to be found. At first the Boers tried to oppose our advance into the mountainous country, but seeing our numbers increase, and hearing of other columns moving round them from the north and south, they gradually came in and surrendered.

On **February 18th** eighteen of them, a hungry and bedraggled lot, came in with a white flag and gave themselves up to us at our camp at Wolvenkop, and during our absence next day, as we were hunting the kloofs at Evergreen and Cascade farms, six more laid down their arms. Meanwhile we had unearthed their carts, wagons, and belongings of all sorts, as most of the inhabitants of Amsterdam had chosen this secluded spot for hiding their property in; and, before we left, Lieut. Crum, of the Mounted Infantry, brought in two more Boers, and Lieut. Lichtenberg another whom they had pounced on during their exploration of the valleys around. Many of the wagons we found had to be burnt, as they had been run by the Boers over the edges of the precipices into the thick bush below, whence, by the help of many teams of oxen, no doubt they hoped to extract them when we were gone. We also captured, whilst here, a great number of cattle, driven down by the Boers in front of our columns to these parts.

The question of our own food supply had already become an acute one, as a convoy, marching from Newcastle in Natal, was to have met us seven days before at Amsterdam, but all the information we could gather was to the effect that three rivers separated us from it, one of them 300 yards wide, another seventeen feet deep and broad in proportion, and we had not so far troubled to inquire about the third. For some time back we had had to put our horses on half rations, and everything, except meat, was down to the same scale. The country, however, produced an ample supply of mealies, both green ones and others, and as beef and mutton was as abundant as could be wished, we in reality cared little for the fate of the convoy.

Colonel Campbell and the rest of our column joined us on **February 20th** at Wolvenkop, and brought orders that we were to march off to Piet Retief at once, but the heavy rain had rendered the Sheila River unfordable, and it was not till the 27th that the column, with some difficulty, got across it and marched into Piet Retief the same day. We passed Col. Alderson's column on the road, and met Colonel Knox's at Piet Retief, while Colonel Pulteney's was also close by, and Colonel Allenby's at Zandsbank, about twelve miles further on. At Piet Retief we learnt what success the other columns had had. There were eight altogether, their commanders' names being:—Smith Dorrien, Campbell, Alderson, Knox, Pulteney, Allenby, Dartnell, and Colville, and the above was the order in which they were spread out from General Smith Dorrien on the north-east to Colonel Colville on the south-west.

The combined successes so far had been:—392 Boers killed, wounded, and captured; 353 surrendered; total, 745. Four cannon captured, including one maxim; ammunition, 161,636 rounds; rifles, 606; horses and mules, 6,504; trek oxen, 4,362; other cattle, 20,986; sheep, 158,130; wagons, 1,604; mealies, etc., 400,000 pounds. And yet we had only skimmed the country in some parts.

We halted a day at Piet Retief, an uninteresting little town, situated in a very fertile tract of country, and marched on **March 1st** to Zandbank on the Assegai River, one of the streams which had so long delayed, and was still delaying, the arrival of our supply convoy. On our way thither a party of twenty Boers, under a field cornet, surrendered to " A " Squadron, who covered the advance of the column. At Zandbank our column halted till April 10th, holding the drifts of the Assegai River near by, whilst other columns scoured the country round Paulpietersburg.

The drift at Zandbank was an important one, as, with Piet Retief held to the west, it shut off any avenues of escape to Boers who might attempt to move to the north out of reach of our southern columns, unless they marched a considerable way into Swaziland, where they did not as a rule care to trust themselves, as the natives were, to a certain extent at all events, on our side. The 18th Hussars did not remain long at Zandbank, but leaving the Mounted Infantry to do the mounted work there, encamped on March 15th at Potgieter's farm, about five miles to the north-east, for the remainder of the time that the column was by the Assegai. For the first few days at Zandbank we patrolled the surrounding country chiefly to collect mealies and any supplies we could lay our hands on, some farms at Idalia, to the north-east, supplying us with considerable quantities. A convoy, the one which we had expected last February, also reached us here, or rather a small part of it did, as the escort had consumed most of our long expected stores.

On **March 5th** we marched off into Swaziland, the native chief of that district, Umchelinga by name, having informed us that some Boers had penetrated into his country. The road we took was an abominable one, and required making a greater part of the way, so that by nightfall we only covered some eight miles, as far as the district called Krough's Concession, heavy rain falling nearly all day.

Next day, **March 6th**, we marched a further six miles to within three of Umchelinga's drift and the Assegai River, and short of our destination, which was Warren store on the further bank, by several miles; but, as the river was up and Colonel Allenby's column had already reached that spot, and were able to communicate with us from the southern bank, there was no need for us to penetrate further into these regions.

Meanwhile General Smith Dorrien's columns had captured sixty of the enemy after a short fight in the country just north of us, and the Boers we were after, having been attacked by Swazis and lost fourteen of their number, had retreated out of Swaziland, and the remaining ten, with their families and wagons, arrived at Zandbank on the 9th and surrendered to us there on our return. The weather was still very bad, and it kept the Assegai River in such flood that movement across it was next to impossible, so for the next few days we had little to do but try and keep the rain out of our sodden bivouacs.

On **March 15th**, the weather having abated and the river gone down considerably, a party of about forty Boers crossed the Assegai at Umchelinga's drift, some sixteen miles below us, early in the morning, and the natives there brought in word to us that they had done so, and were then off saddled, some ten miles off. So at ten a.m. Major Laming, with Major Pollok, Captain Burnett, Lieutenants Wood, Clarke, Wills, and some ninety of our men, together with a few Mounted Infantry and the pompom, set off after them.

We moved north-eastward past Potgieter's farm, and learnt from the natives that the Boers were still at Potgieter's winter farm, situated on an extensive range of hills some five miles further to the eastward. Major Pollok, with Lieut. Wood and a greater part of the force we had with us, was now sent to get between the Boers and Umchelinga's drift and drive them on to our other party, who, with the pompom, held the road where it led down from the hills to the ford over the Umblotana River, the next stream the Boers had to cross on their way northward round our flank. The Umblotana joined the Assegai a few miles below the spot our men with the pompom occupied, and the precipitous nature of the banks of the former river, and the repeated assurance of the natives that there was no path further east that the Boers could cross by, led us to think that in blocking the road itself we had completely hemmed them in between the two rivers, and that Major Pollok's party would soon bring them to bay. There was a track, however, which some of these Boers, who were themselves mostly Swaziland Policemen, knew of, about three miles further to the eastward, and down there, on the approach of Major Pollok's men, they set off, and evaded our retaining party on the main road itself. They had not anticipated, however, our approach from the rear, and Major Pollok was able to capture nine and to kill one of their number before the remaining thirty-two could make good their escape.

It was 9 p.m. before we got back to Potgieter's farm, where our baggage and the rest of the regiment had marched to that day, and our horses, their ration now reduced to two pounds of oats a day, were thoroughly knocked up after their climb over the steep hills and rocks which abound in the country we had been over. The Swazis had been a great help to us in scouting over their difficult country. On every hill top and behind every pinnacle of rock we found these tireless warriors, equipped in their usual costume, as for one of their tribal wars, and ready with all sorts of information; but their statements were never to be relied on, and we found that they were for ever picturing to themselves Boers at every point of the compass, and wishing us to go with them and see if it was so. There is no doubt too that, by believing their statement of the impractability of anyone crossing on horseback the Umblotana River except at the road drift, we had let a greater part of the Boers slip through our hands on that day.

During our absence in this part of Swaziland several more Boers and their families, with wagons and cattle, came in to surrender to the main party of our column, which was still encamped at Zandbank. After this for a while we made no further captures, and the expeditions we went out on from information brought in by our native scouts led to no results. Still we passed a very pleasant time at our quarters at Potgieter's farm, where a company of Infantry had come over to aid us in the night work, which otherwise would have been very hard on our own men, who were out nearly all day and every day patrolling the surrounding country,

Mayall & Co., Ltd.,] [126, Piccadilly, W.
LIEUT.-COLONEL P. S. MARLING, V.C.,
Commanding the Regiment after the death of Colonel Knox.

To the Swaziland Border.

laying up at night on roads the Boers were expected to come by, occupying outlying observation posts and foraging in the neighbourhood.

On **March 31st** Lieut. Wood and fifty men went to a ford over the Assegai River, between Piet Retief and Zandbank, to intercept some Boers who were reported to be going to try and get over there that night. Lieut. Wood and his party, joining another small force of Mounted Infantry on the Piet Retief road, were just in time to capture twenty Boers, seven wagons, and four hundred head of cattle at the drift, the Boers surrendering immediately they saw that they were cornered.

We spent Easter Sunday at Potgieter's Farm, and two days after, on the **10th April**, marched off from that neighbourhood for good, arrived at Piet Retief the same day, and joined up with Colonel Campbell and the remainder of the column. We were met here by Major Pollok and " A " Squadron, who had left us a few days before to go to Annijsspruit on the Assegai River, where the Wakkerstoom road crosses it, there to cover the arrival of a convoy we were expecting. This convoy arrived at Piet Retief on the 10th, and with it Major Marling, v.c., who had left the 18th after the siege of Ladysmith, being invalided home. He now took over command of the regiment from Major Laming, who in turn took command of " C " Squadron. Our horses had suffered considerably through the constant long hours that they had been on duty, and the smallness of the daily allowance of forage. For a long time only two pounds a horse was issued to them; we had lost a good many, but at the same time we had captured a considerable number, and, though many of the captured ones were unsuited to carry our men and their heavy saddles, we still managed to turn out nearly as many mounted men as when we left Middelburg. Other columns had fared much worse than we had, and some of them, 1,000 strong in mounted men when they started, had already come down to 300.

CHAPTER XII.

"BACK TO MIDDELBURG."
APRIL, 1901.

As no more time could be allowed General French for operations in the South-Eastern Transvaal at this period of the war, the columns he had under him were now all directed to return by various routes to the Natal and the Delagoa Bay lines. Only General Smith Dorrien's column, our own, and Col. Allenby's were detailed to go to the northern railway. The small size of our column and the reduced size of Colonel Allenby's, which had lost many horses through horse sickness in the unhealthy low country it had been in beyond the Assegai River, entailed their being amalgamated, Colonel Campbell taking command of the composite column, while Colonel Allenby had the whole of the mounted troops put under him. Colonel Allenby's column consisted of the Scots Greys, Carabineers, half-battalion Lancashire Fusiliers, one pompom, two Elswick guns, one battery of Field Artillery, and two howitzers. This, combined with our own, made a respectable column, rather over-gunned perhaps, and certainly weak in mounted troops, for the Scots Greys and Carabineers together only totalled 400 mounted men, and we and the Mounted Infantry could mount 250 between us.

We halted at Piet Retief from the **10th** to the **15th April**, restocking our supply wagons and patching up our clothes, which had got by now into a very ragged condition.

On **April 15th** we started off, at 6.30 a.m., to Springbok Kraal, on the southern Ermelo road, while General Smith Dorrien marched on our right, and kept roughly parallel with us all the way back. The Boers of the Ermelo, Carolina, and Bethal districts, during our absence in the Piet Retief country, had again collected in large numbers, but they did not seem to be able to assemble so many men as they had done formerly, nor were they quite so ubiquitous. We had heard that they were in force under the Berg which separates the high veld of Ermelo from the lower plateau Piet Retief lies on, and that we should probably meet them by Spitzkop. For the first three days after leaving Piet Retief we saw very few of them, as we were passing over a tract of country very sparsely populated. We halted at the Compies River on **April 16th**, and at Wooikraal on the 17th, just under the Berg where the road from Ermelo descends.

On **April 18th** we started early to march up the pass, the 18th Hussars leading the way. The road wound up a long

Back to Middelburg.

spur to the high ground, where many tributaries of the Vaal take their source, and it was in fact the watershed of South Africa, as the streams on the southern slopes all flowed into the Indian Ocean. On either side of the spur we were climbing up, huge buttresses of almost perpendicular rock ran out to a distance of about 3,000 yards towards the lower country we had come from, steep gullies separating them from the spur we were on. The Boers occupied the flat top of one of these buttresses, which ran out on the south side of the road, but luckily they did not hold the one to the northward. On this southern hill top they had posted a gun and a pompom, and waiting till we had got well on the way up, they opened fire on us, while another of their parties held a position on the road itself to prevent our further advance.

It was a splendid spot for a prolonged defence, but their old ardour in a waiting game seemed by this period of the war to have left them, and as we with little trouble took cover on the northern side of the slope we were on and attacked the Boers holding the road in front, at the same time bringing our many guns to bear on the Boer guns and their position generally, they seemed to have no liking for the task they had taken up, and quickly gave ground to our front, letting us gain the top of the plateau and reach the same level as the ground they occupied themselves. When we had done this their only idea seemed to be to get their guns away in safety as quickly as they could. We could not reach them for some time, as the gully between our spur and the top of the hill their guns were on was a deep one, and ran far into the high country we were now on, but we had got their range, and it looked at one time as if we should prevent them by our fire from pulling their guns away to a place of safety.

The Boers were ever brave in exposing themselves to withdraw their own men or guns from action, and on this occasion they proved themselves equal to the task. The flanking patrol of our advanced guard, consisting of Corporals Goodwin and Sharpe, Privates Capsey, Ryan, and four others, had in the meantime taken, on its own initiative, the task of scaling the buttress of the hill the Boers were occupying, and had slowly ascended the hill side, dragging their horses after them over a most precipitous piece of country. They crested the hill top as the Boers had just got their gun away, and they at once set to work to hurry them on in their retirement.

The regiment itself, having reached the top of the pass, wheeled to the left to attack the Boers in their retreat from their position, while at the same time, from below the pass, Colonel Campbell sent three companies of Infantry to scale the north face of the hill and support Corporal Goodwin's patrol. Our regiment, supported on the right by the Cavalry of Colonel Allenby's column, then hastened round to Smut's farm, through which the Boers in their retreat had passed a short time earlier. They were, however, well away, and, beyond a few snipers in the broken country along the top of the Berg, very little trace of them was to be seen. At Smut's farm one of our men, Private Webster of "C" Squadron, was killed by some of the enemy still lurking in the rocks on a neighbouring ridge, and we buried him next morning at Weldefreden, where we camped at night. The following day we marched to Roodewal, through very swampy country, and took over our supply train from General Smith Dorrien, who had with difficulty up till then brought it along with his own column, encountering very boggy ground on his march.

We crossed the Vaal at Roodewal and reached Van Hendrick Fontein on **April 20th**, a good many Boers having by this time again collected on our front and left flank, but they did not oppose us with any energy. We passed Ermelo next day and fired a few rounds into the town—we had removed all the families on our downward trek—to see if anyone was occupying it, but, beyond a small party of Boers on Boschman's Taffelkop, we got no view of anyone, and we camped a mile or so on the Carolina road, and held Taffelkop with some of the mounted troops. The Boers collected in the afternoon and made an attack on the hill, but they did not follow it up with vigour, and they soon retired for the night, but only to come buzzing behind us next morning when we resumed our march.

The 18th Hussars were covering the front on the next day, **April 22nd**, and throughout the morning had several short skirmishes with a party of about 300 Boers, who were advancing parallel with us up the Kaffir Spruit towards Carolina. As we turned westward, just before we reached Klip Stapel, to take the Middelburg road, we cut their rear party off from those who had already gone on north, and our guns and pompom had some excellent openings given them whilst the Boers crossed an open rise on the opposite side of the Kaffir Spruit.

The whole of this day the Boers had most persistently hung on to the tail of our rearguard, bringing their pompom and light gun into action against our men, but our casualties were few, only four men being wounded during the course of the march. Later in the day the Boers drew off to the west, and we saw very few of them throughout the rest of our march to Middelburg. A certain number of very persistent ones only remained, hanging on to our rearguard, day by day, on the look out for what they might snap up, and also to strip our camping grounds of the many articles, useful and otherwise, which we invariably left behind; ammunition we left among other things, in spite of the stringent orders that were in force to stop us doing so.

By easy stages we marched on to Middelburg, halting at Boschman's Kop, Vaalbank, Pullen's Hope, and Eikeboom, and arrived at our destination on **April 27th**. Between Pullen's Hope and Eikeboom the Boers had attacked us as we were forming the rearguard to the column, but they were in small numbers, or at all events those attacking were few, for one never knew how many were waiting for an initial success to decide them to join in the fray. On this occasion they wounded two of our horses, but with this exception we had no other casualties on our march back.

At Middelburg men and horses had been accumulating during our absence, and we found a most welcome reinforcement of 200 men and 170 horses awaiting us there under command of Captain Gosselin. Out of the 200 horses we had taken with us from Middelburg on February 1st, we had now 136 left. Besides these we had captured fifty-one serviceable ones, making a total mounted strength of 187 when we marched into Middelburg on April 27th, but most of the horses were so weak from low rations that they would scarcely be any real use for a month or so. Nearly all our outlying posts had been sent back to us by now, both those at Wilge River and Bronkhorst Spruit had come in, but other detachments had in the meantime been taken from us, Lieut. Bayford with one party having been sent to Machadodorp, where he got such a bad attack of rheumatic fever that he was shortly afterwards invalided home, and Lieutenants Field and Lyon, with a squadron, were taken on trek with Colonel Douglas' column in his operations round Dulstroom under General Bindon Blood, who had arrived at Middelburg during our absence in place of General Lyttelton, the latter having left to direct operations in Cape Colony.

Whilst out with Colonel Douglas at a skirmish near Dulstroom two of our men were killed, Lance-Corporal R. H. A. Hunter and Corporal George Hood, and four men, Privates McCarthy, Leech, Roach, and Matthews, all of " B " Squadron, were wounded.

CHAPTER XIII.

"WITH GENERAL SIR BINDON BLOOD'S COLUMNS."
APRIL—JULY, 1901.

WE halted at Middelburg from **April 27th** to **May 13th**, thoroughly enjoying a rest after our recent ceaseless movements. During this period we made every effort to collect our scattered forces and re-horse the regiment, and by the 13th we had received one batch of eighty and another of forty horses; we succeeded too in getting Lieutenants Field and Lyon back with their men, and Lieut. Wills back from Groot Oliphant's River, where the last of our outlying posts, with the exception of one at Machadodorp, were stationed. During our stay at Middelburg columns were still at work in the country to the northward, and several hundred Boers and a good many guns had already been captured. Convoys to provision these columns we had had to escort out to Blinkwater, Captain Gosselin and Lieut. Webster taking fifty men, and Lieut. Wills thirty on this duty.

On **May 13th** we marched out of Middelburg, once more on our travels, and this time we took with us the following officers:—Major Marling in command, Major Laming in command of "C" Squadron, Major Pollok in command of "A," Captain Corbett in command of "B," Captain Gosselin in command of "D" (a fourth squadron we made up when sufficient mounted men were available), Captain Burnett, Lieutenants Wood, Field, Clarke, Webster, Wills, Lyon, Lichtenberg, Pilkington, and Captain Hall as Transport, and Captain Hardy as Medical Officer.

Besides these we had 562 non-commissioned officers and men with us and 559 horses and ponies, 478 horses, with thirty-five led ones, actually in the ranks. We left behind at Middelburg about fifty non-commissioned officers and men under Lieut. Dunkley; these included men of the band, who had, up till now, been riding in the ranks of their respective squadrons. Our column marched on the 13th to Pan. Besides ourselves we had with us "T" Battery Royal Horse Artillery, a pompom, and the Seaforth Highlanders, and, further to the south, columns under General Walter Kitchener and Colonel Pulteney were moving parallel to us as we advanced eastward, the idea being to endeavour to capture the Carolina Commando with their cattle and wagons in the country around the Komati River. At the same time columns, under Colonels Benson, Douglas, and Spens, were coming up from Machadodorp and blocking the road to the low veld on the east side. This was as much of the scheme as we were able to fathom.

We marched to Wonderfontein on the 14th, where Lieut. McClintock and seventy-six men joined us, and Colonel Campbell arrived to take over command of the column, which was now to consist of ourselves, two squadrons of the 5th Lancers, the 19th Hussars, "T" Battery, a 5in. gun, two pompoms, and the Seaforth Highlanders. General Blood and his staff attached themselves to the column as well, as we were to be the central one, and he was conducting the combined operations.

On **May 16th** we left Wonderfontein and marched as far as Strathrae, crossed the Komati next day, and arrived at Carolina, meeting hardly any of the many Boers we had come across in that part of the country, when we had crossed it in January with General Smith Dorrien. Two Boers surrendered to us at Carolina.

On **May 19th** we set off with the 19th Hussars, "T" Battery, and a pompom, to go to the extreme edge of the high veld to see if we could find any more of the enemy, but they had nearly all gone far into the low country, and we bivouacked out that night without getting in touch with them at all. Too far away from Carolina to reach it by dark, we stopped for the night with Colonel Benson's column, and very cold we found it on those bleak hill sides without shelter from the winds.

Next day, **May 20th**, we marched back to Carolina, halted there on the 21st, and again marched off on the 22nd to the eastward to the edge of the high veld, and halted at Reitfontein, the 19th Hussars, "T" Battery, a pompom, and four companies of the 60th this time accompanying us. The 5th Lancers, with thirty of our men and thirty-seven horses, the latter mostly requiring a rest, remained at Carolina under Lieut. Pilkington.

On **May 23rd** we marched to Silverkop, where the bush veld began, and at once commenced systematically hunting the kloofs around for stock and wagons. We were rewarded by finding several thousand sheep, ten wagons, and a Boer with some families hidden away in wooded kloofs which were most difficult to get at.

Next day, **May 24th**, we marched to Badplaats, where a hot spring gave us a good opportunity for a general bathe. At Badplaats the dismounted portion of the column halted while the others went on to the Komati River and along its banks for some distance in an easterly direction. The road to Barberton gave us good going till the river was reached, but farther than that, only cattle tracks and Kaffir paths helped us over the rocky bushy country which always abounds in the low veld. At a place called Vergelegen, on the Komati River, we got information of a party of Boers ahead, and, after crossing the river, which there was fairly wide and deep, we came up with them and " A " and " D " Squadrons under Major Pollok and Captain Gosselin, following them up, captured 250 cattle, a lot of ponies, and several hundred sheep. We retraced our steps at nightfall and encamped close to where the Barberton road crosses the river.

On the morrow, **May 27th**, we went off with " B " and " A " Squadrons as far as Thee Spruit, which joins the Komati about ten miles to the eastward, and spent the day in searching the country for Boers, cattle, and wagons, but the former had by now all gone off a long way down the river, and their cattle had most probably been driven away with them. We found fourteen carts and wagons hidden in the bush, and managed to get them burnt before a tropical downpour, accompanied by violent thunder, had time to put the fires out.

Thoroughly wet through, we returned late in the evening to our camping ground of the night before.

On **May 28th** we marched back to Boschoek and joined up with the remainder of our column, which had preceded us there the day before, 1,000 head of cattle and several thousand sheep being the result of our recent raid.

The general operations had so far not been a success, though General Walter Kitchener's column, on the right flank, aided by Colonel McKenzie and Major Royston, 2nd Imperial Light Horse, had succeeded in capturing a certain number of Boers, but it was evident the greater number had slipped through our fingers, and those we were pursuing in the bush veld were not of much consequence as fighting burghers.

Two of our squadrons, " A " and " B," were now ordered to take a convoy to Carolina by Rietfontein, whilst " C " Squadron, under Major Laming, escorted General Bindon Blood to confer with General Kitchener, and thence proceeded to Carolina and Wonderfontein.

We started off with the two squadrons next day, **May 29th**, and left Lieut. McClintock and all the weak horses, about thirty-five of them,, at Silverkop, where the rest of the column remained. As we were marching out of our camping ground Lance-Corporal Gibbs, of " C " Squadron, was accidentally shot by another man of the regiment whilst the latter was cleaning his rifle. The wound proved to be a mortal one, and we buried Corporal Gibbs next evening at Rietfontein.

On **May 30th** Carolina was reached, but we only halted here to pick up General Babington and his staff, as the command of the three Cavalry regiments, 5th Lancers, 18th and 19th Hussars, had just been assigned to him. Changes in our column commanders had grown rather frequent of late. We left Middelburg under Colonel Hughes Hallet, of the Seaforths, passed under Colonel Campbell's command at Wonderfontein, under Major King's during the recent operations, while Colonel Campbell remained at Carolina, and now we were to go under a fresh commander, General Babington.

In spite of it being a soldier's duty to accept without murmur any change of this sort which may fall to his lot, nevertheless so many different "chiefs" in such a short time was a little bewildering, and we were most heartily thankful when another and an early shuffle on the cards brought us back again to Colonel Campbell, under whom we had served so long, and this time we were to remain with him nearly uninterruptedly till his departure for England.

General Babington brought with him Captain Gage, of the 7th Dragoon Guards, as his Brigade Major, and Captain Campbell, of the 16th Lancers, as his A.D.C.

We reached Silverkop on **June 1st** on our return journey, taking with us Lieut. Pilkington and the men and horses we had previously left at Carolina for a rest.

On **June 3rd**, after a wind storm of great severity on the previous day, an icy gale, which was one of the coldest samples of weather we had so far encountered, we marched back to the top of the high veld and encamped on the summit of a barren and burnt hill top, on a farm called Nooitgedaacht, badly situated for water and protection for our horses from the excessively cold winds, which swept that elevated ground. In consequence they fell away a lot in condition, and had we not very soon moved on we should have lost a considerable number. We halted at Nooitgedaacht till June 7th, no plans being forthcoming for the performance of a scheme which affected us in any way.

On **June 6th** Private Clarke, of "B" Squadron, who was out with Lieut. Field's troop, was shot through the head whilst approaching a kopje on which a few Boers had concealed themselves. These Boers were shortly afterwards nearly captured by the remainder of the patrol, but they succeeded in escaping with the loss of some led ponies.

June 7th saw the column, which consisted now of the 19th Hussars, ourselves, and a few guns, at Groenvallei, some three miles **east of Carolina.**

The 5th Lancers did not join us, as had been previously arranged, and as only two squadrons of the 19th Hussars were with us and two of our own, the column was not a very formidable one.

We halted at Groenvallei till June 15th, and whilst we

were there Captain Leveson joined us from England, and Lieut. Purdey from the Cavalry Depôt at Mooi River, where he had been since the siege of Ladysmith.

On **June 11th** we made an expedition, with "C" and "D" Squadrons, to collect families and lay waste the country round Van Wyck's Vlei and Frischgewagt, in the Belfast direction; not an entertaining occupation, but nevertheless necessary under the present system we were adopting of denuding the country of every living thing. One of our men, Private Neal, of "B" Squadron, straying from the position he had been placed in, as a vedette, close to Frischgewagt farm, was held up by the Boers, captured, and sent in to the railway line at Belfast.

On **June 15th** the present weak column we were attached to was broken up, and we once more found ourselves under Colonel Campbell, with four companies of the 60th Rifles, two companies of the Seaforths, two fifteen pounders, and a 5in. gun, while the 19th Hussars and some Infantry left us to form another column which General Babington was to command.

Captain Blore, of the 60th, was now Brigade Major to Colonel Campbell; Captain Sherer, Provost Marshal; Captain Melville, Intelligence Officer; and Lieut. Kennedy, A.D.C.

During the late operations it had been hard for us on the spot to find out what plans were intended to be executed, and it is harder still to recount them otherwise than in a disjointed manner. Just lately we had marched and countermarched considerable distances and taken very few Boers, and now again we seemed to be bent on the same tactics on the west side of Carolina that we had been pursuing with so much zeal on the east.

On **June 15th** we marched to Witbank, between the two branches of the Komati River which form its source, while General Babington's column was in close connection with us to the south. Here we halted a day, and collected a few families from the surrounding farms.

On **June 17th** we turned due south to Vaalbank and joined up with General Babington's column, which was encamped on a most inhospitable piece of very elevated veld. Thence we went on, with the two columns united, through Klipstapel, turned again to the west, and marched to Hartebeeste Spruit, where we met Colonel Beatson's column, and learnt from them of a serious reverse which a part of their column, the Victorian Mounted Rifles, had suffered a few days previously at Wilmansrust. The latter were away from their column, and were attacked in camp at eight p.m. Completely taken by surprise, twenty of their number were killed, thirty wounded, and nearly all the remainder, about

300, captured; 180 horses and mules were killed, and two pompoms, with 1,600 rounds of ammunition, were taken by the enemy. This was annoying to us, to say the least of it, as we had captured by this period nearly all the enemy's guns, and for those still left him he had very little ammunition. Now he was completely equipped again, for a time at any rate.

Perhaps this reverse accounted in some measure for our very cautious tactics of the last few days; if so, we were easily frightened, and the Boers had obtained a greater success over us than the occasion warranted.

On **June 20th** a fresh shuffle was made in the composition of the columns, and at 5 a.m. that morning a force of the 18th and 19th Hussars, 150 Victorians, four guns, one pompom, and 200 Infantry, all under command of General Babington, left Hartebeeste Spruit to endeavour to overtake the Boer Commandants, General B. Viljeon and Muller, who had annexed the two pompoms from the V.M.R. at Wilmansrust.

This was the object of the expedition as far as it was officially made known to us, but we did not quite believe that so pushing a scheme was really intended, as the presence of 200 Infantry, though accommodated with mule wagons to ride on, pretty well nullified this excellent plan. It became more apparent, too, very soon after we started, that we were really to become the usual " escort " to a convoy, a duty in which we were by that time thoroughly proficient, but nevertheless very weary of. We took a long time moving off, and quite stultified the elaborate precautions we had taken to make our departure a secret one, by waiting till morning to get under weigh, and although we turned out some time before, we missed the precious minutes when we could have got away in the darkness. Slowly we pushed along all day and reached Kaffirstaad that night, having taken some ten hours to accomplish about the same number of miles, and it boded ill for any chance we might have had of overtaking the pompoms. A few Boers we saw in front of us, and a cart and a wagon or two, but we stalked majestically on, and took very little note of them.

Next day, **June 21st**, we continued our march, accomplishing five miles, to a place called Hartebeestekuilen, beyond which, as we were almost in sight of the Middelburg railway line, it was unprofitable to proceed. After our arrival there we were ordered off at once to the westward to pursue some Boers, who had come to inspect us from that quarter, but their curiosity was soon satisfied, and they retired still further off, leaving us nothing to do but to return again to our bivouac at Hartebeestekuilen, where we were particularly uncomfortable, as we had brought nothing with us except ourselves and our horses, thinking that the great distance we should have to cover would prevent any baggage keeping up. We might, however, have brought any amount of ox wagons, for, as it turned out, they would not have interfered with our rate of progress.

On **June 22nd** we halted at the same spot, and on the following one, the 23rd, marched back to Kaffirstaad and rejoined Colonel Campbell's column.

On **June 24th** all our four squadrons were despatched to different parts of the compass to devastate the country, and during the day destruction to the extent of fifteen farms and their out-buildings and a great quantity of carts, mealies, and forage, was wrought on this fertile district.

We marched, on **June 25th**, to Schurve Kop, some ten miles to the westward, and on the following day were again detached from Colonel Campbell's column and sent to join General Walter Kitchener's one, which had been moving parallel to us on our left, and was now at Vetfontein.

A good many Boers had been met with by this column, chiefly Bethal and Ermelo men, who, living in the centre of the district between the two railway lines, had never been hustled to the same extent as those who were in closer proximity to our communications and lines of advance. In addition to this they were an excellent fighting commando, and, coupled with many of the Carolina men, were the bravest and most skilful of any Boers we had met.

It was very cold at night now, several degrees of frost being registered, and it was known that the Boers still on commando were in the habit of splitting up at dark and taking shelter in the farmhouses, the greater portion of which in the Bethal district had not yet been destroyed. On this supposition a night march to surprise them was planned, and we joined General Kitchener to take part in this, almost the first of the many night marches, which a little later did so much good by harassing the Boers and thinning them down in numbers. We marched at 8 p.m., with the whole of General Kitchener's column, as far as Kaal-laagte, where the bulk of his column outspanned for the rest of the night.

The 18th Hussars and two Maxim guns continued the march at 3 p.m., and we walked by our horses to keep ourselves warm, as the night was bitterly cold. We plodded on till just before daybreak and visited a small deserted farm on our way, thereby wasting some precious minutes which would have been most valuable to us later on. It was unsafe to leave this farm unviewed, and had not our guide in the inky darkness, which on moonless nights just precedes dawn, missed for a short period his landmarks, all would probably still have turned out well, but the first streak of dawn was appearing as we were still some three miles from Banklaagte and Reitpan, the farms we were to surround at daybreak.

We had to hurry on, and the sound of our horses' feet ringing on the frozen ground no doubt alarmed the inmates of the first farm, and the Boers in both were quickly on horseback and away. Our men tried their best, one squadron, under Major Pollok, galloped round the south side, and another party, under Captain Leveson, the north as far as Spion Kop Hill so as to encircle the enemy, while the reserve went direct at the farm itself, but by the time we had got up the birds had flown. They got away shooting off their horses as they went, but it was a foretaste to them of what was to happen later in the year, often with more success to our side, and on this occasion, though they had escaped us, they had had to spring out of their beds and jump in their shirts on bareback ponies and gallop into safety, screened by the misty morning air, but not too happily clad in their light attire for that frosty atmosphere. They had left everything behind them, and we collected a good quantity of cattle, a few ponies, and destroyed the farms and wagons. The Boers soon assembled again to the southward, and, having had a good night's rest themselves, were quite ready to engage us in skirmishes for the rest of the day, in one of which Private Grist, of "B" Squadron, was wounded. About noon we reached Erste Geluk, close to Bethal, and on the north side of that diminutive town, where General Kitchener and his column had preceded us. During the afternoon the Boers were again most persistent in attacking our observation posts.

At night, with this column, a system of defence, called "perimeter outposts," was adopted. This system did not appeal to us very much, but no doubt it had its advantages, which principally lay in a solid line of entrenchments close to the bivouac ground of each unit, forming a complete cordon round the camp, and one very strongly held. A perimeter of this kind was so small that it could afford to be thickly garrisoned, without an unnecessary number of men being employed on piquet duty. On the other hand the locality, which one had to accept as a camping ground, was as a rule so extensive that by adopting this inner line of defence very many absolutely vital positions, even for night work, were necessarily abandoned and open to an enterprising enemy to seize. No doubt they would have received a hot fire if they did do so, but at the same time they would have been able to do indescribable damage to the crowded bivouac they commanded. Consideration for our horses and the confusion that would be spread among them prejudiced us against this form of night outposts, but apparently the enemy had always sufficient respect for this column never to try to take any advantage of the system. With our other columns we had always adopted the usual plan of a chain of posts about 300 to 600 yards away, with inlying piquets ready to support the smaller outposts, choosing at the same time a position for the camp close to, but just under, the top of a rise, if possible at the head of a small depression that marked the commencement of a stream.

On **June 28th** the column remained halted by Bethal while a force, consisting of ourselves, two guns, a pompom, and two Maxim guns, went to the south-east of the town, while another one from General Babington's column, which was halted close by, reconnoitred in a south-westerly direction. We soon came in contact with a considerable number of Boers, who steadily retired as we advanced. When, however, we halted, preparatory to a return to camp, they attacked " A " Squadron, who, with the pompom and Maxims, were leading the advance, most determinedly, and wounded five of their horses; but the men were well posted on the top of the ridge and soon drove them off. The pompom unfortunately jammed after a few rounds, and lost a good opportunity of retaliating on them for their aggressiveness. Having burnt five farms and done other damage, we returned to Mooifontein, where the camp had shifted a couple of miles in our absence.

On **June 29th** we marched back northward to rejoin our old column, and, halting at Legdaar *en route,* next day reached Middle-Kraal, where Colonel Campbell and the supply columns from Middelburg had taken up a position awaiting us. The Boers in small parties followed us up nearly all the way back, and shortly before reaching Middle Kraal, Privates Peden and Prime, both of " C " Squadron, were wounded whilst engaged in skirmishing with them on the right flank.

Very little success had been gained by our columns whilst operating in the disjointed manner they had done of late. The slow rate of our advance, connection barely kept up by day, and much larger gaps still left at night, gave little hope of any great success.

It was now arranged that three columns, ours on the right, General Babington's in the centre, and General Kitchener's on the left, should march in line westward, and clear the country nearly up the Johannesburg-Pretoria line.

On **July 1st** our column started its march and reached Steenkool Spruit, twenty miles away, that evening. Captain Gosselin, who had been unwell for some time, left us at Middle Kraal, and did not again rejoin the regiment. He proceeded to England on sick leave from Middelburg, and stayed there during the remainder of the war, so Captain Leveson, who had joined us at Carolina, took over command of " D " Squadron from him for a while.

On **July 2nd** we continued our march to Zondagsvlei, and Major Pollok, with " A " Squadron, on the left flank, encountered about 100 Boers on the way. Some of them had taken up a position on a kopje to which Privates Berry and Crandon were advancing as scouts to their troop, and when the latter had approached to within what the Boers thought certain range, they opened fire, and wounded Private Berry in two places, while his horse at the same time came down and broke his shoulder. Private Crandon was close by, and galloping to his comrade's assistance, dismounted and succeeded in placing Private Berry on his own horse and bringing him and his rifle away to a place of safety, from under the very noses of the Boers, who subjected him to a heavy fire, but failed to hit either him or his horse. The supporting troop, which had then opened fire on their position, had no doubt unsteadied their aim. For this determined act of gallantry Private Crandon was afterwards awarded the Victoria Cross.

The error in keeping such a large interval between columns was now amply proved, as these Boers were right between us and General Babington, but no communication with him was possible, and no joint movement could be undertaken against them. However, we shelled them pretty heavily as they retired farther to the westward.

Leaving " D " Squadron and the Infantry with Colonel Campbell, we set off next day, **July 3rd**, with one gun and one company of Infantry to get supplies from the centre column, with which the supply column was marching, and found them halted at Onverwacht, and little pleased with the want of success which they had lately met with. Sending the Infantry, " C " Squadron, and the gun back direct next day to Colonel Campbell, who had moved on to Welgelegen on the Wilge River, we marched ourselves with " A " and " B " Squadrons, two squadrons of the 19th Hussars, and a gun and a pompom from General Babington's column, starting before daylight, to Kromdrai, also on the Wilge River, but rather higher up than Welgelegen. General Bindon Blood accompanied us, and took us at such a smart pace that we thought that something definite must have been located. The pace, however, died away to a halt at Kromdrai, and the only important event which then happened was breakfast on the far side of the river, after which we, " A " and " B " Squadrons, turned down the course of the Wilge till we met Colonel Campbell's column at Welgelegen.

From here to Elands River Station, on the Pretoria-Middelburg line, we lost touch altogether with the other columns, as they were making for Springs, which lay a good deal to the south-westward. Our march to Elands River was unproductive of any stirring events, save that on **July 5th**, the day we left Welgelegen, we sighted a few Boers with cattle and wagons moving a long way off round our right flank. Leaving most of the regiment to guard the column, certain troops of all the squadrons were hastily collected to give chase. The Boers themselves, though hotly pursued by Lieut. Lichtenberg and his troop of " C " Squadron, managed to get away, but their wagons and 250 head of very fine trek oxen were captured and brought into our camp.

On **July 5th** we camped at Boschpoort, **July 6th** at Dwarsfontein, **July 7th** at Rooipoort, **July 8th** at Marskop, and on **July 9th** reached Elands River Station at 9 a.m. in the morning, glad to see even the wild civilisation of a roadside station again after two months absence from the railway line.

We certainly had not met with any definite success during the whole of this period, though it was through no want of energy on our part either, as we had scarcely halted for any longer period than that necessary to give our horses and mules their much needed rest, and we had traversed during the two months an immense extent of country; but the system we were working on was at fault, and, though a few months earlier might have been profitable, was now of little value on the vast plains we had to cross. During the last few days of our march we had seen very little of the enemy. They appeared to have deserted that particular part of the high veld, no doubt finding it an easy matter to go off with their flocks and herds to the low country on the north, and live in comfort there for the cold winter months.

The country changed a good deal as we approached Elands River, and the wide open plains of the district south of Middelburg gave place to rocky ridges and fertile valleys between them, with a temperature much warmer than that of parts we had left, and a stony soil by no means good for our horses to move over.

The day after our arrival at Elands River Station we set off down the Elands River to a place called Doornkral, some twelve miles north of the railway. Captain Leveson, who was in command of " C " Squadron, as Major Laming had gone to Pretoria, was in advance, and on nearing Doornkraal he viewed some cattle in the bush country which begins about there. While proceeding to round them up a party of five Boers who were in a farmhouse close by, and who had been, contrary to their custom, quite surprised by our approach, opened fire on his men for a few minutes, but, seeing their retreat was cut off, as they could not get to their horses, and our men were rapidly galloping round to their rear, quickly surrendered. To this decision they were also no doubt hastened by the fact that one of our fifteen pounder guns, coming up with the leading portion of the main body, and seeing at once what was going on, put a few shells into the buildings themselves. One of these shells had in its course killed a Boer, a man who had already surrendered once to our arms, and had then rejoined the enemy again. We found we had amassed also 200 head of cattle and a few ponies, while in the fight itself one of our men, Private Carter of " C " Squadron, was wounded slightly in the foot.

On the next day, **July 11th**, whilst the column halted at Doornkraal, the regiment reconnoitred for about ten miles to the north-east, and a few Boers were met with and some farms destroyed, but the country was chiefly dense bush, and was not thickly inhabited. What Boers there were had apparently shifted, as Lieut. Lichtenberg, with his troop, had had no better luck the night before, when he visited some three or four farms in the neighbouring valley.

On **July 12th** we marched back to Elands River, where a welcome reinforcement of forty-five men and 146 horses was awaiting us under command of Lieutenants Lyon, Sopper, and Jury, the last two officers joining us here on their first appointment to the regiment. In addition we were able to replenish our supply of stores and equipment, which had by this time run very low.

From Elands River we were to march back to Middelburg, and as arrangements were already in progress to get the railway line, which connects the two places, blockhoused, it was improbable we should meet with any excitement on the way. On **July 13th** we left Elands River, and in six days arrived at Middelburg, taking a more northerly course than the railway line followed, and clearing up a good deal of farm produce on our way. We halted at Bronkhorstspruit, Spitzkop near Wilge River Station, Balmoral, Nooitegedaacht near Witbank Station, and at Groot Oliphant's River, and arrived at Middelburg on July 18th. Here we were glad to get a further supply of forty horses, and once more we could put a good strong force of mounted men in the field.

We halted at Middelburg till **July 25th**, very glad indeed of a short rest from incessant " trekking " and its concomitant discomfort. Colonel Knox was in Middelburg with his column during this period. He had marched there from Wonderfontein after a second trek to the Piet Retief district, and now his column was to be sent to Cape Colony to take part there with General French in some large operations in hand.

Meanwhile, on the 25th, we were again attached to Colonel Campbell's column, and left our own camp to join his troops on the north side of the Klein Oliphant's River, close to the town.

A special corps was at this time being formed called the "Corps of Scouts," recruited from several different regiments, and consisting of special men and picked horses only, and we, among others, had to detach 100 men and the like number of horses, under command of Lieutenants Field and Lyon, to join this force.

EASTERN TRANSVAAL SCOUTS.

The information I can give about the above is rather vague, as I cannot recollect any of the dates. Our work, as it turned out, was principally night marches during the time we were attached to Colonel Benson's column, and our force consisted of 100 men each of the 18th and 19th Hussars, and of the 3rd Mounted Infantry and W.A.M.I., besides some Infantry and guns. We left Middelburg on July 25th, and nothing of importance occurred until we reached Twyflaar. From there we made our first night march, and by daybreak had surrounded three or four small farms. We rushed them at once, led by Lieut. Lyon, and captured eighteen prisoners, a few cattle, two wagons, and fifty good horses. We made another night march two days' later, and caught eleven more prisoners with cattle, horses, etc. Our next one was from Smutshoeg to a farm called Mooivlei, and again it was a success. We caught twenty-five men, a few Cape carts, and a good stock of rifles and ammunition. After that we marched to Ermelo and on the next day to Carolina, taking some 250 women with us from out of the former town. Thence we went to Vlakfontein, and made a night march from there, but without any result. During the night our camp was attacked in our absence, but finding it well guarded the Boers made off. We then went back to Carolina again, and made a night march from there to Warmbad in the Komati valley. It was a very hard and trying march, and we only just got to our destination by peep of day. We succeeded in capturing, however, thirty-five men, including a Captain Breytanbach, thirty wagons, 3,000 head of cattle, besides Cape carts, sheep, etc. This party comprised a noted lot of train wreckers, and was always harassing the convoys between Pan and Wonderfontein, and on their capture General Bindon Blood sent us a message of congratulation. We marched back to Carolina, and from there took all the women and children, together with the prisoners, into the line at Wonderfontein. We also removed the garrison, burnt what provisions were left, and evacuated the place for the time. Nothing of much importance occurred after this. We made a couple more night marches, but without success, as the Boers were always very much on the look-out. We captured, however, a few prisoners on our way to Roodepoort, where we halted for two days. Here I took some volunteers, and put in order the graves of Lieut. Cawston and our men who had been killed close by; we put a good fence round the spot, and planted some young trees round it. From Roodepoort we retired to Middelburg and rejoined the regiment at Wonderfontein, after an absence of six weeks.

A. COLLIER, Squadron-Sergeant-Major, Rough Rider,

18th Hussars.

This column weakened our numbers considerably, but we still had 536 non-commissioned officers and men, 452 squadron horses, and a total of 534 horses and ponies altogether.

In return for our 100 men and horses we had had to send away, fifty of the 18th Battalion of Mounted Infantry were sent to be attached to us, and two officers came with them. Our column now consisted of ourselves and the Mounted Infantry, four guns, two pompoms, and five companies of the Leicestershire Regiment. There were three other columns to work in conjunction with ours, Colonel Parke's from Lydenburg, Colonel Beatson's, which was to come up from Balmoral, and General Walter Kitchener's from Middelburg. The latter General was to take command of the combined force.

During part of the last "trek" and during this one, Lieut. Lichtenberg was given command of a troop of men specially selected, and with them he was employed by Colonel Campbell on any small expedition it was likely a force of a few men might succeed in better than a larger body. Colonel Campbell had also brought with him a few surrendered Boers, who had taken the oath of allegiance and enlisted in the "National Scouts" to fight on our side, and they were then commanded by a Boer of the name of Erasmus.

On **July 26th, 1901**, we marched off from Middelburg to Wonderhoek, some thirteen miles, and next day a few miles further to Dielfontein, where we were close to the edge of the high veld overlooking the Steelpoort valley. On July 27th, hearing that a part of Viljoen's commando was in the Steelpoort valley, we set off past Schiepad down the hill and advanced some way into the lower country to the northwest, leaving Captain Leveson with part of "C" Squadron, the pompoms, and the Mounted Infantry on the top of the hill we had gone down, and sending Lieut. Lichtenberg and the National Scouts to Vaalkop on the north side of the Steelpoort valley, where some cattle were supposed to be concealed. With the regiment, beyond Blinkwater we saw nothing, the land was apparently deserted, and only a few Kaffirs were about, but though in places one could see for many miles, there were here and there vast stretches of country, which were quite concealed by intervening mountains. Just after descending the berg we nearly surprised two Boers who were resting in a farm there, and we captured from them 150 head of cattle and their two rifles, which in their hurry they had to leave behind. Lieut. Lichtenberg had met with better fortune at Vaalkop, surprising and capturing five Boers and annexing 200 head of cattle, besides destroying a considerable amount of farm produce.

That night we retired back to the high veld, where our column had halted at Driefontein, close to the edge of the berg, and we there spent the next day, which was very windy and cold. Early on the morning of July 29th, at 3 a.m., leaving Lieutenant Clarke's sixty men, and the Mounted Infantry with Colonel Campbell's column, to follow us more leisurely, we set out with 400 of our men, two guns and a pompom, past General Kitchener's camp at Klip Spruit, on an expedition to the northward. At Klip Spruit we joined in with the mounted portion of General Kitchener's column, consisting of the 19th Hussars and West Australian Mounted Infantry, proceeded with them to the Kruis River, and dropped down from the high veld by a little used road, which, running along Bothasberg for some miles, then descends by a very ill-made track to cross the Kruis river at Diepkloof. It was early morning by the time we reached the edge of the hills, and 9 a.m. before we got to Diepkloof. There we had to halt for a while to rest the horses and give the men breakfast, as we had still some miles to go. The Boers, under Commandant Trickhard and General Muller, were spread out in the Blood River valley with a piquet at Rooikraal, watching for us to approach from the Blinkwater direction, and entirely ignoring the more southerly road by which we had descended into the bush veld. Part of their force was also detached farther to the south-west on the other bank of the Oliphant's River to watch Colonel Beatson's column should he advance from Rhenoster Kop, as he was supposed to do in order to carry out the general scheme. At 11 a.m. we set off again from Diepkloof, with the 19th Hussars leading the advance. On reaching Rooikraal they came right on top of the Boer piquet, who, having had no previous notion of their proximity, were so taken by surprise that they made off and forgot to alarm their friends, at that time scattered about the broad valley of the Blood River.

On entering this valley, the exact topography of which few of us had any acquaintance with, the leading troops at once reported that wagons and cattle were in view. Our guns were brought up, and their fire compelled the Boers to abandon their teams. Had the locality been better known to us we should have at once advanced as quickly and silently as possible to hold a "poort" at the lower end, whose possession would have practically enclosed all the Boers in the valley in an immense trap. Unfortunately we fired off our guns and alarmed the country side. At once every Boer and available wagon set off to escape from the Blood River valley and to cross the Oliphant's River at Massips' Drift. The 19th Hussars gave chase, and the guns and our regiment were summoned up from the rear. A good many Boers got away, and some had time to take up a defensive position and delay our advance for a while, but others were not so lucky. Five men of the 19th Hussars rushed the enemy's pompom before they had time to get it in action, and wagon after wagon had to halt and surrender, or was captured before the owners could inspan. It was 2 p.m. before the Boers were first sighted, and a considerable distance had then to be traversed, so there was not much time left us to complete our task. At nightfall our troops were scattered all over the valley hunting for elusive Boers, burning abandoned wagons and tents, and collecting cattle from the scrub jungle around. We had a long day, and did not get to our bivouac, in the Blood River at Buffelsvlei, till long after dark. Thirty-one Boers and twenty wagons, besides the pompom and a considerable supply of cattle, rifles and ammunition, had fallen into our hands.

Early next morning, the 30th, our own regiment, the W.A.M.I., and two guns set off to follow on the track of the Boers. We proceeded some distance down the Blood River, crossed it, and cut across to the right bank of the Oliphant's river, where the road runs to the northward on its way to Massips' drift. Captain Leveson was with the leading troop of " C " Squadron on this day, and his troop, accompanied by Lieutenant Lichtenberg and his " irregulars," pushed on a long way ahead of the rest of the squadron and the main body in rear. On approaching Massips' drift this advanced party came up with some of the Boer wagons and their owners, who had yesterday managed to get away from the Blood River valley. Seeing them about to make for the drift, Captain Leveson charged them with his own and Lieutenant Lichtenberg's troop, and while Lieutenant Lichtenberg's men went after those who took the road to the drift, Captain Leveson and his men turned a little to the right, where another track leads along the right bank of the river. The Boers in front of Captain Leveson showed fight, and it was not till his men had got right among them, bayonetting two of them as they did so, that they surrendered with their wagons, some fifteen of them in all. These men were sent back with an escort of six men and the led horses to meet the column, while Captain Leveson, with the remainder of his troop, now comprising only a few men, dismounted to hold Lieut. Lichtenberg's right, as that officer had suddenly been assailed by a good many Boers when close to the drift.

The Boers retreating from the Blood River had joined up at Massips' drift with General Muller's commando, which had been on the left bank of the Oliphant's River all the time. It was hoped that Colonel Beatson's column would march up the left bank of the Oliphant's and block the drift, but all communication had apparently been lost with his column, and, though we did not know it at the time, he was even then well on his way to another part of the country altogether. The body of men under General Muller was a good fighting corps, and was composed of a mixture of many different commandos, mostly men from the larger towns, principally Pretoria and Johannesburg, and of a considerable number of foreigners as well.

They soon saw that our leading troops were unsupported, and crossing the river to the right bank, attacked our men with great vigour, about 500 of them joining in the fray. One of their parties was sent round to the right of our men to cut them off from the advancing column while the main body endeavoured to capture Lieut. Lichtenberg from the front. The flanking party coming on the prisoners Captain Leveson had captured, drove off the escort, released nearly all of them, and then returned to take part in the other attack on Lieut. Lichtenberg and his men, failing to capture, as they did so, Captain Leveson, Sergeant-Major Baldry, and Private Brown, who, with one prisoner they had taken, were withdrawing the way they had come, unable any longer to remain in the forward position they had taken up. Lieut. Lichtenberg and his men were now in a very tight place, surrounded by the Boers on three sides and by the river on the other, and quite cut off from any support from the regiment, which was some eight miles in rear. Seeing that he could not defend himself in the open he quickly retired to a depression in the river bank, where an overflow of the stream had hollowed out a semi-circular bed, sufficiently deep to hold his men and horses and give cover to them, while with the river flowing close to his rear and a flat open piece of ground immediately in his front and flank, he had a veritable fortress for refuge in. In this trench Lieut. Lichtenberg and twenty-one men held out for three hours until our main body, advancing along the road, was able to overcome the Boer opposition and relieve him.

Meantime many furious attacks were made on his stronghold. At first, not knowing its exact locality, the enemy advanced across the open, where his men with little trouble were able to pick them off at distances of two to three hundred yards, but rapidly perceiving their mistake, they retired to the bush and opened a heavy fire on the edges of the river where they imagined his men were hiding, and at the same time brought into action a pompom they had on the further bank. But the shells passed harmlessly over our men's heads, the bullets from the many marksmen, concealed in the surrounding bush, were unfortunately much more deadly. Again and again the Boers endeavoured to rush the troop, but the belt of open was too much for them, and, dragging their wounded away, they slowly began to disperse when the rest of the regiment came up, its advance retarded by the thick bush and the uncertainty of what exact force it had to reckon with. The Boers immediately in front of Lieutenant Lichtenberg's men did not appear to keep one another well informed of the exact locality he was in, for a few of those who had been captured by Captain Leveson and afterwards released by their friends took the main road down to the drift to cross to their commando on the left bank. In doing this they had to pass close to the very spot Lieut. Lichtenberg and his men were concealed in, and as they rode by, unwarned by their comrades of the danger threatening them, they were suddenly greeted by a well-aimed volley from the rifles of our men in the backwater. Boers and horses, including among the latter some of our own they had captured, were in a moment struck down, and they realised too late into what a trap they had moved.

Meanwhile the regiment was near at hand, still impeded by the slow progress of the flanking patrols through the thorny jungle and by the guns, whose safety it was impossible to jeopardise in the thick bush. We had met on our way up several messengers with rather alarming accounts of the annihilation of our advanced parties. Most of the "National Scouts" had come back, having shown no particular relish for the close fighting going on in front, though one of them, Kruger by name, had stopped and fought gallantly with Lieut. Lichtenberg in the river bank. They all brought bad news of the state of affairs in front, and it seemed that, at any rate, a great number of Boers had been encountered. As we neared Massips' drift the Boer pompom opened fire on us from the left bank of the river, and we brought up, as soon as possible, our guns into action against it. In a very short space of time we had compelled them to cease firing and continue their retreat down the opposite bank of the river whilst we pushed on down our bank some way in pursuit. Just before emerging on to the rather less wooded portion of country there is round Massips' drift, we met Captain Leveson, Sergeant-Major Baldry, and Private Brown, driving their solitary prisoner in front of them, and from them learnt more about what was taking place in front.

Captain Leveson, during his retreat, had been hit in the face with a rifle bullet, and had now to be sent back in a light ambulance to camp; he quickly recovered from his wound, and was in his place again among us before we left the bush country.

As we passed the drift Lieut. Lichtenberg's men emerged

from their hole and gave us still further details of the events of the morning. The Boers had now continued their retreat so far and so fast that any further advance was not considered judicious, for at any moment they could, by prearranging a halting place, lie up and await us in ambush, cut off a few men, and then retire again.

Halting beyond Massips' drift we set to work to count our casualties and get the wounded sent back to the rear. Lance-Corporals J. McGinley and F. Morgan had been killed, the former with Lieutenant Lichtenberg in the river bed, and the latter in the open with Captain Leveson. Private G. Porter was so badly wounded that he died on the 31st at Rooikraal; Lieutenant Lichtenberg was dangerously wounded in the stomach, and Corporal Shoeing-Smith Carrington was very badly and Private Hogbin slightly wounded. We buried our two Corporals, whose death was a great loss to us, close to the drift. They were gallant men, thoroughly well up in their work.

Account of the attack on Lieutenant Lichtenberg's troop at Massip's Drift, **30th July, 1901**, written by one of the troop :—

At 4.30 a.m. on the 30th July, 1901, we started towards Massip's drift, our strength being thirty men and twelve loyal burghers. When we had gone some distance down the Blood River valley, the country became so thickly wooded that our flanking scouts had to draw in, and as we wanted to push on we galloped in files down the only track there was leading to the drift. When we had gone about eight miles we came on three Boers forming a piquet, and we rushed them, Private Thorndyke catching one by the throat, while the others jumped on their horses and got away. Two men were sent after them, and they managed to bayonet one of the Boers, but could not catch the other one.

We kept steadily on, and when we arrived some 4,000 yards from Massip's Drift we caught sight of the dust of a convoy a few miles in front, and almost at the same time some Boers opened fire on us from the right flank. Corporal Carrington, Privates Brown, Woollard, Jones, Hood, and Still were sent to attack the Boers on the right and capture a wagon they were defending while the remainder of the troop pushed on to the drift. We were almost immediately met by a heavy fire from both flanks and front, just as we were advancing over rather an open piece of country, in the middle of which lay a clump of trees. We galloped for the trees, but some 150 Boers forestalled us, and we had to turn to the left and make for the bed of the Oliphant's River, where we got excellent cover for ourselves and horses. We lost neither men nor horses on the way, in spite of a continuous stream of bullets, which kept kicking up the dust on all sides of us. Eleven of the loyal burghers left us hurriedly before we started for the river bed, and we saw no more of them.

The Boers kept up a heavy cross fire at us for about ten minutes after we reached the river, and we could not show our heads above the bank to fire a shot, but as soon as they ceased we looked up, and saw that the party who had gained the trees first,—the trees were about 300 yards from us,—were now galloping at us in a mass, shouting "Hands up," "Surrender." We gave them magazine fire for an answer, hardly putting our rifles to our shoulders to fire, and the Boers, I am sure, will never forget it. We were at once overjoyed at our success, and had fixed bayonets to meet the rush, and were laughing at the Boers, when the latter again opened fire from the flank and shot Corporal McGinley dead, wounded Privates Black and Hogbin, the latter being struck in the fingers and a knife in his pocket split in two. Corporal Vesey had a bullet through his helmet, while Burgher Kruger was shot through both breasts, but continued firing back till he was again shot in the thigh and rolled down the bank. Lieut. Lichtenburg received a shot through the sole of his boot, one on the tip of the foresight of his carbine, and one through his stomach.

We quickly got back to the nullah and formed a circle round the edge of it. The Boers almost at once again attempted to gallop up to our position, and an old man and a boy reached as close as six yards from us, but were both killed. They then opened fire on us with their pompom, but the shells passed harmlessly over our heads. Meanwhile Corporal Carrington and the men with him, who had charged and captured the Boer wagon on our right before we became engaged, having accomplished their object with the aid of Captain Leveson and a few more men, had retired with their prisoners, but Viljeon's commando at once attacked them, and in turn most of them found themselves prisoners and their horses as well.

Viljeon sent six of his men with fifteen of our horses back to his column, and on their way back these men came galloping past our position. We could hear them coming, but could not see them owing to the trees, and we thought at first they were a troop of our men, and we jumped up to give them a cheer. As soon as they passed the trees, about twenty yards from us, they pulled up to a dead halt, as they were so surprised to see us. We were surprised too, but recovered first, and our men in the nullah at once opened fire, and in less time than it takes to write it nothing was left standing. Then everything became still for about a quarter of an hour or so, till a movement commenced again in our immediate front, and we could hear men talking in a low voice, but the grass being very long we could not see them. We thought they were creeping up to make a rush on foot, so we laid in wait for them for about an hour and a half, but we found out afterwards that they were taking away their dead and wounded. The Boers commenced to retire after this, and very shortly we saw their main body moving off at a walk on the opposite bank of the river, and "A" Squadron advancing on foot from the direction we had come from.

We followed up the Boers with rifle fire till they got 1,000 yards away, but had not much ammunition to spare after that distance.

Corporal Vesey now went to inform Major Pollok of what had happened, and thence on to Major Marling, and we were very soon released from the position we had held for nearly four hours.

Roll of those present with Lieut. Lichtenburg:—

Lieut. Lichtenburg.
Sergeant Stevenson.
Sergeant Fidkin.
Corporal Randall.
Corporal Vesey.
Corporal McGinley.
Corporal Williams.
S.S. Moore.
Private Beard.
Private Black.
Private Gallacher.
Private Hogbin.

Private Law.
Private Mitchell.
Private Spence.
Private Parsons.
Private Porteous.
Private Porter.
Private Wallace.
Private Wardley.
Private Waller.
Corporal Catford.
Corporal Waldeck, I.L.H.
Burger Kruger.

Near by were also buried the bodies of four Boers, whom the enemy had not been able to take away with them in their retreat. We also burnt four wagons and took two back with us, as we wanted them for our own use.

It was necessary to search the bush for a considerable distance around, as many of the enemy, wounded by our men's fire, had crawled away into it, but we did not succeed in finding any, and their friends had, we hoped, got hold of them, for very shortly after the grass caught alight, and long and dry as it is in that district, soon so thoroughly searched the country side that little chance would have been left for anyone to escape from it. It became too an element we had to contend with for the safety of our guns and wagons on their road back. The spot where the Boers had lain concealed, shooting at our men, and where others had fallen, dropping their rifles and cartridges, were quickly indicated by the constant splutter of small arm ammunition exploding in the fire ring as it steadily swept over the country.

Lieut. Lichtenberg's defence had been a most gallant one, and all the non-commissioned officers and men with him had behaved most bravely, Sergeants Stevenson and Fidkin proving themselves, as they had often done before, men of great courage and resource. The same must also be said of all the other non-commissioned officers and men who comprised the twenty-three defenders of this improvised fortress. Lieut. Lichtenberg and Sergeant Stevenson, for their conduct on this occasion, received respectively the Distinguished Service Order and the Distinguished Conduct Medal.

Kruger, the National Scout, was badly wounded whilst helping in the defence of the river bed, but later on he recovered and accompanied us in our future work. The exact Boer losses we could not discover for certain, but they must have been heavy ones. We met one of their flag of truce bearers a few days later, and inquired from him what casualties they had suffered, and, needless to say, we met with the invariable reply to all questions of that nature, "one killed and two wounded," and his equanimity was by no means upset when we pointed out that we should be happy to show him where, at all events, four of his countrymen were hidden away, for he only smiled at us by way of retort.

Our force withdrew about midday from Massip's drift to another Diepkloof, situated this time about half-way back to the Blood River among very thick bush.

On July 31st we marched back to the Blood River and up the valley to Buffelsvlei,, where we had camped on the night of the 29th, the W.A.M.I., making a tour across the high hills, which shut in the valley on the north side, rejoined us

18th Hussars Patrol in Bush Veldt near Massips Drift, July, 1901.

Light Cavalry.

at Rooikraal the next day, whilst Lieut. Dugdale, who had rejoined us from Colonel Knox, when we were last at Middelburg, hunted the kloofs at the base of these hills, and with Sergeant Coxen's patrol captured four Boers, burnt some wagons, and chased another small party before he joined up with us at Buffelsvlei.

We marched back on **August 1st, 1901**, to Diepkloof on the Kruis River, leaving a squadron behind for some time to await a flag of truce brought in by two Boers, Field Cornet Pienaars and a man named Wolhuter, who had a letter from Commandant Muller to say that we had taken their ambulance. They were a good stamp of Boer, and we had a long talk with them about the war. They seemed very confident of being able to continue operations, and said we should soon hear of more active movements in the Eastern Transvaal, which turned out to be quite true, as Louis Botha at that very time was meditating his raid into Natal. At heart these Boers seemed tired of the war, but said that they would fight as long as their leaders ordered them to.

We picked up the W.A.M.I. at Rooikraal; they had captured two of the enemy and two wagons on their way, whilst Lieut. Webster, with a troop of "C" Squadron, on the hills to the south, brought in about 150 cattle, and the National Scouts a great number of sheep. We halted the next day at Diepkloof, and detached Major Pollok and "A" Squadron to join the W.A.M.I. and one squadron of the 19th Hussars in an expedition up the Tautesberg Mountains, which lay between us and Roos Senekal. They set off at 9 p.m. to ascend the Tautesberg by the track leading up from the direction of Blinkwater on the south-east. They had a difficult task to perform by night, for the climb up the mountains was a very trying one over the wretchedly bad track they had to follow. Whilst this force slowly wound its way up the southern face of the berg, Colonel Aylmer and two other squadrons of the 19th Hussars went to the southern end of Doornhoek, a valley running into the Blood River close by Buffelslei, to block its northern exits. There were, however, many tracks on the high plateau which covers the top of the Tautesberg, and it was impossible to block every avenue of escape. However, the force with Major Pollok succeeded in capturing thirteen Boers with twelve rifles and about 1,000 rounds of ammunition, and burnt two wagons, while the 19th Hussars accounted for one Boer whom they shot on their part of the hill. Major Pollok did not rejoin the regiment till next day, when we had left Diepkloof and marched to join Colonel Campbell at Roodepoort, a farm at the junction of the Kruis and Selons rivers. The road to this spot was a very bad one along a deep gorge; it crossed many precipitous dongas, and was flanked on either side by high rocky hills covered by thick bush, which it was impossible to thoroughly explore. The country was very thinly inhabited, and, apart from the fighting commando which was with Commandants Muller and Trichardt on the Oliphant's River, there were very few Boers about, and those who were there were only too anxious to avoid us among the deep kloofs in which they had taken refuge.

At Roodepoort we found Colonel Campbell had selected a clearing for his camp and piquetted the surrounding hills with Infantry posts.

Lieut. Clarke joined us again here, while Lieut. Jury was sent in with a few mounted men and half the M.I. to help escort a convoy to Middelburg.

On totalling up our captures, we found they now amounted, in the last few days, to fifty-six prisoners, one pompom, and fifteen Boers killed and thirty wounded, 4,000 rounds of small arms ammunition, 270 rounds of pompom ammunition, sixty-one saddles, thirty ponies, 500 cattle, and forty-five wagons.

At Roodepoort we halted till **August 6th**, when we marched back again to Diepkloof, only to return to Roodepoort again on **August 8th**. The country all around was mountainous bush veld, and, beyond the few direct tracks up and down the various dongas, there was no ground where horsemen could move about out of a walk, so that, except patrolling to the Oliphant's River and to Kaffir Kraal, on the east side of Kitchener's camp, there was less work to do during our few days halt in this camp than we had had for a long time.

On **August 9th** we marched at 5 a.m. with nearly the whole regiment,—Captain Leveson, now convalescent, and Lieut. Pilkington, with a few men and the Mounted Infantry being left behind,—down to the Oliphant's River and along its right bank to Kalkfontein, getting there a little after midday and halting for further orders. We were to meet Colonel Beatson at this spot on his way from Rhenoster Kop to the western side of Massip's drift, where he was to carry out the original idea of blocking that drift, a plan which would have been so eminently useful a few days previously. But, as already has been mentioned, Colonel Beatson was nowhere near us, having entrained at Middelburg for distant parts, and he had no intention of coming our way, so we waited in vain at Kalkfontein for a sight of the dust of his advancing column. Why we were to meet him and hold the western side of Massip's drift was not quite clear, as the Boers were never to be caught twice as we had caught them in the Blood River valley, and they certainly never had any intention of returning there till we had left that part of the bush veld for good.

As there was no sign of Colonel Beatson or his column, we had to send messengers to General Kitchener at Diepkloof, over twenty miles away, to find out what we were to do. Corporal Sharpe and Private Capsey undertook this task, as our native runners had returned at once saying that the road was blocked by Boers. The former successfully accomplished their journey, leaving our bivouac at 5.30 p.m., and returning at 2.30 a.m. next morning.

Our orders were to take on the work which Colonel Beatson's column had been intended to do. Colonel Beatson's column was being reinforced by our regiment, as it was considered he would not be strong enough by himself to tackle the combined commandos of Muller and Trichardt, totalling as they did some 800 men. This assumption did not seem to apply to us, so, taking our fresh orders as a compliment, we crossed the river at Kalkfontein at 5 a.m. on the 10th, and, following the track on the west shore of the stream, marched down to the crossing at Massip's drift, and arrived there at 9.30 a.m., the hour we were ordered to meet General Kitchener and his column, who were also marching on Massip's drift *via* the Blood River valley. Had we met the Boers we should no doubt have had a stiff fight, for in that thickly-wooded country it was almost always a question of meeting a whole commando or no one at all, but we did not meet a soul, and our progress was as rapid as it well could be. General Kitchener arrived at 11.30 a.m., with the 19th Hussars and the W.A.M.I., his baggage and convoy following him later, escorted by a few mounted men and Infantry on wagons. The Boers, as a matter of fact, had come no nearer Massip's drift than the far bank of the Moose River, the next stream of any size which enters the Oliphant's River on its left bank, and thinking that even too near for real comfort, had already retreated to the Elands River valley, a river still further away to the northward.

Our plans having come to nothing at Massip's drift, we were hard put to to know what next to do. If we followed the Boers in that thick country we should no doubt meet them ultimately, and they would most assuredly lie up for our advanced people, and, after dealing with them, would again retreat much quicker than we could follow. It was impossible now to come at them from even two sides, and the policy of following them on the narrow front, on which we were compelled to move, along the little winding single track which led through the forests of thorn trees, was open to many objections.

On **August 11th** we halted for a while whilst Captain Corbett, with " B " Squadron, proceeded along the left bank of the Oliphant's River, and a squadron of the 19th Hussars along the right bank, to see what they could find out. However, at 7 a.m., from native information, it seemed very certain that the Boers were somewhere along the left bank, so the 19th Hussars were recalled, and Captain Corbett and his squadron sent on and told to wait for us, whilst we all saddled up and went off to support him as far as the junction of the Moose River. There we received information that the Boers had trekked not so very long before in a north-westerly direction. We pushed on after them across a waterless tract of level sandy country, thickly covered with thorn trees, and now and again broken by low ridges and rocky hills. At Uyskraal we cut into the road which leads from Erstefabricken to Commissie Drift on the Oliphant's river, and from the top of a ridge we could see the rear of a Boer convoy on the opposite side of the Eland's river, disappearing in a northerly direction, over some high hills, and moving in the direction of Pietersburg. We crossed the Eland's River near Uyskraal and endeavoured to make for the point on the hills in the distance where we had seen the wagons, but our knowledge of the country was at fault, and it was impossible to force a road through the thick jungle; we only tore our clothes to pieces, and gained no apparent headway once we were off the main road. Evidently the Boers had thought that we should advance along the road itself, which, following the Eland's River, leads to a crossing a good deal higher up, where another branch road would take us in the direction the wagons had gone. Some of them had, following out this idea, secreted themselves in the dense cover there was on the left or northern bank of the Eland's River, and were waiting our advance down the road, which passed within very close rifle range of the bank they were on. This time their plans were frustrated, as our regiment, leading the advance, crossed the Eland's River, as previously stated, close to Uyskraal, and set off to try and cut through the jungle direct to the Pietersburg road. On the way we met the Boers who were lying up on the bank of the river, and they, hearing us coming, cleared off, firing a few rounds to give themselves time to get away.

We did not plunge very far into the depths of the jungle, but returning to the ford at Uyskraal, halted there for awhile to rest our horses and to think matters over. It was decided to send the 19th Hussars and W.A.M.I. on to Commissie Drift that night, in the hope that all the Boers had not retreated from that locality on their way northward, but events proved that this expectation was not to be fulfilled. The 18th Hussars remained behind at Uyskraal, retiring a little from the drift to some higher ground near a Kaffir kraal, and passed the night there, awaiting the arrival of the supply column, which, miles in rear, was plodding its way slowly through the heavy sand. It did not arrive that night, and it was 10 a.m. next day before it put in an appearance, and then most of the mules were incapable of going any further without rest. A few good teams were sent on with supplies to the 19th Hussars at Commissie Drift, under escort of Major Laming's squadron, while the remainder of the regiment escorted the balance at 2 p.m., and camped that night about two miles short of the drift itself, where they joined up next morning with the 19th Hussars, and the entire force encamped on the right bank of the river in a fairly open spot by the side of the drift.

We were now in the heart of the bush veld, and, at this time of the year, a journey along the banks of the Great Oliphant's River well repaid the trouble it took to get there. We had left the rocky mountainous district, which characterises the descent from the high to the low veld, where the tributaries of the great river by which we were now encamped forced their way in many deep cut ravines to the lower ground, through which the main river then takes its course. In place of the mountains an immense plain, broken here and there by ranges of well-wooded and lofty kopjes, spread for many miles to the north and north-west; a country with little or no water, but covered in nearly every direction by thorn bush of the most aggressive character. Here and there grew large mimosa trees, giving welcome shade from the sun, which, even at that time of the year, was a power to be reckoned with. Only along the water courses, all of which, with the exception of the Oliphant's River itself, were reduced to a series of mere pools by the long drought, did larger trees take the place of these ubiquitous thorn bushes. The valley of the Oliphant's itself was covered with a tropical growth of forest trees and vegetation of many different kinds, and their shade and beauty lent a welcome contrast to the glaring sandy tracks and aggressive barrenness of the regions to the west. Along the river all sorts of game—birds, beasts, and fishes—were to be met with; they seemed to have justly recognised the one spot in that thorny wilderness where a winding oasis of vegetation and the perpetual flow of a deep stream would give them all they desired. In this quiet shady spot we halted for two days whilst our scouts endeavoured to find out the enemy's locality and plans. They had without doubt set out along the Pietersburg road, but it was a doubtful question whether they would be able to find any water in sufficient abundance there for their vast herds of cattle.

The natives of the country told us there was hardly any, and apparently the Boers soon came to that conclusion themselves, for, finding we had left the road open at Uyskraal, they once more descended into the Eland's River valley, determined to keep near the many pools there were in that river bed until we had left that territory, and they could return to the Oliphant's River itself.

At Commissie Drift we amused ourselves shooting and fishing, and met with considerable success in both directions. Our numbers were now increased by the arrival of the 4th Mounted Infantry and the wagon Infantry, who constituted the greater part of the escort to our convoy. Some of the latter had been left at Massip's drift to hold that important crossing till our return, as it was impossible to get wagons across the river between Commissie and Massip's drift.

We just had enough men, all combined they totalled about a thousand, to allow of our making a strong attack, with a good chance of success in fair fight, on the combined commandos in front of us, and it was apparent to all that our policy was to keep together for this purpose. On the other hand the Boers without their wagons, which they always took great care to keep two days marches from us, were much more mobile than we were, and it was highly improbable that, unless we could anticipate their plans and lie up for them, they would give us any opportunity of coming on them in force, but would endeavour to draw us after them and attack us piecemeal if possible.

This simple but very necessary course of combined action was apparent to everybody, but we nevertheless fell into, and with difficulty extricated ourselves from, a very risky venture from which common prudence should have restrained us.

On **August 13th** Major Pollok went out with "A" Squadron to try and capture some parties of Boers who still remained in our neighbourhood, but they had hidden themselves so securely that no trace of them was to be found. On August 14th we did nothing, but on the 15th the 19th Hussars were sent back to Vryskraal, distant about ten miles from Commissie Drift, and early next morning we followed them with a small party of the W.A.M.I., the 4th Mounted Infantry, and the wagon Infantry, about 600 men in all, and reached Vryskraal at about 11 a.m., where we halted for two hours to rest, water and feed the horses. The 19th Hussars had received orders to follow the Erstefabrieken road and see what they could find of the enemy's movements in that direction. The road followed the Eland's River for a considerable distance, and was joined near Slangboom by the one along which the Boers had retired in the Pietersburg direction, and farther on by other roads from the north, some of which, no doubt, the main fighting force of the Boers had returned by on its march back to the Eland's River. The

19th Hussars were doing just what the Boers must have wished them to do. They were composed, like ourselves, of three squadrons, but were considerably weaker in numbers, and in their reconnaissance along the river had to leave one squadron to protect their wagons, which were moving along westward as well. Just before we got to Vryskraal information was received that a considerable force of Boers were ahead, and orders were then sent to the 19th Hussars, by messenger, to tell them to wait for us, and we endeavoured to transmit this message to them by heliograph at the same time. But they had already started, and were even then being drawn on by a skilfully placed decoy of a few cattle, which the Boer commandos had left in their rear, for our message reached them too late, while the heliograph, hidden a great deal by the bushes, failed to attract their attention.

We moved on at about 1 p.m. along the road after them, and were advancing quietly past Slangboom, examining the many traces the Boer forces had left behind them at the junction of the roads where they had halted before turning off to the north, when messengers arrived back from the 19th Hussars to say the regiment had captured some cattle and were advancing again a long way ahead. In a few minutes more messengers came in with urgent requests for help, reporting that their regiment had been led into an ambush, and were holding their own with difficulty. General Kitchener at once despatched Major Marling with the 18th Hussars to go to their help. As we advanced at a fast pace down the Eland's valley road we met messengers, one after the other, with still more urgent appeals for assistance, and we dashed on as rapidly as we could. Some four miles west of Slangboom we came on the baggage column of the 19th Hussars, which consisted of some eight or nine wagons and a few carts, hurrying as fast as it could back in our direction, urged on by every effort of the native drivers, while already, close to the last wagon, a brisk rifle fire, our own and the enemy's, was kept up.

It appeared, as we learnt afterwards, that the two reconnoitring squadrons had pushed on ahead of the convoy, and had overtaken some cattle the Boers were hiding under a ridge of high ground which crossed the road at right angles at Vrieskraal. The road, a mile or two previously, had changed to the left bank of the river, after passing over, what was for that part of the country, a particularly open piece of ground, more especially so where the ford over the river was situated. The line of hills formed an excellent position, and the enemy had posted their pompom on it while they waited on the crest for the advance of the 19th Hussars across the open. The " 19th " saw the cattle beyond the drift and gave chase, losing, as they did so, most of their formation, and, on gaining the lower face of the hills on which the Boers were placed, were met by a furious outbreak of fire from the whole length of the crest, whilst several parties of Boers, now certain of their prey, commenced to gallop round their flanks so as to surround them. Any formation that was left among the advanced squadrons of the 19th Hussars was broken by the onslaught of the Boers, and small parties only, who had escaped capture at the first rush, retired back towards their transport. The squadron with the latter had already become aware of the critical nature of the fight, and had had to use most of their men to cover the north flank of the retiring wagons, against which an encircling party of Boers were already advancing. A short stand was made by the men with the Colt gun, but the Boers pushed on, and the " 19th " had barely time to take the gun itself off the stand and gallop with it for safety to the rear.

In the meantime other parties of Boers were advancing by the left flank, or the south side of the road, but the bush was much thicker here, and it luckily prevented them moving with any celerity. Matters had reached this critical stage when our leading squadron, galloping past the last of the retreating wagons, were just in time to throw themselves off their horses and advance as quickly as possible to the left front and flank, firing heavily as they did so, to repel the Boer skirmishers at the moment when the latter had almost got their hands on the wagons. Our troops were coming up in rear too with the guns, and the latter quickly opened fire, bursting their shrapnel just in front of us, and the Boers, knowing that the bush would give little cover from fire, though it would from view, retired almost as quickly as they had come. We followed them up dismounted through the thick shrub for about three miles, till we came to the remains of the Colt gun, the carriage of which, burnt by the Boers, was still smouldering on the roadside. Here an open stretch of country commenced, and contenting ourselves with shelling the patches of dust we could see in the distance, we halted whilst what remained of the scattered squadrons of the 19th Hussars could be collected and brought back to camp at Slangboom, where we had directed the convoy to halt for the night.

The Boers had had the best of it by a long way; the 19th Hussars had lost three men killed and three wounded, and but for our arrival, in the very nick of time, would have lost the whole of their baggage, while in the end a great proportion of, if not the entire force, would have been captured. As it was, their losses in this latter respect were very considerable, and must have handicapped them severely until they could get a fresh supply of horses and arms.

Private F. Birmingham, of "A" Squadron of our regiment, was hit through the brain, and although he lived for a few hours, died next day, while Private Pollok and Private Strivens were wounded in the fight. Private Birmingham had been one of the party of three men sent with Sergeant Bond from Vrieskraal to carry a message to Colonel Aylmer of the 19th Hussars, to tell him to wait for us. This party had just got up to the rear of the advanced squadron of the 19th Hussars, at the time the latter were almost completely enveloped by the Boers, and they very narrowly missed either capture or being shot as they rode up.

It took us till nightfall to collect the scattered remnants and wounded men, and it was long after dark when we got back to our camp in the thick bush at Slangboom. This effort on our part, with its almost inevitable result, seemed to steady us considerably, and, in the words of the diary from which most of this account is taken, "we dropped Viljoen like a hot potato."

Next day, **August 17th,** we set off on our return march to Rooikraal, halting at Uyskraal on the 17th, Massip's drift on the 18th, Buffelsvlei on the 19th, and arrived at Rooikraal on the 20th. The Boers seemed in no hurry to interfere with us in any way, and there hardly seemed any need for the undignified scamper in which we withdrew across the Oliphant's River, more especially so as we halted for three days at Rooikraal after we got back. The Boers, of course, boasted that they had driven us out, and, on the face of it, it looked rather as if they had done so; but what really affected us most were the long distances we had had to march through the heavy sand, which had served to knock up both our horses and our already heavily taxed mules.

We found Colonel Campbell's column awaiting us at Rooikraal and anxious to learn what successes we had had. We were unable to unfold much of a tale, and their own success in capturing twenty-seven Boers during our absence forced us to believe that we had not really greatly distinguished ourselves. At Rooikraal we reformed into our respective columns, General Kitchener camping a few miles from us at Diepkloof, and we all halted until, after a consultation between General Kitchener, Colonel Campbell, and Colonel Parke, whose column was on the Tautesberg, it was decided to march to Blinkwater on the Steelpoort River.

So on **August 24th** we set off and arrived there next day, halting at Waterval for the night. Captain Leveson and Lieut. Pilkington had rejoined us at Rooikraal, but we had to send away Lieut. Purdey and an escort to take a convoy into Pan. General Kitchener left with this convoy, and Colonel Campbell took over command of both columns, which were encamped together at Blinkwater. Very soon after our arrival some furious storms broke over the camp, and we could see that the commencement of the wet weather was at hand. One of these storms stampeded about forty of our horses, and, though Lieut. Webster and a party of men spent all the day and a greater part of the night looking for them, they were unable to recover all, and nineteen remained missing, among which number, as always happens, there were some very good horses indeed.

On **August 26th** Colonel Campbell, leaving a small force at Blinkwater, took with him the 18th Hussars, one company W.A.M.I., three companies of the Leicestershire Regiment, two guns and a pompom, and marched at 7 a.m. to Middelkraal, the place we had camped at near Witpoort on our march from Lydenburg to Middelburg with General Lyttelton. Nothing was met with *en route,* but Captain Leveson and Lieut. Clarke, taking a small patrol in the direction of Houtenbeck, brought in a Boer whom they had surprised in a tent, and Major Pollok captured and drove in about forty head of cattle from the Dulstroom direction. The next day we marched, at 6.30 a.m., up on to the strip of high veld, which lies on the western slopes of the Steenkampsberg, and forms here an isolated spur of high ground, jutting out almost as far as Roos Senekal.

The change in temperature was very marked, and we appreciated it after the rather sultry weather we had been having in the bush veld.

The West Australian troops had anticipated us by a night march on to this plateau, and when we got there we found they had captured six Boers and some wagons, and that the remainder of the enemy had already taken alarm and retired some way to the northward, along a road which led to Lydenburg, where we followed them for a considerable distance, destroying in our course a great quantity of property and removing from the farms numbers of the inhabitants. We halted that night at Houtenbeck, after having established communication with Colonel Parke's column, which had entered this tract of country from the Roos Senekal direction.

Next day, **August 28th**, we marched back again to Blinkwater, halting for the night at Witpoort,, where we found the fields of young wheat at just the right stage for grazing our horses and mules on. This was a godsend to us, as every particle of grazing had been burnt in the Steelpoort valley, and it was too early yet for the young grass to put in an appearance.

Whilst we were halted at Witpoort, Major Laming went with his squadron up the Steelpoort valley, and on his return

With Gen. Sir Bindon Blood's Columns.

reported that Field Cornet Grobelaar, with 150 men, were at Schoongezicht farm, about sixteen miles to the south-east.

We halted at Blinkwater on the 29th and 30th, sending Captain Corbett with a squadron to Enkeldoorn, a few miles up the valley, to reconnoitre in that direction, and see what he could from the tops of the hills, whilst our native boys searched for Grobelaar's commando.

At 8 p.m. on **August 31st** we set out on a night march to try and surprise them. We took the road by Witpoort and on to the high veld at Witboys, where we surrounded a farm at 1 a.m.; there we found a Boer ambulance and a doctor with it, so, to avoid the chance of the latter giving any alarm of our approach, we took him on with us for the rest of our march, and released him in the morning. The way we were marching was a very roundabout one; we wished to avoid approaching the farm at Schoongezicht from the north-west, as it was most probable the Boers would have a piquet on that side, and to ensure our getting round them we had to go as far as Swartkoppies and almost to the Dulstroom-Belfast road. The night was a fine one with a good moon, and the weather cold, but as we had to walk most of the way up and down the bad roads the latter did not inconvenience us much, and by early morning we had covered nearly thirty miles and were well to the south-east of Schoongezicht.

Meanwhile the W.A.M.I. had advanced up the Steelpoort valley to the south side of the farm, and the Leicesters, starting later in the night, had approached it from the north and north-west sides. It seemed that our force made rather too big a detour, and that we had not been properly informed of the exact farm on Schoongezicht, where most of the Boers were, as there were two or three farms of the same name within the one farm boundary, and as we descended from the high veld down to the particular one we had chosen to attack, we left out another, which was of more importance, on our right flank. The Leicesters captured five Boers and the W.A.M.I. two more in the farms we were approaching, but the main body of the enemy, slipping round our right in the darkness, escaped, and at once commenced to attack our patrols, one troop of " A " Squadron being in close contact with them for a short time. Sergeants Pearce and Brown were with the troop and were both slightly wounded, and Private Clarke rather more seriously so. Three horses were killed and two more were wounded, the Boers getting up very close to the led horses before the latter could gain cover from their fire.

We halted at Schoongezicht for breakfast and to rest our horses, collecting families and removing farm produce whilst we were there, and at 11 a.m. moved back to Blinkwater, followed for a certain distance by the Boers, who, from the tops of the surrounding hills, fired at us as long as they could. We got back to camp about 4 p.m. with our horses, weary after their long night and day, for they had covered nearly fifty miles altogether, and the roads were as bad as they could possibly be.

On **September 2nd** we left Blinkwater and set off for the railway line, leaving any further operations, which might be necessary on the northern side, to Colonel Parke and his column to deal with. Our road lay to Wonderfontein, at the very head of the Steelpoort valley, and on the edge of the high veld. We halted at Sterkloop and Hartebeestehoek, and between these places Corporal Sharpe, of "A" Squadron, captured a Boer single-handed on the right flank, as the latter, with two others, were trying to slip round our column.

We reached Wonderfontein and the railway on September 4th, and set to work to get ourselves refitted with horses and stores, a plan we had always to adopt whenever we touched the line, as the wear and tear on the mounted troops increased more and more as the war went on.

Colonel Knox's column had been broken up shortly before this and sent to Cape Colony to help to form other small columns down there, and our Colonel himself, not wishing to wait for the command of another one, returned to Wonderfontein to take charge of the regiment again. Lieutenants Field and Lyon and the hundred men who had been with Colonel Benson's column, attached to the Corps of Scouts, rejoined us also. They had done very well, and succeeded in capturing a good many Boers.

CHAPTER XIV.

"Wonderfontein to Vryheid."

LIEUTENANTS Lichtenberg and Purdey rejoined at Wonderfontein, the former officer now practically cured of his dangerous wound, having made a very rapid recovery. An accumulation of many mails and our refitting arrangements gave us plenty to do for the next few days we were halted.

We received eighty remounts, but had to send sixty horses into Middelburg, as they were useless for further work for some time to come. Besides these, some eighty horses of "B" Squadron picked up some tulip grass whilst they were out grazing, and out of this number seven died, and twenty-three were so ill that they had to be left behind, while the remainder were useless for work for some time to come. Tulip grass at that time of the year was a most dangerous herb, hard to distinguish, without a careful examination, from the early shoots of the young grass which began to come up in the centre of the valleys in the spring. All animals would greedily devour it as a change from the dry, burnt-up stuff they had been subsisting on for so long, and in a few hours its poisonous effect soon told fatally alike on horses, cattle, and mules.

On **September 8th, 1901,** our rest at Wonderfontein came to an end. General Kitchener returned from Pretoria to take command of the two columns, his own and Colonel Campbell's, and we started at 4 p.m. that afternoon on a fresh trek, southward this time, the object of which we never quite understood from the start. The strength of the regiment, after the various changes which had recently taken place, was now 638 officers, non-commissioned officers, and men, and 577 horses, but of the latter we only had 429 fit for duty, as we were compelled to take a great number of sick ones along with us, and we had besides some thirty to forty ponies used in carts and ridden as second chargers by officers.

Major Laming left us at Wonderfontein to take up an appointment as second in command of the 24th Battalion of Imperial Yeomanry, a corps he shortly afterwards commanded. Lieut. Field joined him, as his adjutant, a little later on. This left us with the following officers for our forthcoming trek:—Colonel Knox, Majors Marling and Pollok, Brevet-Major Burnett, Captains Corbett and Leveson, Lieutenants Wood, Field, Clarke, Dugdale, Purdey, McClintock, Webster, Pilkington, Lichtenberg, Wills, Lyon, Sopper, and Jury, with Captain Hardy, R.A.M.C., and Lieut. Tasker, c.v.s., while Lieut. Dunkley, our Quartermaster, remained at Middelburg to look after the band and detachment we had there. The balance of " B " Squadron, not affected by tulip poisoning, together with Lieut. Dugdale and twenty-four men of " C " Squadron, remained behind, to march next day with Colonel Campbell's part of the column, while " A " and " C " Squadrons set off in the afternoon and formed rear-guard to General Kitchener's force.

Between Wonderfontein and Strathrae the heavily-loaded wagons of the convoy got constantly bogged, until at 10 p.m. some of them became irretrievably so, and we had to spend the night out guarding them, till daylight showed us a way round the many sloughs that abounded in that part of the country. General Kitchener, during the next few days, split up the two columns into what was meant to represent a very mobile portion and a slower moving part, but the first did not prove itself a much quicker machine than the second, and we, with the former, arrived very little ahead of the latter at Ermelo on September 12th. Very few Boers indeed had been met with, and their entire absence seemed a little uncanny, and gave a foundation for the report brought in by our scouts that Louis Botha had collected all the Boers from those districts to take part in a descent he was making on Natal, the project which our friends of the flag of truce in the bush veld had no doubt been alluding to when they said we should soon hear of more stirring events in the South-Eastern Transvaal.

On our way to Ermelo we halted at Strathrae, Vaalbank, and Klipstapel, and the weather, which had been threatening to break up for some time, now changed, and very wintry gales with almost continuous rain caused us to live for a time in great discomfort, while our animals suffered still more severely from the cold. No definite plan of campaign had as yet been formulated for us to adopt, and we really represented nothing but one column adrift in the immense open country of the Eastern Transvaal. At Ermelo we halted till the 16th, completing whilst we were there probably as much destruction as any column had previously done in so short a space of time, for on our departure only one house remained intact out of the many well-built residences in that pretty town. It proved to be a useless work of destruction, as within a short time the town was occupied by our troops, and the blockhouse line from Standerton to Carolina ran through it.

From Ermelo we marched to Schimmelhoek on the Amsterdam road, and from there, on August 17th, to Bankop, collecting some 300 head of cattle and a great quantity of sheep, but meeting with few Boers and only capturing one on our way. Whilst we were occupied in this very indecisive

Wonderfontein to Vryheid.   189

manner round Ermelo, the Boers under Louis Botha had penetrated as far as the Buffalo River, the border of Natal on the northern side, had heavily worsted Major Gough and his Mounted Infantry near Vryheid, captured his two guns, and had it not been for the flooded state of the Buffalo River, they would no doubt have immediately invaded Natal and done an immense amount of damage in that Colony, whose frontiers were very weakly defended indeed.

Urgent messages now began to reach us, asking what we were doing at Ermelo, and telling us to make all haste to Volksrust, and from there to join in with many other columns, already on their way to try and hem in the Boers who had ventured so far from their own districts. So back we had to march with all the haste we could, and, leaving Bankop on **September 18th**, we reached Roodeval, where the road crosses the Vaal River, that night, and next day continued our progress to Ermelo. Here we had to re-sort the column, and leave Lieut. Purdey with all the weak and sick horses as escort to the ox wagons, which, with the Leicesters, were to follow us, while the 18th and 19th Hussars, the W.A.M.I., and the Infantry of General Kitchener's column, accommodated with mule wagons, went on ahead, as fast as the transport mules could travel, to Volksrust.

We left Ermelo on our march southward on **September 20th**, and accomplished twenty-two miles that day, halting at Beginderlyn on the Vaal; on the 21st we reached Amersfoort after a nineteen mile march, losing on the way five horses and four mules from exhaustion, and next day we got to Zandspruit on the Natal railway line. The ox convoy behind had suffered severely, and they lost a great number of oxen, horses, and mules on their hurried march; the supply of forage was very short, as yet no grass had grown up for the cattle to graze on, and the weather, above all, was so bitterly cold that exposure to it in their present weak state caused more deaths among them than anything else. Still we were ordered to hurry, and we did so, but after reaching Zandspruit our pace, for some reason or other, at once slackened. On **September 23rd** we only marched as far as Volksrust, and on the next day to Charlestown and Laing's Nek, where the ox convoy, or what remained of it, caught us up.

We had here to send away eighty-six horses to Newcastle, as they were unfit for further work, and this loss in horse-flesh, together with the arrival of Sergeant Jordan and a dismounted draft of forty-six men from England, obliged us to send off to the Remount Depôt at Newcastle for a further supply of horses, so Major Marling, taking with him most of the men who were dismounted, left us at Charlestown to see what he could manage in the matter. From Laing's Nek we marched on the 25th to Ingogo Station and Donga Spruit, and from there next day to Wool's Drift on the Buffalo, where Major Marling rejoined with 123 horses he had managed to collect. Colonel Garrett's column, which consisted of New Zealanders and Queenslanders, and which had been railed down from the Western Transvaal, also caught us up at the drift, and both columns proceeded together to Kweekspruit, a few miles short of Utrecht town.

General Kitchener had been placed in command of the whole of the columns which were to operate from the north against Louis Botha, and so Colonel Campbell assumed command of the one we were with, which consisted of ourselves, the 19th Hussars, and W.A.M.I., while what Infantry we had with us generally followed with the ox wagons and supply column, a march in rear.

Early on **September 27th** we marched into Utrecht and halted there for the day, continued our easterly move at 8 p.m. that night, and ascended the hill above the town and halted at 11.30 p.m., after we had succeeded in getting all the wagons up the very stiff ascent by which the road leads to Knight's farm at the summit.

Colonel Garrett's column kept with us, and together next morning we went on to Mooihoek, and on the 29th reached Vryheid after a twenty-two miles march.

Very few Boers during all this period were met with, but there were still a small number in the rough country around the Scurveberg, which lay on the south side of the road between Utrecht and Vryheid.

Just before we reached Vryheid, Sergeant Leonard, of " B " Squadron, wished to water his horse at a small deep pool, and the animal, missing its footing in endeavouring to drink from the bank, fell headlong in, on the top of its rider. Sergeant Leonard must have been killed on the spot, as he never rose to the surface, and all efforts to find his body that evening were of no avail. It was not until a search party from Vryheid went out next day that they were able to do so, and his body was recovered and buried at Vryheid on October 1st.

At Vryheid the columns halted for two days, waiting for a convoy from Dundee to come in and refill the wagons. A force, consisting of " B " and " C " Squadrons of our regiment, 200 men of the 19th Hussars, 200 West Australians, two guns and a pompom, all under Colonel Knox, were sent to meet the approaching convoy. They did this at Bembas' Kop on the Blood River, and receiving sixty wagons of supplies, marched back again on October 1st to Vryheid. At 1.30 a.m. next morning both columns were again set in motion to proceed eastward. It was known that Louis Botha and his men, after approaching the Buffalo near Landsman's drift, had turned south along the left bank, and, apparently abandoning their intention of entering Natal itself, had determined on their abortive attack on Forts Itala and Prospect in Zululand. After this they had drawn off in the direction of Babamango Mountain, and it seemed probable that our columns would now be able to get between them and Piet Retief, or whatever point they should make for on their way back to the high veld, when General Bruce Hamilton's columns, which were now on their way from Dundee, should drive them out of that part of Zululand in which they had taken refuge.

During the early hours of **October 2nd** we marched some distance and reached a place called Rietvlei, on the Zululand road, some seventeen miles from Vryheid, at nine in the morning. A long plateau of high veld ran out from Vryheid as far as, and a little beyond this spot, bordered on the south side by a high range of mountains which continued on still farther eastward, and by another range on the north which ended close by, at Waterval, which was Louis Botha's own farm. Directly in front of us, that is to the east, the ground, after rising for a short distance on to a still higher plateau, dropped away suddenly into the hot valleys of what in former days was Zululand, before the Boers took possession of it and called it "conquered territory." This was indeed an ideal place on which to lie in wait for the Boers, for from the southern range of mountains we could easily detect their approach from the southward, and, should they chose to move round further to the east, then by occupying the extremity of the northern range, beyond Waterval Farm, we could head them there, and come on their flank from the westward. But Rietvlei itself was not nearly far enough advanced, for it was nearly a day's march from Waterval, and out of striking distance.

Soon after our arrival some Boers were reported in the country to the south of us, and we had to saddle up again and dash off to hold the lofty hill tops, over which the road to the south passed. A body of some three to four hundred Boers were advancing as we topped the summit, but before they had committed themselves to a very near approach they evidently got wind of our presence, and turned off to the east to look for a better route.

The importance of occupying this southern range was at once manifest, and "A" and "B" Squadrons, with a part of "C," were ordered to remain on the summit until arrangements could be made at the camp at Rietvlei to post permanent Infantry piquets on the hill tops. The Boers retired during the afternoon, and in their place a thick mist and steady drizzle set in on the lofty mountain heights, and when the other troops of the column had slowly withdrawn to camp, our men were left in their damp eyrie, where, as night set in and the mist increased, they were invisible to friend and foe alike. As they had been ordered to hold the positions till the Infantry relieved them, they had to resign themselves to another night's work without any food for themselves or forage for their horses, as the Infantry soon lost their way in the fog, and it was early morning before they arrived and our men could get back to camp. There is no doubt but that we should have pushed on next day to a more easterly position near Waterval farm, but we did not do so, contenting ourselves with a move on the day after, **October 4th**, to Geluk, where the high ground we had come along ends in the steep slopes which lead down to the lower country towards Zululand.

We drove a few Boers off the plateau, the New Zealanders of Colonel Garrett's column having a skirmish with them, in which two on both sides were killed and one wounded Boer picked up, while a considerable body of the enemy were seen at the foot of the hills. Their presence there should have warned us that they were rapidly gaining ground to the northward, and would probably employ that night for their final move round the front of our columns, but we still took no steps to prevent it. In fact, on **October 5th**, we halted at Rietvlei, and it was not till the next day that our force was put in motion to again explore the country to the east. Colonel Garrett's and part of our column was then directed to proceed to Waterval, while our regiment itself was sent to the high ground by Geluk. We met no Boers in this direction; they had all succeeded in outflanking us, and were now on Waterval farm in a strong position holding the northern range of hills with their rearguard, whilst their carts and led ponies wound along the Paulpietersburg road through the low country, which lay between Waterval and the Pivaan River. They had already accomplished their object and gained a secure line of retreat to any place they might wish to proceed to in the Eastern Transvaal.

Though we did not meet with any Boers at Geluk, Colonel Garrett's men very soon came across them as they approached Waterval farm, where the strong position the enemy had taken up prevented any further progress until a proper attack could be made on them. We were ordered to turn northward from Geluk and advance direct on Waterval. When we had done so, we quickly saw from our position on the high ground the nature of the check which the main column had received. Meanwhile orders were sent us to cover the right flank, as it was reported that another party of Boers with a gun were advancing from the eastward, a report which was absolutely, without foundation, as the enemy's rearguard to the north was the only force left to contend with. To aid the advance of the main column we opened fire with two guns we had with us on the hills above Louis Botha's farm. These hills form a long ridge, whose highest point is at Cherry Emmett's farm, the next one to Louis Botha's on the south-east side, and they run in a north-westerly and south-easterly direction behind Waterval.

Between us and Colonel Garrett's column was a very deep ravine, across which our guns could not move, but which our squadron could just scramble over, so to help the main column, which was practically "held up" in front, we despatched "A" Squadron, under Major Pollok, over the ravine to advance by way of Cherry Emmett's farm, seize the high ground there, and then carry along the ridge north-westward until their outflanking movement should relieve the pressure on the main advance.

Our position on the northern end of Geluk farm was on a level with the top of the ridge at Cherry Emmett's farm, and as the ground at the latter spot was open veld, our shrapnel would cover Major Pollok's advance till he gained the summit of the hill, and when he had gained this point he would command the lower portion of the ridge, which, as it was much more rocky, our gun fire had little effect on.

Major Pollok crossed the ravine, and was directing his steps on the part of the ridge in question, when he was diverted from his object by an appeal from some New Zealanders, who, drawn into action near a kopje a few yards from Louis Botha's house at Waterval, were being hard pressed by the enemy posted in front of them and about half way down the ridge, which Major Pollok was directed to attack. It was impossible to refuse aid to the Colonials, and Major Pollok's men soon had their hands so full of work against the centre position of this ridge, that they were unable to make any demonstration against the higher ground, which lay more to their right. In fact they had all their work cut out to hold their own, and in spite of a furious cannonade delivered by our guns on the enemy's position, the squadron gained no ground, and it soon became evident that it was useless butting against such a strong rampart of rock the enemy had there to protect them. One troop of the squadron, under Lieut. Pilkington, had already got into so advanced a position that their right flank was considered insecure, and as the losses they were sustaining were disproportionate to the result, they were withdrawn, but had considerable difficulty in getting back. Repeated requests

o

for more troops to be sent to the right flank, to complete the task " A " Squadron had set out upon, at last brought round a mixed force of mounted men to the south-eastern extremity of the range, and, once there, matters assumed a more prosperous turn.

The Boers had, however, already waited longer than they had intended to, as their one idea was to get away to the high veld again, back to their own farms and districts, and it was only their leader's determination to check us at this very strong position that had kept them engaged so long. Almost at the same time that Major Pollok withdrew his men from their attack the Boers left the position, and in a short time we could see many hundreds of them appearing and disappearing along the road to the northward on their way to the Pivaan River. All our available men were sent on to join in the last turning movement on the right, and on gaining the summit of the ridge they pushed on, without meeting any opposition, after the Boer rearguard, till the latter disappeared and retreated at a great pace in a northerly direction.

What was left of the regiment and the guns still at Geluk had now to retrace their steps by an eight mile round to cross the head of the ravine and join the main column. It was after dark when Goudhoek, Emmett's farm, was reached, and very late that night before we could bury those who had fallen in the day's fight. Lieut. Pilkington had been killed during the hottest part of the engagement, shot through the head, whilst gallantly placing his men in the most forward part of the position to be taken up, actually a part of the ridge on which the enemy themselves were placed. Corporal Faulkener and Lance-Corporal D. Sharpe, both of " A " Squadron, were also killed at the same period of the fight, and Corporals Durkin and Hall and Privates Lyons and Howard were all more or less severely wounded. Corporal Faulkener had been promoted during the war for his gallantry in the field, and Lance-Corporal Sharpe had shown himself, on many occasions, one of our best fighting men.

The fight had not been a very successful one for our side; we had attacked the Boers when every chance of cutting them off from their northern march was past, and their occupation of a very strong position rendered any success very problematical. At the same time we probably inflicted fairly heavy loss on them, as from the position taken up by our guns we again and again swept the ridge they were occupying until we had hardly a round of ammunition left.

LIEUTENANT F. E. C. PILKINGTON, M.A.

CHAPTER XV.

"THE SLANGAPPIESBERG."

THE next day, **October 7th, 1901**, we marched after the Boers, encamping for the night at Diepkloof, where the road dips down to a patch of low veld, extending to the Pivaan River and beyond it to the northward.

The part of the Transvaal we were on the point of leaving was a particularly fertile tract, and Louis Botha had selected a very good site indeed for his farm. High in altitude, very cool and healthy, it was exceptionally well watered, and was already covered with immense plantations of wattle trees, just then bursting into flower, and relieved by their many different shades from too great uniformity. The farm house, a well-built one, had unfortunately met with the same fate so many others had already encountered.

We continued next day our journey northward, and arrived on **October 8th** at Mahlone, and on the 9th at Ersteling, where we had to halt and await the arrival of a convoy from Vryheid. The road from Waterval was a very bad one, more of a watercourse than anything else; it taxed the endurance of our mules and the stability of our transport wagons to their utmost. The country was, in some parts, where we descended into the many valleys leading to the Pivaan River, bush land covered with thorn trees, and in others, where we laboriously ascended the steep hills which lay between the river beds, broken rocky highland.

The Boers had made good their retreat, and we only saw a few scattered local parties as we passed through this country.

Captain Leveson, with " C " Squadron, had been sent on October 8th to meet the convoy coming from Vryheid, but the latter, taking a more westerly road to the one on which he was directed to move, reached us at Ersteling without meeting him, and the squadron had to march to Vryheid and back for no purpose.

On **October 11th**, after refilling our wagons, we crossed the Pivaan River by the bridge and reached Paulpietersburg, which consisted of a small cluster of houses of very recent erection, with a newly-built church in their midst. We learnt here that the main body of the Boers had passed through two days previously, with two guns, and had gone on to Piet Retief, but that the local Boers who had joined them on their march down had left them again, and scattered in smaller forces into the Pongola bush and Slangappiesberg range. The Pongola River, ahead of us, was in flood, and necessitated our remaining for three days at Paulpietersburg, and it was not till **October 15th** that we managed to cross the river and camp at Mooiplaats on the northern side, while Colonel Garrett's column encamped a little to the east of us. His men had seen a few wagons and Boers moving towards the Swaziland border, and to aid him in their capture Colonel Knox, with the 18th Hussars, was directed, the next day, to join forces with him and give chase to the Boers. We overtook Colonel Garrett at Cometjse, close to the border, at 10 a.m. on October 16th. He reported that the Boers, who numbered over a hundred, with some carts and wagons, had turned southward into the mountainous country north of the Pongola River.

We had already marched a long distance that day, but we inspanned again in the afternoon and set off once more on their tracks, reaching Pipe Klipberg that night, where Col. Garrett's Australians had engaged the Boers on the previous day, and had captured two of their number. Early next morning, 4.30 a.m. to be accurate, we started again on their trail, and left our camp at Pipe Klipberg with a few troops to guard it. At Oranjdal we came up with the enemy; the road, which for the last few miles was losing even all vestige of a track, disappeared now for good and all, and evidently the Boers had been unable to get their carts and wagons any further. They had no hesitation in abandoning them, and after lying in wait for our troops on a very formidable kopje, which the New Zealanders approached with a recklessness they must quickly have repented of, they broke into scattered parties and disappeared among the many kloofs which the country abounded in, towards Swaziland. These men were the Swaziland commando, and knew the country perfectly. They had only waited for our guns to shell them and for our advance in force before splitting up and retiring by the mountain paths they knew so well. We collected and burnt thirteen of their wagons and carts, found one of their wounded, whom they had left behind, and then marched back to our camp at Pipe Klipberg for the night.

October 18th was a day of continuous rain, and as our orders were to rejoin Colonel Campbell at once, we had a wet time of it. From 6 a.m. we marched till 5 p.m. with hardly a halt back along the same road as far as Cometjse, then, taking a more westerly direction, we reached Normandie on the Piet Retief-Paul Pietersburg road, whence we proceeded to Mooiplaats, and encamped for the night near the drift over the Pongola River.

Colonel Campbell had left with the remainder of our column on the previous day for Slangappiesberg, and we had to set to work to try and catch him up. Parting company with Colonel Garrett's column, we turned to the north-west, and marching all day across Tafel kop and the outlying spurs of the Slangappiesberg, reached Marienbad at 6.30 in the evening, most of our time and energy having been expended *en route* in hauling our carts and wagons up the rough stony tracks which wound over the hills. At Marienbad we expected to meet Colonel Campbell, but he had left a few hours before our arrival in order to encamp nearer the lofty main range of the Slangappiesberg, and as we could not get our transport any farther that night, we halted on the Luneberg-Piet Retief road and joined up with him at Rooikraal on the morrow.

General W. Kitchener had collected five columns, Colonel Pulteney's, General G. Hamilton's, Colonel Stewart's, Col. Garrett's, and our own, to search the wooded kloofs and mountain summits of the range on the west. The Boers had so often hidden securely here, when hard pressed by our columns in the open, that it was probable they would again trust to our inability to thoroughly search the mountain. Along the northern and north-eastern side ran the chain of blockhouses which had just been completed from Wakerstroom to Piet Retief, and against this line our five columns, from the southern points of the compass, were to drive what Boers were concealed ahead.

Colonel Campbell had reconnoitred the berg on the day of our arrival, **October 20th,** and on the morning of the 21st we set out to ascend the eastern slopes and hunt out the kloofs, the other columns doing the same work on the spurs which lay opposite them. There were not, however, as many Boers as we expected; it seemed to be chiefly a hiding place for their cattle and sheep, and a retreat in which they hid their families and wagons. In one of the densest parts of the thick scrub jungle, growing in the kloofs at the foot of the berg, we found a Boer laager, and, close by it, traces of the guns captured from Major Gough's troops a month previously at Blood River Poort. Following up the trail Captain Leveson's men succeeded in unearthing the two guns, their limbers, and a wagon, together with a certain quantity of shells, and, harnessing some of the squadron horses to the poles, dragged them away to our camp. Private Thorndyke, of " C " Squadron, was most instrumental in finding the guns themselves, tracing them to the hollow bank of a small stream, where they had been hidden below the level of the water.

Continuing our search along the lower slopes of the mountain, we systematically hunted every likely hiding place, and were rewarded for our pains by the capture of nearly a thousand head of cattle. We explored till nightfall, meeting, on the top of the mountain, troops from the other columns who had on their side pursued the same plan of campaign. Darkness found us too far from our camp to return to it that night, and leaving Lieutenants Lichtenberg and Jury on the summit of a high, detached hill, on the southern side of the main range, to prevent any Boers breaking back, we spent a wet night ourselves on some high ground close by, intending to resume our search on the morrow. But the weather on **October 22nd**, the next day, was too bad to admit of any effective work being done in that high altitude, heavy clouds covered the Slangappiesberg, and soon put a stop to any idea of continuing the search, so we returned to Rooikraal in the afternoon, and waited till the 23rd before re-ascending the mountain. On that day we went up by a different route, taking the north-eastern face of the Berg as our objective, while the other troops advanced up from the southern side. This time we completed the task which had been set us, but gained very little result for our pains; what Boers had been up there were able in the thick weather, which came on during the night of the 21st, to slip away between the blockhouses, at that time unfurnished with connecting wire fences, and to drive a good deal of their cattle with them.

The W.A.M.I., now under the able command of Major Royston, succeeded in capturing eight Boers, and we found a few cattle and sheep abandoned on the hill top. Altogether the five columns had captured forty Boers and 5,000 head of cattle.

Having halted another day at Rooikraal for a convoy of supplies which Capt. Leveson with " C " Squadron had gone for, we marched on October 25th to Luneberg, *en route* for Wakerstroom and Volksrust, thereby abandoning further operations in that part of the country. We halted on our way back, on October 26th, at Elandsberg Nek, October 27th at Wonderhoogte, October 28th at Wakerstroom, and on the 29th reached Volksrust. For almost the entire way our road was a very bad one, and led up and down those enormous mountains which, either as spurs of the Drakensberg, or the main range itself, make progress for wheeled transport extremely difficult. It took us from early dawn to sunset to get from one camp to another, and we were glad of a short rest at Volksrust, which was the first we had had since leaving Wonderfontein at the beginning of September.

We had completely failed in the great object we had been sent to accomplish, and our inability to strike a decisive blow at the Boer commandos was very soon to be felt by the late Colonel Benson and his column during their unsuccessful engagement at Brakenlaagte with many of the same men, who had just lately so easily avoided our columns at Waterval.

CHAPTER XVI.

"NIGHT MARCHES AND CONVOY WORK."

FROM **October 29th** to **November 2nd, 1901**, we halted at Volksrust, and re-equipped ourselves with horses and stores of all kinds. The past wet weather and long marches through the bad country we had been in had greatly reduced our number of horses, and we required a good many remounts to put ourselves straight. From the 8th Hussars, who were quartered at Volksrust, we got fifty good horses, giving them, in their place, fifty of our bad ones, an exchange they must have hardly considered a fair one. From the Remount Depôt we got nearly 250 more, and our strength, after sending away all those who were unsuited for further hard work, was 609 horses and thirty-three ponies.

Skin disease, aggravated by the wet weather and the poor rations of forage we had lately had, had broken out to an alarming extent among our horses and mules, and there were very few of them altogether free of this weakening scourge. On November 2nd we left Volksrust for Standerton, where we arrived on November 4th, halting at Paardekop and Platrand on the way.

Colonel Campbell had now taken up permanent command of the column, which was to be, for the future, entirely a mounted one, always with the exception of those men of the Cavalry, whom bad fortune or want of horse management compelled to follow on foot with the wagons, when they could not get a lift on the empty ones there might be to spare .

The reverse suffered by the late Colonel Benson's column necessitated some vigorous measures being adopted against the commandos of the Eastern Transvaal, who had lately shown so much activity and success. At last it was realised that either a systematic sweeping of the country into strongly held line of blockhouses or surprises by night marches were the only two plans offering adequate hopes of success. The days of following the Boers with columns loosely connected by day, and halted, miles apart, by night, were at last past, and, as the country was not yet ready for the driving system, we were now to rely on the second of the two courses, namely, night marches, which had been so successfully employed by the column of the late Colonel Benson.

On **November 7th** we left Standerton, marching that day, with Colonel Allenby's column on our left, to Welbedacht, and from there to Joubert's Vlei. The country on the high veld we found in a very sodden condition, and our wagons were constantly breaking through the crust of the ground and sinking up to their axles in the mud. The Boers were now in full occupation of the Eastern Transvaal right up to the line of Constabulary posts, which at this period of the war were spread over the country from Heidelberg on the south to Eland's River on the north, the only hindrance to their occupation of the whole territory being the Wakkerstroom-Piet line of blockhouses. The immense area, which was still left open to them, was, however, quite enough for their purposes.

The general plan of campaign which we were now about to undertake was to drive the Boers out of the eastern end of the country enclosed by the Natal and Delagoa railway lines, and by night marches of the combined mounted men of several columns pounce on their laagers as opportunities offered. Our movement was to be a slow one from east to west, and none of the enemy were to be permitted to slip round our flanks into the country we had passed through. At the same time, as we advanced and cleared each district, the Constabulary posts were to be pushed forward until they reached the line of the Waterval River and Steenkool spruit, that is from Val station on the Natal railway to Witbank on the Delagoa line. General Bruce Hamilton was given command of four columns wherewith to accomplish this object, namely, Colonel Allenby's, Colonel Campbell's, Colonel Rawlinson's, and Colonel Mackenzie's. During the greater part of the operations he had use of the above four columns, though at one time some of them were called off elsewhere, and at another fresh columns joined in as well.

Our column having reached Joubert's Vlei, marched on from there to Goodehoep and Trickhartsfontein, where we turned still more to the westward, joined Colonel Allenby, and reached Ruigtekuilen on **November 11th**, a central position on the high watershed which bisects the country between the two railways for many miles east and west.

It was not deemed necessary to advance any nearer the Constabulary line than that point, as from the information we had gathered almost the whole of the Boer commandos were now well to our eastward. A good many of the enemy had been met with near Goodhoep, and on the 9th we had to make one long detour to the right flank to pick up a man of the W.A.M.I., who had been attacked by about a hundred Boers and had had one of their number wounded.

As we marched westward from Trickhartsfontein the usual rearguard skirmish took place, the Boers from the Bethal direction following us up for some time, and one of their bullets hit Major Pollok in the wrist, but the wound was not severe enough to keep him from duty.

The country continued to be in a sodden condition, and very heavy thunderstorms occurring at intervals gave it little chance to dry. A halt was made at Ruigtekuilen from **November 11th** to the **17th**, while a combined mounted force from Colonel Allenby's and Campbell's columns was despatched to the country east and south-east of Bethal to locate the main laagers of the Boers. Colonel Knox in the meantime was sent with "A" Squadron and one troop of "B," six companies of the Durham Light Infantry and two guns, to Greylingstad on the Natal railway, to escort a large convoy, the supply wagons of both columns, there and back. This party reached Greylingstad in two days, halting at Boshmansfontein, and at Witpoort four miles off the railway, They started back on November 15th, halting again at Boshmansfontein, and reached Rietkuil on November 16th and Ruigtekuilen on November 17th. Finding the main column had left there the previous day, they continued their march on the 19th to Rooiport, twelve miles west of Bethal, and there rejoined Colonel Campbell again.

"C" Squadron and three troops of "B," all under command of Major Marling, had on November 12th proceeded with Colonel Allenby's and Colonel Campbell's mounted troops first to Rooiport, where they halted for the night, then on as far as Bekkersrust, nearly thirty miles to the eastward, returning back on the same day to Rooiport. This was a hard day's work, and necessitated for many of our men a sixty miles' journey, with a lot of wearying rearguard fighting thrown in on the return march, for the Boers, as usual, rapidly dispersed before us as we advanced, ready to attack us when we retired in our turn. The horses were very much knocked up, and our strength reduced considerably by the day's work. On **November 20th**, after a day's rest, we marched to Bethal, leaving Lieut. Clarke, with eighty men and about that number of horses, for two days at Rooiport, to hold a strong position there till he could be relieved by other troops.

Colonel Rawlinson's column joined us from the south at Bethal, and Colonel MacKenzie's was encamped a few miles off at Vaalkop on the north.

On **November 22nd** Colonel Knox left us to go to England on three months leave, and little did we realise when we bid him adieu on the afternoon of that day at Bethal that it was the last time we should see him, and that he would not return, as we all hoped, to take the regiment to England.

General Bruce Hamilton had divided the columns under him into three parts, (a) those horses which were fit for any nature of hard work, (b) those only fit for convoy work, and (c) those for the present unfit for any work. The first two of these divisions were now to be made use of, and General Hamilton, working on the information which Colonel Wools Sampson, his Intelligence Officer, had procured with his unequalled corps of native guides, set out on the first of his many night marches against the sleeping laagers of the Boers. The Boer forces changed so often in composition and character, that it is very hard to say how many commandos and leaders were actually then in the Eastern Transvaal, or of how many men their commandos really consisted. Chris Botha, P. Botha, Britz, Prinsloo, Grobelaar, P. Viljoen, Erasmus, and other commandants and field cornets, had followings of fifty to five hundred men in this district, but, with the exception perhaps of those under Britz and P. Viljoen, they seemed to rapidly melt away as we approached, and to lack any further initiative for attack since their last successful fight at Brakenlaagte.

Starting at 6.30 p.m. on **November 22nd**, we marched all night and reached Knapdaar on the Groot Oliphant's River at daybreak. Grobelaar and his commando had evidently only left the farm that morning, but their scouts had got wind of our advance, and had time to warn their friends to get away. From Knapdaar to De Witte Krans on the Klein Oliphant's River we moved at a gallop, to see if it was possible to come up with the commando, but they had made good their escape, and hardly a Boer was visible anywhere, so, after resting during the day at De Witte Krans, we retired towards evening back to Knapdaar to rejoin our transport, which, as " B " force, had followed in our footsteps from Bethal. That night we were to have made another night march, but the presence of a Boer outpost on the road by which we wished to move stopped us, and we rested instead, moving next day, the 25th, to Spoien Kop, and on the following one to Bethal.

On **November 27th** Colonel Campbell left us, proceeding to England on three months' leave, and his column was broken up into two parts, Colonel Wing, R.H.A., taking the 19th Hussars and W.A.M.I., and Colonel Simpson, R.A., ourselves, two companies of Infantry, two guns and a pom-pom. This arrangement remained in force till January 15th, when the columns were again amalgamated for good, as the small number of mounted men available, after escort duties were deducted, had handicapped each division very severely. Our own small column was particularly unfortunate, as we only had the one mounted regiment to draw on, and the consequence of this was that we were soon chosen to act almost as a permanent escort to convoys between Ermelo and Standerton, and thereby missed several of the first successes General Bruce Hamilton's troops achieved.

In consequence of Colonel Knox's departure on Nov. 22nd, Major Marling, v.c., had then assumed command of the regiment, while the squadrons remained as before under Major Pollok, Captain Corbett, and Captain Leveson; there were not sufficient mounted men at this period to allow of a fourth squadron being formed.

On **November 27th** we started at 6.30 p.m. on another night march, this time in a northerly direction, selecting Rietkuil on the Steenkool Spruit as our destination. Again we were to be disappointed, for after marching all night we could find no trace of any Boers, and learnt that they had left that locality a few days previously. After resting for breakfast, we set off on our return march of some twenty-two miles, in the heat of the day, and were back in Bethal by 1 p.m., with our horses weary and nothing gained by our long night march.

We rested at Bethal till **December 2nd**, giving our horses as little work as we possibly could, for, to accomplish the long distances by night and day we now had to undertake, it was most necessary to give our animals all the rest we could in between times. The absence of any Boers within a ten mile radius, except a stray observation post or so, also compelled us to forbear wasting horseflesh in unprofitable moves.

In fact a great change had long since come over the country, the constant harassing of this portion of the Transvaal, and the frequent capture of small numbers of the enemy's men, had altered the whole outlook. It was seldom now possible for one's eye, as it roved round the smooth topped ridges, to be stopped by the suspicious specks on the sky line we had formerly been so accustomed to find.

The strength of our weak column was now still further diminished by the loss of Captain Leveson and " C " Squadron, who were sent to escort a convoy from Bethal to Standerton, and they did not rejoin us for some time, but as our forthcoming duties did not necessitate our undertaking any very important work, this was of not so very much consequence. The presence of so many columns at Bethal and the great length of the night marches we were making soon convinced the Boers that it was unsafe to remain anywhere within a day's ride of that town, and compelled them to seek spots further westward where our movements did not extend to. To checkmate this move, we set off on **December 1st** for Ermelo, halting at Spoien Kop and Riet Vlei on the way, Colonel Wing's column marching with us on the left flank, and Colonel Rawlinson's on the right. The Boers had been waiting for this advance in order to slip past us, as they were used to do of old, and occupy in peace the country we had left, and which we generally never returned to for many a day.

At Ermelo our regiment was at once detailed for the Standerton convoy work, and at 4.30 a.m., on **December 4th**, set out for Brakfontein, outspanning at Kaffir Spruit for our midday halt. Within a few miles of us General Hamilton, with the remainder of the mounted men, marching all night, had surprised three laagers in succession. The Boers had thought themselves quite safe after they had got round the right flank of our columns and back into the country we had come from, but they were soon to learn they were safe nowhere when halted for any considerable period. Out of the three laagers ninety-three prisoners, 2,200 rounds of ammunition, 250 cattle, and 6,000 sheep were captured.

During the morning of **December 4th**, on our march to Standerton, Private Brooks, of the 21st Lancers, attached to "B" Squadron, had been shot dead by a small party of Boers hiding in a rocky kopje he had had to approach while he was employed as a scout to the flank guard of the squadron, and we buried him that night at Brakfontein. Next day we marched to Uitkyk, which the blockhouse line had already reached, and we passed the small column, which was engaged in building the houses, just beyond Blesbok Spruit.

December 6th saw us halted within three miles of Standerton awaiting the return of the wagons which, when filled, were to be escorted back to Ermelo. By coming ourselves to Standerton we succeeded in getting 230 horses from the remount depôt, and a few men and horses from our Middelburg supply, but out of the former we were obliged to send back forty-four at once, as they were quite useless for the work we had to do. By **December 8th** the wagons were re-filled, and we started off back to Ermelo, where we arrived on **December 11th**, after halting at Uitkyk, Morgenzan, and Kaffir Spruit.

General Bruce Hamilton had continued his successes in the Bethal direction, and near Trickhartsfontein, after a long night march, he had completely surprised another laager, and captured 131 Boers and 4,000 head of cattle.

Ermelo was being rapidly converted into an immense depôt, and, as fast as possible, supplies were to be pushed up into it from Standerton. After waiting two days, during which several Boers surrendered at Ermelo, we were ordered to march back again with the convoy to the head of the blockhouse line on the Standerton road, while from there onwards it was considered safe for the wagons to move with a small escort, consisting of Lieut. Lyon and twenty-five men, with the Infantry, from post to post. Having spent the night at Brakfontein, we reached the blockhouses at Morganzan on **December 14th**, where we found Colonel Spens' column encamped, and we joined our camp on to his. We had met "C" Squadron during our march; they had been employed on the same work as we were, escorting another convoy to and from Ermelo.

At Morganzan we heard the result of another successful night march undertaken by General Bruce Hamilton. Moving at dusk from Ermelo he had reached De Witte Kranz, on the Klein Oliphant's River, at daybreak, and making a detour to approach the enemy from the north, where they would least expect an attack, had completely surprised one laager in the mists of the early morning, had captured a gun, and scattered the occupants of a second laager to the four winds. Commandant Grobelaar, with the majority of the second commando, had, however, made good their escape.

Whilst we were waiting at Morganzan for the return of the wagons from Standerton, Colonel Spens arranged with Colonel Simpson a plan of action against a scattered commando of some 200 Boers, who had taken up their quarters in the valley of the Blesbok spruit, between the blockhouse line and Bethal. "A" and "B" Squadrons, with the pompom, were to march by a circuitous route, northwards and north-westwards, to the Bethal end of the spruit, while Colonel Spens' men, starting later in the night, beat up the valley from the south.

We left our camp at 8 p.m. on **December 14th**, and marched for hours through the night, gradually wheeling to the west to gain our right positions. About one in the morning our guide was at fault, and for two precious hours we had to remain halted until our exact locality was ascertained. This check spoilt the execution of the original plan, and Major Pollok, with "A" Squadron, in spite of a rapid advance at the first streak of dawn, was unable to reach the farthest westerly point, which had been selected for his squadron to occupy, before the column advancing from the south had alarmed the country side. Colonel Spens' men had captured twelve Boers, and in taking them Major Gough, who was in command of his mounted troops, had been severely wounded.

The main body of the enemy had slipped away north just before we got to our positions, and, seeing that we had completed our forward movement, the more enterprising of them returned to attack our rearguard as soon as we should move off back. A small party of them advanced and hid in a donga to wait till we moved and there would be less chance of us retaliating; but, unluckily for them, we had seen them through our glasses, and, accurately divining the actual place in which they and their ponies were concealed, we brought the pompom to bear on them, and sent Major Pollok and

"A" Squadron across the Blesbok Spruit to capture them in the side valley where they had taken shelter. The pompom shells at once stampeded their ponies, with the exception of one or two of the well trained ones, who refused to go far. Hastily mounting the latter, two of the Boers, under a continued fire from the pompom and long range volleys from our men, who were escort to it, very gallantly did their best to round up the frightened steeds of their dismounted companions. They had miraculous escapes, but succeeded in bringing back several ponies before Major Pollok's men, climbing the opposite slopes of the valley, appeared on the summit and opened fire. Three Boers were captured and brought back to our camp at Morganzan, where, with Colonel Spens' troops, we arrived at 2 p.m.

It was **December 20th** before the convoy returned to us from Standerton, and after a rest at Morganzan, which had done our horses a good deal of good, we moved off with the wagons on that day to escort them as far as Ermelo. There was, however, little escorting required, as the blockhouses had now reached Kaffir spruit within a short day's march of Ermelo, and by daylight the Boers did not care about approaching too close to the well-built posts on this line.

A commando under Britz to the south, well hid in the hilly country by the Vaal River and round Blauw Kop, had on the 19th inflicted considerable loss on the ill-fated Mounted Infantry of Spens' column, some of whom had been engaged in the unlucky episode with Major Gough at Blood River Poort a short time previously. They had set out on another night march from Morganzan just before we left, and in the early morning of December 19th, after they had off-saddled, were surprised by the Boers, and suffered a loss of forty killed and wounded and a hundred captured.

The roads were again very bad through heavy rain, and we struggled with difficulty to Uitzicht on the 20th, and Kaffir Spruit on the 21st. We were unable to get the wagons over the spruit as it was running so high, and the Engineers with the column had to set to and make a bridge before they could cross. There were sufficient troops now collected at Kaffir spruit to escort the convoy the remainder of the way without our help, and as some wagons had to be sent to Colonel Spens' column, now at Berginderling bridge on the Vaal, we were made use of for this duty. We reached his column on **December 23rd**, after a two days' halt at Kaffir Spruit, remained the night with him, and proceeded next day along the main road to Ermelo and reached that town on Christmas Eve, meeting with no adventures *en route*. By this time we were very weary of so much convoy work with its uninteresting concomitants, and especially of the dreary

18th Hussars on Convoy Duty, Kaffir Spruit, on Ermelo-Standerton Road, 1st Dec., 1901.

stretch of road littered with dead cattle we had so constantly to move over, and we had been endeavouring to get back to the main columns for a considerable time. From now onwards we managed to escape any further duty of this description, and were really very lucky to have got off with so small a share.

General Bruce Hamilton, with the bulk of the Ermelo columns, was away from the town on our arrival, as an unprofitable expedition to the south-east had kept him busy for the past few days.

Christmas Day was celebrated by the regiment as auspiciously as was possible. A good dinner procured with difficulty, by the aid of the ox convoy, from less stormy parts, was shared by all, and our spirits kept up by the oft repeated hope that " this time next year " we should be celebrating the occasion in a far different manner.

We halted at Ermelo until **December 29th**, when General Bruce Hamilton and the other columns having returned, we set out on an expedition to the Swaziland border, which was to take us ten days to accomplish. At 7 p.m. that night we started, together with the mounted men of Colonel Rawlinson's column, chiefly composed of the 2nd Mounted Infantry, Colonel Stewart's Johannesburg Mounted Rifles, Colonel Wing with the 19th Hussars and W.A.M.I., and Colonel Williams with some Australian troops, to march to Bankop, some twenty-three miles distant on the Amsterdam road. The Vaal was in heavy flood, and it took a long time to get a pontoon bridge thrown over it in the middle of the night, and, even when completed, the bridge was too short, and we had to jump our horses from the end of it into the flooded land by the bank. This took us a long time to do, but, though day was breaking before we were all across to the eastern side, we found the Boers had relied so much on the river and their knowledge that we were resting for Christmas, that they were not nearly so wide awake as usual.

The 18th Hussars were leading the advance, and at Schimmelhoek, some time after day had broken, surrounded a farm and captured seven Boers with their ponies and cattle. We learnt from them that most of the commandos had split up for the present to go to their homes for the new year. We had left Lieut. Purdey with fifty men to assist in bringing our wagons and baggage after us to Bankop, but the bad state of the country so delayed their march that we saw nothing of them that day, and it was 4 p.m. on the following one before they began to come into sight.

In the meantime constant rain on the cold hill sides of Bankop had, together with lack of food for ourselves and our horses, converted us into a very bedraggled crew, and we were glad to get in motion again, although it was the middle of the night, on **December 31st**, when we made another start for the Swaziland border. The first few hours of the morning were taken up in extracting the wagons out of some fearful bog holes into which they had inadvertently strayed during the darkness, but the fog which hung over the high land, when the day broke, almost served our purpose as well as night, and, on crossing the Usutu River, near Davidale, the leading troops captured twenty-two Boers, who, with their wagons and cattle, were endeavouring to escape northward out of our reach. It was late in the day before we got all our troops across the Usutu and into camp at Davidale, and we were none too pleased at a summons to turn out again at 6 p.m. for another night march. But we soon settled down to it, and with the mounted troops of Colonel Rawlinson's column and the J.M.R., we moved south down the steep berg to the lower country which lies round the Compies River and Amsterdam.

The march was a well executed one, though the night was as dark as it well could be, and the country most difficult to move over at night, for at dawn we had covered nearly thirty miles and completely occupied the neck of a bend in the Compies River, where some Boers were said to be concealed. Further investigation proved that our information was correct. " A " Squadron advanced on the left, while " B " and " C " made a detour to the right to prevent their breaking away up the stream, while other parties of mounted men, prolonging the line still further to the right, gained touch with the river on their side. A stiff climb brought us out on to the top of some hills, which filled up this bend of the river, and " A " Squadron soon came on the most considerable party of the Boers, who, sheltered in a valley, were busy getting ready their morning meal, and evidently sure of their immunity from attack in such an out of the way district. They soon woke to the hopelessness of their cause, and, after a little spasmodic firing, surrendered with their flocks and herds.

There were some other scattered parties to be collected inside our cordon, and on totalling them up we found we had captured fifty Boers and a good number of cattle and sheep. Ex-Commandant Erasmus was among the prisoners, and his seizure was of particular interest to us, as, after the battle of Talana in the early days of the war, his men had surrounded Maritz's farmhouse near Dundee, when Colonel Moller and a party of " B " Squadron had taken refuge there on their way back to General Symons' camp.

After a halt for breakfast and rest at the Compies River, we marched back to Davidale, where Colonel Wing and his men had also returned from a night march they had undertaken on the north side of the camp the night before, capturing during their outing twenty Boers. These successes made us ready for any amount of work, and snatching what sleep we could during our brief halts, we were ready again at 7 p.m. on that night, **January 4th**, to try our luck this time to the eastward, past a place called Lichfield Store, where some Boers were reported. But our good fortune had forsaken us for a time, and we had to return empty handed, after a rough march through broken country, back to camp, where we arrived at 1 p.m. on the next day. There we met General Bruce Hamilton, who had also been out with other troops on the preceding night, and had succeeded in capturing six Boers; this brought our total to well over a hundred captures.

CHAPTER XVII.

"NIGHT MARCHES IN THE EASTERN TRANSVAAL."

January—March, 1902.

OUR men had had practically no rest or sleep since December 30th, and had the enemy executed a night attack on January 5th they would have found us hard to arouse. But the few there were still lurking in that part of the country were rapidly endeavouring to put as much distance between themselves and us as they could, and so we enjoyed a well earned rest that night and the two following days.

On the **8th January, 1902**, we marched back to Outshoorn near Ermelo, where we arrived on the 10th, after halts at Kliprug, Schimmelhoek, and Jan Hendricksfontein; at the latter spot we had two horses shot by a small party of Boers who had followed us up when we were rearguard to the column. At Ermelo we picked up Lieut. Jury and the men we had left behind with sick horses, also Captain Leveson and Lieut. Bayford, the latter having just arrived out from England after six months' sick leave. Halting a day at Oudshoorn, we set off at 6 p.m. on the night of **January 11th** on an expedition to Knapdaar, on the Groot Oliphant's River, where a large commando, under P. Botha, had collected during our absence on the Swaziland border. The distance we had to traverse was almost beyond us, and our information not quite so exact as it might have been, so, though we just accomplished the journey by marching all through the night with hardly a halt of any description, we expended our energy surrounding the wrong farmhouse at daybreak, and found we were still three or four miles short of the Boer laager. The latter had received an alarm too through one of their piquets we had surprised, but not completely captured, during the night, and they were up and away as we rode down the Groot Oliphant's valley in the early morning. We gave chase as far as Kaffirstad, some six miles beyond Knapdaar, and, in spite of our bad start, succeeded in capturing thirty-six of them, together with a fair number of wagons and cattle.

The pace since daybreak had been a fast one, the "18th" pressing on on the right and Colonel Spens' men on the left, and the plains of the Oliphant's River were dotted with groups of men, who had either halted for a time to fire on the retreating Boers, or were escorting back the prisoners as they were captured, while our main wave of mounted men gradually expended itself against the high slopes of the valley to the northward. It was impossible to continue the chase; we had then marched over forty miles without a halt, and had had a long gallop thrown in at the end, so we drew off our squadrons and retired to some shady plantations at Knapdaar there to pass the remainder of the day, with what little food for ourselves and horses we had been able to bring with us.

It was now a question of either remaining at Knapdaar a night and resting our horses there without any food, or of marching them back, weary as they were, to Ermelo as soon as possible, for on this march we had been accompanied by no second column of wagons. It was decided to lie out for the night and return early next morning, and, at 3 a.m. on **January 13th**, we dragged our hungry horses along what seemed a never-ending road back to Ermelo, followed for twenty miles by a small but most persistent commando of the enemy, who gave our horses no rest.

We were on rearguard, and had to accommodate our pace to that of some wagons we had captured and were bringing back with us; these wagons had started empty, but before we got in they were all filled, as high as they could be piled, with saddles and saddlery off the many horses we had had to shoot, before we at last in the heat of the day crawled into Ermelo. Thirty-seven of our own horses had to be destroyed in this way during the harassing march; other corps had suffered in the same manner, and quite 150 must have been lost in the combined columns. We were not allowed to leave animals of any description behind us on the road, and so a tragic fate befel the luckless quadruped who, exhausted by the efforts it had been called upon to perform, was unable, though perhaps for a time only, to respond to any further appeal.

Colonel Wing, with the remainder of General Hamilton's mounted men, had also been away on a night march, and had met with much the same success as we had. He captured Commandant Woolmarans and forty-two Boers, and had not had so far to go for this result.

Another rest for our horses was absolutely necessary, and four days were given us to recoup in, but, as will be seen by a glance at the table showing the waste of horseflesh incurred at this period, we were asking too much for all but the best animals to perform; short halts, though sufficient for really good horses, were almost useless to the great majority, who could only stand this excessive marching, with heavy weights on their backs, if long spells of rest were given them to recover in; on the other hand the success of the operations was the signal for their continuance, and the result was considered more than proportionate to the wastage.

During the few days we were at Ermelo, Colonel Simpson

left us for the Orange River Colony, and we joined the 19th Hussars and the W.A.M.I. again, to serve under Colonel Wing for the remainder of the war.

In spite of the great number of Boers we had captured, totalling as they did, with those who had surrendered, nearly 1,000 men, the country was still unsafe to move about in much beyond the range of our outposts, and a small party of men from Colonel Spens' column were at this time ambushed within a few miles of the town.

At 6.30 p.m. on the night of **January 18th** we undertook another night march to the country under the berg at Windhoek, on the Piet Retief road. This time we crossed the Vaal at Camden, as the river was fordable there, and from that point made our way to the edge of the berg, dropping down into the low country by Waaikraal just as morning broke and a heavy mist with drizzling rain came on. We were unexpected, and twenty-six Boers, after some slight resistance, together with 700 head of cattle, fell into our hands; but twenty more, whose whereabouts we had been ignorant of, escaped from us, in the mist, out of a farmhouse we had not examined. We had covered as usual a lot of ground, and had to halt on the Berg till our horses were rested, and it was not till midday that we started on our return journey through the boggy country which lay between us and the Vaal. Rain came on soon after we set out, and the river was reached at dusk with no sign of its abatement, and, though at one time it had been decided to halt there for the remainder of the night to give the horses a rest, the weather kept so bad that at 8 p.m. we saddled up again and waded on, many times wet through, back to our camps at Ermelo, where we arrived at 11.45 p.m. that night, our men, in spite of their discomforts, beguiling the return journey with every song in their repertoire.

During **January 20th** and **21st** we remained halted by Tafel Kop, the hill outside Ermelo, under which our camp was situated.

General Bruce Hamilton had now decided to act with smaller and more scattered forces and cover thereby a greater extent of country, and the large combinations of mounted men we had employed up to this time were done away with, as their *raison d'être* was gone. The country was parcelled out among the several columns, and Colonel Wing's and Colonel Williams' ones were given the Bethal-Steenkool Spruit-Carolina district to work in, and it was at first proposed to form depôts at these spots and dash out and return to them according as circumstances dictated; but this scheme, however, did not hold good for long.

To take up our new campaigning grounds we marched on **January 22nd**, leaving Sergeant Brown and thirty men to do mounted work for the Ermelo garrison, along the Bethal road as far as Reinhoogte. The baggage of both columns, with most of the troops, marched unopposed along the road, and outspanned at Kaffir Spruit on the way. " B " and " C " Squadrons of the 18th Hussars, having started at 9 p.m. on the preceding night, deviated to the northward, and after a fruitless night march to Middelplaats, rejoined the main column at the camp at Reinhoogte. The Boers they were on the track of were themselves engaged in a midnight expedition to worry the Standerton blockhouse line, an amusement they were frequently engaged in at night, and it was not till their return to their own farms in the early morning that anything was seen of them. Our squadrons then endeavoured to draw them on to a kopje, on which our men had taken up a position, but, failing in this, they gave chase till their further progress was stopped by a wire fence, which gave the enemy time to make good their escape, leaving one prisoner in our hands.

There was a very bad drift over the Riet Vlei spruit near our camp at Reinhoogte, and " A " Squadron were kept there till 9 p.m. that night guarding the wagons and helping them up the steep banks. We were now getting a large share of the wet weather due at this time of the year, so the difficulties with the transport were heavy, and all through the next day we made little progress in the mud and rain, and only reached Hamelfontein at the end of that day's march (January 23rd).

From there Captain Wood, with 110 men of " A " Squadron, of which he had command during Major Pollok's absence on leave, visited some neighbouring farms after midnight, but found no trace of any Boers, while the following night nearly the same result attended the efforts of the whole column, which " B " and " C " Squadrons this time accompanied.

The camp had been moved on **January 24th** to Kuilfontein, a short distance to the north, where the latter expedition to the Groot Oliphant's valley was undertaken from, but Colonel Allenby's column had, without our knowledge, moved close to the points we selected for our raid, and, beyond surprising and capturing two despatch riders, one of whom was wounded in the scuffle, and nearly running our noses into a friendly camp, we obtained no definite result for our trouble. In fact the days of successful night marches were already on the wane; the Boers, harried beyond measure by our sudden and unexpected appearances, had now adopted a plan of perpetual motion by night, which quite checkmated our well thought out arrangements. They would reach a farm at nightfall, where perhaps our native spies would locate them and report their presence to us; but, at 9 p.m. or later, when they had finished their evening meal, the order would be passed round to saddle up, and the whole commando would silently fade away in the darkness of the night to other farms, whose locality, fixed on as a rendezvous by one or two of the leaders, was kept a profound secret even from the rest of the commando itself. An hour before daybreak a second move would take place, and again the silent cavalcade would proceed on its wanderings, halting for that day, after a short march, if it was seen that none of our ubiquitous columns were in the vicinity, only to repeat the same tactic on that and the following nights.

It will be seen that the adoption of these tactics made our success a most problematical one, and that, once the Boers discovered a column was in the neighbourhood, it was a waste of time and horseflesh to attempt any surprises by night. At the same time it cannot be doubted that indirectly they brought pressure to bear on the enemy, some of whom, wearied beyond endurance by the constant night work, at last refused to obey their leaders any longer, and, secretly detaching themselves from their commandos, rode into our posts and surrendered.

On **January 25th, 1902**, we moved our camp back to Banklaagte, close to Spoien Kop, and from there, on the next night, Captain Wood, with "A" Squadron, again visited some neighbouring farms, but met with no better success than he had had before. This was aggravating, as Colonel Allenby, with his column, had passed by our camp the night before, and continuing in the Ermelo direction, had quite taken the wind out of our sails by capturing nearly 100 Boers within fifteen miles of where we were.

We left Banklaagte next day, the **27th January**, and marched to Bethel, where for some reason, which we could not fathom, a small and much harassed garrison had been established. They had no stores of provisions and forage which we could draw on, but instead had themselves to be supplied by convoys from the blockhouse line, and, as this duty was a hazardous one for the small escort which as a rule could only be furnished, they remained in their isolated and strongly entrenched posts, living on scanty supplies, monarchs of the ruined town of Bethel indeed, but of hardly a square yard of country beyond. We halted there for two days, and we must have been a godsend to the garrison, who usually saw no one but Boers from week end to week end, whereas these latter, during our halt there, betook themselves off elsewhere. However, we could not prolong our stay, and on the night of the 29th we had to be off on another night march to a farm called Oshoek, where General Bruce Hamilton had made his capture of nearly one hundred Boers six weeks before. It was deserted, and so was the next one, Klipfontein, which we reached an hour later, just as the sun rose, but on topping the ridge beyond we saw a commando, our old friends of the Blesbok spruit, just emerging out of a farm some two miles away. We gave chase, endeavouring to encircle them at the same time, but it was too much to ask of our wearied horses, who had marched almost without a halt since 7 p.m. the night before, and the Boers gradually drew ahead, leaving three of their number in our hands. After an off saddle, and a rest for breakfast for ourselves and a feed for our horses, we continued again on our course, and rejoined the convoy at Witbank, where it had marched direct that morning from Bethel.

Any further operations which we might have contemplated in the district originally assigned to us were now abandoned on receipt of orders to march westward into the country lying beyond the S.A.C. posts, which now extended from Val Station on the Natal Railway to Witbank on the Delagoa line.

General Gilbert Hamilton was working from Springs with two small columns inside the triangle made by the Constabulary line and the railways, but he was not making much headway against a combined commando under P. Viljoen, Erasmus, and Grobelaar, which, having broken through the blockhouse line, a very weak one, was resting secure in the wide area to the westward.

To reach those parts some long treks lay before us, so we started on at once and reached New Denmark on **January 31st**. From there Colonel Wing decided on another night march to surprise the farms which lay ahead of us, but farm after farm we found uninhabited and destroyed, and at daybreak had had no successes to chronicle. Just as we were pulling up two Boers appeared on the right flank through the mists of the morning, and a small party of West Australians gave chase. They captured one of them, but the other completely defeated them. After he had galloped for a long way and distanced most of his pursuers he halted, dismounted, and shot dead two of them, wounded two more and two horses, and rode away unharmed himself, leading off with him a captured pony.

We reached in the meantime the Constabulary line, and halted there to rest for a while. This line was not a series of blockhouses with wire fences joining them together as the Ermelo-Standerton one was, but simply a succession of fortified posts, and it is doubtful if they were of any great value to us. The Boers passed freely through the line, and beyond reporting the fact that they had crossed and thereby locating them to a certain extent, the Constabulary could do but little. As they occupied farm buildings and tents with a semi-circular hollow wall round the east side of them, instead of blockhouses, they required a considerable force of men to guard each post, and, as their numbers decreased, the outlying ones had to be abandoned and larger gaps created between the permanent posts. Had the line been wired up and held in the same manner as the Ermelo-Standerton one, it would have been a great help to us then and later on in the big drives.

The baggage of our two columns reached Roodebank that day after a long march, during which they had found a Boer hidden in an ant bear hole. We joined up with it at 1 p.m. and continued on our way east next morning, over a desolate country, to Nooitgedaacht, twenty-two miles distant, where we arrived at 5.30 p.m. on **February 2nd.**

Every effort had been made to convert the triangle of country we were now marching through into an uninhabitable wilderness. Kaffirs had been removed, their kraals demolished, farms destroyed and their occupants taken to the concentration camps, nearly but not quite all the crops cut down, and cattle, sheep, goats, and every living animal driven away from the country side. It would seem that no body of men could have existed in this barren district, but yet they did so, and even brought their cattle and wagons with them, their plan being to quarter themselves near one of the towns on the railway and draw what necessities they wanted from the concentration camp there and live on their cattle, and the fruit and vegetable they still found in the country and the buried mealies they had hidden. Their existence, however, must have been a precarious one, and especially so when they were hustled from pillar to post by the presence of several columns in their neighbourhood, as it fell to their lot to be at this period.

We left Nooitgedaacht next morning (February 3rd), and had not proceeded far when we learnt that P. Viljoen and his commando were in the country to the northward, with General Gilbert Hamilton and his two columns in pursuit of them, and that the former were marching south and would pass between us and the Constabulary line. Stopping our eastward march we turned almost back on our tracks, and leaving the baggage to follow us to Blesbok Spruit, a farm which lay about ten miles west of the centre of the S.A.C. posts, we set off with two squadrons of our men under Captains Leveson and Wood, together with some 19th Hussars and W.A.M.I., to endeavour to head the Boers, while **Colonel Williams'** column followed us as a support.

We sighted the enemy and their wagons at about 1.30 p.m., and at once gave chase, with "C" Squadron in the van and "A" Squadron and a gun close behind. Had our horses only been in better fettle we should have captured them all, about 200 as they were in numbers, but we had covered such long distances the last few days, and even that morning had gone fifteen miles before we met with them, that our horses could not go the pace we asked them. The enemy did their best to delay us, dismounting at every hill top to shoot at us as we advanced, but, as fast as we could, we pressed on, and in four miles had captured their wagons and cattle, and, taking on our best horses only, continued the pursuit till we could go no further.

By that time General G. Hamilton's men had come down from the northward on the left flank of the Boers, now completely scattered over the country side, and, thus broken into several parties, the greater number of them managed to get away to both south and north, not liking to cross in the daytime the Constabulary line. We stayed the pursuit at Zondagskraal within sight of the S.A.C., as we had no horses left to follow any further, while the mounted troops of Colonel Williams' column, whom we expected to prolong our line to the right, were too far behind to be of any assistance. Fifteen Boers and all their cattle, wagons, and carts, with the exception of one of the latter, which we could still see disappearing to the south-west, fell into our hands, and General G. Hamilton's men captured some other Boers and cattle on our left. One of the officers of the W.A.M.I. had been killed as we were approaching the wagons, but no other casualties had occurred, whereas the Boers had suffered considerably in wounded, our men having knocked several over at the last position they had reached, and where we had got quite close to them in their retreat.

We now had to get our wagons refilled, and set off next day (February 4th) for that purpose to Brugspruit on the Delagoa Bay railway, and arrived there on the 5th after a night's halt at Goedegevonden, where we crossed the route we had taken with Colonel Campbell in July of 1901. Remounts were very necessary, as we had to send in 105 worn-out horses to Middelburg, but we could only obtain sixty, out of which we had to send back twelve as worthless, and the balance were a very poor lot indeed. However, we got some of our old horses out of Middelburg, which had been sent there for a rest, and at the same time collected a fresh supply of stores and clothing, and got officers and men back from the few days' leave which had been given them, and sent others in their places. General Gilbert Hamilton's column was now some two days' march from us to the south-west, and, on **February 8th**, we were directed to march west parallel with the railway, and endeavour to circumvent what was left of P. Viljoen's commando, which, lying somewhere south of Bronkhurst Spruit, was shut in by General Hamilton on the south and by our column on the east side.

We reached Heuvelfontein that night, and, starting at 3.30 a.m. next morning, explored the country along the Wilge River without any success, nor could we find any trace of the Boers up to Brakfontein on the west side of the river, where we halted for the night. There we learnt that Prinsloo, with about 100 men, was still ahead of us, and next morning, at daybreak, we started off by Hollander Pan to Bronkhurst Spruit, which we crossed at Tweefontein, and searched the farms on the far side, joined there by General Hamilton's men from the southward. There we found traces of the Boers, and learnt soon after from twelve prisoners we picked up out of a farm in which they had hidden, in the hope that we should pass them over in the thick trees which grew there, that Prinsloo and the rest of the commando had skirted round our right flank during the night, and passed between us and the railway. They had rather easily given us the slip, and it was useless just then to try and follow them, so we had to wait for a time till a new plan could be formulated for their capture.

Next day, **February 11th, 1902**, we marched to within a mile of Bronkhurst Spruit Station, passing close to the graves of the men of the 94th Regiment, who had been killed there during their march from Middelburg to Pretoria in the first Boer war. Information was now obtained that the Boers were on the east bank of the Wilge River, and at 7.30 p.m. of the day on which we reached Bronkhurst Spruit we set off again, and, marching all through the night, crossed the Wilge River just south of the station of that name, and turned down the right bank of the river as far as Witpoort farm, but could find no trace of any of Prinsloo's men. At daybreak we recrossed the river and kept southward almost to Dwarsfontein silver mines, where we again met General Hamilton's columns, who had also made a night march in that direction. But if the enemy had been there they had cleared out some time before, and as we could see nothing of them we retraced our steps to Tweefontein on the Bronkhurst Spruit, and halted there for three days to consider fresh projects.

The river ran close by our camp, and though it afforded excellent fishing for our spare hours, yet it was not a very suitable place at that time of the year to fix a camp in, owing to the prevalence of horse sickness, and we were lucky not to suffer more than we did from its proximity. But the spruit had other dangers, and one of our men, Private Myles, of

"C" Squadron, whilst bathing there, was drowned in a pool of the river before assistance could reach him.

At 2.30 p.m. on **February 15th** we marched off to Brakfontein in a heavy storm of rain, having been ordered to leave the country west of the Constabulary line to General Gilbert Hamilton, and proceed at once to Carolina. It was a long trek there, the days were hot at that time of the year, and the march promised to be an unexciting one in the extreme.

On **February 16th** we started on our journey, past the silver mines at Dwarsfontein, and over the Wilge River to Zaiwater, having outspanned for two hours *en route*. Next day we reached the Constabulary line at Steenkool Spruit, where Major Pollok joined us and took up command of the regiment, as Major Marling had to go on sick leave at Bronkhurst Spruit and he did not rejoin again, except for a few days at the beginning of March, till the 15th April.

Major Pollok had been endeavouring to overtake us for some time; he was bringing 140 remounts for us, and had also with him Lieutenants Webster, Wood, and Grigg, the two latter joining the regiment for the first time on appointment. This party, together with some men of the other regiments and some Infantry with a lot of baggage, had marched from Standerton to meet us at Ermelo, and missing us there, set off to Bethel, but we had already left that spot, and to cut us off they had come along the Constabulary posts to Witbank to wait for us to cross that line on our way to Carolina. Reinforced by this contingent, but no longer accompanied by Colonel Williams' column, we left Steenkool Spruit on the 18th, and made a long hot march to Boschmanskranz, where "C" Squadron fruitlessly pursued a few Boers, said to be a party of Grobelaar's commando, who were hanging about our right front. On **February 19th** we reached Koffiebank on the headwaters of the Komati, after another long march which entailed a strain on our transport animals owing to the heat of the day.

The Boers almost always, after we left camp in the morning, came down to the ground we had been occupying and searched it to see if they could find anything of any value to them, and we used to hide sometimes for them, but rarely did so for long, as it delayed the march considerably. That day, however, a regular trap was set for the ones we had seen the day before, and Captain Leveson, with "C" Squadron, hid in a pan there was on the top of a hill just by the camp, and a party of Australians concealed themselves in a farmhouse near by. But only two of the Boers came up, and a small party of our men, having seen them, lay hid till they should approach nearer, but the Boers altered their course, came first of all on the whole squadron concealed in the pan, and, seeing their mistake, at once bolted and were away before anyone in the pan could see them. The small party who had first seen them realised too late that they had discovered the ambush, and had wheeled about. The Boers, pursued by a few ill-directed shots, rapidly gained cover in a fold of the ground, while the squadron hastily mounted and gave chase for a mile or two. Captain Leveson then slackened the pace, ordered the troops to stop further pursuit, and collected them with the exception of Lieutenant Lichtenberg's men, who could not be checked simultaneously with the others. Before Lieut. Lichtenberg could collect all his party, one of them, Private Sparks, detached from the others, had received a mortal wound from some of the enemy, who had opened fire to check our men's advance.

Captain Leveson's squadron now followed in the track of the column, and overtook it near Koffiebank; they brought with them the wounded man, who died that night of his injuries, and was buried next day at Carolina, when the column arrived there. This was the last casualty in the field we were to have in this war, and with it we had suffered a loss of forty-eight killed and ninety-five wounded in all.

At Steynsdraei, near Carolina, we halted for two days, and picked up Sergeant Brown and thirty-four men, who had been doing duty at Ermelo. On **February 23rd** we started off again along the Wonderfontein-Ermelo blockhouse line, and arrived at the latter place on the 25th, halting for a day and night at Smutsoog, where a telegram reached us from England with the sad news that our Colonel had died at home of pneumonia.

We could hardly believe that the painful intelligence was correct, and to verify it we asked for a repetition of the telegram. There was, however, no doubt that our Colonel was dead, and the Regiment, from the senior officers to the last joined troopers, sadly rued the loss.

The officers and soldiers of the British Army have, one readily grants, many natural abilities for the work of their profession, and we may urge, without boastfulness, that they carry out their military duties, more often than not, with zeal, intelligence, and success. Moreover, we can never admit that the officers of our Army are ever lacking in those manly qualities which befit them for the leadership of their men, or in that kindly disposition which leads them to study the comfort of those under their command and to ameliorate their lot. A glance at the improvements the last few years have effected in the interior economy of our regiments and batteries will quickly convince us that our decision can be well maintained. In spite of the correctness of these views,

Smutzog, 23rd February, 1902.

Smutzog, 14th August, 1900.

there are yet few of us who are at heart and soul entirely devoted to our profession, who will give up all social and industrial pursuits to devote our whole thoughts and ideas to the consideration of a soldier's life, which, though the noblest of professions, and one hallowed by the memories of noble deeds, still often becomes monotonous in time of peace through the regularity of the minor duties that have to be carried out.

It may truly be said that our late Colonel was one of the few brilliant exceptions to the ordinary run of military men. His whole thoughts and abilities were centred on the regiment. It came naturally to him to live with it, think of it, and work for it all and every day. He carried out his schemes for its betterment quietly, unostentatiously, and often without their authorship being guessed except by those behind the scenes. His knowledge of soldiers and their manner of enjoying the barrack life which was open to them, enabled him to enter into their system of amusement and to carry out schemes, which others would only have attempted by methods strained and unpalatable. He held this art not only by his appreciation of character, but also by his acquaintance with military duties, the minutiae of which he knew so well; and this, coupled with his unceasing energy and sound knowledge of the broad principles of mounted work, gave him full right to be considered the beau ideal of a light Cavalry soldier. Those who have seen him busily scheming for better conditions in barracks, or who have watched him at the head of his men, looking so well his part, can best appreciate the full extent of the loss which we now had to deplore.

Camping for the night at Bushman's Tafel Kop, our regiment was ordered next day to escort a convoy, which we were to find at Kaffir Spruit, on the Standerton road, to Colonel Mackenzie's column at Berginderlyn Bridge. We reached Kaffir Spruit that day, and having met the convoy in the afternoon, took it on on the 27th, the next day, to Colonel MacKenzie, returning to Kaffir Spruit again at nightfall. The rest of the column joined us here, and most of them, together with "A" Squadron of the "18th," were ordered off at once to march during the night and line up near Blauw Kop with General Plumer's columns, cover the whole country between the Standerton blockhouse line and the railway, and during the next two days sweep westwards the country in the triangle formed by the railway and the blockhouses.

The other two squadrons of the "18th" were detailed to bring the column baggage along the road to Standerton. The "drive" was not a great success, as little connection was kept up between the forces, and most of the Boers slipped through; our column, however, captured eight, and the others forty Boers on the south side of the Vaal. Lieut. Archer Shee, of the 19th Hussars, and two Australians were wounded during the second day's work, and as the former was Brigade-Major to the column, his place was filled by Lieut. Dugdale of our regiment, who kept this appointment till the end of the war.

The headquarters of the regiment halted on the night of **February 28th** at Blesbok Spruit, and on March 1st at Leow Spruit, where the column re-united, and moved on next day to Verblyden, a farm seven miles from Standerton.

We managed to get twenty-three remounts from the depôt there, but had to send in thirty sick horses, and we were now unable to mount a considerable number of our men, who had to follow on foot with the wagons.

On **March 3rd, 1902**, our column was ordered to join up with General Plumer's and undertake a night expedition into the Orange River Colony after De Wet, who, harassed by the late successful " drive " in the northern part of that country, was supposed to be now in hiding in the country near Cornelia. We left Verblyden at 3.15 p.m. with 250 men of our regiment and all officers except Captain Wood and Lieut. McClintock. The former remained behind to bring on a light convoy after us, and the latter was left in charge of the dismounted men and others, who were not to join in the night march, but remain near Standerton.

Colonel Marling had rejoined the previous day, and had command of the regiment during the march, but his bad health compelled him to return to sick leave immediately after it was finished.

Passing through Standerton with the other mounted troops of our column, we halted at 4 p.m. under Stander's Kop until nightfall, and were joined there by General Plumer's force. As soon as it was dark the large combined column, totalling altogether nearly 2,000 mounted men, started on its march with the 18th Hussars in advance, reached Roberts' Drift on the Vaal about midnight, and waited there for some two hours till everyone got safely across the river. From the Vaal we went on southward to within a few miles of Cornelia, reaching Venter's Spruit at daybreak, but the Boer commando was nowhere to be seen, only about a dozen of the enemy were met with, whom we fruitlessly pursued for a short distance. At 7 a.m. we halted for an hour, and then, intending to wheel round to the right and retire back to the Vaal, we started again, but had not gone far before we were directed to turn about and move to the east bank of Venter's Spruit, where some Boers were reported; but we could not come up with them, and after another halt at 2 p.m. for an hour, we dragged our weary horses back to Roberts' Drift, which we reached at seven that night after twenty-eight hours in the saddle, with only three short halts thrown in. We must have covered sixty miles of country at least and had nothing to show for it, except one wounded Boer we picked up in a farmhouse we passed by. Our horses were, however, in very hard condition just then, and only five succumbed on the way back, but the other regiments were not so fortunate, and the road was dotted at very short intervals with their dead bodies. At Roberts' Drift we found the light convoy awaiting us, and were able to rest our horses there the next day, and recruit their numbers from the ranks of the Victorian Mounted Infantry, who were returning to Australia on completion of their term of service. We got fifty-eight horses of a very good stamp from them.

CHAPTER XVIII.

"THE COMMENCEMENT OF THE 'DRIVES.'"

March, 1902.

ON **March 7th**, 1902, we crossed the Vaal to Bultfontein on the Orange River Colony side, and left General Plumer and the Victorians behind. A new column was now formed, and this, under Colonel Vialls, was to work with ours and three others, which were under Colonels Damant, Kiers, and Wilson, with the idea of driving the country in an easterly direction towards the Natal border.

A line of blockhouses ran from Vrede to Botha's Pass, and the three columns mentioned were to join up from the right of ours to the north side of this blockhouse line, while Colonel Vialls' was to prolong the line on our left up to the Vaal river, and keep along the Klip River after its junction with the Vaal. The scheme did not promise much success, as the whole north side of the Vaal and the Klip was left unsearched, while at night the line was broken, and only the drifts over streams, which luckily here flowed north and south, were watched. However, it was new country to us, and we looked forward to exploring the former Free State after being so many months in the Transvaal.

On **March 8th** we marched to Groenfontein on the Spruit-onder-drift, to take up our position in the driving line, and next day started off, keeping indifferent connection with the columns on our flanks, and reached Driefontein on the Commando Spruit that night. This was the first proper drive in which we had as yet participated. When the connection was systematically carried out it was a most imposing sight to see the unbroken line of mounted men, fading in the distance into a sinuous wave, advance at a uniform pace over all obstacles, now crossing a hill top, now dipping in a broad donga, preceded by scattered scouts and followed by compact supports at regular intervals. The difficulty of keeping touch, and at the same time of not forsaking the exact limit of country allotted to each regiment, was soon brought home to us; it was easy enough to rule off a strip of the map and to issue orders that our right was to pass over the exact points the line went through, and the next regiment's left was to act in the same manner, but it would have required astronomical instruments to have fixed the exact position of the line at many points where no easily recognised landmarks were at hand. Later on better orders for the guidance of columns in conducting these drives were issued, and they more nearly approached the method in which, years before in India, the regiment had been practised while moving across the country in "reconnoitring or screening" formation.

Our first day's march was unproductive of any good, for, except some semi-wild ponies and a large herd of several hundred blesbok, nothing particular was met with. The ponies we were ordered to destroy, a task which we did not relish at all, while for the blesbok we had no such commiseration, and forty-six fell to an indiscriminate fire we poured into them as they recklessly galloped along our line.

It was dark on the night of **March 9th** when we pulled up for our halt at Commando Spruit, and barely light the next morning when we started on our way again eastward. Before us lay the mountainous country of the north-eastern district of Vrede and the summits of the Gemsbokhoekberg, and once across the spruit we had our work cut out ascending and descending the hill sides, and at the same time endeavouring to keep up communication with the other columns. These mountains of the high veld broke the unending similarity of the usual rolling plains, and, though wild and remotely situated, they were well watered, and contained some fertile farms hidden in the deep cut valleys which furrowed into the mountain sides. The Boers, as was only natural, had slipped round the left flank of Colonel Viall's column, between whom and the Natal railway was a large stretch of unguarded country, covered with the hills of the Versamelberg range, in which many army corps could have escaped unseen. Some of them even came round by the rear of the driving line and attacked the baggage column as it was following with a small escort under Captain Leveson behind us, and five unwary men of the 19th Hussars, left some way in rear, were captured and relieved of most they possessed. The columns swept on nearly up to the edge of the Berg at Botha's Pass, and then the line broke up and rallied.

Our column marched back to look for the baggage, as we had heard that there were some Boers about in rear, but we took the wrong road, and night came on before we discovered that the convoy was all right, and already at Leeuwdam on the Klip River, where we might have awaited it quietly. Only five Boers had been collected by the combined columns, but a good quantity of sheep and cattle were taken on the last day's drive. Volksrust was the next point to be made for, and on **March 12th** we arrived there, crossing the Versemelberg by Alleman's Nek as we had done with General Buller nearly two years' before. All the columns came into the railway line there, and as Volksrust was a fairly civilised place and full of many of the luxuries of civil life, the town no doubt was a little relieved when the thirsty columns continued once more on their march. Having got together the scattered parties of our regiment, including Lieut. Jury and sixty-eight horses and men from Carolina, Lieut. McClintock and the men from Standerton, who had not started on the last trek, and a few others, who had been straying over the country looking for us, we set off again on March 12th for Paardekop, where we arrived on the 14th, halting at Zandspruit on the way.

We had been very aimlessly roving the country side for the past month with no settled occupation, darting here, there, and everywhere across the veld, sometimes acting by ourselves, at others joining in with any set of columns we came across, and for a little while longer we were to pursue the same tactics.

The break up of General Bruce Hamilton's operations at Ermelo and the dispersal of the different columns he had under him, had made the undertaking of a second set of combined movements in the Eastern Transvaal a difficult matter to arrange. The Standerton-Ermelo-Carolina-Wonderfontein line of blockhouses was, however, now completed, and this, with the Constabulary posts from Vaal to Witbank, divided up the country in fairly equal paddocks, so the old columns, and some fresh ones besides, were ordered to collect and form up to drive these enclosures in that systematic manner which now, above all other methods, was to put a finish to this never-ending war. We had at Paardekop 512 men, and of these could only mount 322 in the ranks; seventy to one hundred men were almost always dismounted, beyond the permanently employed men, who engaged in various necessary duties, numbering roughly 100 more. The other regular regiments were as badly off for horses as we were, and in consequence we grudged the drain on the remount depôts the new Yeomanry occasioned, when it left the men we had trained for so long in their legitimate work dismounted for the sake of others we knew could have had little opportunity to gain knowledge of the duties, in which time and experience could almost alone give proficiency.

At 9.45 p.m. on the night of **March 15th** Colonel Wing set out with most of his mounted men, including 250 of our regiment, Lieutenants Bayford and Lyon being left behind to bring on the balance, to surprise some farms in the valley of the Kaalspruit, where it joins the Vaal north-east of Standerton. The farms were empty of all but a decrepid old man, who had already been captured and rejected by many another column, and we returned after destroying them to meet our baggage at Potfontein, where it had arrived from Paardekop on the morning of March 16th *en route* for Blauw Kop. The column was now trekking northward to meet two

The Commencement of the Drives.

other ones under Colonels Parks and Williams, who were marching on Bethel from the Middelburg railway line. Blauw Kop was reached next day, and Morganzan, on the Standerton-Ermelo blockhouse line, the following one, the 18th March.

Here we undertook another night march. Starting from Morganzan at 8.30 p.m., we made a fruitless expedition to Hamelfontein against a man called Tafel and a small commando he had with him, but a fog came up in the early morning and stopped our pursuit just as we had nearly succeeded in surrounding him in a farm house, from which he in consequence escaped. We were thoroughly weary of these night expeditions by now; they had of late been such constant failures, and it was such a strain on both men and horses, with none of the former excitement of a long gallop at the first streak of dawn and the capture of laagers and their occupants, to reward us for our weary march through the never ending night. They were conducted almost always in the same fashion; Kaffir scouts obtained either from friendly natives, their own actual observation, or from spies among the Boers, intelligence that so many of the enemy were encamped on a certain farm, and they communicated it at once to our columns.

The information was kept absolutely secret, and orders were sent round to the different regiments to have ready a certain number of men, generally at an hour between 6 and 8 p.m., and at the time fixed the column would march away in absolute silence into the dark of the night. The Kaffir guides led the way, followed closely by the advanced troops of the leading regiment, and then at a short distance by the remainder of the column, which marched usually on a narrow front and covered in consequence often some miles of road. No smoking was allowed and very little talking, and after an hour or so of this procession through the inky darkness, matters grew very monotonous, and one yearned to stop anywhere, get off, and sleep for ever so short a period. Failing this the men rode along on their horses in a semi-unconscious state, and the latter, some fast walkers, others slow in their paces, lost their places in the ranks, and, pushing forward among the leaders and guides, had to be held back by their rudely awakened riders, or, dropping to the rear, were whipped up by the small party left behind each squadron for that purpose.

The pace was a continual walk, and if the column was a very long one, the rear portion would be engaged the whole night in trotting up to close the gaps which kept forming by the inevitable stretching out of the troops in front. Sometimes the weather was cold, and one had to get off and walk to keep warm, but this could only occasionally be done, as one could not walk as fast as the horses, and moreover every moment was precious, and if once connection was lost the chain we depended on was broken in the darkness. More usually the nights were warm, and we were tormented the whole way by myriads of mosquitos and sand flies, whose only virtue was that they kept us awake. On occasions a halt for ten minutes was called, generally to allow the rear to close up or a spruit to be crossed, and at once every man threw himself off his horse and lay stretched on the ground, in puddles of water or on the dry, wherever he was, and fell into a deep sleep, from which sometimes even the advance of the column as they moved forward failed to arouse him, and the services of the rear party were again in request.

The second, third, and sometimes even the fourth night march on consecutive days were the occasions on which attacks of drowsiness especially overtook us, and it was most wearying work contending with them, especially when constant marches and changes of camp during the day had prevented us getting rest to make up for the lack of it at night.

Just before dawn, if we were near the located laager, we halted, and two portions of the column were instructed to move, the one by the right flank and the other by the left, while the centre waited until the flanks should be deemed to be far enough forward, when a general advance was made and the laager rushed; the main body secured its occupants with the cattle and wagons, whilst the advanced parties continued on in pursuit of those who had escaped. This was the orthodox plan that is to say, but circumstances more often altered these estimable dispositions, and generally, when the locality of the laager was reached, more or less of an undignified scramble took place, and a howling mob of men galloped at it as hard as they could.

We halted for three days at Morgenzan, and were joined there by two squadrons of the 8th Hussars under Colonel Duff. With this reinforcement we set off for Bethel, to join up with Colonels Park and Williams, and also to escort a convoy of provisions to the garrison there. The neighbouring Boers were on the look out for this convoy, but did not expect an escort of such a size, and when they attacked the rearguard, during an outspan we made in the middle of the day, they were rather surprised to see so many of us. We could not spare much time for them, as it was a long march to Bethel, and we had only one day to do it in, as the garrison there were getting very short of food, and anxious for our arrival.

We had left behind us at Morgenzan seventy men and

The Commencement of the Drives.

about forty sick horses, under charge of Lieut. Grigg, while Captain Corbett left us there to go to Standerton on sick leave.

Reaching Bethel on **March 22nd, 1902**, we halted there next day, and on the 24th marched at 2 a.m. to get into line with the columns under Colonels Park and Williams, which had come down from the north by the west side of Bethel. We were to join up with them and drive the country towards Standerton. This was not a very profitable piece of work to set out upon, as we all well knew that the Boers were already behind us, in the Ermelo direction, when we started. However, we lined up with the other two columns, and left Lieutenants Clarke and McClintock, with 120 men, to follow behind as escort to the baggage and convoy. We drove right up to Standerton, but only succeeded in capturing five Boers between us, and our own column got none at all; the only people who saw any were the baggage guard, who were followed up by a few of the enemy for a short distance.

On **March 25th** we halted at Verblydyn farm, about seven miles out of Standerton, and remained there till **March 30th**, collecting horses and men and enjoying a little rest in a very secure position between the blockhouse line and the Vaal River. Here Lieut. Lichtenburg rejoined us, and several officers and non-commissioned officers were given short periods of leave, as we made it a practice from now onwards to give everyone in turn a few days rest from the incessant trekking which the regiment was called upon to perform.

We succeeded in extracting thirty-five horses out of the Standerton Remount Depôt, and received nine more of our old ones from Middelburg, where they had been resting for awhile, and in addition we got a further supply of seventy-three, which once more swelled our numbers to a respectable size.

At 9 a.m. on **March 30th** we marched to Leuwspruit, the first large post on the Ermelo blockhouse line, and waiting there till after dark we set out at 11 p.m. for the valley of the Blesbok Spruit on another fruitless night march. We had not proceeded far on our way when our guide mistook his direction a little and led us very close to the blockhouse line, so close that we could plainly distinguish the dark outline of the little forts for a few seconds as we topped a rise. Our mistake was brought home to us very quickly; volleys, independent, and Maxim fire was opened on us by the watchful occupants of the blockhouses, as, favoured slightly by a fold in the ground, we made an undignified retreat into the darkness of the night and collected our scattered forces for a fresh advance in a better chosen direction. Two men of the 19th Hussars were wounded through this unfortunate mistake.

At daybreak on **March 31st** there was no sign of any Boers, and Colonel Wing, after halting for a while for "breakfast," marched us off to Mooifontein Farm, from where we were to start on a march to Ermelo, in connection with the two columns of Colonels Park and Williams, with our own forming the right of the line. We might have almost as well saved ourselves the trouble of getting into line, for we kept no connection between the columns, and the Boers paid very little attention to us.

On **April 1st** our column marched to Sukkelaar, the 18th Hussars on the left flank, with the exception of Captain Leveson's squadron, which was attached for the day to the 8th Hussars, placed under Colonel Duff's command, and sent to the right flank. Only a few Boers were sighted. Next day, **April 2nd**, we continued our march at 7 a.m. and reached Sprinbokfontein, the regiment changing to the right flank on this occasion. We left Captain Wood to bring on the convoy, which marched in the centre, while the mounted troops were split up into two halves, Colonel Wing accompanying one half and Colonel Duff the other. Captain Wood found two wounded Boers in a farmhouse which he passed with his squadron.

From Sprinbokfontein we went next day, **April 3rd**, to Rietvlei, the regiment taking its turn on the left flank, while Captain Wood's squadron was detached on this occasion to accompany Colonel Duff on the right. From Rietvlei we reached Ermelo on the following day and halted there on the **5th of April**, and on the **6th** our column, together with that of Colonel Park's, marched out of Ermelo and reached Welgelegan, a farm north-east of that town, situated on the Vaal River, close to its source.

Early next morning, **April 7th**, at 4 a.m., in a thick fog, "A" and "B" Squadrons went on to Lake Crissie, and from there to Lake Banagher, where a few Boers were seen. They were too far off to give us any chance of capturing them, so we off-saddled for a short time, and at about 10 a.m. set off on our way to Lake Vryheid, where "C" Squadron, under Captain Leveson, had already preceded us with the convoy. On our way back we sighted a few Boers with a considerable herd of cattle, and we promptly gave chase. The Boers had the legs of us, but the cattle fell an easy prey, and a couple of Dutchman's Kaffirs, whom for a long time we mistook for Boers, were also captured after an exciting chase.

CHAPTER XIX.

"DRIVES IN THE EASTERN TRANSVAAL."

April, 1902.

WE were now right in the middle of the so-called Lake district, a tract of country we had passed over in our march with General French's troops early in 1901; but the Lakes were nothing else but very large pans of inconsiderable depth; they were, however, covered with a great number of wild fowl at this period of the year, and afforded plenty of sport to those who had guns with them.

We had been brought up through this district in order to get into our places in a big drive which was about to take place from the Pretoria-Delagoa Bay railway to the Standerton one, the right flank of the line having the Constabulary posts, which reached from Witbank on the north to Vaal station on the south, to rest on, while the left flank moved along the Carolina-Ermelo-Standerton blockhouse line, which was now quite completed. We had moved in a circuitous manner in order not to alarm any Boers who might be in the pen we were about to drive, and on reaching Carolina it became necessary to move the columns westward to take up their places in the line.

On **April 8th** we had reached Carolina, and on the 9th made a short march to Vaalwater, allowing Colonel Park's column, which was to be on our west flank during the drive, to get ahead of us. On the 10th we reached Kromdrai, on the Klein Oliphant's river, having chased some imaginary Boers, who turned out to be some of Colonel Park's rearguard, on our way.

On **April 11th** we arrived at Diehoek, about fifteen miles south of Middelburg, where we drew up in line, with Colonel Williams' columns on our right and Colonel Spens' on our left, and we faced south for the night. Here the seven columns were connected in one continuous line, and trenches, 150 yards apart, were dug for the men in the advance squadrons to hold.

These drives were henceforth to be conducted in a more workmanlike manner. The columns taking part in them were each given a certain narrow strip of country for which they were to be responsible, and one column was made the directing one by which all the others had to march. Before starting the drive the line was formed, and a certain proportion of each column was detailed for the actual line itself, supported at regular intervals by larger bodies of men.

Usually half a squadron was in the driving line and half in support, while a special escort was detailed to bring on the baggage some way in rear of the general advance.

At night the driving line entrenched itself, some six to eight men forming a post, and trenches were dug about 100 to 200 yards apart, and connected by lines of obstacles usually consisting of wire entanglements, and if time allowed the front was wired up as well.

At early dawn the line moved on, some signal from the directing column, usually the firing of two shots in quick succession from a gun, giving the office to the other columns on the flanks, and instantly a continuous line of mounted men moved slowly across the country to sweep it as they advanced. It was truly an imposing sight when standing on some eminence one watched as far as the eyes could see, the thin black line zigzaging and waving over the immense expanse of the Eastern Transvaal. What must it have been to anyone inside the net! Scattered as the Boers then were, with very little time given them for preconcerted plans, the sight of this endless moving wall must have made them think that at last the game was up.

There would seem no loophole for escape, lines of blockhouses vigilantly guarded on flanks and rear, and an ever approaching, closely connected wave of mounted men in their front, would give very little hope of further success in this great game of hide and seek. But in spite of their difficulties a good many still succeeded in breaking through at one point or another. The great length of line which had to be kept up was a source of increasing anxiety, and the maintenance of the touch was a most difficult matter, for a slight increase of pace at any one point produced a furious gallop not many miles away, and then a gap occurred, and often only with difficulty could the line be once more united.

At these gaps the Boers, could they but know where they were going to occur, might break through, and indeed without the gaps a determined body of men could easily have ridden down the slight opposition the driving line itself could offer, and then escape through the intervals between the supports. Luckily the enemy were ignorant of where these gaps were, and the moral strength the vast driving line itself carried with it deterred them from making, except on rare occasions, attempts to charge through.

So much for the system on which we were now to work, and of which the columns under General Bruce Hamilton were to gain their first experience in the forthcoming drive from Middelburg to Standerton. With reference to our own column, we had been given about six miles of front to cover, and the 19th Hussars and ourselves divided this distance

The Advance Line (18th Hussar Section) near Vlaklaagte on April 14th, 1902.

18th Hussars crossing a Drift.
[See p. 238.]

between us. Along our own extent of front "C" Squadron was placed on the right, "B" in the centre, and "A" on the left. Each squadron occupied the actual "line" with about half its strength, while the remainder was laagered in rear of the centre of its own immediate extent of front, and the headquarters of the regiment camped with the centre squadron. The advanced line occupied trenches, which were dug before dark some 150 yards apart, and as far as possible the intervening spaces were blocked with obstacles.

At 6.30 a.m. on the morning of **April 12th,** having extended the driving line so that the men were about ten to twenty yards apart, we set off on our journey southward. At first we had great difficulty in keeping the line intact, as the morning was misty, but later on it became easier to do so, and we arrived at the line of the Groot Oliphant's River about 4 p.m., with the men in our immediate neighbourhood linked up in as good a line as could be expected.

Some Boers had been sighted towards the close of the day's drive, but they had all kept a long way ahead, and it was not our policy to split up any of our force to pursue them. Before sundown we had again entrenched ourselves and held a strong position, which it was improbable the Boers would choose to attempt to break through. There was very little firing during the night, though the slightest movement in front provoked it, and, once started, the whole line would take it up and often spend hours at it before they became convinced that there was no cause for alarm. And this was particularly the case if the night was a dark one or foggy.

Next morning, **April 13th,** we continued our drive in the same order as before, starting at 7 a.m., and marching in heavy rain till about 2 p.m., when we reached a farm called Elandsfontein, with the line in excellent order, and took up our position as before for the night. It turned foggy after dark and difficult to see more than a few yards to the front, and in consequence some heavy shooting went on, but it did not appear that there were any considerable number of the enemy in our immediate neighbourhood, although a few shots were fired at us at one period of the night.

Owing to the thick fog we could not make a start next morning, **April 14th,** till 7 a.m., which was unfortunate, as we had a very long way to travel, and it was 5.30 p.m. before we reached our destination, Vlaklaagte, on the Natal railway line, and which also marked the finish of the drive. Our own share of the spoils was not a large one, as we only succeeded in capturing two Boers, but Colonel Spens' column and the Ermelo blockhouse line did better, and we found that we had in the combined operations collected 136 Boers, killed one and wounded another. Horses and men were quite beat on the termination of the day, and everyone slept soundly that night by the little station on the Natal railway line.

We halted at Vlaklaagte next day, **April 15th**, and were rejoined by Colonel Marling, who had recovered sufficiently to take over the regiment from Major Pollok, who had commanded it in his absence.

Next day, **April 16th**, we marched to Zandbaaken, on the Constabulary line of posts which ran from Val Station to Witbank; it was only a short march, and we did not start till nearly 3 p.m., and arrived at our destination at dusk. The plan of campaign which was now to be put into execution consisted in driving the country from the Natal line northward, taking in this time the tract of country which lay west of the Constabulary posts, bordered by that line on the east and the Elandsfontein-Pretoria railway on the west. Two extra columns had come from Springs to help at the western end of the line, and three of the original columns of General Bruce Hamilton's were despatched along the Constabulary posts to fill up the many large gaps there were between them. This Constabulary line was not connected up like the blockhouse ones with continuous wire fences, and at night it was a very easy matter for the Boers to slip through.

It fell to our lot to form part of this flanking line to the general advance, and, as we had the permanent posts to aid us, a much larger extent of front was given to each regiment to watch. We were the rear regiment of the column which had this chain of posts to guard, and we placed the squadrons in the following order from the south :—" C " in rear, then " B," then " A," the latter reaching as far north as Langverwacht, where the next regiment took up the line.

Nothing of moment occurred during the night, and the following morning, **April 18th**, at 6.30 a.m., we moved farther along the Constabulary Posts, and at evening had got the leading squadron as far as Uitkyk, with the others about $2\tfrac{3}{4}$ miles in rear respectively. The headquarters of the regiment were at Dieplaagte, near the S.A.C. Headquarters, and in this position another uneventful night was spent.

On **April 19th** we pushed on " A " Squadron to Roodebloom and " C " to Uitkyk, and halted again for the night, which, being a foggy one, produced a lot of intermittent firing, chiefly at an imaginary enemy. Our rear squadron at night kept touch with the right flank of the driving line, and there was a nasty angle between them, which had to be well rounded off in selecting the posts for the night positions. Next morning we marched on to Steenkool Spruit, while the driving line swept past us up to the Middelburg railway, only to find that there had been a gap on the left, and in consequence an escape of the greater number of Boers who were at one time inside the net. The tract of country lying between Springs and Pretoria had not been properly driven, and there the Boers had quietly slipped round to safety and gained the south of the advancing columns. Our total captures only comprised eight Boers, and we were very downhearted at the ill-success of our exertions, for the work was a very harassing one, and we had little or no rest day and night while the actual drive was in progress.

Apparently Lord Kitchener was not well pleased either with our want of success, and we were promtly ordered to turn about and drive the same extent of country back again up to the Natal line. So after a day's halt at Nauwpoort, a farm six miles south of Witbank, to allow the supply column to go into the line and fill up, we retraced our steps on the **22nd April** by Steenkool's Spruit to Boselkrantz, near Vaalkop, making a march of twenty miles so as to get well ahead of the driving line when they should start on the morrow. We had been joined by half of the 8th Hussars in the morning.

Next day, at 6 a.m., **April 23rd**, we all marched eastward to remove the Bethel garrison. It was no sinecure holding such an isolated post as theirs, cut off as they were for weeks together from any intercourse with the outside world.

The garrison was well packed up, and ready to accompany us back to the Constabulary line at 6 a.m. next morning, **April 24th**, and making a long march of twenty-four miles we reached Wildebeestefontein towards evening, after outspanning for a short time at Trichardsfontein in the middle of the day. The drive south was to have commenced next day, and we were originally intended to hold the S.A.C. line on the night of the 25th, but for some reason it was put off till the following day, a fact we appreciated, as the weather was very wet and misty.

On the 24th we had lost Private Doherty on our march to Wildebeestefontein, but he turned up next day when we were halted there.

On **April 26th** we started off south, keeping well ahead of the driving line, which had now started on its way from the northern railway. We lined the Constabulary posts that night from Langverwacht to Vaalbank, nearly the same position as we had occupied on the night of the 17th, and we found our old trenches very useful, and had little or no digging to do in consequence. No Boers appeared, however, and on the next day we did not see any either. We had, in fact, an uneventful march to Val Station, which we reached about 3 p.m. on the afternoon of April 26th, and we learnt there that the Boers, in the country our columns had been driving, had crossed the railway line near Heidelburg, and got into the district to the south.

CHAPTER XX.

"DRIVES IN THE FREE STATE."

April—May, 1902.

WE halted at Val Station from the **26th April** to the **2nd** of **May, 1902**, an almost unprecedented respite from the continuous trekking of which we had become so heartily weary. Almost the entire time since May, 1900, when we left Ladysmith behind us for good, had seen us plodding over miles and miles of this everlasting veld, wondering what the real feelings of the wandering Jew were and if ours at all resembled his, until at last we almost grew resigned to our system of perpetual motion, and felt quite strange at its cessation.

For some time back we had heard a great deal about peace negotiations whenever we came anywhere near a railway, but so often before had we been deluded into prospects of a termination of our monotonous existence, that we really had paid, up till now, very little attention to the various reports and rumours with which we were furnished by the people on the lines of communication. We thought that they lived only for the arrival of the daily mail train and the crop of anecdotes which came along with it, and we usually politely swallowed their information and went our way in unbelief. Now, however, matters had progressed to such an advanced stage that we could not help our spirits rising again at the prospect of peace, a prospect now a more tangible one than it had ever appeared before. The peace delegates were out with the various commandos, and were to meet together again at Vereeniging on the 15th of May to discuss what success they had met with. It is hard to describe our feelings for the next few weeks while the issue of those negotiations hung in the balance, but I think that, though few of us openly expressed our fervent wishes for a reconciliation,, we never at any time during the succeeding days had them very far away from our hearts.

During our stay at Val Station we succeeded in collecting seventy fresh horses from the Standerton remount depôt, and by the "states" of the regiment at this period of the war it will be seen that hardly ever had we been so strongly mounted, while at the same time our horses were now in very excellent condition and our men very highly trained.

Besides the Standerton horses we got a few from Middelburg as well, and we also sent all our spare men, those we were unable to procure horses for, to Standerton to await

Officers of the Regiment who saw the beginning and end of the War.

Troop Horses that went through the whole Campaign.

remounts. For this duty Lieut. Grigg, Squadron Sergeant-Major Power, and seventy men were taken from our headquarters at Val Station, and Lieut. King and seventy men, who had lately arrived at Middelburg from England, were despatched there as well. Captain Wood was detailed to take charge of the whole detachment on his return from leave.

At 1.30 p.m. on **May 2nd**, having received orders to get under weigh again, we marched out of Val Station on what was to be our last " trek " against our friends the enemy. Orders for this move had come very suddenly, and in consequence a good number of both officers and men, who were away on short leave to Standerton, got left behind, and a few of them only managed to catch us up at Goodehoep, near Greylingstad, where we encamped for the night.

The plan of campaign for our present operations was to be a " drive " from the Standerton-Elandsfontein railway to the Heilbron-Frankfort blockhouse line, and on to the Kroonstadt-Lindley one from there. The following columns were to take part in it:—Rimington's, Lawley's, Nixon's, Barrett's, Spens', Mackenzie's, Duff's, and Allenby's, and they were to be in that order from the right. Our column, Colonel Duff's that is to say, as that officer now had command in place of Colonel Wing (who had not yet recovered from an accident he had received), had about eight miles of front to cover, of which the 18th Hussars took the four miles on the right.

We started off in a thick fog early on the morning of **May 3rd**, long before the line could be put into anything like cohesion, and our column was at the commencement left a considerable distance in rear, as we were uncertain whether or not a start would be made in the mist. But most of the columns did start, so we had to make up considerable leeway for the first ten miles, and we did not completely gain our proper forward position in the line till we reached Barnard's Kop, which had previously been agreed upon as our first halting place. From there onwards to the Vaal River we kept a very steady unbroken line, and slowly crossed the great stretch of country we had to cover. It was late when we reached the river, and our position for the night lay some four miles to the south of it. The river was only fordable at the drifts, which were, in places, some miles apart, and the line in consequence got very much broken up, and it was too late that night to hope to reform it properly. Our column took up a position as well as it could on the ground which had been assigned to it for the night, but communication with the other columns was utterly impossible, as they had disappeared, we could not tell where, in the darkness.

Our regiment occupied a long line of front just south of the Vaal River, where each section halted on its own ground, kept its horses with it, and formed part of a continuous chain of "march outposts." The night was a fairly cold one, and we had no kit or food of any sort except what we had brought on our horses, for our baggage had to turn off to the eastward to cross the Vaal River by a good ford there was at Villiersdorp, the nearest town in that part of the country. At it was midnight almost before they got there and crossed the river, it was quite impossible to hope for any food supplies from them.

Early on the morning of **May 4th** we set off again on our march southward to the Heilbron-Frankfort blockhouse line, but again it was foggy, and in our endeavours to gain touch with Colonel Mackenzie's column on our right, we lost a lot of time, and were some way behind the general line of advance when the fog lifted and showed us the true state of affairs. We then moved on quicker and gained our lost distance, getting touch with the columns on our right and left.

To the eastward there was no line of blockhouses running north and south, and to endeavour to prevent the Boers slipping out to that flank, Colonel Allenby's column had been sent on well ahead of the left of the line to form an advanced flank. The line itself covered a hundred miles of country, so it was only possible for those Boers within a day's ride of the left flank to attempt to escape that way, even supposing they knew the general disposition of our forces when we started.

Very few Boers had, however, been sighted so far, but along the Vaal and the Wilge valleys a few stray ones were picked up, and no doubt some slipped through the meshes of our net when opportunities occurred. Our regiment caught five Boers and ten horses while crossing the Wilge River, and the 19th Hussars also caught five more soon afterwards. From the Wilge River onwards we kept the line intact, and all day continued our way over the great rolling stretches of country which had consisted of mealy fields before the war, and were, on that account, very bad to ride over.

Hour after hour we plodded on till we arrived at the blockhouse line at nightfall. From many miles away we could see the little tin roofs of the circular forts glittering in the sunlight, and, though we kept steadily on, the intervening distance did not for a long time seem to grow very perceptibly less, for both ourselves and our horses were tired and hungry. However, once at the blockhouses our troubles were practically over; we telephoned up the line to find the best places to halt for the night, where we could get some food for our men and forage for our horses, and were told to go to a place called Krom Spruit, where there was a headquarters' camp of one of the regiments holding this line of communications. There we were hospitably entertained by the owners of the blockhouses, who provided us with food for ourselves and horses, and lent us a few blankets to keep out the cold, which by now had increased considerably at night. The ground was hard and stony, but after our long hungry day we very soon forgot everything in a hearty sleep. We learnt too before we did so that the combined columns had succeeded in capturing a total of eighty-six Boers.

About 1.30 p.m. next day (**May 5th**) our baggage reached us from Frankfort, where it had marched to from Villiersdorp on the preceding day. Very little time was given the mules to rest in, for at 3 p.m. we were off again to take up a fresh position for the continuance of the drive on the morrow to the Kronstad-Lindley line. Only our own regiment had halted at Krom Spruit, as the others would have had to come out of their way to do so, and each regiment of the column now marched to its own particular spot for the combined operations of the next day.

Again it was necessary to provide for the proper blocking of the country to the eastward of the advancing columns, for there was no line of blockhouse there, and to do this successfully a chain of stationary mounted troops was to be established along the Liebenberg Vlei, a river which ran in a deep channel from south to north across that part of the country. In order to deceive the Boers the troops of General Lock Elliot's columns, who were given that line and the country between Lindley and the Liebenberg Vlei to watch, ostensibly set off on a night march on May 5th in a southerly direction from Lindley, where they were encamped, and when they had proceeded a short distance on their way they wheeled about, and then marched in a north-easterly direction in order to gain the different blocking positions they were really intended to take up.

The position of our regiment on the night of the **5th May** was close by Jackal's Kop, some four miles south-west of Krom Spruit, and we halted there with each squadron ready to move off to its allotted ground in the morning, "A" on the right, "B" in the centre, and "C" on the left of the line.

At 5.30 a.m. next morning, **May 6th**, we started off in hot haste, as Mackenzie's column on our right had gone on before we had, and it was not till we had covered some ten miles at a fast pace that we were able to make good our part of the line. We could see that there were a few Boers ahead of us when we had our usual half-hour halt at 10.30 a.m. in the neighbourhood of Eland's Kop, but they were apparently retiring as we advanced.

The drive then went on steadily till about 3 p.m. in the afternoon, the interest increasing as we approached nearer to our destination, which, for our column, was a point about ten miles east of Lindley, for a considerable number of Boers had now collected in our front, and there was a good deal of firing going on along the stopping line, distinctly audible from where we were. At this period of the day we heard from our right that Colonel Mackenzie's column had been charged by about 300 Boers, and that most of them had broken through the line, and "A" Squadron, who were next to Mackenzie, were sent off to render what help they could.

It transpired that nearly a thousand Boers had collected in front of us, and that they had broken into two parties, one marching east to cross the Liebenberg Vlei, and the other south-east to cross our positions between Lindley and that river, as they both thought those tracts of country unoccupied. Those who made for the Liebenberg Vlei contrived, through bad management on the part of the blocking line, to get across the river and away with very little loss, but the other party ran their heads into a very well watched line of defence, and they suffered very considerable loss before they could extricate themselves.

Seeing that they could not pass in that direction, and knowing that our line of columns was close on their heels, they were now heavily pressed to determine what course to pursue. The bolder among them wished to charge our line, but a good many were not so keen about it, and in the end it resulted, as we have already seen, in some 300 attacking Colonel Mackenzie, whilst the balance, about 130, remained in a farmhouse and surrendered to that officer when he was able to continue his march.

The day's work was now practically over, for we were close against the blocking line, and soon after 4 p.m. we rallied our squadrons and marched off to Groenvallei, a farm six miles from Lindley, where arrangements had been made for rationing all the columns at our end of the line, for our own transport had not accompanied us, but had gone to Frankfort to stay there till we should return. Again it was nearly dark before we got our camp fixed up and learnt the varied experiences of the day. No doubt we had done the Boers considerable damage, eleven killed and 221 captured, some of whom were wounded, representing the total; and the hard knock they had met with—both those who attempted to cross the blocking line and those who charged Mackenzie's column—must to a certain extent have shattered their morale. It required a great deal of courage, there is little doubt, for them to decide on such bold tactics, and though they were by no means lacking in nerve, yet the constant drain on their

Drives in the Free State. 241

resources these hazardous methods entailed would ere long deprive them of their gallant leaders, whose daring was necessary for the accomplishment of the task.

During our day's march, the longest, I think, we had ever had at this class of work, it was thirty-five miles in a straight line, many of our horses and nearly all the pack animals we had with us had fallen a good deal behind. Throughout the night the stragglers kept dropping in, some of whom had been picked up by the Boers *en route* and relieved of most of their valuables, and by morning only four men of "A" Squadron were still deficient.

The next day, **May 7th**, we halted at Groenvallei, and gave our horses a much needed rest, while we gathered from the neighbouring troops the different events of the late "drive." There were many tales to tell, for it had been quite an exciting time whilst it lasted, and we came to the conclusion that there were still many Boers in this part of the country, and that they had not been harassed to anything like the extent they had been in the Eastern Transvaal, which was for so long our own particular theatre of war.

Our halt was of the briefest duration, for on the 8th we received orders to march at 1.30 p.m. to Geelpan, in company with the 8th and 19th Hussars, so as to get into position for a drive to the Heilbron-Lindley line to catch the Boers who had broken back. Half-way there Major Pollok and "A" Squadron were ordered to retrace their steps, in order to escort a convoy we had just met back to Groenvallei, and they were to go straight to their position in the driving line after they had done so. The 8th and 19th Hussars left us at Geelpan and went on to Damspruit to extend the line to the eastward, and our own regiment turned north to take up its position for the morrow. We were now close to the Brandwater basin, and could see the lofty mountains of the range which bordered Basutoland, glittering with its snowcapped peaks to the southward. It looked a difficult country to fight in, and so the columns in that district said they had very recently found it to be.

At 5.30 a.m. on **May 9th** we started back in a very ragged line on our northward drive. Mackenzie on our left we could not get touch with for many miles, and only two squadrons of the 19th Hussars joined up with us on the right; the rest, with the whole of the 8th Hussars, went off into space, and it was only by accident we ever discovered them again.

It took us some time, too, to find Major Pollok and "A" Squadron, who were keeping touch with Colonel Mackenzie's column on the left. We traversed nearly the same ground we had marched over on May 6th, but we made little progress

R

up to Eland's Kop, which we reached at 10.30 a.m. for the usual halt. Here we managed to join up with Colonel Mackenzie, but the 8th Hussars were still nowhere to be seen, and it was evident too that we should never reach our destination before nightfall. Later in the day we came across four men posted on rocky ground which lay across our front, and behind them a considerable number had taken up a position on a lofty hill. Boers we thought they must be, and this conclusion was strengthened by the fact that the first ones we saw opened fire on our scouts as they approached, so we proceeded to attack them, and had wounded one of the four and one of their horses and had captured the remainder before we discovered that they were the missing 8th Hussars, who had mistaken their road, advanced right across our front, and then halted to have a look round. Their main party narrowly missed being assailed by our united columns.

By nightfall we had only reached a point about four miles north of Klipfontein, and we halted there till next day, still some eight miles short of the blockhouse line. Our column had seen no sign of any of the enemy during the day, but it was reported that about 200 of them had slipped through one of the many gaps in the line. At 6 a.m. on **May 10th** we marched in, cold and hungry, to Deelfontein, close to Frankfort, on the blockhouse line, and there had a good meal and a general clean up, as we found our baggage awaiting us in a ready made camp, which was a luxury we were not very often accustomed to.

The Regiment *en route* to Durban and England.

The Regiment leaving Durban for England.

LIEUT.-COLONEL P. S. MARLING, V.C., ACTING ADJUTANT MAJOR C. BURNETT, REGL. SERGT.-MAJOR SIMMONDS, AND N. C. OFFICERS OF THE REGIMENT who were present at the conclusion of the War.

CHAPTER XXI.
"PEACE."
May, 1902.

AT Deelfontein we halted till the **12th May**, our one engrossing topic of conversation being the peace negotiations, which now appeared even to the most sceptical of us, to have assumed a very favourable form. In fact we learnt that nearly, if not quite all, the commandos had sent, or were sending, representatives to the Vereeniging conference, at which the terms of peace were to be discussed.

It was with light hearts and a very contemptuous disregard for any small discomforts, which might await us on our further march northward to Greylingstad, that we set out from Deelfontein on **May 12th** to march along the Wilge River, with orders to act only against the men of Ross' commando; for it was believed, wrongly however, that that warrior had set his face against any peace terms and had refused to come in. For everyone else an armistice had been proclaimed.

We had not gone far before we became mixed up with a few straggling Boers, and we commenced to attack them. They were very indignant, and sent in a white flag to ask why we were not abiding by the armistice. We told them why, and they promptly informed us that Ross had left for Vereeniging two days ago, and they demanded back their sheep which we had driven off. A wire to Lord Kitchener satisfied us that we had been rightly informed, and we were ordered to cease fighting and hand back the sheep. The first we did readily enough, but it was beyond our power to do the second, as they were most of them already in the stew pot.

We camped that night, **May 13th**, at Middlebult, and marched next day to Zandfontein on the north bank of the Vaal River, and from there by two easy stages to Greylingstad, halting at Vlakfontein *en route*. It was capital fun just marching in perfect peace through the country; we wandered miles beyond the flank guards, shooting all manner of game in a district particularly well stocked with it, we felt suddenly that a heavy responsibility had been taken off our shoulders, and the world seemed to have opened again before us, wearing a different aspect to that very monotonous, yet highly uncertain one, it had worn for so long.

The news at Greylingstad was the same as we had gathered at Frankfort. The peace conference was on and that was all, so we settled ourselves down to a quiet peaceful

time, till further developments should take place. In the
meantime many officers and men were sent on leave to make
the most of the rest which was given us. We sent some
forty horses, used up by the recent " drive," into Standerton,
and got thirty-three from there in their places. The four
missing men rejoined us too. One of them had been captured
by the enemy, but the others had succeeded in finding their
way back unmolested. From the **16th May** onwards we led
a peaceful existence, day followed day with nothing eventful
to mark its progress, and yet no one complained of the
monotony.

June 1st was a Sunday, and Sundays in South Africa had
differed very little from ordinary days for the past three
years, and we did not think, when we rose for our day's work,
that this would be a very memorable one in our lives.
But we were soon to hear the news that made it so. At 8
a.m. on that morning Colonel Wing sent round a telegram
he had just received from Lord Kitchener to say that peace
had been signed late the previous night at Pretoria. There
was peace once more in South Africa, and what this meant
to those of us at Greylingstad that Sunday morning we can
never really find words to express.

There was little outward enthusiasm shown on the receipt
of the news, but nothing can describe our feelings when the
publication of this momentous telegram was once made
known. Many thoughts crowded through our brain. We
were relieved at last from the physical toil we had had so long
to undergo. We were relieved too from that ceaseless
anxiety which naturally attached itself to those who held
positions of responsibility. We had won our fight, of that
there could be no doubt, and the odds, though in our favour
at the end, had likewise been against us at the start. We
could not help, too, sympathising, some of us at all events,
with our conquered foes, very many of whom had won our
respect, and who had invariably fought so well and shown
such dogged determination.

Above all though, I think that, to the 18th Hussars in
particular, the most vivid feeling which ran through their
hearts was that the regiment had, in defeat and victory, in
sickness and good health, in varied country and under many
leaders, ever upheld its old traditions, and emerged from its
struggles with a complement of officers and men of whom
anything could be asked, and, if within human accomplishment, it would be fulfilled; that the regiment, too, was one
whom commanders asked for and reckoned as a valuable
addition to their columns. And, in spite of our toil and discomforts, we thanked God that this should be our reward for
Three Years' War in South Africa.

APPENDIX A.

Extract from the diary of an Officer, taken prisoner on October 20th, 1899, describing his captivity as a prisoner of war in Pretoria.

IT was originally my intention to write in the form of a diary a daily account of my personal experiences during the war. For a title " With Buller to Pretoria " might have done well, but circumstances have caused me to alter my plans as well as the title, and now my feeble attempt at recording the life of a prisoner in the hands of the Boers must henceforth go by the title of " To Pretoria without Buller."

To try and render a cheerful or even interesting account of a period devoid of all pleasure or excitement is no easy task, and beyond my faculties. Let therefore the preface to the following be taken as a humble apology.

When I first took up my residence in the Staats Model School I was one out of about fifty officers confined within its precincts. In four months our numbers had swelled to over a hundred, and " the cry is still they come." As each batch of prisoners arrives our hope of an exchange receives a rude shock. Besides, the harrowing, depressing accounts of defeat and disaster brought in by fresh arrivals are not calculated to relieve our drooping spirits. Naturally we hear the worst side; each tells his own little tale of woe, what actually came under his notice, and, naturally too, the only account he can possibly give.

We meet all types. There is the cheerful prisoner who says things are going swimmingly for us, the doleful one who predicts the downfall of the British Empire. Then we have the prisoner who knows nothing, and the one who professes to know all that is going on; all are mobbed, as they enter our prison gates, for news, which promptly is repeated with numerous embroideries. Our criticisms are then aroused, and in measure they are doubtless severe, but this excess is perhaps excusable, as we bitterly feel our present situation. Could we but have one short period of our lives to act again, now that we have thoroughly rehearsed it, we would allow no such combination of circumstances to again take place, as those which landed us, in some cases so easily, in the Staats Model School at Pretoria.

The Model School is a big stone building situated in the heart of Pretoria. It consists of a number of class rooms and a gymnasium. In the former we sleep, about nine to a room, and in the gymnasium we stretch our limbs. We have made the largest class room our dining room. In front and behind there is a verandah, or stoep as they call it in this country, and in which we sit and watch the people of Pretoria pass by.

Between the verandah and the railings, which separate us from the road, there is a ten foot pathway, which we use in our daily walks round and round the building. Nine times round, we have calculated, constitute a mile. Behind we have a small compound, or plot of ground, which is choked up by the presence of Zarps' tents and those of the soldier servants, our two tin bath rooms and cook house. The force of Zarps which guard us is thirty strong; three are posted in front of the building, three behind, and two on the left, for we are situated at the corner of a road. Our right is flanked by Burke's hospital, from which we are separated by a wall of iron sheeting. Ropes are stretched across the road to prevent carriages or horsemen from passing, whilst those on foot are made to keep to the other side of the road.

We get exercise in various ways. A gymnastic class is very energetic of a morning; many, however, content themselves with walking round and round, and they must seem to passers-by to very much resemble lunatics at exercise. A big unoccupied room serves as a fives court, and fives is a grand game to keep oneself fit. We find it such hot work that a very light attire, consisting merely of a towel round our loins, is our costume for the game.

We breakfast at 8.30 a.m., lunch at 1 p.m., tea at 4.30 p.m., and dine at 7 p.m. The intervals between meals are taken up in reading, writing, card playing, chess, or taking some form of exercise. But often we lean up against the railings of our prison and watch the passers-by, whom we have got to know quite well by sight, and whom we have christened with suitable names.

There is "Iris," a sweetly charming young fairy, who seldom fails to cast a hasty roguish glance as she sails by, and whose sweet smiles have won her the admiration, as well as played havoc with the hearts of many susceptible prisoners. A big, fine, strapping lady, much bedecked, and whose complexion gives rise to a soupçon of artificial colouring, treats us to a rather haughty stare; she we called the "Gendarme." "Marceline," the neat little dressmaker, trips across the road, displaying a dainty little foot and ankle, and whose gathered up skirt insinuate lace and frills. "Haut Ecole," an amazon of vast dimensions in trailing habit and top hat on a long-suffering, raw-boned beast, causes us a little merriment as she bumps round the corner. "Twee," a pretty little fair-haired girl, with fresh rosy cheeks, followed by her smartly trimmed poodle; "Trilby," "Annie," and "Julu," the nurses from next door; "John Bright," and many more whose familiar faces have helped to while away the time in prison.

By 11 p.m. most of the establishment has retired to bed. We have elected a committee to superintend the running of our mess. They receive our orders, and almost anything we wish to buy is procurable in the town, but at treble its proper price. Our gaoler takes the orders, and in the capacity of middleman makes his little bit. As we are supplied by the S.A.R., free gratis, with only one tin of bully beef, a loaf of bread, besides potatoes, tea, coffee, sugar, and salt per man per diem, and as this meagre fare is insufficient, we augment the diet by purchasing meat and vegetables, etc. Our rate of messing varies from 2s. 4d. to 3s. a day.

Every Sunday divine service is held by the Rev. Hoffmeyr, a clergyman of the Dutch Reformed Church, whose home is near Capetown. He was taken prisoner by the Boers for political reasons, and kept confined in Zeerust jail for over three weeks. He has good cause to hate the Boers, in whose hands he had been illegally detained since October 15th, 1899. Mr. Hoffmeyr is a favourite of everyone of us; he likes to look on the bright side of things, and does his best to cheer us up. He is an ardent sympathiser of the British cause, and a most loyal subject of Her Majesty's. He is a good preacher and possesses a fine strong voice, which quite smothers the effect of the harmonium.

We can join the town library by paying a subscription of 15s., half of which is on deposit, and we become entitled for one book at a time for three months. A Kaffir officiates as cook, and although no great chef, he does his best, but is handicapped by the lack of necessary ingredients which we cannot afford to provide him with. We are teetotallers, but not from choice, and water is our sole beverage. There are times when something stronger would be vastly appreciated.

A word concerning our jailer, Mr. Opperman, and his assistant, Dr. Gunning. The former is the typical low class Boer official, ignorant, narrow-minded, and indolent. Dr. Gunning is of a different stamp altogether. He is a Hollander, a harmless individual, and really ready to oblige. But he is as innocent as an unborn lamb, and quite believes the atrocities he has told him. He fills a fairly lucrative post in Pretoria, and, in order to save his own skin, must appear Pro-Boer, but, if truth were known, I am inclined to think he is not the rabid Boer sympathiser he would have us believe. He is fully conscious he lives in a land of deceit, where each suspects his neighbour, and where the actions of all citizens are closely watched. No wonder therefore he must be ever on his guard whilst this espionage is systematically carried out.

Dr. Gunning is in charge of a museum, which I should say chiefly contained rubbish, and he is also the director of the Zoological Gardens. Some time ago he got into serious hot water by imprudently accepting a lion Mr. Rhodes sent him. This was an offence which took a deal of forgiving.

Although the news to be found in the newspapers is scanty and unreliable, yet we should like occasionally to peruse the columns of these local rags. Why we are not allowed to do so beats all comprehension! Our fate is to be kept in utter ignorance of the doings beyond our prison walls! However, an occasional *Standard and Diggers' News* or *Volkstem* is smuggled in to us by some more friendly disposed person.

Among this community of ours are some engaged in literary productions; we have a playwriter and a poet, historians by the score and of varied merits, whilst the walls of several rooms testify to the presence of no mean artists and caricaturists. Great excitement is caused by the advent of letters. Batches of them occasionally arrive, but as the censors do not hurry themselves, it is a question of days, weeks, and sometimes months before they reach us. All English newspapers sent us, whether illustrated or otherwise, are kept by the S.A.R. authorities; none reach our prison, where they would be so appreciated. This is indeed a country of deceit and falsehood.

You have to be shut up as we are to understand the awful depression which bad news occasions. Rumours of it are most disquieting. Our reverses at Stormberg and Colenso were trying times, and it was maddening to watch the Boers rejoice over these victories. How anxiously we followed General Buller's movements. Would he ever get to Ladysmith? Would he again recross the Tugela? These were questions we anxiously discussed. Then came the Spion Kop disaster; matters looked desperate and almost hopeless, but, in spite of it all, we pinned our faith to Buller and to British pluck and determination.

The Boers themselves were cocksure we should never relieve Ladysmith. The newspapers talked of it as the "doomed city," and big head lines announced the last hour had struck. The time of the Platrand fight was the worst we experienced. It was actually given out Ladysmith had fallen, and the excitement in Pretoria was intense.

Appendix A.

Over the way there lives an English family, the Cullingworths, to whose kindness we are deeply indebted. After a time we opened up communication with them, for it was quite evident they were strong sympathisers. In spite of the very great risk they ran, for were it known I dread to think of the consequences, the two daughters signal over to us the true and latest news which they get from the "dogman." The latter is also an Englishman, and a never to be forgotten benefactor. He is employed as a superintendent in the Government Telegraph Office, and, consequently, becomes acquainted with true and reliable news before anyone else. We call him the "Dogman" owing to his being generally accompanied by a fine St. Bernard. He it is who taught the girls over the way the "morse code." They regularly, every morning, signal over to us from the hall of their bungalow the latest news. It is very risky work, but they are so clever at it, and post their little brother and sister to keep watch outside, and to let them know should anyone be approaching the house, or should the Zarp on sentry close by leave his post, to stroll down the road towards the house. Whenever anyone passes the house they are thus warned in time to stop signalling, and when once more the coast is clear they start off again with the message they have to send. From the gymnasium we are able, through the window, to read the message. So now we are posted up with news two or three days ahead of the newspapers themselves!

All telegrams from the seat of war are first sent to Kruger, which, after they have gone through a process of doctoring at his hands, are dished up in as palatable a form as the cunning old man thinks judicious for the eyes of his people to see. This is often a hard job; it is not easy to turn a complete defeat into a skirmish of no significance, still I have seen this repeatedly done with remarkable ingenuity.

Of course the farce cannot be kept up long, and the truth gradually leaks out, and even the *Volkstem,* in a half-hearted way, finds itself obliged to own up. It was long after Kimberley was relieved that the news was published. It was denied at first, as was also Cronje's surrender, and when the latter information was made public every effort was made to minimise the importance of our victory. Cronje, the papers had said, had surrendered with 2,000 men after having inflicted terrible losses on the enemy! They cunningly withheld the real facts for days.

The Boers are the most gullible people imaginable. You have but to pick up the *Standard and Diggers' News* or the *Volkstem* any day to understand the ignorant class of people these vile rags have to cater for. It is inconceivable how, in this nineteenth century, so unreasoning and ignorant a race of white people exists. All the ridiculous nonsense printed finds ready believers, the shameful stories of British cruelty and injustice, and the most diabolical deed of horror, supposed to have been committed by our soldiers, find credence.

On the **16th March, 1900,** our long threatened removal from the Staats Model School was accomplished. The latter place was required as a hospital for wounded Boers. It was not all to our taste being ejected from our quarters, and we had a crude suspicion our new ones would compare unfavourably with the old. So it proved. After our breakfast our belongings were carried off to the building outside Pretoria especially built for our reception. We followed in hired carriages, escorted by the Hollander commando recently returned from the front. Many people turned out to see us " trek," and more than one English sympathiser mingled in that crowd. Our friends over the way waved us a farewell, and by their audacious display of open friendship attracted the attention of the Zarps. These latter were furious and quite unable to conceal their indignation, but had they seen the red, white, and blue ribbons and rosettes the girls displayed when their backs were turned their wrath would have been tenfold greater.

We were not impressed with our new abode. Though we had not certainly expected to find a comfortable or inviting country residence, we had still little anticipated being lodged in a tin shed fit for cattle only. A big tin building, whitewashed on the outside, a veritable whitened sepulchre, containing a dormitory eighty-five yards long, in which all of us try to sleep, and a room with four long deal tables and forms, in which we take our meals. Out of the eating room one steps into a small kitchen on one side and a pantry on the other. The flooring consists of red sand, over a part of which a narrow strip of oilcloth is stretched. The ventilation for 150 people is quite inadequate. In cold weather it will be like a vault. Windows are small, few, and placed high up out of reach. Five bathrooms are situated at the western end of the sleeping room. The whole interior of the shed is illuminated by electric light, which is switched off at 10 p.m., when we have to resort to candles.

Outside a portion of the veld is at our disposal to wander about in, but it is not a big space. There are no trees to shelter us from the sun's rays and no verandah to offer shade. We have more room out of doors than we had at the school; it is also healthier, and the air we breathe is purer. Barbed wire entanglements surround us and mark our boundaries, and rows of electric lights light up the outer darkness at night. Zarps guard us as vigilantly as ever. Just beyond

Appendix A. 251

the entrance gate stands the Commandant's tin shanty, around which the Zarps not on duty sit and chatter.

Whilst at the School we caught sight of the outer world, but here we have none of this harmless recreation. With nought to distract us a feeling of despondency prevails; we begin to realise we are a band of segregated confined outcasts! What we miss most, however, is our usual supply of news, for now we know not what is happening.

On getting here a petition to the S.A.R., strongly protesting against our present treatment and pointing out many objections to this building, was drawn up and signed by every officer, but, just like many former petitions, was never favoured with an answer.

We have frequently suggested being let out " on parole." But this the Boers do not understand. The word of an Englishman is not to be trusted by people whose own code of honour is of a most elastic kind.

We are treated from our hill to a grand panoramic view of Pretoria. Partly hidden away among trees we can discern most of the public buildings. The Courts of (In) Justice, the Houses of Parliament, over which perches the emblem of Liberty, a gilded angel, who, with uplifted finger, proclaims a doctrine little practised in the halls below; the Town Hall: the Artillery Barracks with their up-to-date fittings; the Grand Hotel; the Kaffir location; Kruger's Church, where he occasionally thumps the pulpit when preaching to a congregation as fanatical as himself. In the distance, Sunnyside, a suburb of Pretoria, thickly dotted with little tin-roofed bungalows, peacefully reposes. In the foreground of this pleasing picture lie the Zoological gardens, which, I fancy, contain nothing more ferocious than a few homely rabbits. In the background rise green hills, studded with Mimosa shrub, and on which are erected the very latest pattern forts to protect the town, but which will never be defended.

To add to other attractions, our prison grounds are infested by snakes; five venomous specimens have been slaughtered within the last four days. I fully expect one night to find some loathsome reptile wishing to share my bed. Toads, frogs, rats, and various kinds of insects have already shown a partiality for our dwelling, but a snake is an intruder whom we cannot submissively entertain.

No member of the Committee, appointed over us to administer to our wants, takes the trouble to come near us, and it is only very occasionally we get a short visit from one of them, who then professes it is not in his power to assent to our demands. We are under the thumb of a most objectionable and ignorant Boer, whose hatred of the British has thus a fine chance of displaying itself. No proper censorship seems to exist, and in consequence our letters are not delivered to us till they have been several weeks, and in some cases months, in Pretoria. Cablegrams are similarly treated, and often have been kept back a long time before being posted. Letters from our men at Waterfall, which is twelve miles from Pretoria, have taken fourteen days and longer to reach us!

The food supplied us daily consisted of ½lb. meat, bread, potatoes, coffee, tea, salt, and pepper. Consequently nearly all we eat we buy. Extortionate prices are charged, and we have to submit to be systematically swindled.

The Roman Catholic priest, Father de Lacey, a most worthy gentleman, who showed kindly interest to the men, and to whom he offered his ministration weekly, was ultimately forbidden access to the prisoners at Waterfall, and admittance to the Model School was also denied him. He had been extremely shocked at the state he found the men in and at the way they were looked after. It was his attempt to alleviate their sufferings by small donations, and the steps he took to have their condition improved, which won him the displeasure of the Government.

The sick soldiers in hospital on the Racecourse were in such a disgraceful condition from neglect and want of proper care, that a subscription to relieve them from their miserable plight and supply them with necessary comforts and more suitable food was secretly got up by the few English sympathisers, and to which we officers contributed close upon £100.

The Zarps who guard us are a set of cruel, foul-mouthed, blaspheming brutes, who, without provocation, have repeatedly insulted us. Our own vermin infested shed I have already described, but it is more difficult to picture the horrors of Waterfall, where our men were confined, or to write about the hardships, the captivity of squalor and wretchedness our men have to endure there. That a nation of people, who take pride in ever vaunting their Christian principles, should treat their prisoners of war in so inhuman a way is a disgrace to civilisation.

The want of sanitary arrangements has made itself severely felt. Much sickness prevails. The drinking water is impregnated with disease breeding germs. The hospital is full, enteric cases predominate, and deaths frequently occur. The solitary doctor in attendance is quite unable to cope with all the work which claims his attention, consequently many of the patients have little chance of recovery. The ration of meat issued to the men is but half a pound twice a week; on the other days they must exist on mealy pap, the staple food of the Kaffirs. Soap was unobtainable for 2½ months!

The Happy Valley: the Gully by the Klip River, Ladysmith.

Memorial erected to Officers and Men of the Regiment
who died or were killed during the War.

[See p. 293.]

The majority of the men are in great need of boots, and many are going about with hardly a covering to their feet!

Shortly after our change of quarters Mr. Opperman, the Commandant, and the Zarps who guarded us, were sent away to the front. Dr. Gunning, Assistant Commandant, was dismissed at the same time. Their places were taken by the Hollander corps, with a Mr. Westerlink as the new Commandant. The latter seems a decided improvement on Opperman, and gives us the impression of being truthful and honourable, qualities very rare among the officials here; he is civil and ready to oblige, but firm in the resolve to carry out his instructions and the strict orders the Committee have given him conscientiously and to the very letter. He obeys his orders in a straightforward manner, which is not offensive. The first day he addressed us in the following words:—
" I hope, gentlemen, we will get on well together, and that the only point on which we will disagree is the subject of escapes. You can do your best to escape, and I will try my hardest to prevent you."

Opperman and Gunning had been dismissed in disgrace, for it was the opinion of the authorities that through their want of vigilance three officers had effected their escape. They were also held responsible for all the damage done to the Model School. The authorities were very wild over the state they found " the School " in after our removal, and considered a grave outrage had been committed. The electric light had been tampered with, a few cupboards had been burst open, and the walls of the rooms defaced by drawings and maps. But what they looked upon as an unpardonable and abominable sacrilege was a very clever and lifelike caricature of " Oom Paul." He was represented, Bible tucked under arm, in stove pipe hat and with family gingham, striding off to Bloemfontein, with coat tails flying, to encourage his burghers; and as a pendant to this was his return in hot haste, with eyes bulging out of his head, hat blown off and hair on end, closely pressed by Lord Roberts himself! The Boers have little sense of humour; they did not like our little joke, and showed very little appreciation of our artistic efforts.

The huge map of the Transvaal, Free State, and Natal, and also Cape Colony, embracing the whole seat of war, carefully drawn and painted on the wall of the room, was quite a remarkable piece of work. Little red flags and blue ones, pricked in, marked accurately the progress of the war from day to day, and the various positions of the relative armies.

The guard-room at Malta carefully preserves the clever and well-executed drawings on its walls, but the S.A.R. is evidently not anxious to keep any memento of her prisoners of war, so an application of whitewash quickly removed all trace of our handiwork.

Mr. Churchill's escape, followed by the miraculous disappearance of Captain Haldane, Lieut. Le Mesurier, and Mr. Brockie, and their ultimate flight from our prison, caused the authorities to keep an even stricter eye on us than before, and every precaution was taken against our holding communication with outside sources. Every single article which finds its way into the building is overhauled; everything is searched, even the milk bottles are minutely examined! Every man, whether white or black, whose business brings him through the gate of the precincts of our prison, is strictly watched to prevent any kind of communication taking place.

March 28th, 1902.—From now onwards I shall recount our doings in diary form. Last night we heard bells tolling in the town, and as to-day we noticed all flags at half-mast high, we concluded some important personage had died. We have just been informed that it is General Joubert who is dead. We hear thirty of our men have arrived at the hospital on the racecourse from Waterfall, all suffering from enteric fever, three of them being in a dangerous condition. The hospitals at Waterfall are full.

March 29th.—This afternoon we heard the booming of the guns firing the salute as General Joubert's corpse was being conveyed to the railway station. A wreath from the British officers, prisoners of war at Pretoria, was sent, " but not accompanied by a letter of condolence to Mrs. Joubert," as the *Volkstem* stated.

March 31st.—The papers to-day announce a Boer victory near Bloemfontein and the capture of British guns and prisoners. We do not believe this as yet.

April 4th.—The majority here are still disinclined to believe in the Boer victory at Sannah's Post and the capture of our guns, besides eleven British officers taken prisoners. But I fear, as the report is announced so circumstantially, it is only too true. I have in fact backed my belief to the extent of a pound, which I would willingly lose ! I have been a prisoner so long now that I am able to judge fairly accurately whether what the papers say is true or not by the way the announcements are made.

April 5th.—Alas ! I was right. This morning early thirteen officers, mostly gunners, marched in as prisoners, and besides this numerous addition to our number, three officers, who were also taken at Sannah's Post, have been sent to Burke's hospital in the town, as they were wounded. The officers corroborate the *Volkstem* account of our defeat near Bloemfontein and the capture of seven guns and 430 men. It is a sorry tale they have to tell, and someone has blundered again badly.

April 6th.—More bad news. A brilliant victory for the Boers, according to the papers, and the capture of over 400 more prisoners! The enforced inactivity which now has set in has given the Boers time to recuperate, and the successes they have lately gained have had the effect of making them more uppish than ever. Their tails are up once more! The *Volkstem* talks of Lord Roberts being forced to evacuate the Free State, and compares the forthcoming retreat to that of Napoleon from Moscow!

April 9th.—The State Attorney and some of the Committee paid us a visit this afternoon. Evidently the petition we sent a few days ago brought about this visit. The usual promises were made, and of course they had the impudence to express surprise on hearing we did not get our own letters regularly, and that we were barred from getting English newspapers. The State Attorney could not but acknowledge we were living in great discomfort. I knew by now how much to trust in their promises. The son-in-law of General Joubert also came to thank us on behalf of the deceased's General's widow for the wreath we sent.

April 10th.—From several sources we have heard that the Boers have received a big defeat lately; it may though only be town rumours. A couple of English workmen, who came to see about the drain pipes, managed, when the sentry over them was not watching closely, to whisper us the news. The *Volkstem* has nothing about a British victory.

April 11th.—It is quite impossible to make any sense out of the *Volkstem*. This evening it is quite funny reading. The British, Brabant's Horse, are reported as " surrounded on five sides." I read " it is probable General Villebois is dead; he was buried with full military honours yesterday! "

April 12th.—Eight officers, mostly of the Royal Irish Rifles, arrived here as prisoners, having been captured by General De Wet at Moster Hoek.

April 13th, Good Friday.—The newspapers contain absolutely no war news. I was much amused to-day by the scare caused by a rough kind of sun dial, which had been made by some of us and planted in the ground. Two Hollanders, with rifles ready, very slowly and cautiously approached our wooden erection, which I suppose they took for some diabolical infernal machine of destruction. Then they suddenly summoned up courage and pounced on our ignorant toy. It was quickly demolished and flung far out of harm's way.

April 18th.—In Pretoria life is intolerable, and the English who still remain live in constant dread of expulsion, and can never consider themselves safe from tyranny.

April 20th.—Lord Rosslyn (war correspondent) was brought in to-day. He was captured along with the Royal Irish at Moster Hoek, but since his arrival in Pretoria has been kept at the Hospital on the Racecourse. From sick men's accounts, those who have lately come from Waterfall, he quite bears out all the terrible suffering there. Another subscription is being got up to help our men at Waterfall. A high wire netting is being put up all round our grounds and in front of the barbed wire fence. Spikes have been put into the top bar of the gate. Prices are rising in Pretoria, and we prisoners have to pay very high for all we buy.

April 22nd.—The total amount subscribed by us towards the Waterfall Fund is £700. 16s. 7d.

April 29th.—We hear that the Boers are getting the worst of it all along the line, and are again beginning to lose heart. The *Volkstem* gives absolutely no news, an ominous sign of their discomfiture. Owing to the help of certain sympathisers the prisoners at Waterfall are faring better now. The Boers are very indignant over the Johannesburg explosion, which they put down to the British. To-day the Wesleyan minister, the Rev. Goodwin, held service here in the afternoon, under the watchful eye of a Hollander sentry. Two or three days ago a Mr. Kirkwood, one of the South African Light Horse, was brought here from the Pretoria jail, where he had been confined for about 3½ months. He was taken prisoner at the same time as Mr. Grenfell in Natal. A newspaper is to be started for private circulation. Rosslyn has undertaken the duties of editor, and it is hoped the paper will make a weekly appearance. Contributions are not wanting at present, and the paper is to be plentifully illustrated.

May 6th.—Another prisoner has turned up, a subaltern of the 9th Lancers, from whom we have gleaned little news. Yesterday, however, we got great tidings. From a parson who called to see us we heard the British troops were close to Kroonstad, the enemy had been routed and smashed up, the Irish Brigade cut up, and Colonel Blake taken prisoner. The German commando existed no longer; two commandos, the Bethel and Standerton ones, had refused to fight any longer, and another was wavering. The Boers were in a panic, and a great meeting was at that moment taking place in the market square, where Kruger was to address the crowd. The British had entered the Transvaal, and were marching north of Fourteen Streams towards Mafeking. This was indeed great news, and I felt as if I could jump out of my skin for joy! The Raad meets to-day; I wonder what will be decided. In a rather half-hearted way the *Volkstem* rather implied that they had had a bit the worst of the fighting lately.

May 10th.—A selling lottery was got up yesterday on the date of our release. The winner will get about £50 or over. The dates put up for sale ranged between May 15th and August 15th. The average price of dates put up fetched 10s. The 24th May went for twenty-three shillings. Kruger and his clique are trying their hardest to inspire the Burghers to further resistance, but they are beginning at last to get rather tired of his exhortations and of listening to his biblical quotations, which in vain he tries to render applicable to the present state of things. The Boers are being commandeered everywhere, and under escort forced away to fight. Their ranks must now be filled with very unwilling partisans. In Pretoria everybody has been commandeered, and of late raids have been made in the middle of the night, citizens woken up, taken away then and there, and marched to the front. The other evening there was a performance given in the theatre here, and at the close of the play a number of policemen entered the building and commandeered a great many out of the audience. The general opinion is that the British will be here in a month's time. I hear we are in Kronstadt, but the *Volkstem* does not own up to it. There are now hardly any British subjects left in Pretoria; only quite a few have been allowed to remain, and over 400 have lately been put over the border.

May 20th.—Yesterday we had athletic sports. Three times round the running track within our birdcage constitutes a mile. Considering how very unfit we all are, I wonder greatly anyone was able to run at all. There is a very disquieting rumour abroad that we prisoners may any day be, with practically no warning, suddenly removed north, to either Lydenburg or Barberton. The mere thought of it is too awful. To think that almost within the hearing of our own guns we should be taken away to a spot fifty miles from a railway station. It is too horrible to contemplate. What an obstinate, pig-headed, fanatic old man Kruger is! The lady burghers are urging their husbands and the young bloods to fight to the last, and they even seriously suggest going to the front themselves. A corps of Dutch amazons! Think what is in store for our men when confronted by these furious viragoes.

May 25th.—Yesterday being the Queen's Birthday, we drank the Queen's health with great enthusiasm. I hope they heard us away in the town. The Commandant told me all the men at Waterfall fell in at 11 o'clock in the morning and sang the National Anthem. It must have been an imposing sight, 4,000 men assembled together singing for all they were worth. In the afternoon we had athletic sports. We sent the following telegram to Her Majesty:—" The officers, non-commissioned officers, and men and civilians, prisoners at Pretoria, offer your Majesty their loyal and dutiful congratulations on your birthday."

May 28th.—I have felt quite miserable to-day. The Commandant told us that it was quite possible we might be suddenly moved up north to Pietersburg, about 150 miles north of Pretoria. He advised us to lay in a store of provisions in case it was decided we should be moved. We hear a report that our scouts have entered Johannesburg and that our forces are at Krugersdorp, which is thirty miles west of Johannesburg. I doubt very much our being at Johannesburg yet, but fighting is certainly going on this side of the Vaal. This afternoon I clearly heard guns in the far distance; it was a beautiful calm day for hearing, and the slight breeze was in the right direction.

May 29th.—To-day we could hear guns quite distinctly. We are all very excited in hopes of our coming release. Our advanced guard entered Johannesburg yesterday, and the morning train from Pretoria went half-way there to-day, but had to return. Our troops may arrive any moment. The men who guard us are nearly all on our side, and it would not be very difficult to gain their help in escaping now, but it is hardly worth it, as our hope of freedom is so high.

I hear there has been great excitement in the town all day, and many are leaving to trek north. There is a report Kruger himself is leaving. The American Consul came to-day to see us. It appears that on the Queen's birthday the men at Waterfall raised a Union Jack which had been smuggled in, and there was some row and commotion when it was pulled down by the authorities. As the Boers fear the men breaking out and wrecking Pretoria, the authorities decided to remove them to Middelburg, but the men have openly declared that they refuse to be moved, and would rather die first.

The authorities are in a dilemma and fear bloodshed, as they say they will have to employ force to move the men. So they sent the American Consul, as head of a deputation, to request that we officers should use our influence with the men and get them to go quietly, and that a few of us should go with a guard to Waterfall for this purpose. Colonel Hunt, who is the senior officer, after consulting with other officers here, sent back word that he could not comply with the demand, and that he strongly urged the authorities to allow the men to remain at Waterfall, for we thought it more than likely that the men would overpower the guard and that blood would certainly be shed; but if on the other hand the men were left where they were, some of us would be ready to proceed to Waterfall to restore order there, and we should be responsible for their behaviour. The Government took our hint, and have requested us to send twenty officers to Waterfall to preserve order there. The officers immediately went to get ready, and left on " parole " by special train.

We heard the following startling news, viz., that Kruger and the Government had hurriedly left Pretoria for Lydenburg, that the town was not to be defended, and that Lord Roberts was expected to march in with his troops tomorrow! The Commandant, who also came in, said a few words; he asked us to help him in doing his duty, and that he hoped we should understand his extraordinary position. He had to be responsible to his Government for our safety, and to-morrow he would be responsible to Lord Roberts. It was a wonderful evening, and one I am likely never to forget. We are practically, to all intents and purposes, free men, but we mean to stick to our word and remain under the Commandant's care until the British troops arrive. I don't expect I shall sleep to-night for excitement! I hear that Kruger addressed the people in the market place to-day, and declared he would die fighting in streets of Pretoria. He must have changed his mind, however, as he left shortly afterwards, taking with him every bit of gold handy.

May 30th.—All day we have been listening to guns, but no British troops have yet arrived! From a newspaper correspondent, captured yesterday at Johannesburg, and who arrived here to-day a prisoner, we hear that the Boers are running away in every direction and that no fight is left in them. Lord Roberts, he says, will arrive to-morrow. Pretoria is a city of the dead! I have been watching all day ox waggons, piled up with furniture and household goods, leaving the town, and crowds are trekking north in a great hurry, driving herds of oxen before them.

May 31st.—Another disappointment, as the British troops have not arrived, but they are not far off, and this evening I hear they are but six miles away. We have heard no guns to-day, but we have on the other hand been treated to the sight of numerous fleeing commandos. All the morning we saw them streaming through Pretoria, and through field glasses we could occasionally catch sight of guns. One commando passed quite close to our prison grounds. They took little notice of us; only one man said " Your friends are quite close." It was marvellous to me none of these Boers had a single bad word for us. How would other beaten armies have behaved under similar circumstances? I daresay a shot or two would have come our way, and we should certainly have been jeered at. I hear the town this morning was looted by German Jews; cartloads of Government stores were taken and carried away. Four looters were shot, and we heard the shots quite distinctly.

June 3rd.—We have been in a fever of excitement for several days! It was last Tuesday, five days ago, we heard guns so plainly and thought the British forces would enter Pretoria the next day. Pretoria was in a panic, shops were being broken open and the contents thrown about the streets, the Government stores were looted, and the people helping themselves to everything they could lay their hands on. Men and women, Kaffirs and boys, were busily engaged, heaping up in carts, wheelbarrows, and every mode of conveyance all manner of loot, and quarrelling noisily over the proceeds of their robbery. The town was full of armed Boers coming and going, all very scared and anxious to get away from the front.

The inhabitants of Pretoria, not engaged in looting, were flying from the town. Clouds of dust denoted a general trek north was taking place. Ox wagons, loaded up with every conceivable piece of household property, great herds of cattle, mounted men, women dragging children along after them, were streaming out of the town travelling north and eastwards.

The Government had fled the previous night quite unexpectedly. Kruger had bolted with two millions of gold! He had driven to the first station out of Pretoria, where he had taken train, but outside his house the two sentries still remained, unconscious of the President's departure. Boxes containing bars of gold had formed part of his baggage, and been thrown hastily into the train after him. The officials were furious on finding that the President had decamped without settling their salaries, and that the cheques he had left behind for the purpose were worthless.

Everybody was quite certain that Lord Roberts would make his entry into Pretoria the next day. But we were a little too premature, and our days of captivity were not yet at an end.

Things have now calmed down, and the town resumed its normal aspect, though the frequent appearance of the Boer warriors riding about the place hints to the presence of commandos in the neighbourhood. We are told that Lord Roberts made his entry into Johannesburg on Thursday, but where he is exactly at present is only conjecture. Rumours are more plentiful now than they have ever been.

The twenty officers who went out to Waterfall are not having a very lively time of it I expect. They took no kit

Appendix A. 261

with them, as they expected to be free men the next day. I hear that the cause of the men at Waterfall being obstreperous was owing to no food having been supplied them for two days. They tore down the posts and wire entanglement and seized some oxen which were outside, and in a few minutes the latter were cut up and rationed out, the posts being used as fuel to roast the meat.

We are now daily, I may say hourly, expecting a big fight to come off. Imagine the suspense we are going through! Any day, any moment, we may be free! I have been waiting thirty-two weeks for that day!

June 4th.—At eight o'clock this morning we first heard guns firing very close, and then, in spite of a strongish wind, could distinguish the sound of rifle fire and the spit of a Maxim. Soon afterwards we saw a shell, a good British shell, burst on a hill the other side of a valley about seven miles from our tin house. This was followed by many others, chiefly shrapnel, directed at a redoubt lately built by the Boers, which we saw was occupied by a number of the enemy. Bigger guns, either Howitzers or Naval guns, opened fire on the forts, and we had the pleasure of seeing lyddite shells bursting all over the hills, several falling clean into the fort on the hill overlooking the racecourse. What an exciting day we have had! Picture to yourself anxious, yet jubilant prisoners, sitting in camp chairs in the confines of their prison, surrounded by wire entanglements, calmly smoking while watching the furious bombardment going on a few miles off.

We could discern numbers of spectators on the nearer hills watching the bombardment, and they must have been running no small risk. The *Volkstem* appeared for the last time early to-day, and contained a tissue of lies. It is quite funny reading.

June 5th.—It was with a feeling of supreme contentment and intense happiness we went to bed last night, for we felt certain that Lord Roberts and his forces would enter Pretoria on the morrow. The town, we heard, would not be defended. The Boers had evacuated their positions at nightfall, and retired with all their guns in a north-easterly direction. We were a happy band of captives last night; the thought of being liberated on the following day was quite intoxicating. I could hardly realise I should be free, free after being over eight months a prisoner. The thoughts of coming happiness crowded through my brain as I laid my head on the pillow, and so excited was I that it was some time before I dropped off into a blissful slumber.

At about 1 a.m. I was woken up by hearing our Commandant shouting out to us to get up and dress at once, as we were to pack up our belongings and be ready to march off in two hours time to a railway siding four miles away. Never as long as I live shall I forget that night. Imagine our feelings of horror on hearing that we were to be moved at the last moment and be taken off by the retreating Boers. What would be our fate! No doubt it meant trekking from place to place, having to put up with every kind of discomfort and hardship, and leading a life of utter misery for months.

It was more than we intended to stand, and we therefore determined not to submit passively to be removed. So accordingly, when the Commandant came into our dormitory to hurry us up, we plainly told him we had no intention of obeying his orders, that rather than be moved we would be shot, and, in short, he and his men could do their worst, but, whatever happened, we were resolved to resist. The Commandant began by trying to persuade us, he ridiculed our offering any resistance, and told us he had received his orders and would see they were carried out. We then made the Commandant a prisoner, and a few of us acted as guard over him to prevent his leaving the building. When his assistant came in we also made him a prisoner. Then we talked matters over with them, and plainly showed we were very serious in our intentions, and quite resolved not to be removed.

We gradually talked them over to our way of thinking, and explained that the next day British troops would set us free, and that by standing by us now their own position would be considered in a better light by our own authorities. I think he only really wanted a loophole to get out of complying with the orders he had received from General Botha.

At last the Commandant said that if we let him out on "parole" he gave us his word of honour he and his guard would in no way assist at our removal, and that he would go outside to the twenty mounted Boers, who were waiting to escort us to the railway siding, where the train to take us away was, and tell them that he had given us his word not to let us be removed. After considering the matter over we trusted him and let him out. On his explaining the above to the Boers drawn up outside, they abused him in very forcible language and then galloped off in the direction of the town, shouting out as they left that they would soon return with a Maxim gun and a commando to take us away. What an anxious night we spent! Every moment we expected to hear Boers approaching.

Under the circumstances it was well-nigh impossible to sleep, though most of us went back to bed. I had dressed

Appendix A. 263

myself in uniform, over which I had slipped my suit of mufti, for I had every intention of making a bolt for it on the first opportunity had the worst come off. In the darkness and confusion in removing us I might perhaps have slipped away unperceived and hidden until the Boers had passed by, when I intended to find a refuge in the Kaffir location just outside Pretoria.

It seemed an interminable night; would morning never come? Had our Commandant really played fairly, or would our hopes of liberty be shattered at the very last moment? How I welcomed the first streak of daylight! Safety now seemed assured, and most probably only a few hours separated us from liberty!

At about eight o'clock we thought we could see troops away in the distance, and through field glasses we thought they were men dressed in khaki, but it was a misty morning, and it was hard to distinguish what was really causing so much dust. From the formation they were moving in I thought they must be British troops, but we were by no means certain, and still entertained fears of Boers coming to take us away.

It was whilst we were still speculating over this column of men, moving far away towards Pretoria, that we suddenly caught sight of two officers in khaki galloping up the road which led to our "Birdcage." Then, and then only, we knew that our deliverance was at hand. In a moment hats were flying in the air, and we were all shouting and cheering like madmen. As the two horsemen approached we recognised them to be Winston Churchill and the Duke of Marlborough, and instantly the gate of our prison flew open and we 180 imprisoned officers were streaming out and flocking round our two deliverers. We learnt from them the town had surrendered the previous night, and British troops were now entering Pretoria. A few seconds had sufficed to produce a complete transformation scene!

Our guard we disarmed, and they and the Commandant were placed inside our prison grounds, whilst our soldier servants slipped on the bandoliers and picked up their rifles, and were acting as sentries over them. Both sentries and our former guard seemed quite satisfied with their lot; the former, with broad grins on their faces, were posted all round, where our former Hollander sentries had stood. We then, amidst great cheering, ran up on the flagstaff outside the Commandant's house the Union Jack, which some officer had cleverly manufactured out of a Transvaal flag found in a cupboard in the Model School, and which he had kept concealed for this happy day.

We were free! Free to walk about and go where we pleased! It seemed too good to be true. How often I had wondered how our deliverance would come about. In the end it reminded me of the Gilbert and Sullivan order of things, the situation was so extremely comical. From our prison we made our way to the square in the town, to view there the state entry of the British troops into Pretoria, and to meet many old friends we had been separated from for so long. Among the crowd I noticed many faces which had become so familiar to us in the Model School. Pattison, the dogman, the Cullingworth family, were all there with beaming faces, and with them numerous others whom we cordially greeted. Those like Bridal, Malan, and Opperman were no longer in Pretoria, those whom we had good cause to hate, and who merited severe punishment, had fled with the Government. Mr. de Souza, the Secretary to the Commandant-General, one of the chief members of the S.A.R. Prisoners' Committee, but one who had really done us no harm, had remained in Pretoria, and Dr. Gunning, our Assistant-Commandant in the Model School, was also in town ready to welcome the advent of British troops.

APPENDIX B.

Roll of Officers of the 18th Hussars, showing the Engagements in the Boer War at which they were present.

Rank and Name	Commencement of the War	Dundee and Talana Hill	Ladysmith during the Siege	Gen. Buller's Column Advance to Lydenberg and Bergendal	Middelburg and surroundings, October, 1900, to February, 1901	To Piet Relief under Gen. French, Swaziland Border, and back to Middelburg	Operations under Sir Bindon Blood in Eastern Transvaal	Northern Transvaal under Gen. W. Kitchener	S.E. Transvaal under Gen. W. Kitchener	Eastern Transvaal under Gen. Bruce Hamilton	Orange River Colony and Eastern Transvaal, February and March, 1902	Orange River Colony and Eastern Transvaal, April and May, 1902
Lieut.-Col. Moller, B. D.[1]	Yes	Yes	…	…	…	…	…	…	…	…	…	…
Major Knox, E. C.[2]	Yes	Yes	Yes	Yes	Yes	Yes	Yes	No	Yes	Yes	…	Yes
,, Marling, P. S., V.C.	Yes	Yes	Yes	No; Sick Leave	No	Yes	Yes	Yes	No; with 24th Batt. Imp. Yeo.	Yes	Yes	Yes
,, Laming, H. T.	Yes	Yes	Yes	Yes	Yes	…	…	Yes	Yes	…	Yes	…
,, Greville, H. F.[3]	Yes	Yes	No; Prisoner of War	…	…	…	…	…	…	…	…	…
Capt. Pollok, W. P. M.	Yes	Yes	Yes	No	Yes	Yes	Yes	Yes	Yes	Yes	Yes	Yes
,, Davey, Hon. H. S.[4]	Yes	Yes	Yes	…	…	…	…	…	…	…	…	…
,, Corbett, C. H.	No; Depôt	No; Depôt	No; Depôt	No; Depôt	Yes	Yes	Yes	Yes	Yes	Yes	Yes	No; Leave
,, Welby, M. S.[5]	No; Leave	No; Leave	Yes	Yes	Yes	Yes	Yes	Yes	Yes	Yes	Yes	Yes
,, Burnett, C. K.	Yes	Yes	Yes	Yes	Yes	Yes	Yes	Yes	Yes	Yes	Yes	Yes
,, Leveson, C. H.	No; W. Africa	No; W. Africa	No; W. Africa	No; W. Africa	No; W. Africa	No; W. Africa	…	…	…	…	…	…
Lieut. Haag, E. C.	Yes	Yes	Yes	Yes	Yes	No; S.A.C.	Yes	No; Sick	…	Yes	…	…
,, Gosselin, J. H.[6]	Yes	Yes	Yes	Yes	Yes	No; detch. Middelbg.	…	…	…	…	Yes	No; Leave
,, Stewart, N. St. V. R.	Yes	Yes	Yes	Yes	Yes	No; Gen. Lyttelton's Staff	Yes	Yes	…	Yes	Yes	Yes
,, Wood, J. L.	Yes	Yes	Yes	Yes	Yes	Yes	Yes	Yes	Yes	Yes	Yes	Yes
,, Field, C. D.	Yes	Yes	Yes	Yes	Yes	No; Duistroom	Yes	Yes	No; with 24th Batt. Imp. Yeo.	…	…	…
,, Thackwell, C. J.[7]	Yes	Yes	Yes	Yes	Yes	…	…	…	…	…	…	…
,, McLachlan, A. C.[8]	Yes	Yes	Yes	Yes	Yes	No; lines committa.	No; Leave	…	…	Yes	…	…
,, Bayford, E. H.	Yes	Yes	Yes	Yes	Yes	Yes	…	No	No	Yes	Yes	Yes
,, Cape, H. A.[9]	Yes	Yes	Yes	Yes	…	…	…	…	…	…	Yes	…

Name									
,, Dugdale, J. G. ...	No; Leave	Yes	Yes	Yes	Yes	Yes	Yes	Yes	Yes
,, Cawston, C. F.[10]	Yes	Yes	...	Yes	...	...	...	...	...
,, Purdey, M. S. ...	No; Leave	No; Leave	No; Mooi River	No	Yes	Yes	Yes	Yes	Yes
,, Webster, G. V.	No; Depôt	No; Depôt	Yes	Yes	Yes	Yes	Yes	Yes	Yes
,, McClintock, J. H. J. ...	No; Depôt	No; Dep. Mooi Riv.	Yes	No; detch. Dalstroom	Yes	Yes	No	Yes	Yes
,, King, D. M. ...	No; Depôt	No; Depôt	No; Maritzburg.	No; Sick	No	No	No	No	...
,, Pilkington, F. E. C.[11] ...	No	No	No	No; lines communtn.	Yes	Yes	Yes	Yes	Yes
,, Wills, A. S. ...	No	No	No	Yes	Yes	Yes	Yes	Yes	Yes
,, Lichtenberg, J. W. ...	No	No	No	Yes	Yes	Yes	Yes	Yes	Yes
,, Lyon, E. L. ...	No	No	No	No; lines communtn.	Yes	Yes	Yes	Yes	Yes
,, Sopper, F. W. ...	No	No	No	No	No	No	Yes	Yes	Yes
,, Jury, E. C. ...	No	No	No	No	No	No	Yes	Yes	Yes
,, Wood, C. L. ...	No	No	No	No	No	No	Yes	Yes	Yes
,, Grigg, R. S. ...	No	No	No	No	No	No	Yes	Yes	Yes
Capt. & Q.-M. Baker, J.[13]	Yes	Yes	Yes	Yes	...	...	...	...	...
Lieut. & Q.-M. Dunkley, F.[13]	Yes	Yes	Yes	...	...	...	...	...	...
Lieut. & R.-M. O'Kelly, P.[14] ...	...	...	...	...	...	...	...	...	...

WARRANT OFFICERS.

Name									
Rgt.-Sgt.-Mjr. Simmonds, H.	Yes	Yes	Yes	Yes	Yes	Yes	Yes	Yes	Yes
Bandmaster Payne, J.[15] ...	Yes	Yes	...	...	...	...	...	...	...

[1] Taken prisoner at Dundee.
[2] Died 18th February, 1902.
[3] Taken prisoner at Dundee; did not rejoin Regiment again for duty.
[4] Invalided home.
[5] Died of wounds, 5th August, 1900.
[6] Invalided home.
[7] Invalided home.
[8] Sent home, not being allowed to take further part in S. A. Campaign.
[9] Sent home, not being allowed to take further part in S. A. Campaign.
[10] Invalided home ; died of wounds, 3rd February, 1901.
[11] Killed in action, 6th October, 1901.
[12] Retired.
[13] With Depôt at Middelburg, October, 1900, to end of war. Quartermaster after Captain Baker's retirement.
[14] Appointed Riding Master at end of the war.
[15] Remained with Depôt at Middelburg, October, 1900, to end of war.

APPENDIX C.

Roll of N.C.O.'s and Men who served in South Africa during the period 1st October, 1899, to 31st May, 1902.

"A" SQUADRON.

Regtl. No.	Rank and Name.	Remarks.
2643	S.S.M. Anderson, C.	...
3235	S.Q.M.S. Franks, W.	...
4070	S.S.M. Meyer, F.	...
3341	S.S.F. James, H.	...
3162	Sergt. Bond, T.	...
3170	„ Cole, J.	...
3503	„ Shakespeare, W.	...
3579	„ Dudley, S.	...
3588	„ Pearce, W.	Wounded, 1st September, 1901.
2703	„ Baker, H.	Wounded, 2nd February, 1901. Invalided, 13th March, 1901.
3484	„ Adams, W.	Invalided, 22nd November, 1900.
3605	„ Webb, H.	Killed in action, 6th January, 1900.
3689	„ Hart, W.	...
3954	„ Brockwell, C.	Died, 26th January, 1900.
4024	„ Chowles, A.	...
3708	„ Kimmister, J.	...
4217	Corpl. James, A.	...
3983	S.S.F. Smith, G.	...
4329	Sergt. Warren, E.	Wounded, 4th October, 1900. Invalided, 29th November, 1900.
4027	„ Barton, S.	...
4384	„ Hourigan, W.	...
4009	„ Nye, G.	...
4144	Corpl. Hamilton, F.	...
3189	„ Collins, H.	...
4006	„ Lelliott, A.	Invalided, 5th June, 1901.
3362	Corpl.-S.-S. Wells, C.	...
4279	S.S. Allen, J.	...
4289	„ Wiltshire, T.	...
4008	Trpt. Denny, T.	...
3896	„ Seppings, D.	...
4680	Pte. Adkins, W.	Invalided, 10th November, 1900.
4504	L.-Corpl. Attree, W.	Invalided, 6th April, 1900.
4611	Pte. Aylmore, F.	...
4350	Corpl. Baggott, W.	...
4764	Pte. Bailey, H.	Wounded, 6th January, 1900.
4367	„ Barnes, J.	...
4671	Corpl. Barnes, W.	...
4661	Pte. Bath, W.	...
4643	„ Beatwell, W.	Wounded, 14th October, 1900. Invalided, 8th, January, 1901.
3858	„ Bennett, J.	...

Regtl. No.	Rank and Name.	Remarks.
4723	Pte. Bennett, C.	
4716	„ Birmingham, F.	Killed in action, 18th, August, 1901.
4388	Corpl. Bott, C.	
4447	Pte. Bowers, W.	
4197	„ Brain, W.	Invalided, 21st March, 1900.
4587	„ Brown, P.	
4666	„ Brown, E.	
4703	„ Brockwell, A.	
4500	Corpl. Bryant, J.	
4556	Pte. Burt, T.	
4732	„ Burt, W.	
4773	„ Burton, W.	Died, 22nd December, 1899.
4097	„ Bushell, T.	Killed in action, 20th October, 1899.
3938	„ Campbell, D.	
4380	„ Cann, A.	
3891	„ Capsey, W.	
4469	„ Cherrill, E.	
3819	„ Clutterbuck, T.	Invalided, 23rd June, 1900.
4016	„ Cogan, M.	Wounded, 20th October, 1899.
4516	„ Cook, J.	Invalided, 14th November, 1901.
4705	„ Coppendale, S.	
4080	„ Crandon, G.	
3940	„ Croxton, G.	
4617	„ Curley, M.	
3865	„ Cutler, E.	
4017	„ Davie, G.	
3902	„ Davis, T.	Wounded, 6th January, 1900. Invalided, 21st March, 1900.
4452	„ Deacon, T.	
4535	„ Deacon, W.	Invalided, 4th August, 1900.
4471	„ Denny, W.	
3814	„ Draper, H.	
3821	„ Donaldson, S.	
4631	„ Easom, W.	
4231	„ Edwards, E.	Invalided, 23rd May, 1900.
4394	„ Edmonds, E.	Died, 12th January, 1900.
4777	„ Ennis, R.	
4710	„ Evans, T.	
4725	„ Farnham, C.	
4665	Corpl. Faulkner, F.	Killed in action, 6th October, 1901.
3877	Pte. Gay, I.	
4791	„ Gibson, T.	
4726	„ Gilbert, J.	
4576	Corpl. Gill, C.	Wounded, 6th January, 1900. Killed in action, 2nd February, 1901.
4769	Pte. Greig, G.	
4743	„ Grinham	
3790	Corpl. Hall, G.	
4408	Pte. Hall, E.	Wounded, 6th October, 1901.
4351	„ Hancock, A.	
4045	„ Harkness, A.	
4685	„ Hansford, H.	
3945	„ Harling, R.	Invalided, 14th November, 1901.
4275	„ Harrison, J.	
4190	„ Hart, J.	

Appendix C.

Regtl. No.	Rank and Name.	Remarks.
4758	Pte. Hart, C.	Wounded, 20th November, 1899. Invalided, 18th April, 1900.
4485	,, Hawkins, H.	...
4154	,, Haynes, J.	...
4331	,, Hickman, E.	...
3847	,, Hills, C.	...
3883	,, Holdgate, H.	Invalided, 3rd December, 1900.
4637	,, Halland, T.	...
4135	,, Hughes, T.	...
4354	,, Hughes, T.	Wounded, 2nd February, 1901. Invalided, 10th March, 1901.
4061	,, Hurle, M.	...
4359	,, James, W.	Invalided, 11th December, 1900.
4786	,, Jenkinson, A.	...
4049	Corpl. Jones, J.	...
4688	Pte. Kindred, E.	...
4537	,, King, F.	...
3752	,, Kinnard, F.	...
4551	,, Langlands, W.	Killed in action, 20th Sept., 1900.
4698	,, Lewis, T.	...
4570	,, Little, H.	Died, 17th September, 1902.
4038	,, Loader, W.	...
4108	,, Longley, W.	...
4251	,, Loughlin, J.	...
4767	,, Loveday, T.	...
3866	,, Marchant, G.	Wounded, 20th October, 1899.
4114	,, Mason, W.	...
4204	,, Masters, E.	Wounded, 20th October, 1899. Invalided, 30th July, 1900.
3977	,, McBain, J.	...
3934	,, McIntyre, D.	...
4139	,, McNeil, W.	...
4712	,, Moore, T.	Wounded, 6th April, 1901. Invalided, 7th May, 1901.
4533	Corpl. Morcom, G.	Wounded, 10th October, 1900. Invalided, 29th November, 1900.
4660	,, Murray, W.	...
4345	Pte. Oakes, E.	Died, 15th February, 1900.
4101	,, O'Brien, P.	Wounded, 20th October, 1899.
4681	Corpl. Pakes, F.	...
4742	Pte. Parker, E.	Wounded, 20th October, 1899.
4779	,, Parlane, W.	...
4797	Corpl. Paterson, W.	...
4450	Pte. Piercy, F.	Invalided, 31st March, 1900.
4636	Corpl. Pike, R.	...
4596	Sergt. Pinn, T.	...
4707	Pte. Poague, H.	Invalided, 25th April, 1900.
4766	,, Pollock, W.	Wounded, 17th August, 1901.
4482	,, Quinsey, G.	...
4713	,, Robinson, R.	...
4319	,, Rusk, J.	Invalided, 6th August, 1900.
4122	,, Ryan, J.	...
3921	Corpl. Sharp, D.	Killed in action, 6th October, 1901.
4655	Pte. Sharp, A.	...
4385	,, Shaw, J.	...

Regtl. No.	Rank and Name.	Remarks.
4760	Pte. Shepherd, F.	...
4629	„ Sherwood, T.	... Invalided, 8th March, 1901.
3990	„ Small, D.	...
4510	„ Smith, A.	... Invalided, 1st July, 1900.
4679	Corpl. Smith, A.	...
4639	Pte. Stamberry, A.	...
4378	Stanley, L.	...
4721	„ Stewart, R.	... Wounded, 20th October, 1899. Invalided, 30th July, 1900.
4771	„ Stewart, D.	...
4796	Sergt. Stork, W.	...
3838	Pte. Taylor, H.	...
4167	„ Taylor, W.	...
4453	„ Thomas, E.	...
4193	Pte. Thomas, H.	...
4277	„ Thomas, R.	...
4789	„ Thompson, R.	... Invalided, 7th September, 1900.
4525	Corpl. Thorpe, A.	...
4082	Pte. Tindle, F.	... Killed in action, 2nd February, 1901.
3823	Corpl. Tomley, T.	...
4600	Pte. Walker, H.	... Wounded, 7th November, 1899.
4737	Corpl. Ward, F.	... Wounded, 6th January, 1900.
4746	Pte. Warren, W.	...
3848	„ Whitelock, W.	... Died, 10th July, 1900.
4178	„ Williams, J.	...
4511	„ Williams, J.	...
4007	Corpl. Willis, A.	... Died, 19th February, 1900.
4800	Pte. Willmore, H.	... Invalided, 31st March, 1900.
4415	„ Wilson, G.	...
4787	„ Woods, R.	...
4086	„ Wright, J.	... Invalided, 7th September, 1900.
4907	S.-M.-I. Gibson, J.	...

"B" SQUADRON.

2884	S.S.M. Power, W.	... Wounded, 8th December, 1899.
3614	F.Q.M.S. Padfield, W.	...
3542	Sergt. Stenson, F.	...
2691	„ Markwick, F.	...
3016	„ Mackinson, E.	... Died, 22nd January, 1900.
2879	„ Tait, J.	...
3342	„ Harris, G.	...
3264	„ Christmas, W.	... Invalided, 21st May, 1901.
3522	S.S.F. Walker, H.	...
3691	„ Shepherd, A.	... Wounded, 21st October, 1899.
4096	Sadd.-Sergt. Pow, R.	...
3471	Sergt. Leonard, W.	... Died, 29th September, 1901.
3343	„ Brown, A.	... Died of wounds, 1st June, 1900
3405	„ Brind, A.	...
3513	„ Collier, A.	...
3856	„ Stephens, G.	...
3947	Corpl.-Sadd. Tamplin, A.	...
3869	Corpl. S.S. Nettleton, F.	...
4124	L.-Sergt. Watson, A.	... Wounded, 8th December, 1899.

Appendix C.   269

Regtl. No.	Rank and Name	Remarks
4113	Corpl. Martin, W.	...
4497	,, Valpy, R.	...
4043	,, Pope, F.	Died, 20th August, 1901.
4278	,, Daunt, J.	...
4249	,, Franklin, G.	Wounded, 20th October, 1899.
3996	,, Lee, W.	...
4241	,, Lugton, J.	...
4582	,. Springall, F.	...
4307	S.S. Cluer, W.	...
4495	,, Hiscock, A.	...
4563	,, Partridge, A.	...
3964	,, Bradford, J.	Invalided, 17th May, 1900.
3369	Trpt. Sutch, J.	...
4374	,, Salmon, C.	Killed in action, 20th October, 1899.
4041	Pte. Allison, J.	Wounded, 20th October, 1899.
4633	L.-Corpl. Arnold, A.	Died, 30th June, 1900.
4765	,, Ashmore, R.	Invalided, 21st September, 1900.
4744	Pte. Austen, E.	Wounded, 20th November, 1894. Invalided, 11th May, 1900.
4352	,, Baines, A.	...
4392	,, Barnes, F.	Wounded, 20th September, 1900. Invalided, 25th November, 1901.
4026	L.-Corpl. Beard, F.	...
3973	Pte. Beattie, G.	...
4621	,, Bell, H.	...
4623	L.-Corpl. Bick, G.	...
4341	Pte. Bird, A.	...
4137	,, Blayden, S.	...
4390	,, Bleakley, S.	...
4709	,, Boother, F.	...
4792	,, Bowman, A.	...
4753	,, Borthwick, A.	...
4287	,, Box, E.	...
4440	,, Bridge, D.	...
4110	,, Bryant, J.	Wounded, 20th October, 1899.
4234	,, Burkett, J.	...
4754	,, Byrne, J.	...
4161	,, Caddis, D.	Died of wounds, 5th Sept., 1900.
4402	,, Cahill C.	...
4794	,, Campbell, M.	...
3824	,, Carmichael, D.	...
4568	,, Cawthorne, W.	Wounded, 20th November, 1899. Invalided, 21st March, 1900.
4667	,, Chapman, A.	...
4752	L.-Corpl. Claridge, P.	Killed in action, 8th Dec., 1899.
4381	Pte. Cleary, M.	...
3928	,, Clinch, W.	...
4308	L.-Corpl. Colegate, F.	...
3884	Pte. Collins, G.	...
4423	,, Connolley, W.	Invalided, 21st December, 1901.
3972	,, Coombs, W.	Invalided, 26th October, 1900. Invalided, 23rd January, 1902.
4729	,, Critton, C.	Invalided, 19th April, 1900.
3956	,, Davis, J.	Wounded, 20th October, 1899.
4466	,, Dean, H.	Died, 15th March, 1900.

Regtl. No.	Rank and Name.	Remarks.
4668	Pte. Dineen, A.	Killed in action, 9th October, 1900.
4491	L.-Corpl. Earle, H.	...
4370	Pte. Fallon, A.	...
3952	,, Felhan, T.	...
4603	,, Fielding, W.	...
4115	L.-Corpl. Flatt, G.	Invalided, 26th November, 1901.
3820	Pte. Fulcher, A.	...
4283	L.-Corpl. Germaine, A.	...
4689	Pte. Goater, E.	Invalided, 27th June, 1900.
4632	,, Greaves, B.	...
4468	,, Greenfield, F.	...
3853	,, Harman, A.	...
3958	,, Harris, W.	...
4057	,, Harrison, W.	Invalided, 1st April, 1901.
4236	,, Hawkins, A.	..
4091	,, Head, F.	Invalided, 30th July, 1900.
4212	,, Hepburn, C.	...
4399	,, Hider, T.	...
4496	L.-Corpl. Hiscock, A.	...
4376	Pte. Hogg, E.	Invalided, 7th September, 1900.
4762	,, Hopkins, T.	...
4751	L.-Sergt. Howard, W.	Wounded, 8th Dec., 1899. Killed in action, 24th Dec., 1900.
4358	Pte. Hudson, T.	...
4646	,, Hunt, C.	...
4435	L.-Corpl. Hunter, R.	Killed in action, 16th April, 1901.
4433	Pte. Hurlston, J.	...
4274	L.-Corpl. Irvine, F.	Wounded, 20th October, 1899.
4761	Pte. Jackson, R.	...
4686	,, Jones, J.	Invalided, 24th February, 1902.
4449	,, Josey, S.	...
4368	,, Kearney, P.	...
4227	,, Lane, W.	...
4532	,, Lead, W.	...
4674	,, Leeder, H.	...
4790	,, Leith, W.	...
3923	,, Linden, T.	...
4037	,, Malcolm, J.	...
4075	,, Matthews, G.	Wounded, 16th April, 1901.
4333	,, Matthews, W.	...
4313	,, Maton, E.	Wounded, 8th December, 1899. Invalided, 27th June, 1900.
4406	,, Mc Fudgeon, A.	...
4550	,, Mc Leod, D.	...
4215	,, Mc Pherson, J.	...
4125	,, Millgate, F.	...
4172	L.-Corpl. Millar, J.	Wounded, 20th October, 1899.
4272	Pte. Millar, J.	Invalided, 11th May, 1900.
4226	,, Mitchell, C.	...
4065	,, Morgan, W.	...
4254	,, Mitchell, G.	...
4011	,, Neighbour, R.	...
4098	,, Nicholls, E.	...
4552	,, Nicoll, F.	...
4663	L.-Corpl. Padfield, F.	...

Appendix C. 271

Regtl. No.	Rank and Name.	Remarks.
3746	Pte. Page, S.	Invalided, 29th May, 1900. Died, 4th October, 1900.
4361	„ Parker, A.	
4060	„ Pavitt, J.	
3986	„ Pike, E.	
4328	„ Pullinger, H.	
4656	„ Quayles, A.	
4699	„ Quick, H.	
4031	„ Ratcliffe, H.	
4013	„ Reid, P.	Killed in action, 2nd Nov., 1900.
4708	L.-Corpl. Reeves, W.	
4591	Pte. Renton, R.	
4748	„ Roach, T.	Wounded, 16th April, 1901.
3839	„ Rogers, C.	
4460	„ Rutherford, W.	
4676	„ Saunders, E.	
4783	„ Sawtell, W.	Wounded, 10th June, 1900.
4567	„ Scott, A.	
3587	„ Sefton, W.	
4606	„ Seppings, J.	
4182	„ Shand, G.	
4443	L.-Corpl. Sharp, T.	
4168	Pte. Shiels, J.	Died, 16th August, 1900.
4609	„ Shrubsole, A.	Killed in action, 20th October, 1899.
4747	„ Smith, W.	Invalided, 11th March, 1902.
4386	„ Smith, A.	Invalided, 11th October, 1900.
4412	„ Smith, R.	
4527	„ Stanton, E.	
4199	„ Stevens, W.	Invalided, 12th February, 1902.
4731	„ Stevens, R.	
4662	„ Stevenson, W.	
4290	„ Stewart, W.	Wounded, 8th December, 1899. Wounded, 2nd November, 1900. Invalided, 27th February, 1901.
4319	L.-Corpl. Stringer, W.	
4294	Pte. Talbot, W.	Killed in action, 24th Dec., 1900.
4493	„ Teale, W.	
4216	L.-Corpl. Thomas, C.	
4749	Pte. Thompson, H.	
4518	„ Thompson, C.	
4305	„ Thomson, T.	Wounded, 20th October, 1899. Invalided, 1st June, 1900.
4538	L.-Corpl. Tomlinson, W.	
4701	Pte. Trend, H.	Wounded, 6th April, 1901.
4772	„ Trump, W.	
3560	„ Turner, G.	
4430	L.-Corpl. Vigers, R.	
4010	Pte. Walker, G.	
4682	„ Walker, H.	
4396	„ Wall, J.	
4642	„ Webb, A.	
4589	„ Weir, G.	Wounded, 20th October, 1899. Invalided, 30th July, 1900.
3844	„ Wells, E.	
4346	„ West, H.	Invalided, 8th November, 1901.

272   The 18th Hussars in South Africa.

Regtl. No.	Rank and Name.	Remarks.
4119	Pte. Wilson, J.	...
4221	,, Wilson, G.	... Invalided, 23rd May, 1900.
4481	,, Woodgett, F.	...
4158	,, Woodley, H.	... Died of wounds, 22nd Feb., 1900.
3234	S.S.M. Legge, E.	...
4185	Corpl. Trump, E.	...

"C" SQUADRON.

2734	S.S.M. Mortiboy, G.	...
3278	,, Baldry, E.	...
3665	S.Q.M.S. Marshall, W.	...
2857	S.S.F. Challinor, W.	... Invalided, 10th September, 1901.
2426	S.Q.M.S. Watts, E.	...
3292	Sergt. Smith, A.	...
4784	,, Stevenson, W.	...
3204	,, Sturgess, C.	...
3388	,, Seppings, R.	...
3086	,, Foster, G.	...
3441	,, Batten, A.	... Killed in action, 20th October, 1899.
3304	,, Nest, T.	...
3039	,, Fidkin, J.	... Died, 5th April, 1902.
4441	S.S.F. Tate, H.	...
3985	,, Hamilton, G.	...
3678	Sergt. North, W.	...
3706	,, Birkett, W.	...
3486	,, Coatsworth, P.	...
3929	,, Butcher, J.	...
3546	,, Swabey, H.	...
3984	,, Fortune, D.	...
3337	Corpl. Overton, A.	...
3065	,, Kirkpatrick, C.	... Invalided, 5th June, 1901.
3832	,, Rees, J.	...
4169	Corpl. S.-S. Elvin, P.	...
4247	,, James, W.	...
4288	Corpl. Sadd. Boon, A.	...
3829	Corpl. Jordan, C.	... Invalided, 23rd May, 1900.
4084	,, Wilson, J.	... Invalided, 31st March, 1901.
3574	,, Kennett, J.	...
4306	,, Randall, W.	...
4192	,, Pollard, E.	...
4150	Trpt. Hall, A.	... Invalided, 14th November, 1901.
4558	,, Herniman, G.	... Wounded, 10th June, 1900.
4605	,, Robson, A.	...
4323	S.S. Carrington, H.	... Wounded, 30th July, 1901. Invalided, 25th September, 1901.
4177	,, Tucker, J.	...
4616	,, Moore, E.	...
3881	Pte. Addison, A.	...
4382	,, Austen, E.	...
4634	,, Baigent, A.	... Died, 5th March, 1900.
4298	,, Baker, J.	...
4720	,, Barwell, C.	...
4021	,, Bee, W.	... Wounded, 21st August, 1900. Invalided, 26th October, 1900.

Appendix C. 273

Regtl. No.	Rank and Name.	Remarks.
4793	Pte. Berry, E.	...
4286	,, Bradley, J.	...
4903	,, Brett, A.	... Invalided, 3rd July, 1900.
4152	,, Brimblecombe, F.	...
4487	,, Brown, F.	...
4132	,, Burkett, W.	... Killed in action, 24th Dec., 1900.
4670	,, Calver, E.	...
4696	,, Carleton, R.	...
4262	,, Carter, J.	... Wounded, 10th July, 1901.
4343	,, Clarke, A.	...
4590	,, Claridge, H.	... Invalided, 18th May, 1900.
4371	,, Clayton, C.	...
4219	,, Clegg, F.	... Wounded, 22nd October, 1899.
4512	,, Crouch, W.	... Died, 30th January, 1900.
4196	,, Cutmore, J.	...
4520	,, D'Arcy, W.	...
4717	,, Dawson, W.	...
3946	,, Deal, W.	... Wounded, 8th December, 1899.
4198	Corpl. Dearnley, B.	...
4062	Pte. Doyle, J.	...
3845	,, Drummond, R.	...
4528	,, Drummond, F.	...
3899	,, Duckerin, F.	...
3980	,, Emmett, W.	... Invalided, 3rd June, 1900.
4480	,. Evans, A.	... Wounded, 21st August, 1900. Invalided, 6th October, 1900.
4157	,, Evart, J.	... Wounded, 8th December, 1899. Invalided, 28th August, 1900.
4641	,, Ferguson, M.	...
4314	L.-Corpl. Field, H.	...
4778	,, Finch, W.	...
4377	Pte. Freeman, T.	...
4434	,, Gallacher, J.	...
3988	,, Gidney, T.	...
4628	,, Gould, L.	... Died of wounds, 8th December, 1899.
4711	,, Grace, E.	... Invalided, 17th May, 1900.
4066	,, Greenstock, G.	...
4261	,, Grieve, P.	... Killed in action, 20th October, 1899.
4548	,, Haddock, R.	...
4719	,, Halliday, E.	... Died of wounds, 8th December, 1902.
4702	,, Harding, W.	...
4143	,, Hart, J.	... Invalided, 4th August, 1900.
3890	,, Harvey, F.	...
4536	,, Hayles, S.	...
4365	,, Henderson, W.	... Invalided, 2th May, 1900.
4488	,, Holdsworth, J.	...
4334	L.-Corpl. Holloway, J.	... Invalided, 14th November, 1900. Wounded, 23rd January, 1901.
3816	Pte. Horsfield, G.	...
4044	,, Hurley, T.	...
3633	,, Johnson, R.	... Invalided, 10th May, 1900.
4269	,, Jones, H.	...
4420	,, Jowett, M.	...
4615	,, Kidd, D.	... Wounded, 25th January, 1901.
4700	,, King, G.	...

T

Regtl. No.	Rank and Name.	Remarks.
4059	Pte. Lawrie, G.	...
4795	,, Law, E.	...
4131	,, Lee, R.	...
4683	,, Leek, W.	...
4138	,, Lewis, A.	...
4030	,, Lock, H.	Killed, 20th October, 1899.
4222	,, Maggs, H.	...
4005	,, Mason, J.	Invalided, 12th February, 1901.
3813	,, Maloney, T.	Invalided, 29th May, 1900.
4401	,, Mc Donald, H.	...
4094	,, Mc Ewan, M.	...
4256	,, Mc Gavin, G.	...
4785	L.-Corpl. Mc Ginley, J.	Killed 30th July, 1901.
4165	Pte. Mc Hardy, J.	Killed, 8th December, 1899.
4179	,, Mc Lay, D.	...
4503	,, Mc Lay, J.	...
4036	,, Mc Quillan, F.	...
4780	,, Mc Veigh, W.	Invalided, 29th November, 1900.
3830	,, Meecham, B.	...
4657	,, Meekings, W.	Wounded, 8th December, 1899.
4788	,, Menzies, W.	Invalided, 16th July, 1900.
4229	,, Millbourne, E.	...
3910	,, Molyneaux, A.	...
4362	,, Morgan, H.	...
4036	,, Murray, J.	...
4280	,, Neil, D.	...
3822	,, Nicholl, J.	...
4714	,, Olley, H.	...
4549	L.-Corpl. Padwick, H.	Wounded, 20th October, 1899.
4608	Pte. Pamplin, W.	...
3981	,, Parsons, H.	...
4103	,, Peden, E.	Wounded, 30th June, 1901.
4706	,, Percival, A.	...
4042	,, Peters, F.	...
3818	,, Phillpot, W.	...
4373	,, Pritchard, E.	...
3951	,, Reed, A.	...
4446	,, Rendle, H.	Invalided, 21st March, 1900.
4336	,, Robertson, J.	Wounded, 17th November, 1899.
4263	,, Rose, H.	Invalided, 6th June, 1900.
4465	,, Ross, C.	...
4782	,, Rowe, T.	...
3817	,, Rummie, A.	...
3882	,, Russell, T.	...
4344	,, Scott, A.	Invalided, 30th August, 1900.
4675	,, Sefton, A.	...
4395	Sergt. Sexton, A.	Wounded, 20th October, 1899.
4239	Corpl. Sheeham, T.	Wounded, 8th December, 1899.
4635	Pte. Sherwood, J.	...
4356	,, Sibbick, J.	...
3750	,, Smith, F.	...
4741	,, Smith, J.	...
4208	,, Soper, J.	...
4156	,, Spence, W.	...
4559	,, Standen, F.	Invalided, 10th November, 1900.

Appendix C. 275

Regtl. No.	Rank and Name.	Remarks.
4757	L.-Corpl. Stannard, F.	Invalided, 16th June, 1900.
4467	Pte. Stevens, W.	...
4203	„ Still, G.	...
4104	Corpl. Strange, J.	...
4461	Pte. Swan, S.	...
4353	L.-Corpl. Tallboy, H.	...
4798	Pte. Taylor, R.	Died, 7th January, 1900.
4299	L.-Corpl. Thomson, A.	Invalided, 11th October, 1900.
3939	Pte. Thomas, R.	...
4614	„ Thorndyke, W.	...
3812	L.-Corpl. Todd, H.	...
4669	Pte. Tomlin, E.	Invalided, 23rd May, 1900.
4578	Sergt. Vesey, C.	...
4727	Pte. Waller, H.	Invalided, 29th May, 1900.
4181	„ Waterston, W.	Wounded, 20th October, 1899.
4426	„ Warren, T.	...
4451	L.-Corpl. Watts, H.	...
4282	Pte. Webster, S.	Wounded, 8th Dec., 1899. Killed in action, 18th April, 1901.
4347	„ Weir, J.	Died of wounds, 9th Dec., 1899.
4123	„ White, C.	...
4397	„ White, G.	...
4482	„ Whitter, W.	...
3733	L.-Sergt. Williams, J.	...
4348	Pte. Williams, S.	...
3960	„ Wilson, W.	...
4649	„ Wolfe, A.	...
4264	„ Wood, H.	...
4687	„ Woodley, J.	...
4718	L.-Corpl. Woolard, W.	Invalided, 18th May, 1900.
4472	Pte. Hurst, J.	..
4336	„ Robertson, J.	...
3122	Sergt. Coxen, H.	...
2286	„ Stanley, G.	Invalided, 7th September, 1900.
2538	„ Austen, W.	...
2849	Sergt.-Trpt. McManns, W.	...
3173	Pte. Austen, F.	Invalided, 19th April, 1901.
3230	„ Austen, C.	...
3398	Sergt. Baker, A.	Invalided, 13th May, 1900.
3722	Corpl. Baker, C.	...
4607	Pte. Birkenshaw, T.	Killed in action, 2nd February, 1900.
4109	„ Bracey, W.	...
4149	„ Cooper, C.	Wounded, 10th June, 1900.
4206	Corpl. Carroll	...
3360	Pte. Cook, A.	...
4483	„ Davidson, R.	...
3684	„ Denny, W.	...
4439	„ DeBrandt, W.	...
3658	L.-Corpl. Fauvell, C.	...
4799	Pte. Galvin, A.	...
3402	„ Johnson, A.	...
2846	„ James, R.	...
4774	„ Honeybone, C.	...
4759	„ Matthewson, C.	...
4644	„ Medhurst, H.	...

T 2

Regtl. No.	Rank and Name	Remarks
4755	Pte. Mills, B.	...
3477	,, Nice, J.	...
4105	,, Norman, W.	...
4490	,, Povis, R.	...
4756	,, Poppel, R.	...
4624	,, Roffey, E.	...
4610	,, Saunders, A.	...
4678	,, Tracey, A.	Invalided, 20th December, 1900.
4695	,, Vince, J.	Invalided, 27th February, 1901.
4619	,, Wallis, T.	Invalided, 6th June, 1900.
4801	,, Waterson, J.	...
3863	,, Ward, B.	...

N. C. O.'s and Men who proceeded to South Africa with Lieut. McClintock after Siege of Ladysmith.

Regtl. No.	Rank and Name	Remarks
3784	S.-I.-F. Ford, R.	...
3854	Sergt. Batchelor, G.	...
3266	S.-S.-F. Collinson, G.	...
3481	Sergt.-Farr. Clarke, A.	...
3244	L.-Sergt. Skelly, J.	...
3465	Corpl. Goodwin, W.	...
3392	,, Eade, H.	Invalided, 4th August, 1900. Wounded, 10th June, 1901.
3438	,, Tibbs, A.	...
3651	,, Knights, H.	...
3675	,, Shrimpton, A.	...
3794	,, Webb, A.	Invalided, 31st August, 1900.
3779	,, Adams, G.	...
3599	,, Dellar, J.	Invalided, 4th August, 1900.
3390	,, Alexander, A.	Invalided, 2nd February, 1900.
3419	Corpl.-S.-S. Wilkinson, A.	...
3605	,, Hunt, C.	...
3420	,, Tobel, P.	...
3124	Trpr. Williams, J.	...
3429	Pte. Allen, P.	Invalided, 13th May, 1900.
3553	,, Allison, W.	...
4659	,, Anderson, L.	...
3711	,, Barnes, C.	Wounded, 23rd January, 1901. Invalided, 11th March, 1902.
3377	,, Bartlett, T.	...
3728	,, Barwise, G.	Wounded, 25th January, 1901.
3451	,, Bell, H.	...
3248	,, Bird, J.	...
4522	,, Bishop, E.	...
3716	,, Black, T.	...
3900	,, Bott, G.	Wounded, 29th January, 1901.
3620	,, Bowden, G.	...
3591	,, Bradey, E.	Invalided, 27th June, 1900.
3619	,, Brogden, D.	...
4919	,, Brooks, E.	Killed in action, 4th Dec., 1901.
3907	,, Brown, J.	...
3692	,, Burden, J.	Invalided, 17th July, 1900.
3948	,, Casey, J.	...

Appendix C. 277

Regtl. No.	Rank and Name.	Remarks.
3434	Pte. Chalmers, G.	...
3475	,, Champion, T.	...
3411	,, Clarke, H.	... Invalided, 24th October, 1901.
3571	,, Clarke, M.	...
3379	,, Collyer, W.	... Killed in action, 24th Dec., 1900.
3795	,, Collier, S.	...
3443	,, Cook, H.	...
4985	,, Cooney, H.	...
3764	,, Coulter, W.	...
3685	,, Crack, H.	...
3698	,, Creedie, A.	...
3350	,, Eles, H.	...
3962	,, Elms, E.	...
3316	,, Everitt, H.	...
4291	,, Dobbin, G.	...
4023	,, Fisher, M.	...
4126	,, Fisk, J.	... Invalided, 22nd August, 1900.
3660	,, Flynn, W.	...
4431	,, French, J.	... Invalided, 6th June, 1900.
3500	,, Fryer, R.	...
3265	,, Gibbs, P.	...
3371	,, Godfrey, J.	...
3936	,, Gow, J.	... Invalided, 1st July, 1900.
3364	,, Griffen. A.	...
3705	,, Griffiths, G.	...
3540	,, Gray, J.	... Died, 28th June, 1900.
3792	,, Greening, G.	...
3626	,, Hale, A.	... Killed in action, 12th February, 1901.
3422	,, Harding, E.	...
3924	,, Hart, H.	... Invalided, 29th May, 1900.
3224	,, Higgins, C.	...
3355	,, Hopkins, F.	...
3311	,, Howell, E.	...
4418	,, Hunter, R.	... Invalided, 17th May, 1900.
3221	,, Hutchings, W.	...
3653	,, Jameson, W.	...
4515	,, Jones, H.	...
4566	,, Kempster, J.	...
3798	,, Kent, W.	... Invalided, 24th October, 1901.
3239	,, Kier, E.	... Invalided, 21st September, 1900.
3519	,, Laird, T.	...
3289	,, Lanaghan, M.	...
3704	,, Leonard, A.	...
3585	,, Lilley, G.	...
3416	,, Lockyer, G.	...
4053	,, Manklow, N.	...
3440	,, Manley, W.	...
3424	,, Mattheson, E.	... Invalided, 20th September, 1901.
3676	,, Matthews, G.	...
3657	,, Matthews, A.	...
4081	,, McReady, R.	...
4652	,, McGregor, W.	... Invalided, 24th October, 1901.
3718	,, McLaren, N.	...
3715	,, McNally, J.	...
3435	,, Merritt, C.	... Invalided, 14th November, 1901.

Regtl. No.	Rank and Name.		Remarks.
3887	Pte.	Myles, J.	Drowned, 14th February, 1902.
3512	,,	Murphy, W.	Invalided, 24th April, 1901.
3727	,,	Murray, C.	
3775	,,	Murray, J.	
4048	,,	Nevin, M.	Invalided, 16th July, 1900.
3652	,,	New, J.	
3478	,,	Nice, C.	
3797	,,	Nicholls, R.	Killed in action, 2nd February, 1901.
3778	,,	Otway, R.	
3714	,,	Paisley, G.	
3305	,,	Pauline, H.	
3998	,,	Pearce, C.	
3743	,,	Poole, H.	
3872	,,	Porter, G.	Killed in action, 31st July, 1901.
3461	,,	Primmer, A.	
3631	,,	Pritchett, J.	Killed in action, 24th Dec., 1900.
3167	L.-Corpl.	Radnor, C.	Invalided, 23rd January, 1901.
3745	Pte.	Riley, J.	
3699	,,	Rolston, J.	Invalided, 23rd May, 1900.
3613	,,	Rust, P.	Invalided, 6th December, 1900.
3630	,,	Savin, F.	Invalided, 6th August, 1900.
4875	,,	Selkirk, R.	Invalided, 16th July, 1900.
3474	,,	Shipley, J.	Died, 15th April, 1900.
3662	,,	Sladden, R.	Invalided, 19th March, 1900.
3384	,,	Smith, F.	
3397	,,	Slinger, S.	
3777	,,	Saundy, J.	
3286	L.-Corpl.	Stock, S.	Invalided, 5th July, 1900.
4003	Pte.	Sutherland, J.	
3756	,,	Tatton, W.	Invalided, 21st December, 1901.
3584	,,	Taylor, C.	Invalided, 11th October, 1900.
4638	,,	Thew, A.	Invalided, 6th July, 1900.
3772	,,	Toole, J.	
4270	,,	Tribe, G.	Invalided, 8th September, 1900.
4409	Corpl.	Wardley, T.	
3421	Pte.	Weeks, W.	
3372	,,	Whenham, C.	
3755	,,	Whitcombe, C.	
3800	,,	Wilde, W.	Invalided, 11th October, 1900.
4304	,,	Williams, L.	
3604	,,	Wilson, J.	
3776	,,	Wiltshire, J.	
3674	,,	Wright, F.	
3761	,,	Wooster, J.	
3406	,,	Wyatt, F.	
3356	,,	Youart, F.	Invalided, 22nd August, 1900.
3723	,,	Owen, F.	Killed in action, 29th January, 1902.

N.C.O.'s and men who joined at Ladysmith, 26th March, 1900, under command of Lieut. G. V. Webster.

3350	Corpl. Abbott, R.		
3317	Corpl.-S.-S. Pegg, G.		
3498	Corpl. Smith, J.		Invalided, 29th May, 1900.
3754	Pte. Anderson, W.		

Appendix C.   279

Regtl. No.	Rank and Name.	Remarks.
3459	Pte. Brown, J.	Invalided, 11th October, 1900.
3408	„ Clark, H.	Invalided, 7th September, 1900.
3276	„ Davis, J.	Invalided, 7th September, 1900.
3332	„ Gibbons, W.	Wounded, 2nd February, 1901. Invalided, 16th May, 1901.
3227	„ Grinham, E.	Died, 23rd May, 1900.
3058	„ Hackney, J.	...
3656	„ Holyome, J.	...
3281	„ Lill, W.	...
3339	„ Morgan, J.	Invalided, 8th October, 1900.
3343	„ Mould, J.	Invalided, 21st September, 1900.
3468	„ Phillips, J.	Invalided, 16th July, 1900.
3216	„ Plews, L.	...
3228	„ Roberts, E.	...
3485	„ Sandford, C.	...
3256	„ Seabrooke, A.	...
3298	„ Smith, F.	...
3288	„ Smith, W.	...
3297	L.-Corpl. Spicer, G.	...
3378	Corpl. Tatford, S.	...
3243	Pte. Baldwin, J.	...
3523	„ Coogan, A.	...
4142	„ Gorman, S.	Invalided, 14th August, 1900.
3494	„ Grint, F.	...
3729	„ Higginbottom, T.	Invalided, 16th July, 1900.
3873	Corpl. Hood, G.	Killed in action, 16th April, 1901.
3598	Pte. Kay, T.	Invalided, 14th November, 1900.
3516	„ Kaatze, A.	...
3213	„ Leonard, S.	Invalided, 16th June, 1900.
3413	, Martin, F.	Invalided, 7th September, 1900.
3202	„ Mitchell, G.	Invalided, 11th October, 1900.
2823	„ Neale, H.	...
4407	„ Phillips, E.	...
3380	„ Savage, W.	Invalided, 4th August, 1900.
3259	„ Snelling, C.	Invalided, 31st January, 1901.
3445	„ Strivens, A.	Wounded, 17th August, 1901. Invalided, 24th October, 1901.
3217	„ Till, C.	Invalided, 28th August, 1900.
3508	„ Walsh, W.	Invalided, 11th May, 1900.
3514	„ White, A.	...
3724	„ Patient, A.	...
3586	„ Pierce, A.	...
3361	L.-Sergt. Warwell, R.	...
3573	Pte. Dugdale, F.	Invalided, 23rd May, 1900.
3549	„ Fern, F.	Invalided, 23rd May, 1900.
2714	„ Griffen, A.	...
3455	„ Mansfield, W.	Invalided, 29th November, 1900.
3267	„ Matthews, F.	...
3831	„ Parker, W.	...
3282	„ Parsons, G.	...
3232	„ Shearman, H.	...
3852	„ Simmonds, E.	Invalided, 17th April, 1900.
4151	„ Smith, H.	...
3224	L.-Corpl. Swallow, C.	...
3315	Pte. Taylor, J.	...

The 18th Hussars in South Africa.

Regtl. No.	Rank and Name.		Remarks.
3209	Pte. Turner, O.	...	
3313	„ Wheeler, T.	...	Invalided, 16th July, 1900.
3212	„ Yates, W.	...	
3219	L.-Corpl. Pulford, W.	...	
3340	Pte. Wilson, J.	...	
3791	„ Holyoak, W.	...	Invalided, 10th April, 1900.

N.C.O.'s and men who joined the Regiment at Zandspruit, 22nd June, 1900.

5186	Corpl. Durkin, E.	...	Wounded, 6th October, 1901. Invalided, 9th November, 1901.
4815	Pte. Bonaker, W.	...	
4813	„ Brooks, J.	...	
4846	„ Butterfield, G.	...	
4811	„ Collett, F.	...	
4819	„ Day, C.	...	Invalided, 4th March, 1901.
4843	„ Dorey, W.	...	
4857	„ Forrest, J.	...	Invalided, 18th May, 1901.
4802	„ Griffen, G.	...	
4847	„ Hurcom, T.	...	Died, 29th December, 1900.
4728	„ Jones, T.	...	
4697	„ Knight, F.	...	
4808	„ Lightening, F.	...	
4803	„ Lyons, W.	...	Wounded, 6th October, 1901.
4817	„ Marshall, R.	...	
4850	„ Mitchelsom, C.	...	Invalided, 24th February, 1902.
4825	L.-Corpl. Morgan, T.	...	Killed in action, 30th July, 1901.
4804	Pte. Pallen, F.	...	
4694	„ Plummer, E.	...	
3495	„ Prior, A.	...	
4832	„ Quinn, F.	...	
4845	„ Rough, E.	...	
4257	„ Small, J.	...	Invalided, 21st December, 1901.
4734	„ Wallace, F.	...	
4828	„ Watson, A.	...	
4809	„ Webb, C.	...	
4833	„ Woolaston, H.	...	
4834	„ Knight, H.	...	
4814	„ Gibbs, C.	...	Died, 29th May, 1901.
4135	„ Hughes, R.	...	

N.C.O.'s and men who joined the Regiment at Middelburgh, November, 1900.

2506	L.-Corpl. Ritchie, J.	...	
3142	„ Tipping, T.	...	
3308	„ Cluney, S.	...	
3104	Pte. Barber, J.	...	
3172	„ Barnes, W.	...	
3049	„ Bee, S.	...	Invalided, 27th February, 1901.
2372	„ Beswick, T.	...	

Appendix C. 281

Regtl. No.	Rank and Name.	Remarks.
3113	S.-S. Bloxsome, G.	...
2405	Pte. D'Acres, M.	...
2425	,, Elton, J.	... Killed in action, 23rd January, 1901.
3175	,, Handscombe, A.	... Invalided, 7th September, 1901.
4842	,, Harman, W.	...
4906	,, Howlett, H.	...
3094	,, Hope, E.	... Invalided, 31st January, 1901.
2478	,, Hughes, W.	...
3132	,, Hawkins, R.	...
3121	,, Kemp, S.	...
4848	,, Lewington, H.	...
4823	,, Marchbank, F.	...
3073	Corpl. Speight, J.	...
3080	Pte. Smith, W.	...
4851	,, Smith, W.	...
4879	,, Sheehan, M.	... Wounded, 2nd February, 1901.
2440	,, Simmonds, J.	... Died, 4th February, 1902.
2271	,, Warren, W.	... Invalided, 12th October, 1901.
4810	,, Woolmore, H.	...
3099	,, Wood, G.	...
3072	,, Whitely, W.	...
3050	,, Ashton, J.	...

N.C.O.' and Men who joined the Regiment at Middelburg (under command of Captain C. H. Corbett), 14th January, 1901.

3908	Sergt. Brown, H.	... Wounded, 1st September, 1901.
3995	L.-Sergt. Lee, T.	...
4805	Pte. Boyes, E.	...
4816	,, Pawley, W.	...
4822	,, Norris, W.	...
4830	,, Carter, E.	...
4831	,, Symons, F.	...
4838	,, North, H.	...
4852	,, Duff, W.	...
4853	Boy Webb, A.	... Invalided, 4th May, 1901.
4858	Pte. Dowling, E.	...
4862	,, Cripps, E.	...
4867	,, Randle, A.	...
4868	,, Oran, F.	... Invalided, 20th May, 1901.
4870	,, Manlove, T.	...
4872	,, Harrison, J.	...
4876	,, Rogers, J.	...
4881	,, Tassell, C.	... Invalided, 9th September, 1901.
4883	,, Pollard, W.	...
4887	,, Bates, A.	...
4893	,, Mainstone, J.	... Invalided, 27th December, 1901.
4884	,, Millburn, C.	...
4888	,, Drayson, L.	...
4899	,, Cattrall, A.	...
4904	Boy Steele, W.	...
4905	,, Smith, J.	...
4909	Pte. Holness, J.	... Died, 30th May, 1901.

Regtl. No.	Rank and Name.	Remarks.
4910	Pte. Lugton, W.	...
4939	„ Brown, J.	...
4915	„ West, O.	...
4920	„ Levi, W.	...
4921	„ Stride, J.	...
4922	„ Lock, J.	...
4924	L.-Corpl. Walter, A.	...
4929	Pte. Wharton, W.	... Invalided, 9th November, 1901.
4930	„ Roome, W.	...
4934	„ Parrott, G.	... Invalided, 24th February, 1902.
4945	„ Everest, A.	...
4937	„ Dale, H.	...
4938	„ Palmer, R.	... Invalided, 5th February, 1902.
4942	„ Ellery, R.	...
4946	„ Cannon, A.	...
4947	„ Cox, W.	...
4949	„ Smith, G.	...
4950	„ Cherrill, F.	... Invalided, 21st July, 1901.
4953	„ Welch, F.	... Invalided, 18th January, 1902.
4954	„ Wood, C.	...
4955	„ White, J.	...
4958	„ Carter, C.	...
4959	„ Paton, J.	...
4975	„ Smith, H.	...
4963	„ Vaughan, T.	...
4964	„ Catford, W.	...
4968	„ King, A.	..
4966	„ Parker, A.	...
4967	„ Davies, W.	...
4969	„ Griesel, J.	...
4970	„ Ives, F.	... Invalided, 16th June, 1901.
4977	„ Garside, G.	...
4974	„ Laws, F.	... Invalided, 9th March, 1902.
4976	„ Bowrey, S.	...
4979	„ Clarke, E.	... Wounded, 1st September, 1901.
4980	„ Wright, J.	...
4989	„ Ray, C.	...
4983	„ Roberts, C.	...
4986	„ Meaker, T.	...
4987	„ Taylor, W.	...
4994	L.-Corpl. Brown, S.	...
4990	Pte. Harris, H.	... Died, 29th May, 1901.
4993	„ Bush, J.	...
4995	„ Glover, R.	...
4996	„ Crowe, H.	... Invalided, 17th June, 1901.
4998	„ Fuller, F.	...
4997	S.-S. Hayter, V.	...
5001	Pte. Hives, J.	...
5004	L.-Corpl. Foskett, C.	...
5005	Pte. McCarthy, C.	... Wounded, 16th April, 1901. Invalided, 21st July, 1901.
5006	„ Rockell, H.	...
5009	L.-Corpl. Aldous, H.	... Died, 17th February, 1902.
5014	Pte. Banks, G.	...
5016	„ Prime, E.	... Wounded, 30th June, 1901. Invalided, 25th September, 1901.

Appendix C. 283

Regtl. No.	Rank and Name.	Remarks.
5015	Pte. Horner, W.	...
5019	,, Crowhurst, J.	...
5021	,, Collins, A.	...
5022	,, Healey, H.	...
5024	,, Dowsett, R.	...
5049	,, Martin, D.	...
5026	,, Humm, A.	... Invalided, 20th March, 1901.
5028	,, Parker, F.	...
5030	L.-Corpl. Forrester, J.	... Died, 1st February, 1901.
5031	Pte. Freeman, F.	...
5037	,, Gibbons, A.	...
5033	,, Everest, H.	... Invalided, 16th June, 1901.
5034	,, Elvin, C.	... Invalided, 9th November, 1901.
5036	,, Anderson, C.	...
5042	,, King, C.	...
5043	,, Staton, G.	...
5041	,, Filler, H.	...
5067	,, Sowden, H.	... Invalided, 26th February, 1901.
5047	,, Wiseman, J.	...
5049	,, Stewart, F.	...
5048	,, Watts, H.	...
5052	,, Bruton, W.	...
5053	,, Baldwin, W.	... Died, 2nd July, 1901.
5054	,, Baldwin, E.	...
5051	,, Elliott, A.	...
5055	,, Meredith, H.	... Wounded, 23rd January, 1901 Died, 21st December, 1901.
5057	,, Hassum, H.	... Died, 29th March, 1901.
5064	,, Hobbs, H.	...
5059	,, Coby, W.	...
5060	,, Sparks, W.	... Killed in action, 20th Feb., 1902.
5065	,, Dunford, W.	... Invalided, 29th May, 1901.
5066	,, Broughton, W.	... Invalided, 10th August, 1901.
5069	,, Sykes, F.	...
5071	L.-Corpl. Margetts, T.	... Died, 2nd June, 1901.
5073	Pte. Smith, A.	...
5081	,, Peake, H.	... Died, 25th March, 1902.
5086	,, Perdue, L.	...
5072	,, Lewis, H.	...
5077	,, Snelling, J.	...
5084	,, Monks, W.	...
5088	,, Moore, G.	...
5087	,, Moger, T.	...
5083	,, Bailey, H.	...
5091	,, Smith, J.	...
5094	,, Maloney, T.	...
5095	,, Fairbrother, C.	...
5097	,, Tillman, T.	...
5103	,, Porter, F.	...
5089	,, Still, G.	...
5090	,, Grist, T.	... Wounded, 27th June, 1901.
5096	,, Martin, H.	...
5102	,, Jackson, A.	...
5093	,, Gaines, E.	...
5101	,, Walsh, T.	...

Regtl. No.	Rank and Name.	Remarks.
5108	Pte. McAusland, W.	...
5099	„ Loughlin, J.	... Invalided, 27th February, 1901.
5105	„ Armitt, W.	...
5104	„ Hegley, W.	...
5115	„ Strudwick, H.	...
5113	„ Corton, W.	...
5114	„ Henry, W.	...
5111	„ Rand, A.	...
5122	„ Reid, R.	...
5120	„ Elson, H.	...
5123	„ Harris, W.	...
5128	„ Paul, F.	...
5125	„ Lovett, E.	...
5126	„ Collier, J.	...
5129	„ Howard, E.	... Wounded, 6th October, 1901. Invalided, 24th October, 1901.
5121	„ Woodward, A.	...
5132	„ Clarke, G.	... Killed in action, 6th June, 1901.
5135	„ Stevens, A.	...
5136	„ McEwan, D.	... Died, 10th April, 1901.
5167	„ Buckingham, W.	...
5138	„ Bury, E.	...
5146	„ Turnbull, R.	...
5153	„ Woosey, R.	...
5152	„ Wickham, W.	...
5166	„ Foster, J.	... Invalided, 25th November, 1901.
5176	„ Lees, A.	...
5185	„ Hogben, C.	... Wounded, 30th July, 1901.
5189	„ Easton, G.	...
5196	„ Mc Kenzie, J.	... Invalided, 27th December, 1901.
5214	„ Rose, C.	...
5279	„ Town, T.	...
4806	„ Graham, A.	...
4827	„ Leech, B.	... Wounded, 16th April, 1901. Killed in action, 14th August, 1901.
4854	Boy Davis, P.	... Died, 28th October, 1901.
4859	„ Corp, B.	...
4869	Pte. Fuller, G.	...
4962	„ Hay, W.	...
5013	„ Simpson, C.	...
5464	„ Town, J.	...

N.C.O.'s and men who joined at Middelburg, June, 1901.

3271	S.-S.-F. Mooney, H.	...
4812	Pte. Mann, A.	...
4821	„ French, S.	...
4824	„ Birks, F.	... Invalided, 29th August, 1901.
4839	„ Lee, J.	...
4860	„ Willett, S.	... Died, 10th June, 1901.
4863	„ King, F.	...
4889	„ Hill, F.	...
4890	„ Berry, A.	... Wounded, 2nd July, 1901
4892	„ Gyngell, E.	...

Appendix C. 285

Regtl. No.	Rank and Name.	Remarks.
4895	Pte. Buckingham, H.	...
4894	,, Emonson, W.	...
4898	,, Hall, A.	... Died, 6th August, 1901.
4900	,, Sargeant, G.	...
4901	,, Hood, T.	...
4912	,, Sampson, C.	...
4913	,, Garrett, S.	...
4914	,, Shuttes, F.	...
4916	,, Leyster, H.	...
4917	,, Norris, J.	...
4943	,, Ward, F.	... Died, 5th June, 1901.
4965	,, Tribe, W.	... Died, 23rd February, 1902.
4972	,, Croft, E.	...
5000	,, Unwin, C.	...
5002	,, Croft, J.	...
5008	,, Edgeley, C.	...
5010	,, Parr, C.	...
5025	,, Sporle, R.	...
5027	,, Shearing, T.	...
5045	,, Paul, G.	...
5044	,, Williams, E.	... Died, 18th February, 1902.
5050	,, Wingrove, J.	... Invalided, 14th April, 1902.
5063	,, Weston, B.	...
5070	,, Green, F.	... Died, 27th February, 1902.
5075	,, Watson, W.	... Died, 20th August, 1901.
5085	,, Neale, G.	...
5082	,, Cates, J.	...
5092	,, Gage, F.	...
5100	,, Luff, P.	... Invalided, 24th February, 1902.
5109	,, McKenzie, J.	...
5131	,, Louis, M.	...
5149	,, Moore, H.	...
5188	,, Nixon, J.	...

N.C.O.'s and men who joined at Eland's River, July 12th, 1901.

3682	Sergt. Mill, R.	...
5843	S.-S. Londsdale, R.	...
4418	Pte. Hunter, R.	...
4840	,, Furneaux, T.	...
4885	,, Berry, H.	...
4908	,, Lewis, D.	...
5404	,, Hassard, J.	...
4956	,, Morse, C.	...
4961	,, Cuff, R.	...
5017	,, Densham, W.	... Invalided, 12th February, 1902.
5107	,, Watts, A.	...
5143	,, Brunton, F.	...
5142	,, Scott, A.	...
5145	,, Guscott, S.	...
5150	,, Baird, W.	...
5147	,, Mitchell, W.	...
5148	,, Willats, S.	...
5154	,, Donaldson, R.	...

Regtl. No.	Rank and Name.	Remarks.
5155	Pte. Porteous, R.	...
5163	„ Townsend, W.	...
5169	„ Dewar, D.	... Invalided, 14th April, 1902.
5177	L.-Corpl. Allcock, R.	... Invalided, 10th February, 1902.
5179	Pte. Ferguson, T.	...
5181	„ Cooper, C.	... Died, 21st January, 1902.
5180	„ Benton, A.	...
5187	„ Cattle, A.	...

N.C.O.'s and men who joined August, 1901.

3671	Corpl. Petty, E.	...
5865	Pte. Gooden, W.	...
4855	„ Bear, B.	...
5845	„ Dearing, H.	...
4877	„ Harris, A.	...
4941	„ Eddy, C.	...
5079	„ Summers, J.	... Died, 10th December, 1901.
5124	„ Watts, W.	...
5130	„ Hill, W.	...
5140	„ Nixey, W.	... Invalided, 12th November, 1902.
5157	„ Chapman, C.	...
5162	„ Tolley, A.	...
5170	„ Sheriff, W.	...
5171	„ Lowbridge, W.	... Invalided, 24th February, 1902.
5178	„ Bolston, W.	...
5182	„ Clements, R.	...
5191	„ Lindsay, W.	...
5195	„ Marsh, J.	...
5198	„ Webb, A.	...
5197	„ Smith, N.	... Invalided, 14th November, 1901.
5201	„ Brown, A.	...
5202	„ Arthur, J.	...
5203	„ Frazer, W.	...
5206	„ Sanderson, J.	...
5205	„ Stevens, J.	...
5210	„ Oliver, J.	...
5211	„ Chapman, C.	...
5208	„ Wolstencroft, J.	...
5209	„ Worrall, J.	...
5217	„ Childs, H.	...
5213	„ Walton, H.	...
5219	„ Lowing, A.	...
5222	„ Hume, J.	...
5221	„ Hart, E.	... Died, 23rd February, 1902.
5224	„ Smith, H.	...
5227	„ Stenning, G.	...
5239	„ Eades, B.	...
5237	„ Russell. W.	...
5232	„ Helliwell, F.	...
5236	„ Neller, H.	...
5241	„ Stewart, A.	...
5243	„ Bellingham, F.	... Invalided, 5th February, 1902.
	„ McCafferty, C.	...

Appendix C. 287

Regtl. No.	Rank and Name.	Remarks.
	Pte. Keavey, M.	...
	,, Templeman, G.	...
	,, Harris, G.	...
	,, McLeod, D.	...
	,, Nixon, C.	...
5568	,, Wallace, F.	...

N.C.O.'s and Men who joined the Regiment February, 1902.

Regtl. No.	Rank and Name.	Remarks.
5979	Corpl. Massey, E.	...
5307	Pte. Coppen, R.	...
5309	,, Tanton, G.	...
5315	,, Travers, E.	...
5396	,, Davis, J.	...
5414	,, Pitts, A.	...
5432	,, Cummings, W.	...
5448	,, Howarth, G.	...
5479	,, Ritchie, W.	...
5490	,, Baker, T.	... Invalided, 9th March, 1902.
5560	,, Doherty. G.	...
5515	,, Taylor, W.	...
5501	,, Forrester, A.	...
5502	,, Cowan, G.	...
5510	,, Hawkins, A.	...
5516	,, Santen, C.	... Died, 20th March, 1902.
5525	,, Knubley, D.	...
5511	,, Harvey, H.	...
5503	,, Williams, L.	...
5512	,, Basham, W.	...
5518	,, Smith, A.	...
5519	,, Bickle, H.	...
5527	,, Veitch, J.	...
5579	,, Veal, J.	...
5540	,, Bannister, E.	...
5542	,, Taylor, A.	...
5545	,, Davis, G.	...
5548	,, Malston, T.	...
5549	,, Moxam, J.	... Invalided, 24th February, 1902.
5573	,, Howe, J.	...
5550	,, Wilson, H.	...
5565	,, Hull, W.	...
5566	,, Mills, G.	...
5574	,, Brewer, W.	...
5582	,, Cross, J.	...
5586	,, Meakes, C.	... Died, 20th July, 1902.
5590	,, Bowes, H.	...
5598	,, Wright, G.	...
5610	,, Watson, C.	...
5617	,, Forbes, A.	...
5600	,, Sullivan, F.	... Invalided, 21st March, 1902.
5601	,, Eaves, W.	...
5606	,, Caplin, H.	...
5611	,, Byrnand, F.	...
5612	,, Spacey, A.	...

288   The 18th Hussars in South Africa.

Regtl. No.	Rank and Name.	Remarks.
5619	Pte. Dooley, J.	...
5622	,, Propert, S.	...
5623	,, Gaiger, W.	...
5624	,, Mandy, A.	...
5625	,, Reed, H.	...
5631	,, Ellis, J.	...
5632	,, Gale, T.	...
5657	,, Small, A.	...
5651	,, Forman, A.	...
5653	,, Reed, W.	...
5660	,, Saunders, A.	...
5663	,, Halliday, T.	...
5667	,, Woolger, J.	...
5668	,, Webb, G.	...
5670	,, Perkins, V.	...
5675	,, Hill, W.	...
5676	,, Dalny, G.	...
5684	,, Ackers, J.	...
5690	,, Harlow, J.	...
5687	,, Powell, G.	...
5806	,, Griffen, F.	... Invalided, 14th April, 1902.

N.C.O.'s and men who joined the Regiment from other Departments, etc.

3025	Q.-M.-S. Parsons, W.	...
3763	Corpl. Baker, J.	...
3428	Pte. Elmore, W.	... Invalided, 10th September, 1901.
4653	,, Nicholas, E.	... Died, 14th January, 1901.
3414	,, Wells, E.	... Invalided, 20th May, 1901.

APPENDIX D.

List of Officers mentioned in Despatches, Promoted, awarded Honours, etc.

Rank and Name	Date of Despatch	Remarks
Major E. C. Knox	Sir G. White's Despatch, dated 2nd Dec. 1900	"A thoroughly capable commander, worthy of advancement."
Major H. T. Laming	Gen. Buller's Despatch, dated 19th June, 1900	
Capt. M. S. Wellby	,, ,, ,,	
Capt. E. C. Haag	Gen. Buller's Despatch, dated 9th Nov., 1900	
Lieut.-Col. E. C. Knox	,, ,, ,,	
Major H. J. Laming	,, ,, ,,	"A very good squadron leader."
Capt. & Adjt. C. Burnett	,, ,, ,,	"A thoroughly capable officer."
Capt. E. C. Haag	,, ,, ,,	"An excellent squadron leader and one who well understands South African warfare."
Lieut. C. D. Field	,, ,, ,,	"Very good at reconnaissance, and rendered excellent work as Brigade-Provost-Marshal."
Lieut. C. J. Thackwell	,, ,, ,,	"An excellent promising young officer."
Lieut. C. J. Thackwell	Lord Kitchener's Despatch, dated March 8th, 1901	The report on skirmish at Uitkyk, near Middelburg, 24th December, 1900, noted "The gallant conduct of Lieut. Thackwell, who was at the head of the party"; also "the very excellent services rendered by this officer during the campaign," and stated he "behaved with great gallantry." Lieut. Thackwell was awarded the D.S.O.
Major H. T. Laming	Lord Roberts' Despatch, dated Sept. 4th, 1901	
Capt. C. Burnett	,, ,, ,,	
Capt. E. C. Haag	,, ,, ,,	

u

List of Officers mentioned in Despatches, Promoted, awarded Honours, etc.—continued.

Rank and Name	Date of Despatch	Remarks
Capt. J. H. Gosselin	Lord Roberts' Despatch, dated Sept 4th, 1901	
Lieut. J. L. Wood	,, ,, ,,	
Lieut. C. D. Field	,, ,, ,,	
Lieut. E. H. Bayford	,, ,, ,,	
Lieut. G. V. Clarke	,, ,, ,,	
Lieut. J. G. Dugdale	,, ,, ,,	
Lieut. J. W. Lichtenberg	Lord Kitchener's Despatch, dated Oct. 8th, 1901	Awarded the D.S.O. "for conspicuous gallantry on Oliphant's River, July 30th, in pursuit of Viljoen's convoy, when in face of very superior numbers of the enemy; though dangerously wounded, by his courage and example enabled his small party to hold out for two hours against repeated attacks, and thereby secured capture of a large portion of convoy."
Capt. C. H. Leveson	Lord Kitchener's Despatch, dated March 8th, 1902	Awarded D.S.O. for conspicuous good service in December and January.
Lieut. C. V. Clarke	,, ,, ,,	,,
Lieut. J. G. Dugdale	*London Gazette*, 29th Nov. 1900	Awarded D.S.O.
Major H. T. Laming	,, ,, ,,	,,
Lieut. J. L. Wood	,, ,, ,,	To be Brevet Lieut.-Colonel.
Major E. C. Knox	,, ,, ,,	To be Brevet Major.
Capt. C. Burnett	,, ,, ,,	,,
Capt. E. C. Haag	,, ,, ,,	,,
Lieut.-Col. P. S. Marling, V.C.	Lord Kitchener's Despatch, dated April 8th, 1902	Awarded D.S.O.
Major W. P. M. Pollok	Lord Kitchener's final Despatch, dated June 23rd, 1902	
Capt. C. H. Leveson	,, ,, ,,	,,
Lieut. E. H. Bayford	,, ,, ,,	,,
Lieut. C. D. Field	,, ,, ,,	
Lieut.-Col. P. S. Marling, V.C.	,, ,, ,,	To be Companion of the Order of the Bath.

Appendix D.

List of N.C.O.'s and Men mentioned in Despatches.

Rank and Name.	Date of Despatch.
Sergt. Howard, W.	Sir G. White's Despatch, 2nd Dec., 1899.
S.S.M. Mortiboy, G.	(Attached to Bethune's Mounted Infantry).
F.Q.M.S. Padfield, W.	Gen. Buller's Despatch, 9th Nov., 1900.
Sergt. Howard, W.	Gen. Buller's Despatch, 9th November, 1900.
„ Baker, H.	„ „ „
„ Shakespeare, W.	Lord Roberts' Despatch, 4th September, 1901.
S.Q.M.S. Batchelor, G.	„ „ „
Sergt. Fortune, D.	„ „ „
„ Swabey, H.	„ „ „
„ Butcher, J.	„ „ „
Corpl. Sheehan, T.	„ „ „
Sergt. Sexton, W.	„ „ „
Pte. Stewart, W.	„ „ „
S.Q.M.S. Batchelor	Lord Kitchener's Despatch, March 8th, 1901.
Sergt. Stephens, G.	„ „ „
„ Coxen, H.	„ „ „
Corpl. Valpy, R.	„ „ „
Sergt. Sexton, W.	„ „ „
Pte. Hopkins, F.	„ „ „
Corpl. Speight, J.	„ „ „
„ Faulkner, F.	„ „ „
„ Hall, G.	„ „ „
„ Kidd, D.	„ „ „
Pte. Seppings, J.	„ „ „
„ Smith, W.	„ „ „
Corpl. Stork, J.	Lord Kitchener's Despatch, July 28th, 1901.
Sergt. Baker, H.	„ „ „
S.Q.M.S. Batchelor, G.	„ „ „
Pte. Bleakley, S.	„ „ „
Sergt. Stevenson, G.	Lord Kitchener's Despatch, October 8th, 1901.
Corpl. Wardley, T.	„ „ „
Sergt. Vesey, C.	„ „ „
Corpl. S. S. Moore	„ „ „
S.S.M. Baldry, E.	„ „ „
Corpl. Jones, H.	„ „ „
L.-Corpl. Sharp, D.	Lord Kitchener's Despatch, Dec., 8th, 1901.
Pte. Shaw, J.	„ „ „
„ Warren, W.	„ „ „
Corpl. Durkin, E.	„ „ „
L.-Corpl. Williams, J.	Lord Kitchener's Despatch, March 8th, 1902.
Sergt. Swabey, H.	„ „ „
Corpl. Sheehan, T.	„ „ „
R.S.M. Simmonds, H. A.	Lord Kitchener's Despatch, June 23rd, 1902.
S.S.M. Power, W.	„ „ „
Sergt. Fortune, D.	„ „ „
Pte. Thorndyke, W.	„ „ „
F.Q.M.S. Padfield, W.	„ „ „
S.S.M. Legge, E.	„ „ „

Roll of N.C.O.'s and Men Promoted for Gallantry.

Rank and Name.		Remarks.
L.-Corpl. Sexton, W.	...	Promoted Sergeant, March 8th, 1901.
Pte. Kidd, D.	...	,, Corporal, March 8th, 1901.
,, Spright, J.	...	,, Corporal, March 8th, 1901.
,, Faulkner, F.	...	,, Corporal, March 8th, 1901.
,, Hall, G.	...	,, Corporal, March 8th, 1901.
,, Stork, J.	...	,, Corporal, July 28th, 1901.
,, Wardley, T.	...	,, Corporal, October 8th, 1901.
S.S. Moore	...	,, Corporal, October 8th, 1901.
L.-Corpl. Vesey, C.	...	,, Sergeant, October 8th, 1901.
Pte. Jones, H.	...	,, Corporal, October 8th, 1901.
,, Sheehan, T.	...	,, Corporal, March 8th, 1902.

List of Warrant and N.C.O.'s and Men awarded Distinguished Conduct Medals.

R.S.M. Simmonds, H. A.
S.S.M. Mortiboy, G.
 ,, Baldry, E.
S.Q.M.S. Batchelor, G.
S.S.M. Legge, E.
Sergt. Stevenson, G.
 ,, Swabey, H.

Sergt. Baker, H.
S.S.M.R.R. Collier, A.
Corpl. Williams, J.
 ,, Sheehan, T.
Pte. Stewart, W.
 ,, Bracey, W.
 ,, Morgan, T.

Victoria Cross.

Pte. H. C. Crandon.—On July 4th, at Springbok Laagte, Ptes. Berry and Crandon were scouting towards a kopje, when the Boers suddenly opened fire on them at a range of 100 yards. Pte. Berry's horse fell and became disabled, and he was himself shot in the right hand and left shoulder. Pte. Crandon at once rode back under a heavy fire to his assistance, gave up his horse to the wounded man to enable him to reach shelter, and followed him on foot, having to run for 1100 yards, all the time under fire. (October 18th, 1901.)

APPENDIX E.

List of Officers, N.C.O.'s, and Men Killed and Died of Wounds during War.

No.	Regtl. No.	Rank and Name	Squad.	Date of Death	Place	Remarks
1	3441	Sergt. Batten, A.	C	20th Oct., 1899	Talana	
2	4374	Trptr. Salmon, C.	B	,, ,, ,,	,,	
3	4030	Pte. Lock, W.	C	,, ,, ,,	,,	
4	4097	,, Bushell, T.	A	,, ,, ,,	,,	
5	4609	,, Shrubsole, A.	B	,, ,, ,,	,,	Reported from Pretoria
6	4752	L.-Corpl. Clarridge, R.	B	8th Dec. ,,	Ladysmith	
7	4165	Pte. McHardy, J.	C	,, ,, ,,	,,	Died from wounds received 8th Dec., 1899
8	4347	L.-Corpl. Weir, J.	C	9th ,, ,,	,,	Died from wounds received 8th Dec., 1899
9	4628	Pte. Gould, L.	C	,, ,, ,,	,,	Severely wounded, shell fire, 2nd Dec., 1899
10	2028	,, Owen, A.	B	16th ,, ,,	,,	Died from wounds received 8th Dec., 1899
11	4719	,, Halliday, W.	C	4th Jan., 1900	Waggon Hill	
12	3605	Sergt. Webb, H.	A	6th ,, ,,	Ladysmith	
13	4158	Pte. Woodley, H.	B	22nd ,, ,,	Landspruit	Died from wounds received 8th Dec., 1899
14	4633	L.-Corpl. Arnold, A.	B	30th June ,,	Meerzicht	Died from wounds received 29th June, 1900
15	...	Capt. Wellby, M. S.	B	5th Aug. ,,		Died from wounds received 30th July, 1900. Buried at Zandspruit
16	4161	Pte. Caddis, D.	B	5th Sept. ,,	Dulstroom	Died from wounds received 4th Sept., 1900
17	4551	,, Langlands, J.	A	20th ,, ,,	Badfontein	
18	3348	Corpl. Brown, A.	B	1st June ,,	Heilbron	
19	4668	Pte. Dineen, A.	B	9th Oct. ,,	Near Lyndenburg	
20	4013	,, Reid, P.	B	2nd Nov. ,,	Near Middelburg	
21	4261	,, Grieve, P.	C	20th Oct., 1899	Talana	Death ascertained from evidence taken by a Court of Enquiry

List of Officers, N.C.O.'s, and Men Killed and Died of Wounds during the War—continued.

No.	Regtl. No.	Rank and Name	Squad.	Date of Death	Place	Remarks
22	4751	L.-Sergt. Howard, W.	B	24th Dec., 1900	Near Uitkyk	Buried there
23	4132	Pte. Birkett, W.	B	,, ,, ,,	,, ,,	Died from wounds
24	3379	,, Collyer, J.	B	,, ,, ,,	,, ,,	Died from wounds
25	3631	,, Pritchett, J.	B	,, ,, ,,	,, ,,	
26	4294	,, Talbot, W.	B	,, ,, ,,	,, ,,	
27	2524	,, Elton, J.	C	23rd Jan., 1901	Wonderfontein	
28	3723	,, Owen, F.	B	29th ,, ,,	,,	
29	...	Lieut. Cawston, C. F.	A	3rd Feb. ,,	Roodeport	
30	4576	L.-Corpl. Gill, C.	A	2nd ,, ,,	,,	
31	3797	Pte. Nicholls, W.	A	,, ,, ,,	,,	
32	4607	,, Birkenshaw, T.	A	,, ,, ,,	,,	
33	4082	,, Tindle, F.	A	,, ,, ,,	,,	
34	3626	,, Hale, A.	B	12th Feb. ,,	Uitkyk	
35	4282	,, Webster, S.	C	18th April ,,	Smut's Farm, Ermelo	
36	5132	,, Clarke, G.	B	6th June ,,	Elandsfontein (214)	
37	3873	Corpl. Hood, G.	B	16th April ,,	Dulstroom	
38	4435	L.-Corpl. Hunter, R. H. A.	B	,, ,, ,,	,,	Died of wounds
39	4785	,, McGinley, J.	C	30th July ,,	Welverdiend	
40	4825	,, Morgan, F.	C	,, ,, ,,	,,	Died of wounds received 16th April, 1901 Buried at Pretoria
41	4827	Pte. Leech, B.	B	14th Aug. ,,	Kranspoort	
42	4716	,, Birmingham, F.	A	18th ,, ,,	Vyskraal	
43	3872	,, Porter, G.	C	31st July ,,	Rooikraal	Died of wounds
44	4665	Corpl. Faulkner, F.	A	6th Oct. ,,	Waterval	
45	3921	L.-Corpl. Sharpe, D.	A	,, ,, ,,	,,	
46	...	Lieut. Pilkington, F. E. C.	A	,, ,, ,,	,,	
47	4919	Pte. Brooks. E.	B	4th Dec. ,,	Vitgerzocht	21st Lancers, attached 18th Hussars
48	5060	,, Sparkes, W.	C	20th Feb., 1902	Koffiebank	Died of wounds. Buried at Carolina

Appendix E.

List of Officers, N.C.O.'s, and Men Wounded during War.

No.	Regtl. No.	Rank and Name	Squad.	Date	Place	Remarks
1	...	2nd Lieut. McLachlan, A. C.	B	20th Oct. 1899	Talana	...
2	...	" Cape, H. A.	C	" " "	"	...
3	...	" Bayford, E. H.	B	8th Dec. "	Reconnaissance at Ladysmith	...
4	...	" Thackwell, C. J.	B	20th Oct. "	Talana	...
5	4249	L.-Corpl. Franklin, G.	B	" " "	"	...
6	4395	" Sexton, W.	C	" " "	"	...
7	4110	Pte. Bryant, J.	B	" " "	"	...
8	4305	" Thompson, T.	B	" " "	"	...
9	4101	" O'Brien, P.	A	" " "	"	...
10	4721	" Stewart, R.	A	" " "	"	...
11	4204	" Masters, T.	A	" " "	"	...
12	4181	" Waterson, W.	C	" " "	"	...
13	4172	L.-Corpl. Millar, A.	B	" " "	"	...
14	4247	" Irvine, F.	B	" " "	"	...
15	4016	" Cogan, M.	A	" " "	"	...
16	3956	Pte. Davis, J.	B	" " "	"	...
17	4742	" Parker, W.	A	" " "	"	...
18	4589	" Weir, G.	B	" " "	"	...
19	3691	Sergt.-Farr. Shepherd, A.	B	21st " "	Dundee	...
20	4219	Pte. Clegg, F.	C	22nd " "	Retreat from Dundee	...
21	4600	" Walker, H.	A	7th Nov. "	Ladysmith	...
22	4336	" Robertson, J.	C	17th " "	"	...
23	4758	" Hart, C.	A	20th " "	"	...
24	4568	" Cawthorne, W.	B	20th " "	"	...
25	4744	" Austen, E.	B	" " "	"	...
26	2884	S.S.M. Power, W.	B	8th Dec. "	Reconnaissance at Ladysmith	...
27	4751	L.-Sergt. Howard, W.	B	" " "	"	"
28	4124	L.-Corpl. Watson, A.	B	" " "	"	"
29	4239	" Sheehan, T.	C	" " "	"	"

List of Officers, N.C.O.'s and Men Wounded during War—continued.

No.	Regtl. No.	Rank and Name	Squad.	Date	Place	Remarks
30	3946	Pte. Deal, W.	C	8th Dec., 1899	Reconnaissance at Ladysmith	
31	4157	,, Ewart, J.	C	,, ,, ,,	,, ,,	
32	4657	,, Meekings, W.	C	,, ,, ,,	,, ,,	
33	4282	,, Webster, S.	C	,, ,, ,,	,, ,,	
34	4290	,, Stewart, W.	B	,, ,, ,,	,, ,,	
35	4313	,, Maton, E.	B	,, ,, ,,	,, ,,	
36	4576	L.-Corpl. Gill, C.	A	6th Jan., 1900	Waggon Hill	
37	4737	,, Ward, F.	A	,, ,, ,,	,,	
38	3902	Pte. Davis	A	,, ,, ,,	,,	
39	4764	,, Bailey, H.	B	10th June, ,,	Botha's Pass	
40	4558	Trmtr. Herniman	B	,, ,, ,,	,,	
41	3392	L.-Sergt. Eade, H.	B	,, ,, ,,	,,	
42	4149	Pte. Cooper, C.	B	,, ,, ,,	,,	
43	4783	,, Sawtell	B	,, ,, ,,	,,	
44	2013	,, Grover, W.	B	30th July ,,	Near Meerzicht	
45	...	Lieut. Field, C. D.	C	21st Aug. ,,	Van Wyck's Vlei	
46	4480	Pte. Evans, A.	C	,, ,, ,,	,, ,,	
47	4329	Sergt. Warren, E.	A	4th Oct. ,,	Schoeman's Kloof	
48	4392	Pte. Barnes, F.	B	20th Sept. ,,	Badfontein	
49	3866	,, Marchant, S.	A	20th Oct., 1899	Talana	Reported from Pretoria
50	4549	L.-Corpl. Padwick, H.	C	,, ,, ,,	,,	,, ,, ,,
51	4041	Pte. Allison, J.	B	,, ,, ,,	,,	,, ,, ,,
52	4533	L-Corpl. Morcom, C.	A	10th Oct., 1900	Near Dulstroom	
53	4643	Pte. Beatwell, W.	C	14th ,, ,,	Witpoort	
54	4021	,, Bee, W.	A	21st Aug. ,,	Van Wyck's Vlei	
55	4290	,, Stewart, W.	B	2nd Nov. ,,	Near Middelburg	
56	4033	,, Wilson, T.	B	29th ,, ,,	,, ,,	
57	4084	L.-Corpl. Wilson, J.	C	8th Dec. ,,	,, ,,	
58	3049	Pte. Bee, L.	B	,, ,, ,,	,,	
59	...	Lieut. Thackwell, C. J.	B	24th ,, ,,	Uitkyk	
60	5055	Pte. Meredith, A.	B	23rd Jan., 1901	,,	
61	3711	,, Barnes, C.	C	,, ,, ,,	,,	

Appendix E.   297

62	4334	L.-Corpl. Holloway, W.	C	23rd Jan., 1901	Uitkyk	...
63	3728	Pte. Barwise, G.	C	25th " "	"	...
64	4615	" Kidd, D.	C	" " "	"	...
65	4879	" Sheehan, M.	A	2nd Feb. "	Roodeport	...
66	4354	" Hughes, H.	A	" " "	"	...
67	3332	" Gibbons, W.	A	" " "	"	...
68	2703	Sergt. Baker, A.	A	29th Jan. "	Near Wonderfontein	...
69	3900	Pte. Bott, G.	B	6th April "	Oliphant's River	...
70	4701	" Trend	A	" " "	Amsterdam	...
71	4712	" Moore, J.	B	16th " "	Near Dulstroom	...
72	5005	" McCarthy, C.	B	" " "	"	...
73	4827	" Leech, B.	B	" " "	"	...
74	4748	" Roach, T.	B	27th June "	Near Bankpan	...
75	4075	" Matthews, G.	B	2nd July "	Zondagsvlei	...
76	5090	" Grist, G.	A	10th " "	Doorn Kraal	...
77	4890	" Berry, E.	C	30th June "	Near Boschport	...
78	4262	" Carter	C	30th July "	Welverdiend	...
79	4103	" Peden, E.	C	" " "	"	...
80	5016	" Prime, E.	C	" " "	"	...
81	...	Capt. Leveson, C. H.	C	" " "	"	...
82	...	Lieut. Lichtenberg, J. W.	C	17th Aug. "	Vrieskraal	...
83	4323	Corpl. S.S. Carrington, H.	B	" " "	"	...
84	5185	Pte. Hogbin	A	1st Sept. "	Blinkwater	...
85	3445	" Strivens, A.	A	" " "	"	...
86	4766	" Pollok, W.	A	6th Oct. "	Waterval	...
87	3588	Sergt. Pearce, W.	A	" " "	"	...
88	3908	L.-Sergt. Brown, H.	A	" " "	"	...
89	4979	Pte. Clarke, E.	A	11th Nov. "	Ruigtekuilen	...
90	5186	Corpl. Durkin, E.	A			
91	3790	" Hall, G.	A			
92	4863	Pte. Lyons, W.	A			
93	5129	" Howard, E.	A			
94	...	Major Pollok, W. P. M.				

List of N.C.O.'s and Men who Died of Disease during War.

No.	Regtl. No.	Rank and Name	Squad.	Date of Death	Place	Remarks
1	4773	Pte. Burton, W.	A	22nd Dec. 1899	Intombi	Dysentry
2	4798	,, Taylor, R.	C	7th Jan. 1900	Ladysmith	,,
3	4394	L.-Corpl. Edmunds, C.	A	12th ,, ,,	,,	Enteric Fever
4	3016	Sergt. Makinson, E.	B	22nd ,, ,,	Intombi	Fractured ribs and injury to left lung
5	3954	L.-Sergt. Brockwell, C.	A	26th ,, ,,	Ladysmith	Enteric Fever
6	4512	Pte. Crouch, W.	C	30th ,, ,,	Mooi River	,,
7	3423	L.-Corpl. Turner, W.	C	6th Feb. ,,	Ladysmith	Dysentry
8	4345	Pte. Oakes, E.	A	15th ,, ,,	,,	Enteric Fever
9	4007	L.-Corpl. Willis, A.	A	19th ,, ,,	,,	Dysentry
10	4634	Pte. Baigent, A.	C	5th Mar. ,,	,,	,,
11	4466	,, Dean, H.	B	15th ,, ,,		Enteric Fever
12	3474	,, Shipley, J.		15th Apr. ,,	Mooi River	,,
13	3227	,, Grinham, E.	A	23rd May ,,	Ladysmith	,,
14	3540	,, Gray, J.	B	28th June ,,	,,	Abscess on liver
15	3848	,, Whitelock, W.	A	10th July ,,	Maritzburg	Peritonitis
16	4168	,, Shiels, J.	B	16th Aug. ,,	Twyfelaar	Pneumonia
17	4847	,, Hurcom, J.	B	29th Dec. ,,	Middelburg	Enteric Fever
18	4653	,, Nicholas, E.	A	14th Jan. 1901	,,	Aneurism of Aorta
19	5030	L.-Corpl. Forrester, B.		1st Feb. ,,	Pretoria	Enteric Fever
20	5057	Pte. Hassum, H.	B	29th Mar. ,,	Middelburg	,,
21	5136	,, Mc Ewan, D.	A	10th Apr. ,,	,,	,,
22	4990	,, Harris, H.	C	29th May ,,	Machadodorp	,,
23	4814	L.-Corpl. Gibbs, W.	C	,, ,, ,,	Carolina	Accidentally shot
24	4909	Pte. Holness, J.	C	30th ,, ,,	Pretoria	Enteric Fever
25	5071	L.-Corpl. Margetts, T.	C	2nd June ,,	,,	,,
26	4943	Pte. Ward, F.	C	5th ,, ,,	Middelburg	,,

Appendix E.   299

27	4860	Pte. Willett, S.	B	10th June, 1901	Middelburg	Enteric Fever
28	5054	,, Baldwin, W.	A	2nd July ,,	Wonderfontein	,, ,,
29	4898	,, Hall, A.	C	6th Aug. ,,	Middelburg	Pneumonia
30	4043	L.-Corpl. Pope, F.	B	20th ,, ,,	Rooikraal, Transvaal	Enteric Fever
31	5075	Pte. Watson, W.	C	31st ,, ,,	Middelburg	Drowned
32	3471	Sergt. Leonard, W.	C	29th Sept. ,,	Vryheid	Enteric Fever
33	4854	Pte. Davis, P.	C	28th Nov. ,,	Middelburg	
34	5079	,, Summers, J.	C	10th Dec. ,,	,,	,, ,,
35	5055	,, Meredith, A. J.	C	21st ,, ,,	Standerton	,, ,,
36	5181	,, Cooper, C.	C	21st Jan. 1902	Ermelo	,, ,,
37	2440	,, Simmons, J.	A	4th Feb. ,,	Durban (H.S. Avoca)	Remittent Fever
38	3887	,, Myles, T.	C	14th ,, ,,	Tweefontein	Drowned
39	5009	L.-Corpl. Aldous, H. S.	B	17th ,, ,,	Middelburg	Enteric Fever
40	5044	Pte. Williams, E.	B	18th ,, ,,	Standerton	,, ,,
41	5221	,, Hart, E.	A	23rd ,, ,,	,,	,, ,,
42	4965	,, Tribe, W.	B	23rd ,, ,,	Ermelo	,, ,,
43	5070	,, Green, F.	B	27th ,, ,,	Pretoria	,, ,,
44	5516	,, Santen, C.	C	20th Mar. ,,	Middelburg	,, ,,
45	3039	Sergt. Fidkin, J.	C	5th ,, ,,	Pretoria	,, ,,
46	5081	Pte. Peake, H.	A	25th ,, ,,	Charlestown	,, ,,
47	3746	,, Page, S.	B	4th Oct. 1900	Canterbury, England	Pneumonia
48	5586	,, Meakes, C.		20th July, 1902	Standerton	Enteric Fever
49	4570	,, Little, H.		17th Sept. ,,	,,	Pneumonia

Return of Casualties of the 18th Hussars from October 20th, 1899, to 31st May, 1902.

Killed in action and died of wounds	48
Died of disease	49
Wounded	94
*Taken prisoners	130
Invalided to England	214
Total casualties	535
Number present in South Africa during the War	1233
Percentage of killed	3·89
,, ,, wounded	7·62
,, ,, deaths through disease	3·97

* *Particulars of numbers taken prisoners.*

At Dundee	81
Reconnaissance from Grass Kop	1
,, ,, Zandspruit	4
,, ,, Shoeman's Kloof	2
At Middelburg, December, 1900, and January, 1901	32
,, Badfontein Valley	6
,, Wilge River on train	2
On June 11th, 1901, near Carolina	1
,, May 6th, 1902, near Lindley	1
	130

APPENDIX F.

Strength of the Regiment at different dates during the War.

Date	Officers	Rank and File	Total	Horses
October 28th, 1898	—	—	623	—
September 25th, 1899	18	456	474	—
October 16th, 1900	15	470	485	250
May 13th, 1901	16	562	*578	†493
May 22nd, 1901	16	526	*542	†503
June 26th, 1901	19	526	*545	†482
July, 1901	20	536	*556	†492
September 7th, 1901	21	638	*659	†545
November 11th, 1901	18	651	*669	†609
March 15th, 1902	20	512	*532	†322
April 28th, 1902	21	900	921	†528

* Not including the Depôt at Middelburg, which consisted of usually 50 to 100 men, or of others away from Headquarters.
† Not including ponies.

APPENDIX G.

Officers of the 18th Hussars with the Regiment in Ladysmith during the Siege.

Major E. C. Knox ... ... In command.
  „ P. S. Marling, v.c. ... ... In command of A Squadron.
  „ H. T. Laming ... ... In command of C Squadron.
Captain M. S. Wellby ... ... A Squadron.
  „ Hon. H. S. Davey ... ... Adjutant till January 1st, 1900.
  „ C. K. Burnett ... ... Adjutant from January, 1st, 1900.
Lieutenant E. C. Haag ... ... A.D.C. to Sir G. White.
  „ T. H. Cosselin ... ... Transport Officer.
  „ N. St. V. R. Stewart ... A Squadron.
  „ J. L. Wood ... ... A „
  „ C. D. Field ... ... C „
  „ C. J. Thackwell ... ... B „
  „ E. H. Bayford ... ... B „
  „ G. V. Clarke ... ... C „
  „ J. G. Dugdale ... ... C „
  „ C. F. Cawston ... ... A „
  „ M. S. Purdey ... ... A „
Captain and Quarter-Master J. Baker
  „ W. E. Hardy, R.A.M.C.

At Intombi Hospital.

Lieutenant A. C. McLachlan ... ... B Squadron.
  „ H. A. Cape ... ... C „

APPENDIX H.

Strength of the Regiment leaving Ladysmith for Dundee on 25th September, 1899.

Officers 18	Trumpeters	5
Sergeants 27	Privates	406
Corporals 18		
Total 474		

Roll of Officers of the 18th Hussars present at Dundee, 20th October, 1899.

Lieut.-Col. Moller, B. D.
Major Knox, E. C.
 „ Marling, v.c., P. S.
 „ Laming, H. T.
 „ Greville, H. F.
Capt. Pollok, W. P. M.
 „ Davey, Hon. H. S.
 „ Burnett, C. K.
Lieut. Haag, E. C.
 „ Gosselin, J. H.
 „ Stewart, N. St. V. R.

Lieut. Wood, J. L.
 „ Field, C. D.
 „ Thackwell, C. J.
 „ McLachlan, A. C.
 „ Bayford, E. H.
 „ Cape, H. A.
 „ Clarke, G. V.
 „ Cawston, C. F.
Capt. and Q.-M. Baker, J.
R.A.M.C. Capt. Hardy, W. E.
Vet.-Lieut. Shore, F. H.

APPENDIX I.

Strength of the Regiment in the Field at various dates during the War.

MAY 22ND, 1901.

Officers and Men :—	Mounted	With Transport	With Sick Horses	Dismounted	Sick	Ponies	Total
A Squadron	155	19	...	...	...	...	174
B „	168	15	...	...	...	...	183
C „	149	36	...	...	...	...	185
Total	472	70	...	...	...	...	542
Horses :—							
A Squadron	155	8	...	...	...	5	168
B „	169	4	...	...	...	5	178
C „	149	16	...	...	...	6	171
Total	473	28	...	...	...	16	517

JUNE 26TH, 1901.

Officers and Men :—							
A Squadron	151	29	...	...	...	...	180
B „	160	23	...	...	...	...	183
C „	155	27	...	...	...	...	182
Total	466	79	...	...	...	...	545
Horses :—							
A Squadron	151	8	...	...	...	12	171
B „	160	5	...	...	...	10	175
C „	155	3	...	...	...	11	169
Total	466	16	...	...	...	33	515

JULY, 1901.

Officers and Men :—							
A Squadron	151	27	...	...	...	...	178
B „	146	30	...	...	...	...	176
C „	175	27	...	...	...	...	202
Total	472	84	...	...	...	...	556
Horses :—							
A Squadron	152	11	...	...	...	13	176
B „	146	2	...	...	...	13	161
C „	175	5	...	...	...	16	196
Total	473	18	...	...	...	42	533

September 7th, 1901.

Officers and Men :—	Mounted	With Transport	With Sick Horses	Dismounted	Sick	Ponies	Total
A Squadron ...	165	23	10	20	1	...	219
B ,, ...	145	29	32	17	1	...	224
C ,, ...	159	27	7	21	2	...	216
Total ...	469	79	49	58	4	...	659
Horses :—							
A Squadron ...	165	12	...	Absent	10	14	201
B ,, ...	145	4	...	...	32	9	190
C ,, ...	159	5	...	6 (absent)	7	9	186
Total ...	469	21	...	6	49	32	577

November 5th, 1901.

Officers and Men :—	Mounted	With Transport	With Sick Horses	Dismounted	Sick	Ponies	Total
A Squadron ...	180	37	...	14	2	...	223
B ,, ...	184	32	...	12	...	...	228
C ,, ...	173	40	...	4	1	...	218
Total ...	537	109	...	30	3	...	669
Horses :—							
A Squadron ...	180	12	...	5	4	13	*214
B ,, ...	184	10	...	4	8	10	†216
C ,, ...	173	9	...	4	13	10	‡209
Total ...	537	31	...	13	25	33	639

* Two absent.   † One absent.   ‡ One absent.

April 28th, 1902.

Officers & Men :—	Head-quarters	Middelburg	Standerton	Supply Column	Col. Head-quarters	Hospital	Various Places	Total
A Squad.	179	43	5	...	6	16	25	274
B ,, ...	179	34	16	...	2	16	35	282
C ,, ...	187	35	8	1	2	21	24	278
Total	545	112	29	1	10	53	84	§834
Horses :—								
A Squad.	192	...	...	...	...	...	...	192
B ,, ...	176	...	...	...	...	...	...	176
C ,, ...	160	...	...	...	...	...	...	160
	528	...	...	...	...	...	...	‖528

§ Not including a draft of 67 N.C. officers and men, *en route* to join Regiment.
‖ Not including 36 ponies.

Amount of Transport and Followers with Regiment.

- 1 Conductor.
- 38 Natives.
- 158 Mules.
- 12 Mule Wagons.
- 1 Trolley.
- 2 Water Carts.
- 2 S. A. A. Carts.
- 2 Squadron Carts.

This does not include Cape Carts, as many as twenty of which accompanied the Regiment at times.

APPENDIX K.

Increase and Decrease of Horses from 1st October, 1899, to 31st May, 1902.

Months		Effective	Remounts	Decrease						Total
				Killed and taken by Enemy	Died and Destroyed	Strayed	Abandoned	Destroyed for Chevril	Transferred to Sick Depôts	
1st October	1899	436	22	148	...	...	...	...	31	179
1st November	,,	279	6	...	...	...	...	...	...	...
1st December	,,	285	...	...	17	...	...	...	...	17
1st January	1900	268	1	...	3	...	...	...	...	3
1st February	,,	266	...	...	...	...	...	93	...	93
1st March	,,	173	29	...	14	52	...	...	...	66
1st April	,,	136	318	...	19	...	..	...	23	42
1st May	,,	412	121	...	25	...	...	...	100	125
1st June	,,	408	91	...	17	5	...	...	54	76
1st July	,,	423	99	...	12	...	...	...	67	79
1st August	,,	443	50	...	34	3	...	...	42	79
1st September	,,	414	...	...	27	2	20	...	10	59
1st October	,,	355	238	...	47	...	6	...	...	53
1st November	,,	540	92	...	4	...	...	...	86	90
1st December	,,	542	52	...	21	2	...	...	78	101
1st January	1901	493	51	...	27	...	...	...	30	57
1st February	,,	487	158	...	23	...	...	...	30	53
1st March	,,	592	2	...	22	...	...	...	27	49
1st April	,,	545	173	...	102	...	...	...	53	155
1st May	,,	561	140	...	20	2	...	...	36	58
1st June	,,	643	63	...	63	...	..	...	37	100
1st July	,,	606	221	...	43	...	...	...	136	179
1st August	,,	648	159	...	80	...	...	...	42	122
1st September	,,	685	126	...	111	...	...	...	111	222
1st October	,,	589	384	...	105	...	...	...	116	221
1st November	,,	752	...	...	39	...	...	...	101	140
1st December	,,	612	169	...	40	...	...	...	68	108
1st January	1902	673	135	...	132	...	...	...	106	238
1st February	,,	570	226	...	75	...	...	...	135	210
1st March	,,	586	274	...	48	...	...	...	178	226
1st April	,,	634	71	...	45	...	...	...	60	105
1st May	,,	600	251	...	22	5	...	...	103	130
1st June	,,	721	...	...	.	...	...	...	...	...
			3722	148	1237	71	26	93	1860	3435

In the column, "Died and Destroyed," many horses are shown which were "killed by the enemy." The two columns were not separately kept up after the first month of the war.

Seventy-one horses were left after the siege of Ladysmith.

Thirteen horses of the original number we had at the commencement of the war were left on 31st May, 1902.

APPENDIX L.

Detail of Duties performed by the Regiment at Manchester Fort.

		Total
No. I Piquet ...	1 Sergeant, 2 Corporals, and 18 Men	21
„ II „ ...	1 Sergeant, 2 Corporals, and 15 Men	18
Detached Post ...	1 Sergeant and 6 Men	7
Hussar Post ...	1 Sergeant, 1 Corporal, and 10 Men	12
Fort Guard ...	1 Corporal and 6 Men	7
Gun Sangars at Night	2 Corporals and 9 Men	11
Fort road ...	1 Corporal and 3 Men	4
Guard on Tents	1 Corporal and 3 Men	4
Grazing Guard	1 Corporal and 5 Men	6
		90

In support in rear of Vedettes	46
In Reserve in Fort and Tents (including Men attending Hospital, Servants and Cooks)	90
Total number with Headquarters	226

APPENDIX M.

Special Natal Field Force Order,
by Lieut.-General Sir George White. V.C., G.C.B., etc., Commanding.

ORGANISATION :— Ladysmith, 14th December, 1899.

1.—In order that a Force may be ready organised to move out from Ladysmith for offensive operations at short notice, the following arrangements will be made by Officers Commanding Sections and others concerned, for the defence of Ladysmith during the absence of the Flying Column.

2.—The Flying Column, which will be under the personal command of the Lieut.-General Commanding, will take with it three days' supplies for men and animals in the wagons; one day's preserved meat in addition being carried on pack mules.

3.—Colonel W. G. Knox, C.B., will command the garrison; and the detachment Royal Navy, under Captain the Hon. Hedworth Lambton, will co-operate in the defence of Ladysmith.

Appendix M.

4.—The troops will be divided as follows, and arrangements will be made forthwith by Officers Commanding Sections of the Defence for the troops remaining at Ladysmith to take over their defensive duties immediately the Flying Column leaves :—

TROOPS FOR THE FLYING COLUMN, Under command of the Lieut.-General Commanding		TROOPS FOR THE DEFENCE OF LADYSMITH, Under Colonel Knox	
Commander	Unit	Section	Unit
Cavalry Brigade, under Brigadier-General Brocklehurst.	5th Dragoon Guards. 5th Lancers. 18th Hussars. Imperial Light Horse. Supply Column.	Reserve	19th Hussars. Dismounted portion of Cavalry of Flying Column.
7th Brigade, under Colonel Hamilton.	1st Bn. Devonshire Regt. 2nd Bn. Gordon Highlanders. 2 Cos. 1st Bn. R. Irish Fus. Supply Column.	C Section under O. C. 1st Bn. Manchester Rgt.	2 guns 42nd Battery, R. F. A. Natal Naval Volunteers. 1st Bn. Manchester Regt. 3 Cos. 1st Bn. K. R. R. Corps.
8th Brigade, under Major-Gen. Howard.	5 Cos. 1st Bn. Liverpool Regt. 6 Cos. 1st Bn. Leicester Regt. 2nd Bn. Rifle Brigade. Supply Column.	B Section under O. C. 2nd Batt. K. R. R. Corps.	4 guns 42nd Battery, R. F. A. Two 15 pr. R. F. A. guns under Lieut. Belcher, R.A. 4 Cos. 1st Bn. K. R. R. Corps. 2nd Bn. K. R. R. Corps. 2 Cos. 1st Bn. Leicester Regt.
Divisional Troops.	13th Battery, R. F. A. 21st ,, ,, 53rd ,, ,, 67th ,, ,, 69th ,, ,, 2 guns No. 10 Mountain Baty., R. G. A. 1st Brigade Div. Ammunition Column. 2nd Brigade Div. Ammunition Column. 23rd Co., R.E. & det. Tel. Sec. Natal Carbineers. Border Mounted Rifles.	A Section under senior officer.	Howitzer and Nordenfelt dets. Balloon & Telegraph Secs., R.E. 3 Cos. 1st Bn. Liverpool Regt. Det. 1st Bn. Gloucester Regt. Det. 2nd Bn. R. Dublin Fus.
		The Flats	Natal Mounted Rifles.

Mounted Infantry Companies will accompany their respective battalions, except the Mounted Infantry Company of the Manchester Regiment, which will accompany the 7th Brigade on Flying Column.

All details not mentioned above, and capable of bearing arms, will be available for the defence of Ladysmith, under Colonel Knox's orders.

The Principal Medical Officer will make the necessary medical arrangements.

By order, A. HUNTER, MAJOR-GENERAL.
Chief of the Staff, Natal Field Force.

APPENDIX N.

Special Natal Field Force Order,
By Lieut.-General Sir George White, V.C., G.C.B., etc., Commanding.

Ladysmith, 17th December, 1899.

ALLOTMENT OF THE GARRISON TO THE DEFENCES OF LADYSMITH.

Troops	Section "A," under Col. W. G. Knox, C.B.	Section "B," under Major-Gen. F. Howard, C.B., C.M.G., A.D.C.	Section "C," under Col. I. S. M. Hamilton, C.B., D.S.O.
Troops at the disposal of Commanders of Sections	Cavalry:— 1 Squadron 19th Hussars Artillery:— 13th Battery, R.F.A. 2 Maxim-Nordenfelt guns Infantry:— 1st Bn. Liverpool Regt. Det. 1st Bn. Gloucestershire Regt. Det. 2nd Bn. R. Dublin Fusiliers	Dismounted men of Cavalry Brigade 69th Battery, R.F.A. Two 15-pdr. R.F.A. guns under Lieut. Belcher 1st Bn. Leicester Regt. 2nd Bn. King's Royal Rifle Corps 4 Coys. 1st Bn. King's Royal Rifle Corps	1 Squadn. 18th Hussars Natal Naval Voluntrs. 42nd Battery, R.F.A. 100 Impl. Light Horse (dismounted) 1st Bn. Manchester Regt. 3 Coys. 1st Bn. King's Royal Rifle Corps Dt. 1st Bn. R. Irish Fus.
Reserves under the orders of the Lieut.-General Commanding	Infantry:— 1st Bn. Devonshire Regt. Detachment Royal Navy (disposed as ordered). Three Batteries Royal Field Artillery, and two Ammunition Columns. Detachment No. 10 Mountain Battery, R.G.A. Two 6.3 in. Howitzers. The Cavalry Brigade, less 100 men Imperial Light Horse, and one Squadron each of 18th and 19th Hussars. 400 men Natal Mounted Volunteers. 23rd Field Company, R.E. Detachments of Telegraph and Balloon Sections.	2nd Bn. Rifle Brigade	2nd Bn. Gdn. Highlds.

The remainder of the Natal Mounted Volunteers will be responsible for the defence of the low ground between the Eastern point of Cæsar's Camp and the bend of the river below Helpmakaar Hill.

The Mounted Infantry Companies will be with their respective battalions.

The Infantry forming the "General Reserve" will be furnished with mule wagons, in which they can be rapidly transferred to any point of the Defences that may require support. These wagons will be kept massed under the orders of Officers in charge of Brigade Transport, and the mules kept ready to inspan at once.

On the "Alarm" sounding, the Ball (or Red Lamp) will be run up on the hill above the Headquarter Office and on Cove Hill, and all troops will at once stand to their arms, the "Reserve Infantry" getting into their wagons. The General Officer Commanding Cavalry Brigade, Officers Commanding Brigade Divisions, R.F.A., the O.C. Natal Mounted Volunteers, and Officers Commanding Infantry Battalions of the "General Reserve," will at once report personally at the Headquarter Office for orders. At night, the Cavalry will turn out on their brigade parade ground; during the day they will saddle up at their respective day stations. Officers in Command of Sections will report by telephone to the Headquarter Office the situation in front of their respective sections.

By order, A. HUNTER, MAJOR-GENERAL.
Chief of the Staff, Natal Field Force.

APPENDIX O.

Proclamation to the Inhabitants of the South African Republic.

Whereas by Proclamation No. 1 of 1900, Burghers who had not taken a prominent part in the hostilities, were allowed, upon taking an oath, to return to their homes, and were not dealt with as Prisoners of War, and

Whereas by Proclamation No. 2 of 1900, Burghers to whom Passes and Permits had been granted, might retain their stock, or take them to the Winter Veld, and

Whereas many Burghers have taken the said oath, but have, notwithstanding this oath, taken up arms against the Forces of Her Majesty the Queen, and

Whereas many Burghers who have taken the said oath, have aided and abetted the enemy in raiding trains and destroying property belonging to the Forces of Her Majesty the Queen, or have acted as spies for the enemy, and

Whereas the Government of the South African Republic considers such oath immoral, and has issued a notice warning all Burghers against taking the said oath, and

Whereas it is manifest that the leniency which has been extended to the Burghers of the South African Republic is not appreciated by them, but, on the contrary, is being used as a cloak to continue the resistance against the Forces of Her Majesty the Queen, and

Whereas there are no means of distinguishing the Combatant from the non-Combatant portion of the population:

Now, therefore, I, Frederick Sleigh, Baron Roberts, of Kandahar and Waterford, K.P., G.C.B, G.C.S.I., G.C.I.E., V.C., Commander-in-Chief of Her Majesty's Forces in South Africa, do hereby proclaim and make known as follows:—

1. That from and after this date Sections 1 and 2 of Proclamation No. 1 of 1900 are repealed, except in respect of those Burghers who have already taken the said oath.
2. That Proclamation No. 2 of 1900 is repealed.
3. That all such persons who have taken the said oath, and who have in any way broken such oath, will be punished with either death, imprisonment, or fine.
4. That all Burghers in the districts occupied by Her Majesty's Forces, except such as have already taken the said oath, shall be regarded as Prisoners of War, and shall be transported or otherwise dealt with as I may determine.

5. That all buildings and structures on farms on which the scouts or other forces of the enemy are harboured will be liable to be razed to the ground.

6. That the fine mentioned in Proclamation No. 6 of 1900, Section 2, shall be rigorously exacted where any damage is done to the Railway, and persons are hereby warned to acquaint Her Majesty's Forces with the presence of the enemy upon their farms, and failing to do so, they will be regarded as aiding and abetting the enemy.

GOD SAVE THE QUEEN.

Given under my hand and seal at Pretoria this 14th day of August, 1900.

ROBERTS, FIELD-MARSHAL.
Commander-in-Chief in South Africa.

With reference to Paragraph 6, the Fine therein mentioned shall in no event be less than a sum of 2s. 6d. per morgen on the area of each Farm.

APPENDIX.—P.

ITINERARY OF MARCHES.

No. 1.—(1) From Ladysmith to Dundee with Glencoe Field Force, under Colonel Pickwood, September 25th, 1899, to September 26th, 1899.

(2) From Dundee to Ladysmith with Glencoe Field Force, under General Yule, October 22nd, 1899, to October 26th, 1899.

			Miles
(1) Ladysmith	...	... to Sunday's River	16
Sunday's River	...	... „ Glencoe	21
		Total mileage	37
(2) Dundee	...	... to Vlakfontein	22
Vlakfontein	...	... „ Waschbank River	16
Waschbank River	...	... „ near Sunday's River	12
Near Sunday's River	...	... „ Ladysmith	24
		Total mileage	74

No. 2.—From Ladysmith to Zandspruit with the Natal Field Force. General Brocklehurst in command of the 2nd Cavalry Brigade, to which the 18th Hussars were attached. May 22nd, 1900, to June 21st, 1900.

		Miles
Pound's Plateau, Ladysmith	... to Modderspruit	10
Modderspruit ...	... „ Sunday's River	9
Sunday's River ...	... „ De Aar's Farm	13
De Aar's Farm ...	... „ Kalabash Store	8

Appendix P. 311

		Miles
Kalabash Store	to Ingagane	13
Ingagane	,, Cattle Drift	18
Cattle Drift	,, Inchanga Drift	6
Inchanga Drift	,, Ingkalba Spruit	11
Ingkalba Spruit	,, Wool's Drift	15
Wool's Drift	,, Coetze's Drift	9
Coetze's Drift	,, De Wet's Farm	6
De Wet's Farm	,, Yellowboom Farm	4
Yellowboom Farm	,, Botha's Pass	14
Botha's Pass	,, Gransvlei	12
Gransvlei	,, Alleman's Nek	12
Alleman's Nek	,, Opperman's Kraal	5
Opperman's Kraal	,, Charlestown	11
Charlestown	,, Zandspruit	14

Total mileage 190

No. 3.—From Zandspruit to Lydenburg and Middelburg with General Buller's column. General Brocklehurst in command of 2nd Cavalry Brigade, to which 18th Hussars were attached up to Lydenburg. General Lyttleton in command of column from Lydenburg to Middelburg. August 7th, 1900, to October 16th, 1900.

		Miles
Zandspruit	to Meerzicht	12
Meerzicht	,, Ameersfoort	17
Ameersfoort	,, Mooifontein	10
Mooifontein	,, Berginderlyn	7½
Berginderlyn	,, Rietspruit	12½
Rietspruit	,, Ermelo	4
Ermelo	,, Klipfontein	14½
Klipfontein	,, Vaalbult	16½
Vaalbult	,, Twyfellaar	5
Twyfellaar	,, Van Wick's Vlei	8½
Van Wick's Vlei	,, Geluk	7
Geluk	,, Bergindal	7
Bergindal	,, Machadodorp	15
Machadodorp	,, Helvetia	9
Helvetia	,, Crocodile River	16
Crocodile River	,, Swartz Koppies	31
Swartz Koppies	,, Vrischgewacht	16½
Vrischgewacht	,, Wemmershoek	8½
Wemmershoek	,, Weltrefreden	10
Weltrefreden	,, Lydenburg	3
Lydenburg	,, Krugerspost	17
Krugerspost	,, Lydenburg	17
Lydenburg	,, Spitz Kop	9
Spitz Kop	,, Wemmershoek	6½
Wemmershoek	,, Dulstroom	15
Dulstroom	,, Witpoort	15
Witpoort	,, Schiedpad	10
Schiedpad	,, Hoedspruit	12
Hoedspruit	,, Bankfontein	10
Bankfontein	,, Middelburg	6

Total mileage ... 348

No. 4.—From Middelburg. Reconnaissances in the neighbourhood with small columns under (1) Colonel Payne, November 1st, 1900; (2) Colonel Carleton, November 13th, 1900, and (3) November 28th, 1900; (4) Colonel Campbell, December 7th, 1900.

		Miles
(1) Middelburg	to Klipfontein	17
Klipfontein	„ Middelburg	15
(2) Middelburg	„ Elandslaagte	15
Elandslaagte	„ Scheidpad	19
Schiedpad	„ Bothaville	9
Bothaville	„ Bankfontein	14
Bankfontein	„ Middelburg	6
(3) Middelburg	„ Groot Oliphants' River	11
Groot Oliphants' River	„ Roodepoort	12
Roodepoort	„ Kranspoort	6
Kranspoort	„ Hartebeestefontein	17
Hartebeestefontein	„ Oliphants' River	12
Oliphants' River	„ Middelburg	11
(4) Middelburg	„ Groot Oliphants' River	12
Groot Oliphants' River	„ Kranspoort	18
Kranspoort	„ Roodepoort	6
Roodepoort	„ Groot Oliphants' River	11
Groot Oliphants' River	„ Middelburg	12

Total mileage ... 223

No. 5.—From Middelburg to Carolina and back with General Smith Dorrien's Column. Colonel Henry in command of the mounted forces, of which the 18th Hussars formed part. January 21st. 1900, to January 30th, 1901.

		Miles
Middelburg	to Pan	12
Pan	„ Wonderfontein	15
Wonderfontein	„ Twyfellaar	18
Twyfellaar	„ Carolina	8
Carolina	„ Twyfellaar	8
Twyfellaar	„ Wonderfontein	18
Wonderfontein	„ Pan	15
Pan	„ Middelburg	12

Total mileage ... 106

No. 6.—From Middelburg to Piet Retief and back, with General French's columns. Colonel Campbell in command of the column to which 18th Hussars were attached. February 1st, 1901, to April 27th, 1901.

		Miles
Middelburg	to Bankfontein	13
Bankfontein	„ Roodepoort	8
Roodepoort	„ Boschmansfontein	10
Boschmansfontein	„ De Witte Krantz	10
De Witte Krantz	„ Klipfontein	13½
Klipfontein	„ Bothwell	15¾

Appendix P. 313

		Miles
Bothwell	to Blauwater	6
Blauwater	„ Umpilasi	9½
Umpilasi	„ Bonnie Braes	6
Bonnie Braes	„ Westhoe	12
Westhoe	„ Amsterdam	8
Amsterdam	„ Wolvenkop	13
Wolvenkop	„ Sheila River	4
Sheila River	„ Piet Retief	13½
Piet Retief	„ Zandbank	11
Zandbank	„ Umchinga's Drift	11
Umchinga's Drift	„ Zandbank	11
Zandbank	„ Piet Retief	11
Piet Retief	„ Pampoem's Kraal	10½
Pampoem's Kraal	„ Sprinbokfontein	11
Sprinbokfontein	„ Weldefreden	9
Weldefreden	„ Van Hendriksfontein	12
Van Hendriksfontein	„ Tafelkop	8½
Tafelkop	„ Vogelfontein	13½
Vogelfontein	„ Boschmanskop	8
Boschmanskop	„ Vaalbank	10½
Vaalbank	„ Pullen's Hope	10½
Pullen's Hope	„ Eikeboom	10
Eikeboom	„ Middelburg	12½
	Total mileage	302

No. 7.—From Middelburg to the Komati River, and through Eastern Transvaal to Eland's River, with General W. Kitchener's columns. Colonel Campbell in command of column to which 18th Hussars were attached, for the greater part of the time. May 13th, 1901, to July 18th, 1901.

		Miles
Middelburg	to Pan	12
Pan	„ Wonderfontein	15
Wonderfontein	„ Strathrea	11
Strathrea	„ Carolina	15
Carolina (including a reconnaissance)	„ Nooitgedacht	15
Nooitgedacht	„ Carolina	9
Carolina	„ Silverkop	22
Silverkop	„ Badplaats (Warmbads)	10
Badplaats	„ Vergelegen	9
Vergelegen	„ Thee Spruit & Boschhoek	33
Boschhoek	„ Rietfontein	9
Rietfontein	„ Carolina	18
Carolina	„ Rietfontein	18
Rietfontein	„ Silverkop	5
Silverkop	„ Nooitgedacht	12
Nooitgedacht	„ Groenvallei	8
Groenvallei	„ Frischgevacht	15
Frischgevacht	„ Groenvallei	15
Groenvallei	„ Witrand	13
Witrand	„ Vaalbank	13
Vaalbank	„ Hartebeestespruit	14
Hartebeestespruit	„ Kaffirstadt	19
Kaffirstadt	„ Hartebeestekuillen	8

314   *The 18th Hussars in South Africa.*

		Miles
Hartebeestekuillen ...	... to Kaffirstadt	8
Kaffirstadt	... ,, Schurvekop	12
Schurvekop (night march)	... ,, Erstegeluk	15
Erstegeluk	... ,, Mooifontein (and reconnaissance)... ...	12
Mooifontein	... ,, Legdaar	12
Legdaar	... ,, Middelkraal	9
Middelkraal	... ,, Steenkoolspruit ...	14
Steenkoolspruit	... ,, Zondagsvlei	16
Zondagsvlei	... ,, Onverwacht	9
Onverwacht	... ,, Welgelegen (*via* Kromdrai)	17
Welgelegen	... ,, Boschpoort	5
Boschpoort	... ,, Dwarsfontein... ...	5
Dwarsfontein	... ,, Rooipoort	10
Rooipoort	... ,, Marskop	12
Marskop	... ,, Eland's River ...	6
Eland's River	... ,, Doornkraal	12
Reconnaissance	... at ,, ...	10
Doornkraal	... to Eland's River ...	12
Eland's River	... ,, Bronkhorstspruit ...	10
Bronkhorstspruit ...	... ,, Spitzkop	8
Spitzkop	... ,, Balmoral	8
Balmoral	... ,, Nooitgedacht ...	8
Nooitgedacht	... ,, Groot Oliphant's River	10
Groot Oliphant's River ...	... ,, Middelburg	12
	Total mileage ...	570

No. 8.—From Middelburg to Commissie Drift on Groot Oliphants' River and back to Wonderfontein, with General W. Kitchener's Columns. Colonel Campbell in command of the column, to which 18th Hussars were attached for most of the period. July 26th, 1901, to September 4th, 1901.

		Miles
Middelburg	... to Wonderhoek	17
Wonderhoek	... ,, Dielfontein	13
Reconnaissance	... at Dielfontein	12
Dielfontein (night march)...	... to Buffelsvlei	28
Buffelsvlei	... ,, Massip's Drift and Diepkloof	29
Diepkloof	... ,, Buffelsvlei	14
Buffelsvlei	... ,, Rooikraal	6
Rooikraal	... ,, Diepkloof	6
Diepkloof	... ,, Roodepoort	10
Roodepoort	... ,, Diepkloof	10
Diepkloof	... ,, Roodepoort	10
Roodepoort	... ,, Kalkfontein	13
Kalkfontein	... ,, Massip's Drift ...	13
Massip's Drift	... ,, Vyskraal	14
Vyskraal	... ,, Commissie Drift ...	9
Commissie Drift ...	... ,, Slangboom (and fight)...	32
Slangboom	... ,, Vyskraal	11
Vyskraal	... ,, Massip's Drift ...	14
Massip's Drift	... ,, Buffelsvlei	18
Buffelsvlei	... ,, Rooikraal	6

Appendix P.   315

		Miles
Rooikraal	to Blinkwater	15
Blinkwater	„ Middelkraal	10
Middelkraal (night march)	„ Houtenbeck	18
Houtenbeck	„ Blinkwater	16
Blinkwater (night march)	„ Schorngezicht and back	45
Blinkwater	„ Sterkloop	10
Sterkloop	„ Hartebeestehoek	10
Hartebeestehoek	„ Wonderfontein	10
	Total mileage	419

No. 9.—From Wonderfontein to Vryheid and back to Standerton, with General W. Kitchener's Columns. Colonel Campbell in command of the column to which the 18th Hussars were attached. September 8th, 1901, to November 4th, 1901.

		Miles
Wonderfontein	to Strathrae	11
Strathrae	„ Vaalbank	22
Vaalbank	„ Klipstapel	10
Klipstapel	„ Ermelo	14
Ermelo	„ Schimmelhoek	22
Schimmelhoek	„ Bankop	8
Bankop	„ Roodeval	14
Roodeval	„ Ermelo	16
Ermelo	„ Berginderlyn	19
Berginderlyn	„ Ameersfoort	17
Ameersfoort	„ Zandspruit	18
Zandspruit	„ Volkrust	11
Volkrust	„ Charlestown	3
Charlestown	„ Ingogo	16
Ingogo	„ Wool's Drift	18
Wool's Drift	„ Kweekspruit	8
Kweekspruit	„ Utrecht	8
Utrecht	„ Knight's Farm	7
Knight's Farm	„ Mooihoek	16
Mooihoek	„ Vryheid	22
Vryheid	„ Bombaskop	16
Bombaskop	„ Vryheid	16
Vryheid (night march)	„ Rietvlei	16
Reconnaissance	at Rietvlei	14
Reconnaissance	„ Geluk	14
Rietvlei	to Goudhoek	19
Goudhoek	„ Diepkloof	4
Diepkloof	„ Mahlone	11½
Mahlone	„ Ersteling	15½
Ersteling	„ Paulpietersburg	8½
Paulpietersburg	„ Mooiplaats	15½
Mooiplaats	„ Pipeklipberg	23
Reconnaissance	at Pipeklipberg	14
Pipeklipberg	to Mooiplaats	23
Mooiplaats	„ Marienthal	18
Marienthal	„ Rooikraal	12
Rooikraal (reconnaissance)		15
Rooikraal	to Luneburg	15
Luneburg	„ Elandsberg Nek	20

316   The 18th Hussars in South Africa.

		Miles
Elandsberg Nek...	... to Wonderhoogte	13
Wonderhoogte ...	... „ Wakkerstroom	12
Wakkerstroom ...	... „ Volkrust	22
Volkrust ...	... „ Paardekop	21
Paardekop ...	... „ Platrand	15
Platrand ...	... „ Standerton	15
	Total mileage	668

No. 10.—From Standerton to Ermelo, and operations in that neighbourhood, with General Bruce Hamilton's columns. Colonel Campbell in command of the column to which the 18th Hussars were attached, from November, 1901, to November 26th, 1901; Colonel Simpson, R.A., in command from November 27th, 1901, to January 16th, 1902; Colonel Wing, R.A., in command for remainder of period. November 7th, 1901, to February 5th, 1902.

		Miles
Standerton	... to Joubert's Vlei	22
Joubert's Vlei	... „ Goodehoep	14
Goodehoep	... „ Trickhardsfontein	8
Trickhardsfontein	... „ Ruigtekuillen	15
Ruigtekuillen	... „ Boshmansfontein	17
Boshmansfontein	... „ Witpoort	12
Witpoort	... „ Boschmansfontein	12
Boschmansfontein	... „ Rietkuil	14
Rietkuil	... „ Rooipoort	21
Rooipoort	... „ Bethal	13
Bethal (night march)	... „ Knapdaar and Spoienkop	37
Spoienkop	... „ Bethal	13
Bethal (night march)	... „ Steenkoolspruit and back	48
Bethal ...	... „ Spoienkop	13
Spoienkop	... „ Rietvlei	16
Rietvlei	... „ Ermelo	12
Ermelo	... „ Brakfontein	22
Brakfontein	... „ Uitkyk	21
Uitkyk ...	... „ Standerton	19
Standerton	... „ Uitkyk	19
Uitkyk ...	... „ Morgenzan	13
Morgenzan	... „ Kaffirspruit	18
Kaffirspruit	... „ Ermelo	13
Ermelo	... „ Brakfontein	22
Brakfontein	... „ Morgenzan	9
Morgenzan (night march)	... „ Blesbokspruit and back	39
Morgenzan	... „ Kaffirspruit	18
Kaffirspruit	... „ Berginderlyn	14
Berginderlyn	... „ Ermelo	19
Ermelo (night march)	... „ Bankop	27½
Bankop (night march)	... „ Davidale	24
Davidale (night march)	... „ Compies River and back	38
Davidale (night march)	... „ Lichfield Store and back	33
Davidale	... „ Kliprug	17½
Kliprug	... „ Schimmelhoek	9½
Schimmelkoek ...	... „ Jan Hendrikfontein	17½
Jan Hendrikfontein	... „ Outshoorn	7
Outshoorn (night march) ...	... „ Knapdaar	48
Knapdaar	... „ Ermelo	28

Appendix P. 317

		Miles
Ermelo (night march) ...	... to Windhoek	20
Windhoek (night march) ...	... „ Ermelo	20
Ermelo (night march) ...	... „ Reinhoogte	25
Reinhoogte	... „ Hamelfontein ...	8
Hamelfontein (night march)	... ...	15
Hamelfontein	... to Kuilfontein	8
Kuilfontein (night march)	... „ Groot Oliphant's Valley and back	20
Kuilfontein	... „ Banklaagte	8
Banklaagte (night march)	... ...	15
Banklaagte	... „ Bethal	8
Bethal (night march) ...	... „ Oshoek and Witbank ...	38
Witbank	... „ New Denmark ...	18
New Denmark (night march)	... „ Roodebank	23
Roodebank	... „ Nooitgedacht ...	27
Nooitgedacht	... „ Blesbokspruit and engagement	34
Blesbokspruit	... „ Goedegevonden ...	22
Goedegevonden	... „ Brugspruit	16
	Total mileage	1108

No. 11.—From Brugspruit to Standerton *viâ* Carolina and Ermelo. Column under command of Col. Wing, R.A., February 8th, 1902, to March 1st, 1902.

		Miles
Brugspruit (night march) ...	... to Heuvelfontein ...	15
Heuvelfontein	... „ Brakfontein ...	15
Brakfontein	... „ Bronkhurstspruit ...	15
Bronkhurstspruit (night march)	... „ Tweefontein and back...	18
Bronkhurstspruit ...	... „ Brakfontein ...	15
Brakfontein	... „ Zaiwater ...	24
Zaiwater	... „ Steenkoolspruit ...	13
Steenkoolspruit	... „ Boschmanskop ...	26
Boschmanskop	... „ Koffiebank ...	24
Koffiebank	... „ Carolina ...	15
Carolina	... „ Smutsoog ...	15
Smutsoog	... „ Ermelo ...	21
Ermelo	... „ Kaffir Spruit ...	13
Kaffir Spruit	... „ Berginderlyn ...	13
Berginderlyn	... „ Kaffir Spruit ...	13
Kaffir Spruit (drive) ...	... „ Standerton ...	43
	Total mileage ...	298

No. 12.—From Standerton over Robert's Drift to Botha's Pass and Volkrust Column under command of Col. Wing, R.A. March 3rd, 1902, to March 12th, 1902.

		Miles
Standerton (night march)	... to near Cornelia and Robert's Drift	53
Robert's Drift ...	... „ Bultfontein	5
Bultfontein (drive) ...	... „ Groenfontein	15
Groenfontein „ ...	... „ Driefontein	21
Driefontein „ ...	... „ Leeuwdam	23
Leeuwdam	... „ Opperman's Kraal ...	22
Opperman's Kraal ...	... „ Volkrust	6
	Total mileage ...	145

318 The 18th Hussars in South Africa.

No. 13.—From Volkrust to Ermelo, and into line with Gen. Bruce Hamilton's columns for "drive" to Standerton railway line. Colonel Wing in command of column, to which 18th Hussars were attached. March 12th, 1902, to April 14th, 1902.

		Miles
Volkrust	... to Zandspruit	11
Zandspruit	... „ Paardekop	10
Paardekop (night march)...	... „ Kaalspruit and Potfontein	36
Potfontein	... „ Bleuwkop	16
Bleuwkop	... „ Morgenzan	8
Morgenzan (night march)...	... „ Hamelfontein and back	44
Morgenzan	... „ Verblyden	23
Verblyden	... „ Leuwspruit	5
Leuwspruit (night march)	... „ Mooifontein	17
Mooifontein	... „ Sukkelaar	15
Sukkelaar	... „ Springbokfontein	14
Springbokfontein	... „ Rietvlei	13
Rietvlei	... „ Ermelo	13
Ermelo	... „ Welgelegen	16
Welgelegen (night march)	... „ Lake Banagher and Vryheid	42
Lake Vryheid	... „ Carolina	12
Carolina	... „ Helpmakaar	12
Helpmakaar	... „ Kromdrai	12
Kromdrai	... „ Driehoek	10
Driehoek (drive)	... „ Middelkraal	18
Middelkraal „	... „ Elandsfontein	22
Elandsfontein „	... „ Vlaklaagte	32
	Total mileage	401

No. 14.—From Vlaklaagte to Middelburg railway line and back. "Drives" with General Bruce Hamilton's columns. Col. Wing, R.A., in command of column to which 18th Hussars were attached. April 16th, 1902, to April 26th, 1902.

		Miles
Vlaklaagte	... to Zandbaaken	9
Zandbaaken (drive)	... „ Leeuwspruit	21
Leeuwspruit „	... „ Uitkyk	15
Uitkyk „	... „ Roodebloom	11
Roodebloom „	... „ Steenkool Spruit	13
Steenkool Spruit „	... „ Nauwpoort	12
Nauwpoort	... „ Steenkool Spruit	12
Steenkool Spruit...	... „ Boselkrantz	16
Boselkrantz	... „ Vaalkop	15
Vaalkop	... „ Wildebeestefontein	17
Wildebeestefontein (drive)	... „ Val Station	30
	Total mileage	171

No. 15.—From Val Station to Frankfort and Lindley and back to Greylingstadt with General Bruce Hamilton's columns. Col. Duff in command of column, to which 18th Hussars were attached. May 2nd, 1902, to end of the war.

Appendix P.

		Miles
Val Station (drive)	to Roodepoort	12
Roodepoort „	„ near Villiersdorp	22
Villiersdorp „	„ Krom Spruit	27
Krom Spruit	„ Jackal's Kop	8
Jackal's Kop (drive)	„ Groenvallei	45
Groenvallei	„ Geelpan	13
Geelpan (drive)	„ Sterkfontein	33
Sterkfontein	„ Dielfontein	6
Dielfontein	„ Zandport	14
Zandport	„ Zandfontein	19
Zandfontein	„ Leeuwspruit	18
Leeuwspruit	„ Vlakfontein	14
Vlakfontein	„ Greylingstadt Station	5
Greylingstadt Station	„ Standerton	35
	Total mileage	271

SUMMARY OF MARCHES MADE BY THE REGIMENT.

	Miles
No. 1.—Ladysmith to Glencoe	37
Dundee to Ladysmith	74
No. 2.—Ladysmith to Zandspruit	190
No. 3.—Zandspruit to Middelburg	348
No. 4.—Reconnaissances at Middelburg	223
No. 5.—Middelburg to Carolina and back	106
No. 6.—Middelburg to Piet Rietief and back	302
No. 7.—Middelburg to Komati River and Eland's River, and back to Middelburg	570
No. 8.—Middelburg to Commissie Drift and Wonderfontein	419
No. 9.—Wonderfontein to Vryheid and Standerton	668
No. 10.—Operations in Eastern Transvaal with General Bruce Hamilton	1108
No. 11.—Brugspruit to Standerton	298
No. 12.—Standerton to Robert's Drift and Volkrust	145
No. 13.—Volkrust to Ermelo and Standerton Railway Line	401
No. 14.—"Drives" from Vlaklaagte to Middelburg Railway Line and back	171
No. 15.—Val Station to Frankfort, Lindley, Greylingstadt, and Standerton	271
Total number of miles marched by the Regiment	5331

www.ingramcontent.com/pod-product-compliance
Lightning Source LLC
Chambersburg PA
CBHW021352290426
44108CB00010B/201